Contributions to Finance and Accounting

The book series 'Contributions to Finance and Accounting' features the latest research from research areas like financial management, investment, capital markets, financial institutions, FinTech and financial innovation, accounting methods and standards, reporting, and corporate governance, among others. Books published in this series are primarily monographs and edited volumes that present new research results, both theoretical and empirical, on a clearly defined topic. All books are published in print and digital formats and disseminated globally.

More information about this series at http://www.springer.com/series/16616

Peter Brusov • Tatiana Filatova • Natali Orekhova

Ratings

Critical Analysis and New Approaches of Quantitative and Qualitative Methodology

Springer

Peter Brusov
Financial University Under
the Government of Russian Federation
Moscow, Russia

Tatiana Filatova
Financial University Under
the Government of Russian Federation
Moscow, Russia

Natali Orekhova
High School of Business
Southern Federal University
Rostov-on-Don, Russia

ISSN 2730-6038 ISSN 2730-6046 (electronic)
Contributions to Finance and Accounting
ISBN 978-3-030-56242-7 ISBN 978-3-030-56243-4 (eBook)
https://doi.org/10.1007/978-3-030-56243-4

This Springer imprint is published by the registered company Springer Nature Switzerland AG.
The registered company address is: Gewerbestrasse 11, 6330 Cham, Switzerland

Dedicated to our dear children and to our nice grandchildren

Preface

The monograph develops new modern methodologies for rating of non-financial issuers and of project ratings based on the use of the modern theory of capital cost and capital structure (BFO theory—Brusov–Filatova–Orekhova theory) and of its two perpetuity limits (Modigliani–Miller theory (MM theory) and the modified Modigliani–Miller theory (MMM theory)), as well as modern investment models created by the authors.

In order to modify and improve existing rating methods to increase the objectivity and correctness of rating estimates, the monograph critically analyzes the methodological and systemic shortcomings of the existing credit rating of non-financial issuers and project rating. The modern theory of capital cost and capital structure (BFO theory) for companies of arbitrary age and its two perpetuity limits (Modigliani–Miller theory and modified Modigliani–Miller theory) have been modified for rating needs. The incorporation of financial ratios used in the rating methodology was carried out both in the BFO theory and in its perpetuity limits: in the Modigliani–Miller theory and in the modified Modigliani–Miller theory. A fundamentally new approach to the rating methodology has been developed, which includes the adequate application of discounting, which is practically not used in existing rating methodologies, when discounting the financial flows; the use of rating parameters under discounting of financial flows; and the correct determination of discount rates taking into account the financial ratios.

The proposed improvement of the rating methodology of existing rating systems will improve the accuracy of issued ratings and make them more objective. Using in rating methods the modern theory of corporate finance, tools of well-developed theories of corporate finance (BFO theory and its perpetuity limits) allow us to move in the rating industry from the use of mainly qualitative rating methods to the use of mainly quantitative methods, which opens up new horizons in issuer rating and in determination methods their creditworthiness.

This book is intended for managers and analysts of rating agencies, students, both undergraduate and postgraduate, students of MBA program, teachers of economic and financial universities, students of MBA program, scientists, financial analysts, financial directors of company, managers of insurance companies, officials of regional and federal ministries and departments, and ministers responsible for economic and financial management.

Kronburg, Moscow, Russia Peter Brusov
20 June 2020

Contents

About the Authors

Peter Nickitovich Brusov is professor at the Financial University under the Government of the Russian Federation (Moscow). Originally a physicist, he was the cofounder of (together with Victor Popov) the theory of collective properties of superfluids and superconductors. In the area of finance and economy, Peter Brusov has created a modern theory of capital cost and capital structure, the Brusov–Filatova–Orekhova theory, together with Tatiana Filatova and Natali Orekhova, and has modified twice the Modigliani–Miller theory: for arbitrary company age (BFO theory) and for advance payments of tax on profit (MMM theory). Peter Brusov has been Visiting Professor of Northwestern University (USA), Cornell University (USA), Osaka City University (Japan), and Chung–Cheng National University (Taiwan), among other places. He is the author of over 500 research publications including eight monographs, numerous textbooks, and articles.

Tatiana Filatova is professor at the Financial University under the Government of the Russian Federation (Moscow). In the last 20 years, she has been a dean of the faculties of financial management, management, and state and municipal government, among others, at the Financial University. Tatiana Filatova is coauthor of a modern theory of capital cost and capital structure, the Brusov–Filatova–Orekhova theory, and the author of over 260 research publications including seven monographs, numerous textbooks, and articles.

Natali Orekhova is professor of the Center of Corporate Finance, Investment, Taxation and Rating at the Research Consortium of Universities of the South of Russia. Natali Orekhova has been the leading scientist of the Financial University under the Government of the Russian Federation. She is the coauthor of a modern theory of capital cost and capital structure, the Brusov–Filatova–Orekhova theory, and the author of over 110 research publications including five monographs, numerous textbooks, and articles.

Chapter 1
Introduction

New modern methodologies for rating of non-financial issuers and project ratings have been developed, based on the application of the modern theory of cost and capital structure (BFO theory—Brusov–Filatova–Orekhova theory) and its perpetuity limits (Modigliani–Miller theory (MM theory) and new modified Modigliani–Miller theory (MMM theory)), as well as modern investment models created by authors.

In order to modify and improve existing rating methodologies, to increase the objectivity and accuracy of rating assessments, a critical analysis of the methodological and systemic shortcomings of the existing credit ratings of non-financial issuers and project rating has been carried out. The modern theory of capital cost and capital structure (BFO theory) (Brusov 2018a, b; Brusov et al. 2015, 2018a, b, c, d, e, f, 2019, 2020; Filatova et al. 2008, 2018) has been modified for companies of arbitrary age and its perpetuity limits (Modigliani–Miller theory (MM theory) (Modigliani and Miller 1958, 1963, 1966) and new modified Modigliani–Miller theory (MMM theory)) for rating needs. The incorporation of financial indicators used in the rating methodology, both into the BFO theory and into the Modigliani–Miller theory, has been carried out. Within the framework of the modified BFO theory for rating needs, a complete and detailed study of the dependence of the weighted average cost of capital of WACC, used as the discount rate for discounting financial flows, on the financial ratios used in the rating, on the age of the company, on the leverage level, and on the level of taxation was conducted in a wide range of values of equity cost and debt cost for companies of arbitrary age. This allows us to carry out the correct assessment of the discount rate, taking into account the values of financial ratios.

To assess the creditworthiness of issuers, two models have been created that take into account the discounting of financial flows: a single-period model and a multi-period model.

The incorporation of rating ratios into the modern theory of capital cost and capital structure, the BFO theory, and its perpetuity limit allows the use of powerful tools of these well-developed theories for credit rating of non-financial issuers, while

P. Brusov et al., *Ratings*, Contributions to Finance and Accounting,
https://doi.org/10.1007/978-3-030-56243-4_1

discounting financial flows using the correct discount rates taking into account the values of financial ratios. The quantitative analysis in the rating has been expanded by expanding the range of financial indicators, introducing a number of new financial indicators. All this is a qualitatively new basis for creating a modern methodology for rating of non-financial issuers, and it increases the objectivity and accuracy of ratings.

The authors have modified created by them models of long-term (perpetuity) investment projects and projects of arbitrary duration with various debt repayment schemes (at the end of the project duration, uniform payments of debt) for rating needs.

The incorporation of financial indicators used in the rating methodology (coverage ratios and leverage ratios) into the model of long-term (perpetuity) investment projects and projects of arbitrary duration with various debt repayment schemes (at the end of the project duration, uniform payments of debt) was carried out.

For long-term (perpetuity) investment projects and projects of arbitrary duration with various debt repayment schemes (at the end of the project duration, uniform payments of debt), a complete and detailed study of the dependence of the main performance indicator, NPV, on financial ratios used in the rating (coverage ratios and leverage ratios), on the level of debt financing, and on the project duration in a wide range of values of equity cost and debt capital cost was carried out. This creates a new methodological basis for modern project rating.

The use of tools of well-developed corporate finance theories (BFO theory and its perpetuity limits) opens up new horizons in the rating industry, which gives the opportunity to switch from using mainly qualitative methods for determining the creditworthiness of issuers to using mainly quantitative methods in rating, which will undoubtedly improve the quality and accuracy of the rating score.

Recommendations have been developed to the rating agencies: the Big Three (Standard & Poor's, Fitch, and Moody's), ACRA, European, Chinese, and others on modifying the methodologies for rating of non-financial issuers and for project rating.

1.1 Monograph Structure

The monograph has the following structure. After the Introduction (Chap. 1), the importance of rating and the limitations of existing rating methodologies are discussed (Chap. 2). Chapters 3, 4 and 5 are devoted to an overview of the two main theories of capital cost and capital structure of the company—the Brusov–Filatova–Orekhova theory (BFO theory) (Chap. 5) and its perpetuity limit—the Modigliani–Miller theory (MM theory) (Chap. 3), which are used in the subsequent chapters to modify the currently accepted methodologies for rating of non-financial issuers and project ratings. In Chap. 4 for the first time, results are presented on the modification of the Modigliani–Miller theory to the case of advance tax payments accepted in practice (MMM theory). This modification substantially changes all the main statements of the classical Modigliani–Miller theory.

In the following Chaps. 6, 7 and 8, both theories are used for rating purposes, for which the incorporation of rating coefficients is carried out both within the modern theory of capital cost and capital structure, the BFO theory, and within two perpetuity limits: the Modigliani–Miller theory (MM theory), including the modified Modigliani–Miller theory (MMM theory). This incorporation allows us to use the powerful tools of these well-developed theories for credit rating of non-financial issuers, while discounting the financial flows using the correct discount rates, taking into account the financial ratios.

Within the framework of the modified for rating needs BFO theory, Modigliani–Miller theory (including the modified one), a complete and detailed study was conducted of the dependence of the weighted average cost of capital, WACC, and the cost of equity, ke, used as discount rates for discounting financial flows, on financial ratios used in the rating, depending on the company age (for the BFO theory), of the level of borrowed financing, and the level of taxation in a wide range of values of equity and debt capital costs for perpetuity companies as well as for companies of arbitrary age. This allows for the correct assessment of discount rates taking into account the financial ratios, which is extremely important for issuing the correct credit ratings of issuers.

To assess the creditworthiness of issuers, two models have been created that take into account discounting of financial flows: a single-period model and a multi-period model, which are described in the monograph.

Chapters 9 and 10 describe the modern investment models, created by the authors of the monograph and well tested in the real sector of the economy. These models are modified in Chaps. 11, 12 and 13 for the needs of rating. These chapters are devoted to the analysis of existing project rating. The effectiveness of investment models (both long-term and arbitrary duration) is considered from the point of view of owners of equity capital as well as from the point of view of owners of both equity and debt capital. In this case, the consideration is conducted for two different methods of discounting. In the first method of discounting, operating and financial flows are not separated and both are discounted at the general rate (which, obviously, can be chosen as the weighted average cost of capital WACC). For perpetuity projects for WACC, the Modigliani–Miller formula is used, and for projects of arbitrary duration the famous Brusov–Filatova–Orekhova formula for WACC is used. In the second method of discounting, operating and financial flows are separated and discounted at different rates: operating flows at a rate equal to the equity cost, depending on the leverage level, and credit (or financial) flows at a rate equal to the debt cost, which up to sufficiently large leverage levels remains constant and begins to grow only at sufficiently high leverage level L, when there is a danger of bankruptcy.

Investment models with various debt repayment schemes are considered: at the end of the project term, even repayment of debt during the project implementation period.

In Chaps. 11–13, the models created by the authors for long-term (perpetuity) investment projects and projects of arbitrary duration with various schemes for debt repayment (at the end of the project term, uniform) were modified for the rating needs.

The incorporation of financial indicators used in the rating methodology (coverage ratios and leverage ratios) into the model of long-term (perpetuity) investment projects and projects of arbitrary duration with various debt repayment schemes (uniform and at the end of the project term) was carried out.

For long-term (perpetuity) investment projects and projects of arbitrary duration with various debt repayment schemes (uniform and at the end of the project term), a complete and detailed study was conducted of the dependence of the main performance indicator, NPV, on the financial ratios used in the rating (coverage ratios and leverage ratios), the level of borrowed financing, profitability ratio, cost of equity, and debt capital in a wide range of values of equity and debt capital. This creates a new methodological basis for modern project rating.

The monograph includes a description of qualitatively new effects in the BFO theory, which must be taken into account in the rating. Accounting for these effects is necessary for issuing the correct credit ratings of issuers. Such effects include the effects of the "golden" (Chap. 14) and "silver" (Chap. 15) age of the company and the anomalous effect of depending of the equity cost on the leverage level (Chap. 17), which can modify a company's dividend policy, which may affect its creditworthiness. We describe as well the simultaneous effect of taxes and leverage on the financial condition of the company and its investment program (Chap. 18), and a number of others. When issuing ratings, accounting for inflation is also extremely important. Chapter 16 is devoted to the description of the correct accounting method. In conclusion, recommendations are given to the national rating agency ACRA and international rating agencies, including the Big Three on improving the rating methodology (Chap. 19).

The improvement of the rating methodology of the existing rating systems proposed in the monograph will improve the accuracy of ratings and make them more objective. Using in rating methods the modern theory of corporate finance, tools of well-developed theories of corporate finance (BFO theory and its perpetuity limits—MM theory and MMM theory) allow us to move in the rating industry from the use of primarily qualitative methods to the use of primarily quantitative methods, which opens up new horizons in the rating of issuers and methods for determining their creditworthiness.

References

Brusov P (2018a) Editorial: introduction on special issue on the Banking System and financial markets of Russia and other countries: problems and prospects. J Rev Global Econ 7:i–vi. SCOPUS

Brusov P (2018b) Editorial. J Rev Global Econ 7:i–v. SCOPUS

Brusov P, Filatova T, Orekhova N, Eskindarov M (2015) Modern corporate finance, investments and taxation. Springer International Publishing, Switzerland, 373 p. monograph. SCOPUS. https://www.springer.com/gp/book/9783319147314

Brusov PN, Filatova TV, Orekhova NP, Kulik VL (2018a) Rating: new approach. J Rev Global Econ 7:37–62. SCOPUS. https://doi.org/10.6000/1929-7092.2018.07.05

Brusov PN, Filatova TV, Orekhova NP, Kulik VL (2018b) A "golden age" of the companies: conditions of its existence. J Rev Global Econ 7:88–103. SCOPUS. https://doi.org/10.6000/1929-7092.2018.07.07

Brusov PN, Filatova TV, Orekhova NP, Kulik VL (2018c) Rating methodology: new look and new horizons. J Rev Global Econ 7:63–87. SCOPUS. https://doi.org/10.6000/1929-7092.2018.07.06

Brusov PN, Filatova TV, Orekhova NP (2018d) Modern corporate finance and investments, monograph. Knorus Publishing House, Moscow, 517 p

Brusov P, Filatova T, Orekhova N, Eskindarov M (2018e) Modern corporate finance, investments, taxation and ratings. Springer Nature Publishing, Switzerland, 571 p. monograph

Brusov PN, Filatova TV, Orekhova NP, Kulik VL, Weil I (2018f) New meaningful effects in modern capital structure theory. J Rev Global Econ 7:104–122. SCOPUS. https://doi.org/10.6000/1929-7092.2018.07.08

Brusov PN, Filatova TV, Orekhova NP, Kulik VL, Weil I (2019) Ratings of the investment projects of arbitrary durations: new methodology. J Rev Global Econ 8:437–448. SCOPUS. https://doi.org/10.6000/1929-7092.2019.08.37

Brusov PN, Filatova TV, Orekhova NP, Kulik VL, Chang S-I, Lin YCG (2020) Modification of the Modigliani–Miller theory for the case of advance payments of tax on profit. J Rev Global Econ 9:257–268

Brusov P, Filatova T, Orekhova N, Kulik V, Weil I, Brailov A (2018) The impact of the central bank key rate and commercial banks credit rates on creating and maintaining of a favorable investment climate in the country. J Rev Global Econ 7:360–376. SCOPUS. https://doi.org/10.6000/1929-7092.2018.07.31

Filatova T, Orehova N, Brusova A (2008) Weighted average cost of capital in the theory of Modigliani–Miller, modified for a finite life–time company. Bull FU 48:68–77

Filatova TV, Brusov PN, Orekhova NP, Kulik VL (2018) Ratings of the long–term projects: new approach. J Rev Global Econ 7:645–661. SCOPUS. https://doi.org/10.6000/1929-7092.2018.07.59

Modigliani F, Miller M (1958) The cost of capital, corporate finance, and the theory of investment. Am Econ Rev 48:261–297

Modigliani F, Miller M (1963) Corporate income taxes and the cost of capital: a correction. Am Econ Rev 53:147–175

Modigliani F, Miller M (1966) Some estimates of the cost of capital to the electric utility industry 1954–1957. Am Econ Rev 56:333–391

Chapter 2
The Importance of Rating and the Disadvantages of Existing Rating Systems

2.1 The Importance of Rating

Rating is one of the most important instruments for regulating financial markets, the main task of which is to assess the quality of assets taking into account risk factors, conducted by independent experts. Ratings characterize the creditworthiness of the borrower, predict trends in it, or characterize the investment attractiveness of the project. They play an important role in decision-making, in establishing and maintaining business relationships. We will consider two types of ratings: credit rating and investment attractiveness rating (although there are other types of credit ratings: ratings of banks and banking groups, insurance companies, issues of financial instruments, regional and municipal authorities, and others). A credit rating is a measure of a company's creditworthiness, which is calculated on the basis of its financial condition, security of assets and capital, and exposure to risks. The credit rating expresses the opinion of the agency on the ability and willingness of the creditor (issuer) to fulfill its financial obligations in full and on time.

A credit rating can also talk about the quality of a credit instrument, for example, a company bond, or other debt instrument. The presence of a credit rating gives the company a number of advantages, such as obtaining a bank loan and other borrowed funds, and for the company with a high rating at a preferential rate, obtaining a commodity loan with a deferred payment and others.

The investment attractiveness rating of a project or company is an assessment of the level of satisfaction of financial, production, organizational, marketing, legal and other requirements, or interests of an investor with respect to a specific investment project or company. This type of rating allows you to evaluate the advantages and disadvantages of the investment project, as well as the state of the investment climate in a particular industry or region. As in the case with a credit rating, the presence of an investment attractiveness rating provides several advantages: obtaining financing for an investment project, obtaining a loan, and other types of attracting investments

P. Brusov et al., *Ratings*, Contributions to Finance and Accounting,
https://doi.org/10.1007/978-3-030-56243-4_2

and others. Its presence allows, for example, federal, regional, or municipal authorities to rank the presented investment projects in order to select the pool of the most attractive ones with a view to selecting and financing them.

Thus, credit rating and investment attractiveness ratings issued by rating agencies have a wide range of applications and are an aggregate indicator reflecting the creditworthiness of a company or the investment attractiveness of an investment project.

So, issuer rating plays an important role in the modern economy and finance. At the same time, occasional scandals related to the work of rating agencies indicate serious problems in the rating industry. The subject of the current research is the existing rating systems, their methodologies, and the shortcomings of these methodologies.

The purpose of this monograph is to modify the methodologies of existing rating systems to develop a fundamentally new approach to the rating methodology, the key factors of which are (1) adequate use of discounting when discounting the financial flows, which is practically not used in existing rating methodologies; (2) use when discounting rating parameters; and (3) the correct determination of the discount rate, taking into account financial ratios.

The monograph uses the modern theory of capital structure, the BFO theory (Brusov (2018a, b), Brusov et al. (2015), Brusov et al. (2018a, b, c, d, e, f, g), Brusov et al. (2019), Brusov et al. (2020), Filatova et al. (2018a, b), as well as its perpetuity limit, the Modigliani–Miller theory (MM theory) (Modigliani and Miller (1966), Myers (2001), Modigliani and Miller (1958), Modigliani and Miller (1963)), including the modified Modigliani–Miller theory (MMM theory) (Brusov et al. (2020)). All three theories have been modified for rating needs. As a result of the modification of the methodologies of the existing rating systems, a fundamentally new approach to the rating methodology has been developed, which includes adequate use of discounting when discounting financial flows, which is practically not used in existing rating methodologies; the use of rating parameters for discounting; and the correct determination of discount rates taking into account financial ratios.

The developed approach should be applied by rating agencies throughout the world, both international and Russian, in assessing the creditworthiness of issuers.

A modification of the methodology of existing rating systems will improve the accuracy of ratings and make them more objective. The use of tools of well-developed theories opens up new horizons in the rating industry, which gets the opportunity to switch from using mainly qualitative methods for determining the creditworthiness of issuers to using mainly quantitative methods in rating.

2.2 The Analysis of Methodological and Systemic Deficiencies in the Existing Credit Rating of Non-Financial Issuers

The analysis of methodological and systemic deficiencies in the existing credit rating of non-financial issuers has been conducted by us. We have analyzed the methodology of the Big three (Standard & Poor's, Fitch, and Moody's) and Russian national rating agency ACRA.

2.2.1 *The Closeness of the Rating Agencies*

The closeness of the rating agencies has been discussed by us in a paper (Brusov et al. 2018d) and is caused by multiple causes.

1. The desire to preserve their "know-how." Rating agencies get big enough money for generated ratings (mostly from issuers) to replicate its methodology.

2. The desire to avoid public discussion of the ratings with anyone, including the issuer. It is a very convenient position—rating agency "a priori" avoids any criticism of generated ratings.

3. The absence of any external control and external analysis of the methodologies results in the fact that shortcomings of methodologies are not subjected to serious critical analysis and stored long enough.

2.2.2 *Discounting*

One of the major flaws of all existing rating methodologies is a failure or a very narrow use of discounting. But even in those rare cases where it is used, it is not quite correct, since the discount rate when discounting financial flows is chosen incorrectly.

The need to take into account the time factor in terms of discounting is obvious, because it is associated with the time value of money. The financial part of the rating is based on a comparison of generated income with the value of the debt and the interest payable. Because income and disbursement of debt and interest are separated in time, the use of discounting when comparing revenues with the value of debt and interest is absolutely necessary for assigning credit ratings for issuers.

1. In existing rating methodologies, despite their breadth and detail, there are a lot of shortcomings. One of the major flaws of all existing rating methodologies, as mentioned in our papers concerning ratings, is a failure or a very narrow use of discounting. But even in those rare cases where it is used, it is not quite correct, since the discount rate when discounting financial flows is chosen incorrectly.

The need to take into account the time factor in terms of discounting is obvious, because it is associated with the time value of money. The need to take into account the time factor in terms of discounting is obvious, because it is associated with the time value of money. The financial part of the rating is based on a comparison of generated income with the value of the debt and the interest payable. Because income and disbursement of debt and interest are separated in time, the use of discounting when comparing revenues with the value of debt and interest is absolutely necessary for assigning credit ratings for issuers.

This raises the question about the discount rate. This question has always been one of the major and extremely difficult in many areas of finance: corporate finance and investment; it is particularly important in business valuation, where a slight change in the discount rate leads to significant changes in estimates of capitalization of the company, which is used by unscrupulous appraisers for artificial bankruptcy of companies. As well it is essential in rating, and when assigning a rating to an issuer, and forecasting.

Therefore, as soon as we are talking about financial flows, it is necessary to take account of discounting; otherwise, the time value of money is not taken into account, i.e., any analysis of financial flows should take account of discounting.

2. When we talk about using the rating reports for the three or five (GAAP) years, assuming that the behavior indicators beyond that period are "equal," discounting must be taken into account.

2.2.3 Dividend Policy of the Company

1. Dividend policy of the company must be taken into account (and account) when rating, because the financial policy is taken into account in rating. However, the existing methodologies for ranking estimate only the stability of the dividend policy and do not estimate its reasonableness: how reasonable is the value of dividend payouts and how do they relate to the economically reasonable dividend values.

2. The reasonableness of dividend policy, its score, is determined by comparing the values of paid dividends with their economically reasonable value, which is the cost of equity capital k_e of the company. The calculation of k_e is a rather difficult task.

BFO theory allows you to make the correct assessment of the value of the equity capital cost of the company, and thus to compare values of the dividend paid by the company to their economically reasonable value, it allows you to assess the reasonableness of dividend policy, which is clearly linked to the creditworthiness of the issuer.

3. For example, one of the varieties "cash flow," taking into account the amount of paid dividends (discretionary cash flow (DCF) S&P), should be compared with the economically reasonable dividend values, and this will affect the rating.

2.2.4 Leverage Level

1. Currently the rating agencies take into account the leverage level only from the perspective of assessing of financial stability and risk of bankruptcy. In fact, the leverage level significantly affects the main financial indicators of the company's activity: the cost of equity capital, WACC—in other words, the cost of attracting of capital, as well as the capitalization of the company. The failure of this effect in the analysis of financial reports leads to incorrect conclusions based on it.

Evaluation (by the BFO method) of the influence of the debt financing level on the effectiveness of investment projects for different values of capital costs can be used in the rating of investment projects and investment programs of companies.

2.2.5 Taxation

1. Taxation affects the rating of the issuers. Evaluation (by the BFO method) of the influence of taxation (tax on profit organization rate) on the financial performance of the company and on the effectiveness of investment projects can be used when rating companies and their investment programs, investment projects, as well as in the context of change of tax on profits of the organization rate for forecast predictions and in analysis of country risk.

2. Evaluation (by the BFO method) of the influence of the Central Bank base rate, credit rates of commercial banks on the effectiveness of investment projects, and creation of a favorable investment climate in the country can be used to forecast predictions, as well as in country risk analysis.

2.2.6 Accounting of the Industrial Specifics of the Issuer

Industrial specifics of the issuer in the existing rating methodologies, especially in newly established ones and taking into account the experience of predecessors, are ignored. So in "The methodology of ACRA for assigning of credit ratings for non-financial companies on a national scale for the Russian Federation," creditworthiness is determined by taking into account the characteristics of the industry in which the company operates. To assess of the factor of the industry risk profile, ACRA subdivides the industry into five groups according to their cyclical, barriers to entry, and industry risk statistics, as well as trends and prospects.

The weight of the factor of industry risk profile is determined individually for each group and varies depending on the level of credit risk. This creates a certain rating threshold for companies from industries with high risk and slightly rewards low risk industry.

However, the existing accounting of industry specifics of issuer is clearly insufficient. Ranking methodologies should better integrate industry peculiarities in the organization of finance of issuers. In particular, it is very important to define business needs in working capital, the size of which directly depends on financial soundness indicators: solvency and creditworthiness. The latter is the key indicator in rating.

2.2.7 *Neglect of Taking into Account the Particularities of the Issuer*

In existing rating methodologies, taking account of the particularities of the issuer, features of financial reports, and taxation, legal, and financial system is neglected in favor of achieving full comparability of financial reports; they smooth the distinctions (see Moody's rating methodologies).

2.2.8 *Financial Ratios*

1. A necessary and sufficient quantity and mix of financial ratios are not determined; it appears that such questions are not even raised when evaluating the financial risk; the financial condition of the issuer largely depends on the quantity and quality of financial ratios, their correlation, or independence.

2. Some financial ratios define ambiguously the state of the issuer. For example, the ratio of cash flow/leverage is high at high cash flow value as well as at low leverage value. The question is how these two different states of the issuer, which is attributed to one value of financial risk, really equally relate to credit risk.

3. As recognized in the ACRA methodology "in some cases it is possible that individual characteristics of factor/subfactor simultaneously fall into several categories of evaluation, particularly for qualitative factors. In this case, the score is based on expert opinion, taking into account the most important parameters."

4. In connection with paragraph 3 it should be noted that the formalization of expert opinions is one of the most important tasks in improving the rating methodology, in making a peer review process more objective. There are a few ways to solve this problem: using results of modern theory of measurement, using of the formalism of fuzzy sets, fuzzy logic, and others.

5. Tabulate the composition of various risks, for example, CICRA (in S&P methodology) gives 6×6 matrix, which has 36 elements, i.e., generally CICRA should have 36 different values, but their total number is equal to 6. The question is how this is justified. The fact that the total number is exactly equal to 6 shows that it is not very justified, or there are other considerations, but they must be well grounded.

Table 2.1 Score of funding and liquidity (after ACRA)

		Liquidity assessment				
Assessment of funding		*1*	*2*	*3*	*4*	*5*
	1	1	2	2	3	4
	2	1	2	3	3	4
	3	2	2	3	4	5
	4	3	3	3	4	5
	5	3	3	4	5	5

Similar examples abound. So in "The ACRA methodology for assigning of credit ratings for microfinance organizations on a national scale for the Russian Federation" (Table 2.1) "Score of funding and liquidity" provides 5 × 5 matrix that has 25 elements, i.e., generally should be 25 different states, but their total number is equal to 5. The question is whether it is justified. The fact that the total number is exactly equal to 5 shows that it is not very justified.

6. Tabulation of mixes of different ratios in determining the financial risk has been done not quite correctly:

	FFO/ debt (%)	Debt/ EBITDA (x)	FFO/cash interest (x)	EBITDA/ interest (x)	CFO/ debt (%)	FOCF/ deb (%)	DCF/ debt (%)
Minimal	60+	Less than 1.5	More than 13	More than 15	More than 50	40+	25+
Modest	45–60	1.5–2	9–13	10–15	35–50	25–40	15–25
Intermediate	30–45	2–3	6–9	6–10	25–35	15–25	10–15
Significant	20–30	3–4	4–6	3–6	15–25	10–15	5–10
Aggressive	12–20	4–5	2–4	2–3	10–15	5–10	2–5
Highly leveraged	Less than 12	Greater than 5	Less than 2	Less than 2	Less than 10	Less than 5	Less than 2

ratios at least not completely correlated but used as fully correlated. So, one can see that the two lines

Minimal	60+	Less than 1.5	More than 13	More than 15	More than 50	40+	25+
Modest	45–60	1.5–2	9–13	10–15	35–50	25–40	15–25

do not allow mixing between parameters of lines, although such mixing can occur, for example,

	60+	1.5–2	More than 13	More than 15	More than 50	40+	25+

All these points are limiting the applicability of rating agencies methods. They were introduced by the rating agencies for the purpose of simplifying the procedure of ranking (with or without understanding) and unifying the methods used in different reporting systems of different countries, with the objective of making results comparable.

Mentioned ambiguity of evaluations already occurred when S&P has assigned a rating to Gazprom.

References

Brusov P (2018a) Editorial. Introduction on special issue on the banking system and financial markets of Russia and other countries: problems and prospects. J Rev Global Econ 7:i–vi

Brusov P (2018b) Editorial. J Rev Global Econ 7:i–v

Brusov P, Filatova T, Orehova N, Eskindarov M (2015) Modern corporate finance, investments and taxation. Springer International Publishing, Cham, 373p. https://www.springer.com/gp/book/9783319147314

Brusov P, Filatova T, Orehova N, Eskindarov M (2018a) Modern corporate finance, investments, taxation and ratings. Springer Nature Publishing, Cham, 571p

Brusov PN, Filatova TV, Orekhova NP, Kulik VL (2018b) Rating: new approach. J Rev Global Econ 7:37–62. https://doi.org/10.6000/1929-7092.2018.07.05

Brusov PN, Filatova TV, Orekhova NP, Kulik VL (2018c) A "golden age" of the companies: conditions of its existence. J Rev Global Econ 7:88–103. https://doi.org/10.6000/1929-7092.2018.07.07

Brusov PN, Filatova TV, Orekhova NP, Kulik VL (2018d) Rating methodology: new look and new horizons. J Rev Global Econ 7:63–87. https://doi.org/10.6000/1929-7092.2018.07.06

Brusov PN, Filatova TV, Orekhova NP, Kulik VL, Weil I (2018e) New meaningful effects in modern capital structure theory. J Rev Global Econ 7:104–122. https://doi.org/10.6000/1929-7092.2018.07.08

Brusov P, Filatova T, Orekhova N, Kulik V, Weil I, Brailov A (2018f) The impact of the central bank key rate and commercial banks credit rates on creating and maintaining of a favorable investment climate in the country. J Rev Global Econ 7:360–376. https://doi.org/10.6000/1929-7092.2018.07.31

Brusov PN, Filatova TV, Orekhova NP (2018g) Modern corporate finance and investments, monograph. Knorus Publishing House, Moscow, 517p

Brusov PN, Filatova TV, Orekhova NP, Kulik VL, Weil I (2019) Ratings of the investment projects of arbitrary durations: new methodology. J Rev Global Econ 8:437–448. https://doi.org/10.6000/1929-7092.2019.08.37

Brusov PN, Filatova TV, Orekhova NP, Kulik VL, Chang S-I, Lin YCG (2020) Modification of the Modigliani–Miller theory for the case of advance payments of tax on profit. J Rev Global Econ 9:257–268

Filatova T, Orehova N, Brusova A (2008a) Weighted average cost of capital in the theory of Modigliani–Miller, modified for a finite lifetime company. Bull FU 48:68–77

Filatova TV, Brusov PN, Orekhova NP, Kulik VL (2018a) Ratings of the long–term projects: new approach. J Rev Global Econ 7:645–661. https://doi.org/10.6000/1929-7092.2018.07.59

Filatova TV, Brusov PN, Orekhova NP, Kulik VL (2018b) Ratings of the long–term projects: New approach. J Rev Global Econ 7:645–661. https://doi.org/10.6000/1929-7092.2018.07.59

Modigliani F, Miller M (1966) Some estimates of the cost of capital to the electric utility industry 1954–1957. Am Econ Rev 56:333–391

Myers S (2001) Capital structure. J Econ Perspect 15(2):81–102

Modigliani F, Miller M (1958) The cost of capital, corporate finance, and the theory of investment. Am Econ Rev 48:261–297

Modigliani F, Miller M (1963) Corporate income taxes and the cost of capital: a correction. Am Econ Rev 53:147–175

Part I
Corporate Finance Theories Used in Ratings and in Rating Methodologies

Chapter 3
Capital Structure: Modigliani–Miller Theory

3.1 Introduction

Capital structure is understood as the relationship between equity and debt capital of the company. Does capital structure affect the company's main settings, such as the cost of capital, profit, value of the company, and the others, and, if it affects, how? Choice of an optimal capital structure, i.e., a capital structure, which minimizes the weighted average cost of capital, WACC, and maximizes the value of the company, V, is one of the most important tasks solved by financial manager and by the management of a company. The first serious study (and first quantitative study) of the influence of capital structure of the company on its indicators of activities was the work by Modigliani and Miller (1958). Until this study, the approach existed (let us call it traditional), which was based on empirical data analysis.

One of the most important assumptions of the Modigliani–Miller theory is that all financial flows are perpetuity. This limitation was removed by Brusov–Filatova–Orekhova in 2008 (Filatova et al. 2008, Brusov et al. 2018a, b, c, d), who have created BFO theory—modern theory of capital cost and capital structure for companies of arbitrary age (BFO–1 theory) and for companies of arbitrary lifetime (BFO-2 theory) (Brusov et al. 2015). In Fig. 3.1 the historical development of capital structure theory from the traditional (empirical) approach, through perpetuity Modigliani–Miller approach, to general capital structure theory—Brusov–Filatova–Orekhova (BFO) theory—is shown.

In 2001, Steve Myers has considered the case of one-year company and shows that in this case the weighted average cost of capital, WACC, is higher than in the Modigliani–Miller case, and the capitalization of the company, V, is less than in the Modigliani–Miller case.

So, before 2008 only two results for capital structure of the company were available: Modigliani–Miller for perpetuity company and Myers for one-year company (see Fig. 3.2). BFO theory has filled out the whole interval between $t = 1$ and

P. Brusov et al., *Ratings*, Contributions to Finance and Accounting,
https://doi.org/10.1007/978-3-030-56243-4_3

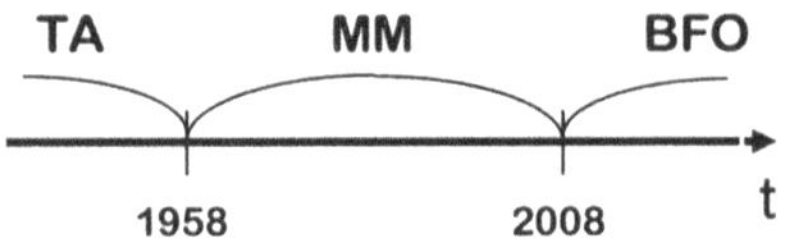

Fig. 3.1 Historical development of capital structure theory (here *TA* traditional (empirical) approach, *MM* Modigliani–Miller approach, *BFO* Brusov–Filatova–Orekhova theory)

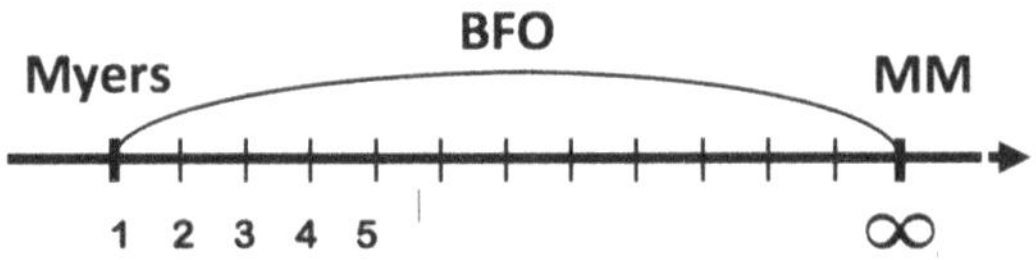

Fig. 3.2 MM theory describes perpetuity limit, Myers' paper describes one-year company, and BFO theory fills the whole numeric axis (from $n = 1$ up to perpetuity limit $n = \infty$)

$t = \infty$. It gives the possibility of calculating the capitalization V, the weighted average cost of capital, *WACC*, equity cost k_e, and other financial parameters for companies of arbitrary age and for companies of arbitrary lifetime. BFO theory has led to a lot of new meaningful effects in modern capital structure theory, discussed in this monograph.

3.2 The Traditional Approach

According to the traditional (empirical) approach, the weighted average cost of capital, WACC, and the associated company capitalization, $V = \mathrm{CF/WACC}$, depend on the capital structure and the level of leverage, L. Debt cost always turns out to be lower than equity cost because the former has lower risk, since in the event of bankruptcy creditor claims are met prior to shareholders claims.

As a result, an increase in the proportion of lower-cost debt capital in the overall capital structure up to the limit which does not cause violation of financial sustainability and growth of risk of bankruptcy leads to lower weighted average cost of capital, WACC.

The profitability required by investors (the equity cost) is growing; however, its growth has not led to compensation of benefits from the use of lower-cost debt capital. Therefore, the traditional approach welcomes the increased leverage $L = D/S$ and the associated increase of company capitalization. The traditional (empirical) approach has existed up to appearance of the first quantitative theory by Modigliani and Miller (1958).

3.3 Modigliani–Miller Theory

3.3.1 Modigliani–Miller Theory Without Taxes

Modigliani and Miller (MM) in their first paper (Modigliani and Miller 1958) have come to conclusions which were fundamentally different from those of the traditional approach. Under assumptions (see Sect. 3.3.3 for details) that there are no taxes, no transaction costs, and no bankruptcy costs, perfect financial markets exist with symmetry information, there is equivalence in borrowing costs for both companies and investors, etc., they have showed that choosing the ratio between the debt and equity capital does not affect company value as well as capital costs (Fig. 3.3).

Under above assumptions, Modigliani and Miller have analyzed the impact of financial leverage, supposing the absence of any taxes (on corporate profit as well as individual one). They have formulated and proven the following two statements.

Without taxes, the total cost of any company is determined by the value of its EBIT (earnings before interest and taxes), discounted with fixed rate k_0, corresponding to the group of business risk of this company:

$$V_L = V_U = \frac{\text{EBIT}}{k_0}. \tag{3.1}$$

Index L means a financially dependent company (using debt financing), while index U means a financially independent company.

Fig. 3.3 Dependence of company capitalization, U_L, equity cost, k_e, debt cost, k_d, and weighted average cost of capital, WACC, in traditional (empirical) approach

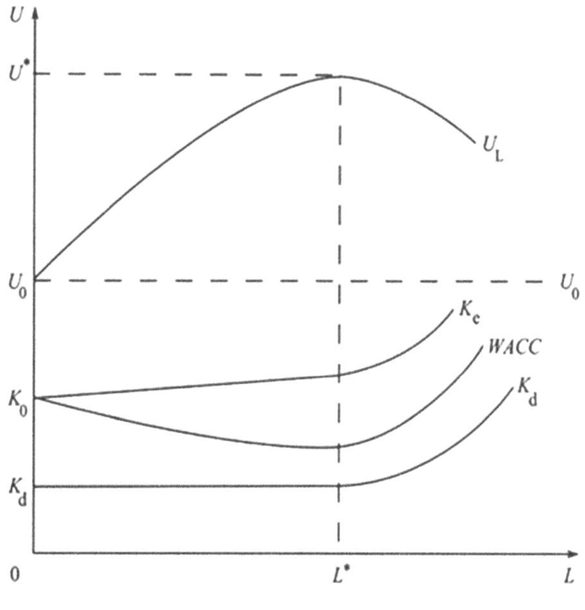

Authors supposed that both companies belong to the same group of business risk, and k_0 corresponds to the required profitability of financially independent company, having the same business risk.

Because, as it follows from the formula (Eq. 3.1), the value of the company does not depend on the value of debt, then according to Modigliani–Miller theorem (Modigliani and Miller 1958), in the absence of taxes, the value of the company is independent of the method of its funding. This means as well that weighted average cost of capital, WACC, of this company does not depend on its capital structure and is equal to the capital cost, which this company will have under the funding by equity capital only.

$$V_0 = V_\mathrm{L}; \quad \mathrm{CF}/k_0 = \mathrm{CF}/\mathrm{WACC}, \quad \text{and thus WACC} = k_0.$$

Note that the first Modigliani–Miller theorem is based on suggestion about independence of weighted average cost of capital and debt cost on leverage level.

From the first Modigliani–Miller theorem (Modigliani and Miller 1958), it is easy to derive an expression for the equity capital cost

$$\mathrm{WACC} = k_0 = k_\mathrm{e} w_\mathrm{e} + k_\mathrm{d} w_\mathrm{d}. \tag{3.2}$$

Finding from here k_e, one gets

$$\begin{aligned} k_\mathrm{e} &= \frac{k_0}{w_\mathrm{e}} - k_\mathrm{d}\frac{w_\mathrm{d}}{w_\mathrm{e}} = \frac{k_0(S+D)}{S} - k_\mathrm{d}\frac{D}{S} = k_0 + (k_0 - k_\mathrm{d})\frac{D}{S} \\ &= k_0 + (k_0 - k_\mathrm{d})L \end{aligned} \tag{3.3}$$

Here,

D	Value of debt capital of the company
S	Value of equity capital of the company
$k_\mathrm{d}, w_\mathrm{d} = \frac{D}{D+S}$	Cost and fraction of debt capital of the company
$k_\mathrm{e}, w_\mathrm{e} = \frac{S}{D+S}$	Cost and fraction of equity capital of the company
$L = D/S$	Financial leverage

Thus, we come to the second statement (theorem) of Modigliani–Miller theory about the equity cost of financially dependent (leverage) company (Modigliani and Miller 1958).

Equity cost of leverage company k_e could be found as equity cost of financially independent company k_0 of the same group of risk, plus premium for risk, the value of which is equal to production of difference ($k_0 - k_\mathrm{d}$) on leverage level L:

$$k_\mathrm{e} = k_0 + (k_0 - k_\mathrm{d})L. \tag{3.4}$$

Formula (Eq. 3.4) shows that equity cost of the company increases linearly with leverage level (Fig. 3.3).

The combination of these two Modigliani–Miller statements implies that the increasing of level of debt in the capital structure of the company does not lead to increased value of firms, because the benefits gained from the use of more low-cost debt capital markets will be exactly offset by an increase in risk (we are speaking about the financial risk, the risk of bankruptcy) and, therefore, by an increase in the cost of equity capital of firms: investors will increase the required level of profitability under increased risk, by which a higher level of debt in the capital structure is accompanied.

In this way, the Modigliani–Miller theorem argues that in the absence of the taxes, the capital structure of the company does not affect the value of the company and its weighted average cost of capital, WACC, and equity cost increases linearly with the increase of financial leverage.

Explanations, given by Modigliani and Miller after obtaining their results, are the following (Modigliani and Miller 1958). Value of the company depends on profitability and risk only and does not depend on the capital structure. Based on the principle of preservation of the value, they postulated that the value of the company, which is equal to the sum of the equity and debt funds, is not changed when the ratio between its parts is changed. An important role in justification of Modigliani–Miller statements is an existence of arbitral awards opportunities for the committed markets. Two identical companies, differing only by the leverage level, must have the same value. If this is not the case, the arbitration aligns business cost: investors of less cost company can invest capital in a company of more value. Selling of shares of the first company and buying of stock of the second company will continue until the values of both companies are equal.

Most of Modigliani and Miller assumptions (Modigliani and Miller 1958), of course, are unrealistic. Some assumptions can be removed without changing the conclusions of the model. However, assuming no costs of bankruptcy and the absence of taxes (or the presence of corporate taxes only) is crucial—the change of these assumptions alters conclusions. The last two assumptions rule out the possibility of signaling theory and agency costs theory and, thus, also constitute a critical prerequisite (Fig. 3.4).

3.3.2 Modigliani–Miller Theory with Taxes

In the real situation, taxes on profit of companies always exist. Since the interest paid on debt is excluded from the tax base, it leads to the so-called effect of "tax shield": the value of the company that used the borrowed capital (leverage company) is higher than the value of the company that was financed entirely by the equity (non-leverage company). The value of the "tax shield" for 1 year is equal to $k_d D T$, where D—the value of debt, T—the income tax rate, and k_d—the interest on the debt (or debt capital cost) (Modigliani and Miller 1963). The value of the "tax shield" for perpetuity company for the entire time of its existence is equal to

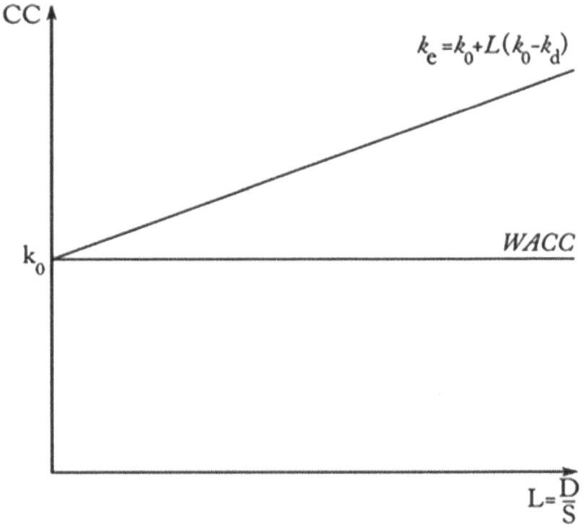

Fig. 3.4 Dependence of equity cost k_e and WACC on leverage level L within Modigliani–Miller theory without taxes

(we used the formula for the sum of terms of an infinitely decreasing geometric progression).

$$(\mathrm{PV})_{\mathrm{TS}} = k_d DT \sum_{t=1}^{\infty} (1 + k_d)^{-t} = DT \tag{3.5}$$

and the cost of leverage company is equal to

$$V = V_0 + DT, \tag{3.6}$$

where V_0 is the value of a financially independent company.

Thus, we obtain the following result obtained by Modigliani and Miller (1963):

> The value of financially dependent company is equal to the value of the company of the same risk group that used no leverage, increased by the value of tax shield arising from financial leverage, and equal to the product of rate of corporate income tax T and the value of debt D.

Let us now get the expression for the equity capital cost of the company under the existence of corporate taxes.

Accounting that $V_0 = \mathrm{CF}/k_0$ and that the ratio of debt capital $w_d = D/V$, one gets

$$V = \mathrm{CF}/k_0 + w_d VT. \tag{3.7}$$

Because the value of leverage company is $V = \mathrm{CF}/\mathrm{WACC}$, for weighted average cost of capital, WACC, we get

$$\mathrm{WACC} = k_0(1 - w_d T). \tag{3.8}$$

From here the dependence of WACC on leverage $L = D/S$ becomes the following:

$$\text{WACC} = k_0(1 - LT/(1 + L)). \tag{3.9}$$

On the other hand, defining the weighted average cost of capital with "tax shield" accounting, we have

$$\text{WACC} = k_0 w_e + k_d w_d (1 - T). \tag{3.10}$$

Equating Eqs. (3.9) and (3.11), one gets

$$k_0(1 - w_d T) = k_0 w_e + k_d w_d (1 - T) \tag{3.11}$$

and from here, for equity cost, we get the following expression:

$$\begin{aligned} k_e &= k_0 \frac{(1 - w_d T)}{w_e} - k_d \frac{w_d}{w_e}(1 - T) = k_0 \frac{1}{w_e} - k_0 \frac{w_d}{w_e} T - k_d \frac{D}{S}(1 - T) \\ &= k_0 \frac{D + S}{S} - k_0 \frac{D}{S} T - k_d \frac{D}{S}(1 - T) = k_0 + L(1 - T)(k_0 - k_d). \end{aligned} \tag{3.12}$$

So, we get the following statement obtained by Modigliani and Miller (1963):

> Equity cost of leverage company k_e paying tax on profit could be found as equity cost of financially independent company k_0 of the same group of risk, plus premium for risk, the value of which is equal to production of difference $(k_0 - k_d)$ on leverage level L and on tax shield $(1 - T)$.

It should be noted that the formula (Eq. 3.12) is different from the formula (Eq. 3.4) without tax only by the multiplier $(1 - T)$ in terms of a premium for risk. As the multiplier is less than unit, the corporate tax on profits leads to the fact that capital is growing with the increasing of financial leverage, slower than it would have been without them.

Analysis of formulas (Eqs. 3.4, 3.9, and 3.12) leads to the following conclusions. When leverage grows:

1. Value of company increases.
2. Weighted average cost of capital WACC decreases from k_0 (at $L = 0$) up to $k_0(1 - T)$ (at $L = \infty$) (when the company is funded solely by borrowed funds).
3. Equity cost increases linearly from k_0 (at $L = 0$) up to ∞ (at $L = \infty$).

Within their theory, Modigliani and Miller (1963) had come to the following conclusions. With the growth of financial leverage (Fig. 3.5):

1. The company value increases.
2. The weighted average cost of capital decreases from k_0 (for $L = 0$) up to $k_0(1 - T)$ (for $L = \infty$, when the company is financed entirely with borrowed funds).
3. The cost of equity capital increases linearly from k_0 (for $L = 0$) up to ∞ (for $L = \infty$).

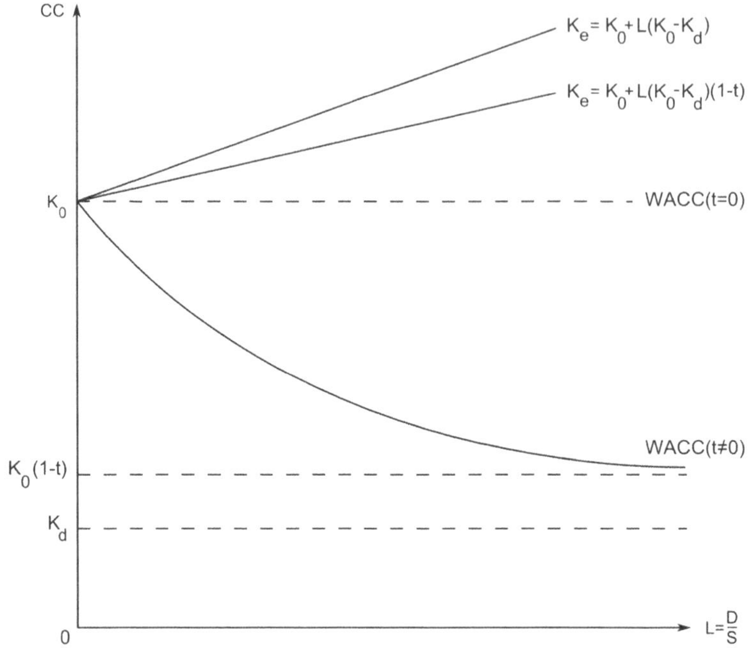

Fig. 3.5 Dependence of equity capital cost, debt cost, and WACC on leverage in Modigliani–Miller theory without taxes ($t = 0$) and with taxes ($t \neq 0$)

3.3.3 Main Assumptions of Modigliani–Miller Theory

The most important assumptions of the Modigliani–Miller theory are as following:

1. Investors are behaving rationally and instantaneously, see profit opportunity inadequated to investment risk. Therefore, the possibility of a stable situation of the arbitration, i.e., obtain the risk-free profit on the difference in prices for the same asset, cannot be kept any length of time—reasonable investors quickly take advantage of it for their own purposes and equalize conditions in the market. This means that in a developed financial market capital, the same risk should be rewarded by the same rate of return.
2. Investment and financial market opportunities should be equally accessible to all categories of investors—whether institutional or individual investors, large or small, rapidly growing or stable, or experienced or relatively inexperienced.
3. Transaction costs associated with funding are very small. In practice, the magnitude of transaction costs is inversely proportional to the amount of finance involved, so this assumption is more consistent with reality than the large sums involved: i.e., in attracting small amounts, the transaction costs can be high, while, as in attracting large loans, as well as during placement of shares at a significant amount, the transaction costs can be ignored.

4. Investors get money and provide funds to borrowers at risk-free rate. In all probability, this assumption is due to the fact that the lender seeks to protect himself by using one or other guarantees, pledge of assets, the right to pay claims on third parties, and the treaty provisions restricting the freedom of the borrower to act to the detriment of the creditor. Lender's risk is really small, but its position can be considered risk free with respect to the position of the borrower and, accordingly, should be rewarded by a risk-free rate of return.
5. Companies have only two types of assets: risk-free debt capital and risky equity capital.
6. There is no possibility of bankruptcy, i.e., irrespective of what the level of financial leverage of the company—borrowers are reached—bankruptcy is not threatening them. Thus, bankruptcy costs are absent.
7. There are no corporate taxes and taxes on personal income of investors. If the personal income tax can indeed be neglected, because of the assets of the company separated from the assets of shareholders, the corporate income taxes should be considered in the development of more realistic theories (which was done by Modigliani and Miller in their second paper devoted to the capital structure (Modigliani and Miller 1963).
8. Companies are in the same class of risky companies.
9. All financial flows are perpetuity.
10. Companies have the same information.
11. Management of the company maximizes the capitalization of the company.

3.3.4 *Modifications of Modigliani–Miller Theory*

Taking into Account Market Risk: Hamada Model Robert Hamada (1969) unites capital asset pricing model (CAPM) with Modigliani–Miller model taxation. As a result, he derived the following formula for calculation of the equity cost of financially dependent company, including both financial and business risk of company:

$$k_e = k_F + (k_M - k_F)b_U + (k_M - k_F)b_U\frac{D}{S}(1 - T), \tag{3.13}$$

where b_U is the β-coefficient of the company of the same group of business risk as the company under consideration, but with zero financial leverage. The formula (Eq. 3.13) represents the desired profitability of equity capital k_e as a sum of three components: risk-free profitability k_F, compensating to shareholders a temporary value of their money, premium for business risk $(k_M - k_F)b_U$, and premium for financial risk $(k_M - k_F)b_U\frac{D}{S}(1 - T)$.

If the company does not have borrowing ($D = 0$), the financial risk factor will be equal to zero (the third term is drawn to zero), and its owners will only receive the premium for business risk.

To apply the Hamada equation, specialists in practice, in most cases, use book value of equity capital as its approach of market value. Nevertheless, the Hamada formula implies the use of market value of the assets.

It should be noted also that the formula (Eq. 3.13) can be used to derive other equations, using which you can analyze the impact of financial leverage on β-factor of company shares.

Equating CAPM formula to equity cost, we get:

$$k_{\mathrm{F}} + (k_{\mathrm{M}} - k_{\mathrm{F}})b_{\mathrm{U}} = k_{\mathrm{F}} + (k_{\mathrm{M}} - k_{\mathrm{F}})b_{\mathrm{U}} + (k_{\mathrm{M}} - k_{\mathrm{F}})b_{\mathrm{U}}\frac{D}{S}(1 - T) \tag{3.14}$$

or

$$b = b_{\mathrm{U}}\left(1 + \frac{D}{S}(1 - T)\right). \tag{3.15}$$

In this way, the assumptions on which Modigliani–Miller theory and CAPM are based, β-factor of equity capital of financially dependent company is equal to β-factor of financially independent company, corrected for tax on profit rate and applied leverage level. Consequently, market risk of the company, measured by a factor b, depends on both the business risk of the company, a measure of which is b_{U},, and on the financial risk b, which is calculated by the formula (Eq. 3.15).

In conclusion, here are the formulas for calculating the capital costs within the CAPM model [in parenthesis, there are formulas within the Modigliani–Miller theory (Modigliani and Miller 1958, 1963, 1966)].

The equity cost for company without debt capital:

$$k_{\mathrm{e}} = k_{\mathrm{F}} + (\bar{k}_{\mathrm{M}} - k_{\mathrm{F}})\beta_{\mathrm{U}}, \quad (k_{\mathrm{e}} = k_0). \tag{3.16}$$

The equity cost for company with debt capital:

$$k_{\mathrm{e}} = k_{\mathrm{F}} + (\bar{k}_{\mathrm{M}} - k_{\mathrm{F}})\beta_{\mathrm{e}}, \quad (k_{\mathrm{e}} = k_0 + (1 - T)(k_0 - k_{\mathrm{d}})L). \tag{3.17}$$

The debt cost:

$$k_{\mathrm{d}} = k_{\mathrm{F}} + (\bar{k}_{\mathrm{M}} - k_{\mathrm{F}})\beta_{\mathrm{d}}, (k_{\mathrm{d}} = k_{\mathrm{F}}; \beta_{\mathrm{d}} = 0). \tag{3.18}$$

The weighted average cost of capital (WACC):

$$\mathrm{WACC} = k_{\mathrm{e}}w_{\mathrm{e}} + k_{\mathrm{d}}w_{\mathrm{d}}(1 - T), \quad (\mathrm{WACC} = k_0(1 - Tw_{\mathrm{d}})). \tag{3.19}$$

The Cost of Capital Under Risky Debt Another hypothesis of Modigliani and Miller was the suggestion about free of risk debt (in their theory, there are two types of assets: risky equity and free of risk debt). However, if we assume the risk of bankruptcy of the company (and, accordingly, the ability to nonpayment of loans), the situation may change. Stiglitz (1969) and Rubinstein (1973) have shown that the conclusions concerning the total value of company do not change as compared to the findings derived by Modigliani and Miller under assumptions about free of risk debt (Modigliani and Miller 1958, 1963, 1966). However, the debt cost is changed. If previously, under assumption about the free of risk debt, it (debt cost) was regarded as a constant $k_d = k_F$, now it is not a constant. This claim is based on the work by Hsia (1981), where based on the models of pricing options, Modigliani–Miller and CAPM, it was shown that if one uses the formula for the net discount income, a term, reflecting tax protection on debt, should be discounted at the rate

$$k'_d = k_F + (k_0 - k_F)N(-d_1)\frac{1}{w_d}, \tag{3.20}$$

where

$$d_1 = \frac{-\ln w_d + k_F t}{\sigma\sqrt{t}} k_F + \frac{1}{2}\sigma\sqrt{t}, \tag{3.21}$$

where t—a moment of payment of a credit and $N(-d_1)$—cumulative normal distribution of probability of random value d_1.

The Account of Corporate and Individual Taxes (Miller Model) In the second article, Modigliani and Miller (1963) considered taxation of corporate profits, but did not take into account the presence in the economy of individual taxes of investors.

Merton Miller (1997) has introduced the model, demonstrating the impact of leverage on the company value taking into account corporate and individual taxes (Miller 1976).

To describe his model, we will enter the following legends: T_C—tax on corporate profits rate, T_S—the tax rate on income of an individual investor from his ownership by stock of corporation, T_D—tax rate on interest income from the provision of individual investors of credits to other investors and companies. Income from shares partly comes in the form of a dividend and, in part, as capital profits, so that T_S is a weighted average value of effective rates of tax on dividends and capital profits on shares, while the income from the provision of loans usually comes in the form of the interests. The latter are usually taxed at a higher rate. In light of the individual taxes, and with the same assumptions that have been made for Modigliani–Miller models previously, the financially independent company value can be determined as follows:

$$V_U = \frac{\text{EBIT}(1 - T_C)(1 - T_S)}{k_0}. \tag{3.22}$$

A term $(1 - T_S)$ allows us to take into account the individual taxes in the formula. In this way, the numerator indicates which part of the operating company's profit remains in the possession of the investors, after the company will pay taxes on their profits, and its shareholders then will pay individual taxes on income from stock ownership. Since individual taxes reduce profits, remaining in the disposal of investors, the latter, with other things being equal, also reduce and an overall assessment of the financially independent company value.

We will assess the financially dependent company under the condition of a double taxation of income investors. To start, let us divide the annual cash flows of financially dependent company CF_L into flows sent to its shareholders CF_e and the flows belonging to debt owners CF_d, taking account of both corporation tax on profits and tax on the income of individuals:

$$CF_L = CF_e + CF_d = (EBIT - I)(1 - T_C)(1 - T_S) + I(1 - T_D), \tag{3.23}$$

where I is the annual interest payments on debt.

The formula (Eq. 3.23) can also be rewritten as follows:

$$\begin{aligned} CF_L &= CF_e + CF_d \\ &= EBIT(1 - T_C)(1 - T_S) - I(1 - T_C)(1 - T_S) + I(1 - T_D). \end{aligned} \tag{3.24}$$

The first term of the equation (Eq. 3.24) corresponds to cash flow after taxes for financially independent company, shown in equation (Eq. 3.22), which shows its present value. The second and the third terms of the equation, reflecting the financial dependence, correspond to cash flows related to the debt financing, which, as previously, is considered free of risk. Their present values are obtained by discounting risk-free nominal rate on debt k_d.

By combining the present values of all three terms, we get the company value by using the debt financing and in the presence of all types of taxation:

$$V_U = \frac{EBIT(1 - T_C)(1 - T_S)}{k_0} - \frac{I(1 - T_C)(1 - T_S)}{k_d} + \frac{I(1 - T_d)}{k_d}. \tag{3.25}$$

The first term in (Eq. 3.25) is identical to V_U in formula (Eq. 3.22). Accounting this and combining two last terms, we get the following formula:

$$V_L = V_U + \frac{I(1 - T_d)}{k_d}\left[1 - \frac{(1 - T_C)(1 - T_S)}{(1 - T_d)}\right]. \tag{3.26}$$

The amount of paid interests by taking into account the taxation, divided by the desired profitability of debt capital,

$$\frac{I(1 - T_d)}{k_d} \tag{3.27}$$

is equal to market value of the debt D. Substituting D in the previous formula, we get the final expression, which is known as a formula of a Miller model:

$$V_L = V_U + \left[1 - \frac{(1 - T_C)(1 - T_S)}{(1 - T_d)}\right] D. \tag{3.28}$$

The Miller model allows you to obtain an estimate of the value of financially dependent company, taking into account the corporate tax, as well as tax on individuals. The Miller formula (Eq. 3.28) has several important consequences:

1. The second term of sum,

$$\left[1 - \frac{(1 - T_C)(1 - T_S)}{(1 - T_d)}\right] D, \tag{3.29}$$

represents the gains from the use of debt capital. This term replaces the tax on profit of corporation rate in the Modigliani–Miller model with corporate taxes:

$$V_L = V_U + TD. \tag{3.30}$$

2. If we ignore taxes, a term (Eq. 3.29) will be equal to zero. Thus, in this case, the formula (Eq. 3.28) is transformed into the original version of the Modigliani–Miller model without taxes.
3. If we neglect taxes on individuals, the considering term becomes $1 - (1 - T_C) = T_C$, so, in this case, (Eq. 3.28) becomes a Modigliani–Miller model with corporate taxes (Eq. 3.30).
4. If the shareholder receives profit only in the form of dividend, and if effective tax rates on income from shares and bonds are equal ($T_S = T_D$), the terms $1 - T_S$ and $1 - T_D$ are shrinking, and the factor for D in (Eq. 3.29) again is equal to T_C.
5. If the shareholder receives dividends, and income from capital, the situation is changed.

   In this case, effective tax rates on income from shares and bonds are not equal. Let us take a look at common case, when individual taxes on income for the company shares are less than individual taxes of creditors. This encourages investors to purchase the shares of the company compared to purchasing the bonds of the company. In this case, $T_S < T_D$. Then factor in D in (Eq. 3.28) β has the form

$$\begin{aligned}\beta &= 1 - \frac{(1 - T_C)(1 - T_S)}{(1 - T_d)} = 1 - (1 - T_C)\alpha = 1 - (1 - T_C)(1 + \gamma) \\ &= T_C + \gamma(T_C - 1) < T_C.\end{aligned} \tag{3.31}$$

It is less than T_C, because $\gamma > 0$, $T_C < 1$; therefore, in this case, the effect of using debt financing, although there is, is less than in the absence of individual taxes. In other words, the effect of tax shields for the company in this case decreases, and it becomes less than the above individual taxes of creditors (individual taxes for the obligations of the company) in comparison with the individual income tax on shares.

6. Let us take a look at case $T_S > T_D$, when individual income taxes on shares are bigger than individual taxes creditors. The factor β takes the form

$$\begin{aligned}\beta &= 1 - \frac{(1 - T_C)(1 - T_S)}{(1 - T_d)} = 1 - (1 - T_C)\alpha = 1 - (1 - T_C)(1 - \gamma) \\ &= T_C + \gamma(1 - T_C) > T_C.\end{aligned} \tag{3.32}$$

It is bigger than T_C, because $\gamma > 0$, $T_C < 1$; therefore, in this case, the effect of the use of debt financing is increased compared with the case of the absence of individual taxes.

7. If $(1 - T_C)(1 - T_S) = 1 - T_D$, then this term is zero, and the effect of using debt financing will also be zero. This means that the benefits of the use of tax shields as a result of the application of debt financing will be fully offset by additional losses of investors, associated with a higher tax rate on interest on income of individuals. In this case, the capital structure will not affect the company value and its capital cost—in other words, you can apply Modigliani–Miller theory without tax (Modigliani and Miller 1958).

In his report, Miller (1976) claimed that companies on average will use issuance of shares and debt securities in such a way as to result in taxation of investors' income to be optimal. In such an equilibrium state will occur equality

$$(1 - T_C)(1 - T_S) = 1 - T_D, \tag{3.33}$$

and thus, as we have pointed out above, capital structure will not affect the market company value and its capital cost. Thus, by Miller, the conclusions on the irrelevance of the capital structure, made on the basis of the original Modigliani–Miller model with zero taxes, remain in force.

Subsequently, researchers adapted and checked the Miller results. Their works, as a rule, have been devoted to the Miller's conclusion concerning the absence of the gains from the use of the debt capital by the company. In the USA, an effective tax rate on the income of shareholders is lower than the one on the income of creditors, but, nevertheless, the product $(1 - T_C)(1 - T_S)$ is less than $1 - T_D$.

Consequently, the companies may receive the benefit from the use of debt financing. However, in the Miller's work, in fact, it has been shown that the distinction of rates of individual taxes on income of shareholders and creditors to some extent compensates the advantages of the use of debt financing, and, in this way, the tax benefits of debt are less than anticipated in an earlier Modigliani–Miller model, where only corporate taxes have been taken into account.

In conclusion, we present in Table 3.1 classification and summary of main theories of capital structures of company.

Table 3.1 Classification and summary of main theories of capital structures of company

Theory		Main thesis
Traditional theory		Empirical theory, existing before appearance of the first quantitative theory of capital structures (Modigliani–Miller theory) in 1958 (Modigliani and Miller 1958, 1963, 1966). Weighted average cost of capital depends on capital structures of company. There is an optimal dependence on capital structures of company
Modigliani–Miller theory (MM)	Without taxes	Capital cost and capitalization of the company are irrelevant to the capital structures of company
	With taxes	Weighted average cost of capital is decreased with leverage level, equity cost is increased linearly with leverage level, and capitalization of the company is increased with leverage level continuously
Brusov–Filatova–Orekhova theory (BFO-1)	For arbitrary age Without inflation	BFO theory (Brusov and Filatova 2011; Brusov et al. 2011a, b, c, 2012a, b, 2013a, b, 2014a, b; Filatova et al. 2008; Brusova 2011) has replaced the famous theory of capital cost and capital structure by Nobel laureates Modigliani and Miller (1958, 1963, 1966). The authors have moved from the assumption of Modigliani–Miller concerning the perpetuity (infinite time of life) of companies and further elaborated quantitative theory of valuation of core parameters of financial activities of companies with arbitrary age. Results of modern BFO theory turn out to be quite different from those of Modigliani–Miller theory. It shows that the latter, via its perpetuity, underestimates the assessment of weighted average cost of capital and the equity cost of the company and substantially overestimates the assessment of the capitalization of the company. Such an incorrect assessment of key performance indicators of financial activities of companies has led to an underestimation of risks involved, and impossibility, or serious difficulties in adequate managerial decision-making, which was one of the implicit reasons of the global financial crisis of 2008. In the BFO theory, in investments at certain values of return on investment, there is an optimum investment structure. As well authors have developed a new mechanism of formation of the company optimal capital

(continued)

Table 3.1 (continued)

Theory		Main thesis
		structure, different from that suggested by trade-off theory
	For arbitrary age With inflation	Inflation not only increases the equity cost and the weighted average cost of capital, but as well it changes their dependence on leverage. In particular, it increases the growing rate of equity cost with leverage. Capitalization of the company is decreased when taking account of inflation
	For arbitrary age With increased financial distress costs and risk of bankruptcy	In BFO theory, with increased financial distress costs and risk of bankruptcy, the optimal capital structure is absent, which means that trade-off theory does NOT work
Brusov–Filatova–Orekhova theory (BFO-2)	For arbitrary lifetime	In perpetuity limit (Modigliani–Miller theory), time of life of company and company age turn out to be the same: both of them are infinite. When we move from the assumption of Modigliani–Miller concerning the perpetuity of companies, these concepts (time of life of company and company age) become different and one should distinguish them when generalizing the Modigliani–Miller theory with respect to finite n. Thus, we have developed two kinds of finite n-theories: BFO-1 and BFO-2. BFO–1 theory is related to companies with arbitrary age, and BFO-2 theory is related to companies with arbitrary lifetime companies. In other words, BFO-1 is applicable for the most interesting case of companies that reached the age of n-years and continue to exist on the market, and allows us to analyze the financial condition of the operating companies. BFO-2 theory allows us to examine the financial status of the companies which ceased to exist, i.e., of those for which n means not age, but a lifetime, i.e., the time of existence. A lot of schemes of termination of activities of the company can exist: bankruptcy, merger, acquisition, etc. One of those schemes, when the value of the debt capital D becomes zero at the time of termination of activity of company n, is considered in Chapter 3 and comparison of results of BFO-1 and BFO-2 have been done.

(continued)

Table 3.1 (continued)

Theory		Main thesis
Brusov–Filatova–Orekhova theory (BFO–3)	For rating needs	A new approach to rating methodology has been developed in this monograph. Part 2 is devoted to rating of non-financial issuers, while Part 3 is devoted to long-term and arbitrary duration project rating. The key factors of a new approach are: (1) The adequate use of discounting of financial flows virtually not used in existing rating methodologies, (2) The incorporation of rating parameters (financial "ratios") into the modern theory of capital structure (Brusov–Filatova–Orekhova (BFO–3 theory) (in Chapter 8) and into its perpetuity limits (MM and MMM (in Chapters 6 and 7). This on the one hand allows us to use the powerful tools of these theories in the rating, and on the other hand, it ensures the correct discount rates when discounting financial flows. The interplay between rating ratios and leverage level which can be quite important in rating is discussed as well. All these create a new base for rating methodologies. New approach to ratings and rating methodologies allows us to issue more correct ratings of issuers and makes the rating methodologies more understandable and transparent
Trade-off theory	Static	The static trade-off theory is developed taking into account tax on profit and bankruptcy cost. It attempts to explain the optimal capital structure in terms of the balancing act between the benefits of debt (tax shield from interest deduction) and the disadvantage of debt (from the increased financial distress and expected bankruptcy costs). The tax shield benefit is the corporate income tax rate multiplied by the market value of debt and the expected bankruptcy costs are the probability of bankruptcy multiplied by the estimated bankruptcy costs
		Does not take into account the costs of the adaptation of financial capital structure to the optimal one, economic behavior of managers, owners, and other participants of economical process, as well as a number of other factors
		As it has been shown in BFO theory, the optimal capital structure is absent in trade-off theory

(continued)

Table 3.1 (continued)

Theory		Main thesis
	Dynamic	The dynamic trade-off models assume that costs of constant capital adjustment are high and thus firms will change capital structure only if benefits exceed costs. Therefore, there is an optimal range, outside of which each leverage changes but remains unchanged inside. Companies try to adjust their leverage when it reaches the boundary of the optimal range. Subject to types of adjustment costs, firms reach target ratio faster or slower. Proportional changes imply slight correction, whereas fixed changes imply considerable costs. In the dynamic model, correct decision on financial structure capital of the company in this period depends on the profit, which the company hopes to receive in the next period
		In BFO theory, with increased financial distress costs and risk of bankruptcy, the optimal capital structure is absent, which means that trade-off theory does NOT work: in static version as well as in dynamic one
Accounting for transaction cost		Accounting for the recapitalization transaction costs for the company, in which these costs are high, leads to the conclusion that it is more cost-effective to not modify financial capital structure, even if it is not optimal, during a certain period of time. The actual and target capital structure may vary because of the tool costs
Accounting for asymmetry of information		At the real financial markets, information is asymmetric (managers of the companies have owned more reliable information than investors and creditors), and rationality of economic subjects is limited
Signaling theory		Information asymmetry may be reduced on the basis of certain signals for creditors and investors, related to the behavior of managers on the capital market. It should take into account the previous development of the company and the current and projected cost-effectiveness of activities
Pecking order theory		The pecking order theory is the preferred, and empirically observed, sequence of financing type to raise capital. That is, firms first tap retained earnings (internal equity) finance, second source is debt, and the last source is issuing new common stock shares

(continued)

Table 3.1 (continued)

Theory		Main thesis
		(external equity). The empirical evidence of nonfinancial firm debt ratios coupled with the decision-making process of top management and the board of directors points to a greater adherence to the pecking order theory
Theories of conflict of interests	Theory of agency costs	Management of the company may take decisions that are contrary to the interests of the shareholders or creditors, respectively; the costs are necessary to monitor its actions. An effective tool for resolving agent problem is the correct selection of compensation package (the share of participation of agent in property, bonus, stock options), allowing us to link revenue of managers with the dynamics of equity capital and to provide motivation for managers to its (equity capital) conservation and growth
	Theory of corporate control and costs monitoring	If asymmetries of information exist, creditors, providing the capital, are interested in the possibility of the implementation of the self-monitoring of the effectiveness of its use and return. Costs for monitoring, as a rule, are borne by the company owners by including them into credit rate. The level of monitoring costs depends on the scale of the business; therefore, with the increase of the business scale, the weighted average cost of capital of the company grows and company market value is reduced
	Theory of stakeholders	Stakeholder theory is a theory that identifies and models the groups that are stakeholders of a corporation or project. The diversity and the intersection of stakeholders' interests and different assessment by them of acceptable risk generate conditions for conflict of their interest, that is, making some corrections into the process of optimizing financial capital structure
Behavioral theories	Manager investment autonomy	Managers implement those decisions, which, from their point of view, will be positively perceived by investors and, respectively, positively affect the market value of companies: when the market value of shares of a company and the degree of consensus of expectations of managers and investors are high, the company has an additional issue of shares, and in the opposite situation, it uses debt instruments. In this way, the financial capital structure is

(continued)

Table 3.1 (continued)

Theory		Main thesis
		more influenced by investors, the expectations of which are taken into account by managers
	The equity market timing theory	Leverage level is determined by market dynamics. Equity market timing theory means that company should issue shares at high price and repurchase them at low price. The idea is to exploit temporary fluctuations in the equity cost relative to the cost of other forms of capital
	Information cascades	In order to save costs and to avoid errors, financial capital structure can be formed not on the basis of the calculations of optimal capital structure or depending on available in different periods of company life funding sources, but borrowing from other companies that have successful, reputable managers (companies' leaders), as well as using (in the wake of the majority) the most popular methods of management of capital structure

References

Brusov PN, Filatova TV (2011) From Modigliani–Miller to general theory of capital cost and capital structure of the company. Finance Credit 435:2–8

Brusov P, Filatova T, Orekhova N, Brusova A (2011a) Weighted average cost of capital in the theory of Modigliani–Miller, modified for a finite life-time company. Appl Financ Econ 21 (11):815–824

Brusov P, Filatova T, Orekhova N, Brusov PP, Brusova N (2011b) From Modigliani–Miller to general theory of capital cost and capital structure of the company. Res J Econ Bus ICT 2:16–21

Brusov P, Filatova T, Orekhova N et al (2011c) Influence of debt financing on the effectiveness of the investment project within the Modigliani–Miller theory. Res J Econ Bus ICT (UK) 2:11–15

Brusov P, Filatova T, Eskindarov M, Orekhova N (2012a) Influence of debt financing on the effectiveness of the finite duration investment project. Appl Financ Econ 22(13):1043–1052

Brusov P, Filatova T, Eskindarov M, Orekhova N (2012b) Hidden global causes of the global financial crisis. J Rev Global Econ 1:106–111

Brusov P, Filatova P, Orekhova N (2013a) Absence of an optimal capital structure in the famous tradeoff theory! J Rev Global Econ 2:94–116

Brusov P, Filatova T, Orekhova N (2013b) A qualitatively new effect in corporative finance: abnormal dependence of cost of equity of company on leverage. J Rev Global Econ 2:183–193

Brusov P, Filatova P, Orekhova N (2014a) Mechanism of formation of the company optimal capital structure, different from suggested by trade off theory. Cogent Econ Finance 2:1–13. https://doi.org/10.1080/23322039.2014.946150

Brusov P, Filatova T, Orekhova N (2014b) Inflation in Brusov–Filatova–Orekhova theory and in its perpetuity limit–Modigliani–Miller theory. J Rev Global Econ 3:175–185

Brusov P, Filatova T, Orekhova N, Eskindarov M (2015) Modern corporate finance, investment and taxation, 1st edn. Springer International Publishing, Cham, pp 1–368

Brusov P, Filatova T, Orekhova N, Kulk WI (2018a) New meaningful effects in modern capital structure theory. J Rev Global Econ 7:104–122

Brusov P, Filatova T, Orekhova N, Kulk V (2018b) A "golden age" of the companies: conditions of its existence. J Rev Global Econ 7:88–103

Brusov P, Filatova T, Orekhova N, Kulk V (2018c) Rating methodology: new look and new horizons. J Rev Global Econ 7:63–87

Brusov P, Filatova T, Orekhova N, Kulk V (2018d) Rating: new approach. J Rev Global Econ 7:37–62

Brusova A (2011) A comparison of the three methods of estimation of weighted average cost of capital and equity cost of company. Financ Anal Prob Sol 34(76):36–42

Filatova T, Orekhova N, Brusova A (2008) Weighted average cost of capital in the theory of Modigliani–Miller, modified for a finite life-time company. Bull FU 48:68–77

Hamada R (1969) Portfolio analysis, market equilibrium, and corporate finance. J Financ 24 (1):13–31

Hsia C (1981) Coherence of the modern theories of finance. Financ Rev 16(1):27–42

Miller M (1976) Debt and taxes. J Financ 32(2):261–275

Miller M (1997) Merton Miller on derivatives. Wiley, New York, NY

Modigliani F, Miller M (1958) The cost of capital, corporate finance, and the theory of investment. Am Econ Rev 48:261–297

Modigliani F, Miller M (1963) Corporate income taxes and the cost of capital: a correction. Am Econ Rev 53:147–175

Modigliani F, Miller M (1966) Some estimates of the cost of capital to the electric utility industry 1954–1957. Am Econ Rev 56:333–391

Rubinstein M (1973) A mean-variance synthesis of corporate financial theory. J Financ 28:167–181

Stiglitz J (1969) A re-examination of the Modigliani–Miller theorem. Am Econ Rev 59(5):784–793

Chapter 4
Modification of the Modigliani–Miller Theory for the Case of Advance Tax on Profit Payments

4.1 Introduction

The first serious study (and first quantitative study) of influence of capital structure of the company on its indicators of activities was the work by Nobel Prize Winners Modigliani and Miller. Their theory has a lot of limitations. One of the most important and serious assumptions of the Modigliani–Miller theory is that all financial flows as well as all companies are perpetuity. This limitation was removed by Brusov–Filatova–Orekhova in 2008 (Filatova et al. 2008), who have created BFO theory—the modern theory of capital cost and capital structure for companies of arbitrary age (Brusov (2018a, b), Brusov et al. (2015), Brusov et al. (2018a, b, c, d, e, f), Brusov et al. (2018g), Brusov et al. (2019), Brusov et al. (2020), Filatova et al. (2018)).

Despite the fact that the Modigliani–Miller theory (Modigliani and Miller (1958, 1963, 1966) is currently a particular case of the general theory of capital cost and capital structure—Brusov–Filatova–Orekhova (BFO) theory—it is still widely used in the West.

In this chapter, we discuss one more limitation of Modigliani–Miller theory: a method of tax on profit payments. Modigliani–Miller theory considers these payments as annuity-immediate while in practice these payments are made in advance and thus should be considered as annuity-due.

We generalize the Modigliani–Miller theory for the case of advance tax on profit payments, which is widely used in practice, and show that this leads to some important consequences, which change seriously all the main statements by Modigliani and Miller. These consequences are the following: WACC depends on debt cost k_d, WACC turns out to be lower than in the case of the classical Modigliani–Miller theory, and thus company capitalization becomes higher than in the ordinary Modigliani–Miller theory. We show that equity dependence on leverage level L is

P. Brusov et al., *Ratings*, Contributions to Finance and Accounting,
https://doi.org/10.1007/978-3-030-56243-4_4

still linear, but the tilt angle with respect to L-axis turns out to be smaller: this could lead to the modification of the dividend policy of the company.

Correct accounting of the method of tax on profit payments demonstrates that shortcomings of Modigliani–Miller theory are serious than thought: the underestimation of WACC really turns out to be bigger, as well as the overestimation of the capitalization of the company. This means that systematic risks arising from the use of modified Modigliani–Miller theory (which is more correct than the "classical" one) in practice are higher than it was suggested by the "classical" version of this theory.

4.2 Modified Modigliani–Miller Theory in Case of Advance Tax Payments

4.2.1 Tax Shield in Case of Advance Tax Payments

Modigliani–Miller theory considers these payments as annuity-immediate while in practice these payments are made in advance and thus should be considered as annuity-due.

To calculate tax shield *TS* in the case of advance tax payments, one should use annuity-due (Fig. 4.1)

$$TS = k_d Dt + \frac{k_d Dt}{(1+k_d)} + \frac{k_d Dt}{(1+k_d)^2} + \ldots = \frac{k_d Dt}{\left(1-(1+k_d)^{-1}\right)} = Dt(1+k_d) \tag{4.1}$$

This expression is different from the case of the classical Modigliani–Miller theory (which used annuity-immediate) (Fig. 4.2)

$$TS = \frac{k_d Dt}{(1+k_d)} + \frac{k_d Dt}{(1+k_d)^2} + \ldots = \frac{k_d Dt}{(1+k_d)\left(1-(1+k_d)^{-1}\right)} = Dt \tag{4.2}$$

Thus, in the former case tax shield *TS* is bigger by multiplier $(1 + k_d)$. This is connected with the time value of money: money today is more expensive than money tomorrow due to the possibility of their alternative investment.

Fig. 4.1 Annuity-due

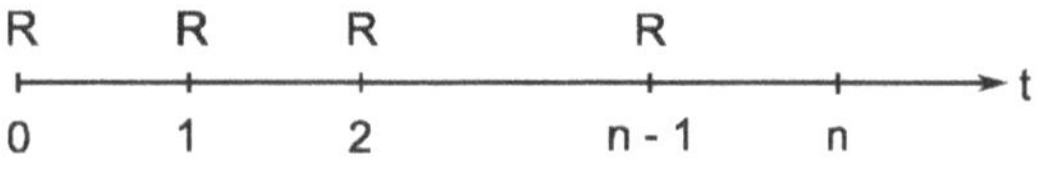

Fig. 4.2 Annuity-immediate

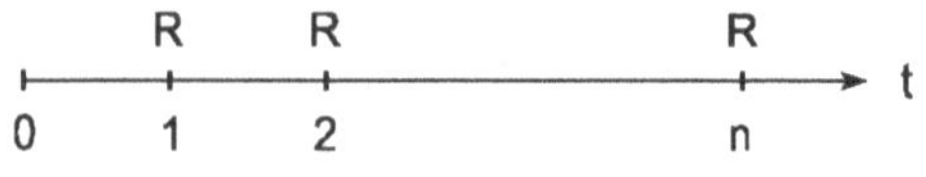

4.2.2 Capitalization of the Company

Modigliani–Miller theorem for capitalization of the company

$$V = V_0 + TS \tag{4.3}$$

takes the following form:

$$V = V_0 + Dt(1 + k_d). \tag{4.4}$$

Thus, we arrive at the following statement, which modifies the original Modigliani and Miller.

The value of financially dependent company making tax on profit payments in advance is equal to the value of the company of the same risk group that used no leverage, increased by the value of tax shield arising from financial leverage, and equal to the product of rate of corporate income tax t, the value of debt D, and multiplier (1 + k_d*).*

Substituting $D = w_d \cdot V$

one has

$$V\left(1 - w_d t(1 + k_d)\right) = V_0$$

$$\frac{CF}{WACC} \cdot \left(1 - w_d t(1 + k_d)\right) = \frac{CF}{k_0}$$

And for WACC we have the following formula:

$$WACC = k_0\left(1 - w_d t(1 + k_d)\right). \tag{4.5}$$

$$\text{At} L \to \infty \quad WACC = k_0(1 - t(1 + k_d)). \tag{4.6}$$

This expression is different from that of the classical Modigliani–Miller theory

$$WACC = k_0\left(1 - w_d t\right)$$

$$\text{At } L \to \infty \quad WACC = k_0(1 - t).$$

From these expressions, it is seen that WACC decreases with L, achieving lower value $WACC = k_0(1 - t(1 + k_d))$ at $L \to \infty$ in the considered case comparing with the classical Modigliani–Miller theory $WACC = k_0(1 - t)$.

This also means also that company capitalization becomes higher than in the ordinary Modigliani–Miller theory (Fig. 4.3).

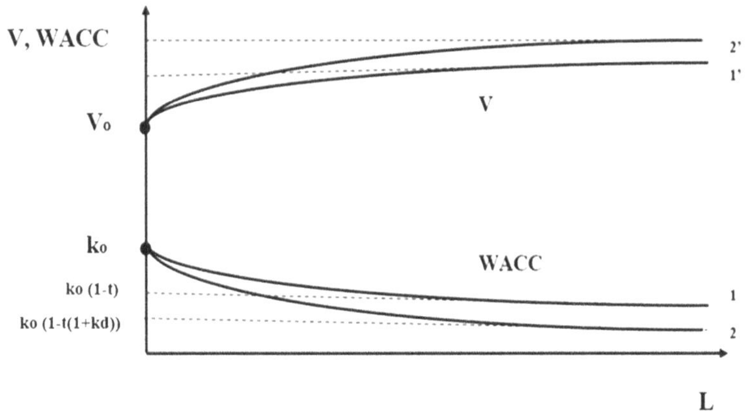

Fig. 4.3 Dependence of company capitalization, V, and WACC on leverage level in the "classical" Modigliani–Miller theory (curve 1′ and curve 1) and in the "modified" Modigliani–Miller theory (curve 2′ and curve 2)

4.2.3 Equity Cost

Let us find equity cost

$$WACC = k_e w_e + k_d w_d (1 - t). \tag{4.7}$$

Equating (4.5) and (4.7), we obtain

$$k_0(1 - w_d t(1 + k_d)) = k_e w_e + k_d w_d (1 - t), \tag{4.8}$$

whence we get the following expression for the equity cost:

$$\begin{aligned} k_e &= k_0 \frac{(1 - w_d t(1 + k_d))}{w_e} - k_d \frac{w_d}{w_e}(1 - t) = \\ &= k_0 \frac{1}{w_e} - k_0 \frac{w_d}{w_e}(1 + k_d) \cdot t - k_d \frac{D}{S}(1 - t) = \\ &= k_0 \frac{D + S}{S} - k_0 \frac{D}{S}(1 + k_d) \cdot t - k_d \frac{D}{S}(1 - t) = \\ &= k_0 + L[(1 - t)(k_0 - k_d) - k_0 k_d t]. \end{aligned} \tag{4.9}$$

Finally, we have for the equity cost

$$k_e = k_0 + L[(1 - t)(k_0 - k_d) - k_0 k_d t]. \tag{4.10}$$

Thus, we arrive at the following statement, which modifies the original Modigliani and Miller theory (Fig. 4.4).

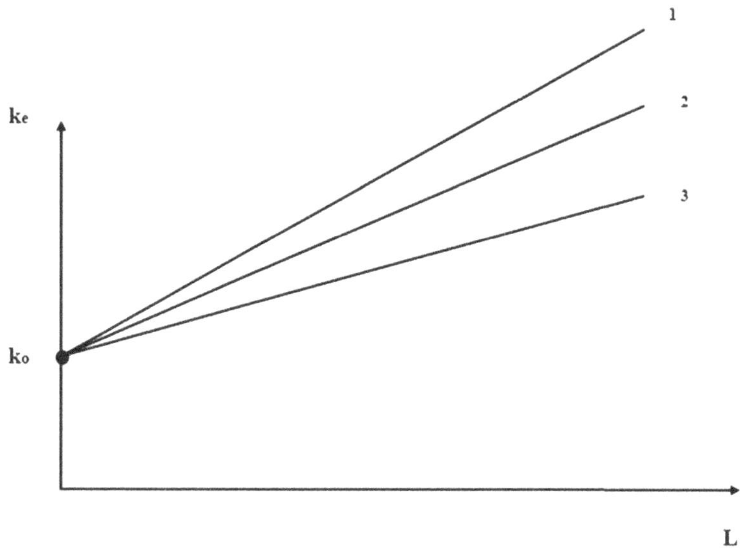

Fig. 4.4 Dependence of equity cost of the company, ke, on leverage level in the "classical" Modigliani–Miller theory (curve 2), in the "modified" Modigliani–Miller theory (curve 3), and for financially independent company ($t = 0$) (curve 1)

Equity cost of leverage company k_e making tax on profit payments in advance could be found as equity cost of financially independent company k_0 of the same group of risk, plus premium for risk, the value of which is equal to production of leverage level L on production of difference (k_0 − k_d) and tax shield ($1-t$), decreasing by the value $k_0 k_d t$.

This means that equity cost dependence on leverage level L is still linear, but the tilt angle with respect to L-axis turns out to be smaller $tg\alpha = (k_0 - k_d) \cdot (1 - t) - k_0 k_d t$.

This could lead to the modification of the dividend policy of the company, because the equity cost is economically sound value of dividends. Thus, company could decrease the value of dividends.

4.3 The Dependence of the Weighted Average Cost of Capital, WACC, on Leverage Level in the "Classical" Modigliani–Miller Theory (MM Theory) and in the Modified Modigliani–Miller Theory (MMM Theory)

Let us compare the dependence of the weighted average cost of capital, WACC, on leverage level in the "classical" Modigliani–Miller theory (MM theory) and in the modified Modigliani–Miller theory (MMM theory). Study of such dependence is very important, because the weighted average cost of capital, WACC, plays the role of discount rate in operating financial flows discounting as well as of financial flows in rating methodologies. WACC's value determines as well the capitalization of the company $V = CF/WACC$. We use Microsoft Excel for calculations.

From Tables 4.1, 4.2, 4.3, and 4.4 and from Fig. 4.5, it is seen that WACC in MMM theory turns out to be lower than in the case of the classical Modigliani–

Table 4.1 Dependence of WACC on leverage level in the "classical" Modigliani–Miller theory

k_o	L	t	WACC
0.2	0	0.2	0.2000
0.2	1	0.2	0.1800
0.2	2	0.2	0.1733
0.2	3	0.2	0.1700
0.2	4	0.2	0.1680
0.2	5	0.2	0.1667
0.2	6	0.2	0.1657
0.2	7	0.2	0.1650
0.2	8	0.2	0.1644
0.2	9	0.2	0.1640
0.2	10	0.2	0.1636

Table 4.2 Dependence of WACC on leverage level in the modified Modigliani–Miller theory (MMM theory) at $k_d = 0.18$.

k_o	L	t	k_d	WACC
0.2	0	0.2	0.18	0.2000
0.2	1	0.2	0.18	0.1764
0.2	2	0.2	0.18	0.1685
0.2	3	0.2	0.18	0.1646
0.2	4	0.2	0.18	0.1622
0.2	5	0.2	0.18	0.1607
0.2	6	0.2	0.18	0.1595
0.2	7	0.2	0.18	0.1587
0.2	8	0.2	0.18	0.1580
0.2	9	0.2	0.18	0.1575
0.2	10	0.2	0.18	0.1571

Table 4.3 Dependence of WACC on leverage level in the modified Modigliani–Miller theory (MMM theory) at $k_d = 0.14$

k_0	L	t	k_d	WACC
0.2	0	0.2	0.14	0.2000
0.2	1	0.2	0.14	0.1772
0.2	2	0.2	0.14	0.1696
0.2	3	0.2	0.14	0.1658
0.2	4	0.2	0.14	0.1635
0.2	5	0.2	0.14	0.1620
0.2	6	0.2	0.14	0.1609
0.2	7	0.2	0.14	0.1601
0.2	8	0.2	0.14	0.1595
0.2	9	0.2	0.14	0.1590
0.2	10	0.2	0.14	0.1585

Table 4.4 Dependence of WACC on leverage level in the modified Modigliani–Miller theory (MMM theory) at $k_d = 0.1$

k_0	L	t	k_d	WACC
0.2	0	0.2	0.1	0.2000
0.2	1	0.2	0.1	0.1780
0.2	2	0.2	0.1	0.1707
0.2	3	0.2	0.1	0.1670
0.2	4	0.2	0.1	0.1648
0.2	5	0.2	0.1	0.1633
0.2	6	0.2	0.1	0.1623
0.2	7	0.2	0.1	0.1615
0.2	8	0.2	0.1	0.1609
0.2	9	0.2	0.1	0.1604
0.2	10	0.2	0.1	0.1600

Miller theory and thus company capitalization becomes higher than in the ordinary Modigliani–Miller theory. It is seen that WACC decreases with debt cost k_d.

Correct accounting of the method of tax on profit payments demonstrates that shortcomings of Modigliani–Miller theory are serious than thought: the underestimation of WACC really turns out to be bigger, as well as the overestimation of the capitalization of the company. This means that systematic risks arising from the use of modified Modigliani–Miller theory (MMM theory) (which is more correct than the "classical" one) in practice are higher than it was suggested by the "classical" version of this theory.

4.4 Conclusions

Despite the fact that the Modigliani–Miller theory is currently a particular case of the general theory of capital cost and capital structure—Brusov–Filatova–Orekhova (BFO) theory—it is still widely used in the West. We generalize the Modigliani–Miller theory for the case of advance tax on profit payments, which is widely used in

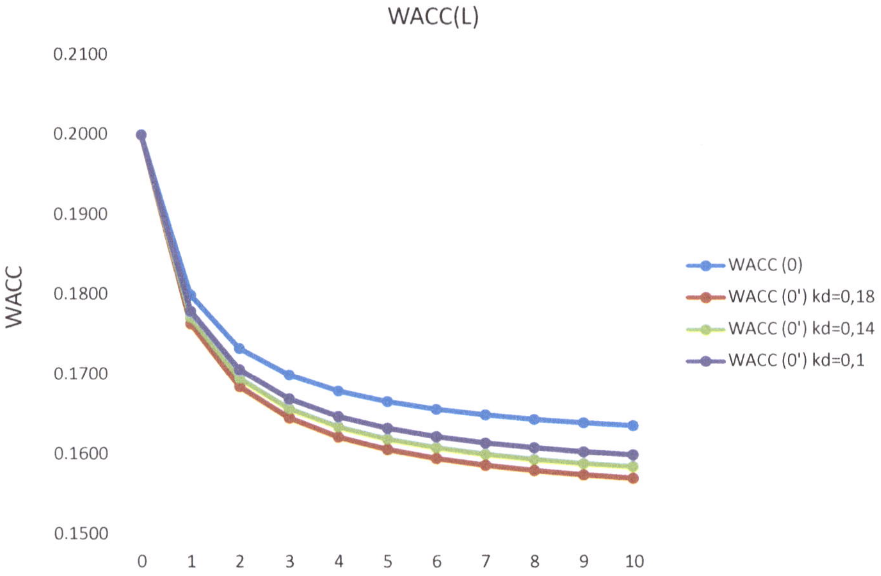

Fig. 4.5 Dependence of WACC on leverage level L: (1) in the "classical" Modigliani–Miller theory (curve WACC(0)) and (2) in the modified Modigliani–Miller theory (MMM theory) at different values of debt cost: $k_d = 0.18$; $k_d = 0.14$; $k_d = 0.1$ (curves WACC(0′))

practice, and show that this leads to some important consequences, which change seriously all the main statements by Modigliani and Miller. These consequences are the following: WACC depends on debt cost k_d, WACC turns out to be lower than in the case of the classical Modigliani–Miller theory, and thus company capitalization becomes higher than in the ordinary Modigliani–Miller theory.

We study as well the equity cost dependence on leverage level L and show that it is still linear, but the tilt angle with respect to L-axis turns out to be smaller in MMM theory $tg\alpha = (k_0 - k_d) \cdot (1 - t) - k_0 k_d t$, than in the classical Modigliani–Miller theory $tg\alpha = (k_0 - k_d) \cdot (1 - t)$. This could lead to the modification of the dividend policy of the company, because the equity cost is economically sound value of dividends. Thus, company could decrease the value of dividends, which they should pay to shareholders.

Correct accounting of the method of tax on profit payments demonstrates that shortcomings of Modigliani–Miller theory are serious than thought: the underestimation of WACC really turns out to be bigger, as well as the overestimation of the capitalization of the company. This means that systematic risks arising from the use of modified Modigliani–Miller theory (which is more correct than the "classical" one) in practice are higher than it was suggested by the "classical" version of this theory.

References

Brusov P (2018a) Editorial. Introduction on special issue on the banking system and financial markets of Russia and other countries: problems and prospects. J Rev Global Econ 7:i–vi

Brusov P (2018b) Editorial. J Rev Global Econ 7:i–v

Brusov P, Filatova T, Orehova N, Eskindarov M (2015) Modern corporate finance, investments and taxation. Springer International Publishing, Cham, 373p. https://www.springer.com/gp/book/9783319147314

Brusov P, Filatova T, Orehova N, Eskindarov M (2018a) Modern corporate finance, investments, taxation and ratings. Springer Nature Publishing, Cham, 571p

Brusov PN, Filatova TV, Orekhova NP, Kulik VL (2018b) Rating: new approach. J Rev Global Econ 7:37–62. https://doi.org/10.6000/1929-7092.2018.07.05

Brusov PN, Filatova TV, Orekhova NP, Kulik VL (2018c) A "golden age" of the companies: conditions of its existence. J Rev Global Econ 7:88–103. https://doi.org/10.6000/1929-7092.2018.07.07

Brusov PN, Filatova TV, Orekhova NP, Kulik VL (2018d) Rating methodology: new look and new horizons. J Rev Global Econ 7:63–87. https://doi.org/10.6000/1929-7092.2018.07.06

Brusov PN, Filatova TV, Orekhova NP, Kulik VL, Weil I (2018e) New meaningful effects in modern capital structure theory. J Rev Global Econ 7:104–122. https://doi.org/10.6000/1929-7092.2018.07.08

Brusov P, Filatova T, Orekhova N, Kulik V, Weil I, Brailov A (2018f) The impact of the central bank key rate and commercial banks credit rates on creating and maintaining of a favorable investment climate in the country. J Rev Global Econ 7:360–376. https://doi.org/10.6000/1929-7092.2018.07.31

Brusov PN, Filatova TV, Orekhova NP (2018g) Modern corporate finance and investments, monograph. Knorus Publishing House, Moscow, 517p

Brusov PN, Filatova TV, Orekhova NP, Kulik VL, Weil I (2019) Ratings of the investment projects of arbitrary durations: New methodology. J Rev Global Econ 8:437–448. https://doi.org/10.6000/1929-7092.2019.08.37

Brusov PN, Filatova TV, Orekhova NP, Kulik VL, Chang S-I, Lin YCG (2020) Modification of the Modigliani–Miller theory for the case of advance payments of tax on profit. J Rev Global Econ 9:257–268

Filatova T, Orehova N, Brusova A (2008) Weighted average cost of capital in the theory of Modigliani–Miller, modified for a finite lifetime company. Bull FU 48:68–77

Filatova TV, Brusov PN, Orekhova NP, Kulik VL (2018) Ratings of the long–term projects: new approach. J Rev Global Econ 7:645–661. https://doi.org/10.6000/1929-7092.2018.07.59

Modigliani F, Miller M (1958) The cost of capital, corporate finance, and the theory of investment. Am Econ Rev 48:261–297

Modigliani F, Miller M (1963) Corporate income taxes and the cost of capital: a correction. Am Econ Rev 53:147–175

Modigliani F, Miller M (1966) Some estimates of the cost of capital to the electric utility industry 1954–1957. Am Econ Rev 56:333–391

Chapter 5
Modern Theory of Capital Cost and Capital Structure: Brusov–Filatova–Orekhova Theory (BFO Theory)

As we discussed in Chap. 3, one of the serious limitations of the Modigliani–Miller theory is the suggestion about perpetuity of the companies. In 2008, Brusov–Filatova–Orekhova (Filatova et al. 2008) have removed this limitation and have shown that the accounting of the finite lifetime (or finite age) of the company leads to significant changes of all Modigliani–Miller results (Modigliani and Miller 1958, 1963, 1966): capitalization of the company is changed, as well as the equity cost, k_e, and the weighted average cost of capital, WACC, in the presence of corporate taxes. Besides, a number of qualitatively new effects in corporate finance, obtained in the Brusov–Filatova–Orekhova theory (Brusov and Filatova 2011; Brusov et al. 2011a, b, c, 2012a, b, 2013a, b, 2014a, b), are absent in the Modigliani–Miller theory.

Only in the absence of corporate taxes, we give a rigorous proof of the Brusov–Filatova–Orekhova theorem that equity cost, k_e, as well as its weighted average cost, WACC, does not depend on the lifetime (or age) of the company, so the Modigliani–Miller theory could be generalized for arbitrary lifetime (arbitrary age) companies.

Until recently (before 2008, when the first paper by Brusov–Filatova–Orekhova (Filatova et al. 2008) has appeared), the basic theory (and the first quantitative one) of the cost of capital and capital structure of companies was the theory by Nobel Prize winners Modigliani and Miller (Modigliani and Miller 1958, 1963, 1966). One of the serious limitations of the Modigliani–Miller theory is the suggestion about perpetuity of the companies. We remove this limitation and show that the accounting of the finite lifetime (finite age) of the company leads to change of the equity cost, k_e, as well as of the weighted average cost of capital, WACC, in the presence of corporate taxes. The effect of leverage on the cost of equity capital of the company, k_e, with an arbitrary lifetime, and its weighted average cost of WACC is investigated. We give a rigorous proof of the Brusov–Filatova–Orekhova theorem that, in the absence of corporate taxes, cost of company equity, k_e, as well as its weighted average cost, WACC, does not depend on the lifetime of the company.

P. Brusov et al., *Ratings*, Contributions to Finance and Accounting,
https://doi.org/10.1007/978-3-030-56243-4_5

5.1 Companies of Arbitrary Age and Companies with Arbitrary Lifetime: Brusov–Filatova–Orekhova Equation

Let us consider companies of arbitrary age and companies with arbitrary lifetime.

In perpetuity limit (Modigliani–Miller theory) ***time of life of company*** and ***company age*** turn out to be the same: both of them are infinite. When we move from the assumption of Modigliani–Miller concerning the perpetuity of companies, these concepts (time of life of company and company age) become different and one should distinguish them under generalization of the Modigliani–Miller theory with respect to finite n.

Thus, we have developed two kinds of finite n-theories: BFO-1 and BFO-2. BFO-1 theory is related to companies with arbitrary age, and BFO-2 theory is related to companies with arbitrary lifetime companies. In other words, BFO-1 is applicable for the most interesting case of companies that reached the age of n-years and continue to exist on the market, and allows us to analyze the financial state of the operating companies. BFO-2 theory allows us to examine the financial status of the companies which ceased to exist, i.e., of those companies for which n means not age, but a lifetime, i.e., the time of existence. A lot of schemes of termination of activities of the company can exist: bankruptcy, merger, acquisition, etc. One of those schemes, when the value of the debt capital D becomes zero at the time of termination of activity of company n, is considered in this chapter below (Eq. 5.5) and comparison of results of BFO-1 and BFO-2 has been done as well.

To start with the case of finite n let us first of all find the value of tax shield, TS, of the company for n-years

$$\mathrm{TS} = k_{\mathrm{d}}DT\sum_{t=1}^{n}(1+k_{\mathrm{d}})^{-t} = DT[1-(1+k_{\mathrm{d}})^{-n}]. \tag{5.1}$$

(We used the formula for the sum of n terms of a geometric progression).

Here, D is the value of debt capital, k_{d} the cost of debt capital, and T the tax on profit rate.

Next, we use the Modigliani–Miller theorem (Modigliani and Miller 1958, 1963, 1966):

The value of financially dependent company is equal to the value of the company of the same risk group that used no leverage, increased by the value of tax shield arising from financial leverage, and equal to the product of rate of corporate income tax T and the value of debt D.

$$V = V_0 + DT. \tag{5.2}$$

This theorem was formulated by Modigliani and Miller for perpetuity companies, but we modify it for a company of arbitrary age.

$$V = V_0 + \mathrm{TS} = V_0 + k_\mathrm{d} DT \sum_{t=1}^{\infty} (1 + k_\mathrm{d})^{-t}$$
$$= V_0 + w_\mathrm{d} VT[1 - (1 + k_\mathrm{d})^{-n}], \tag{5.3}$$

$$V(1 - w_\mathrm{d} VT[1 - (1 + k_\mathrm{d})^{-n}]) = V_0. \tag{5.4}$$

There is a common use of the following two formulas for the cost of the financially independent and financially dependent companies (Modigliani and Miller 1958, 1963, 1966):

$$V_0 = \mathrm{CF}/k_0 \text{ and } \quad V = \mathrm{CF}/\mathrm{WACC}. \tag{5.5}$$

However, these almost always used formulas were derived for perpetuity company, and in the case of a company of finite age (or with a finite lifetime), they must be modified in the same manner as the value of tax shields (Brusov and Filatova 2011; Brusov et al. 2011a, b, c, 2012a, b, 2013a, b, 2014a, b; Filatova et al. 2008):

$$V_0 = \mathrm{CF}[1 - (1 + k_0)^{-n}]/k_0; \quad V = \mathrm{CF}[1 - (1 + \mathrm{WACC})^{-n}]/\mathrm{WACC}. \tag{5.6}$$

From formula (Eq. 5.4), we get Brusov–Filatova–Orekhova equation for WACC (Brusov et al. 2011, 2011a, b, c, 2012a, b, 2013a, b, 2014a, b; Filatova et al. 2008):

$$\frac{1 - (1 + \mathrm{WACC})^{-n}}{\mathrm{WACC}} = \frac{1 - (1 + k_0)^{-n}}{k_0[1 - \omega_\mathrm{d} T(1 - (1 + k_\mathrm{d})^{-n})]}. \tag{5.7}$$

Here, S—the value of equity capital of the company, $w_\mathrm{d} = \frac{D}{D+S}$—the share of debt capital, $k_\mathrm{e}, w_\mathrm{e} = \frac{S}{D+S}$—the cost and the share of the equity capital of the company, and $L = D/S$—financial leverage.

At $n = 1$, we get Myers (Myers 2001) formula for 1-year company

$$\mathrm{WACC} = k_0 - \frac{(1 + k_0)k_\mathrm{d}}{1 + k_\mathrm{d}} w_\mathrm{d} T \tag{5.8}$$

For $n = 2$, one has

$$\frac{1 - (1 + \mathrm{WACC})^{-2}}{\mathrm{WACC}} = \frac{1 - (1 + k_0)^{-2}}{k_0\left[1 - \omega_\mathrm{d} T\left(1 - (1 + k_\mathrm{d})^{-2}\right)\right]}. \tag{5.9}$$

This equation can be solved for WACC analytically:

$$\text{WACC} = \frac{1 - 2\alpha \pm \sqrt{4\alpha + 1}}{2\alpha}, \tag{5.10}$$

where

$$\alpha = \frac{2 + k_0}{(1 + k_0)^2 \left[1 - \omega_d T \frac{2k_d + k_d^2}{(1 + k_d)^2}\right]}. \tag{5.11}$$

For $n = 3$ and $n = 4$, the equation for the WACC becomes more complicated, but it still can be solved analytically, while for $n > 4$, it can be solved only numerically.

We would like to make **an important methodological notice**: taking into account the finite lifetime of the company, all formulas, without exception, should be derived using formulas (Eq. 5.6) instead of their perpetuity limits (Eq. 5.5).

Below, we will describe the algorithm for the numerical solution of the equation (Eq. 5.7).

5.1.1 Algorithm for Finding WACC in the Case of Companies of Arbitrary Age

Let us return back to n-year project (n-year company). We have the following equation for WACC in n-year case:

$$\frac{1 - (1 + \text{WACC})^{-n}}{\text{WACC}} - A(n) = 0, \tag{5.12}$$

where

$$A(n) = \frac{1 - (1 + k_0)^{-n}}{k_0[1 - \omega_d T(1 - (1 + k_d)^{-n})]}. \tag{5.13}$$

The algorithm of the solving of the Eq. (5.12) should be as follows:

1. Putting the values of parameters k_0, ω_d, T and given n, we calculate $A(n)$.
2. We determine two WACC values, for which the left part of the Eq. (5.12) has opposite signs. It is obvious that as these two values we can use WACC_1 and WACC_∞, because $\text{WACC}_1 > \text{WACC}_n > \text{WACC}_\infty$ for finite $n \geq 2$.
3. Using, for example, the bisection method, we can solve Eq. (5.12) numerically.

In MS Excel, it is possible to solve Eq. (5.7) much easily by using the option "matching of parameter": we will use it throughout the monograph.

5.2 Comparison of Modigliani–Miller Results (Perpetuity Company) with Myers Results (1-Year Company) and Brusov–Filatova–Orekhova Ones (Company of Arbitrary Age))

Myers (2001) has compared his result for 1-year company (project) (Eq. 5.8) with Modigliani and Miller's result for perpetuity limits (Eq. 2.8). He has used the following values of parameters:

$$k_0 = 8\% \div 24\%; \quad k_d = 7\%; T = 50\%; \quad w_d = 0\% \div 60\%$$

and estimated the difference in the WACC values following from the formulas (Eqs. 5.8 and 2.8). We did make the similar calculations for 2-, 3-, 5-, and 10-year project for the same set of parameters, and we have gotten the following results, shown in Tables [Table 5.1 (second line (bulk)), Table 5.2 (second line (bulk)), and Table 5.3)] and corresponding figures (Figs. 5.1, 5.2, and 5.3).

Note that data for equity cost $k_0 = 8\%$ turn out to be a little bit uncertain: this could be related to the fact that this value of equity cost is quite close to the value of interest rate of the debt $k_d = 7\%$. For all other values of equity cost, the results are reproducible and very informative and are discussed below.

For a graphic illustration of the results, we use data for $n = 1, 2, \infty$, which adequately reflect the results we have obtained.

5.2.1 Discussion of Results

1. From Table 5.1 and Fig. 5.1, it is obvious that WACC is maximum for 1-year company (project) and decreases with the lifetime (age) of the company (project) and reaches the minimum in the Modigliani–Miller perpetuity case. Dependence of all WACC values on debt share w_d turns out to be linear at any equity cost k_0 for all considered durations of the project (lifetime values of the companies). It is natural for 1-year project because it is described by Myers linear formula (5.8) as well as, in the Modigliani–Miller perpetuity case, described by the formula (2.8), which is linear too, but a surprise for 2-year project, where the formula for WACC (5.7) is obviously nonlinear.

The negative slope in WACC increases with the equity cost k_0.

2. As it follows from the Table 5.2 and Fig. 5.3, the dependence of the average ratios $\bar{r} = \langle \Delta_1/\Delta_2 \rangle$ on debt share w_d is quite weak and can be considered as almost constant. The value of this constant increases practically linear with the equity cost k_0 from 1.22 at $k_0 = 10\%$ up to 5.69 at $k_0 = 24\%$ (see Fig. 5.4).

Table 5.1 WACC dependence on debt share w_d for different values of equity cost k_0 for companies with different lifetime n

k_0	n	$w_d = 10\%$	20%	30%	40%	50%	60%
$k_0 = 8\%$	$n = 1$	7.6%	7.3	6.9	6.6	6.2	5.9
	$n = 2$	**7.52**	**7.08**	**6.6**	**6.17**	**5.67**	**5.21**
	$n = \infty$	7.6	7.2	6.8	6.4	6.0	5.6
$k_0 = 10\%$	$n = 1$	9.7	9.3	8.9	8.6	8.2	7.8
	$n = 2$	**9.51**	**9.05**	**8.59**	**8.13**	**7.64**	**7.16**
	$n = \infty$	9.5	9.0	8.5	8.0	7.5	7.0
$k_0 = 12\%$	$n = 1$	11.6	11.3	10.9	10.5	10.2	9.8
	$n = 2$	**11.51**	**11.02**	**10.54**	**10.07**	**9.6**	**9.09**
	$n = 3$	**11.46**	**10.93**	**10.39**	**9.85**	**9.31**	**8.77**
	$n = 5$	**11.42**	**10.83**	**10.25**	**9.66**	**9.06**	**8.46**
	$n = 10$	**11.396**	**10.786**	**10.1695**	**9.5455**	**8.914**	**8.2745**
	$n = \infty$	11.4	10.8	10.2	9.6	9.0	8.4
$k_0 = 16\%$	$n = 1$	15.62	15.2	14.9	14.5	14.1	13.7
	$n = 2$	**15.52**	**14.99**	**14.5**	**13.98**	**13.47**	**12.96**
	$n = 3$	**15.44**	**14.88**	**14.31**	**13.75**	**13.18**	**12.61**
	$n = 5$	**15.38**	**14.76**	**14.14**	**13.51**	**12.88**	**12.24**
	$n = 10$	**15.34**	**14.67**	**13.99**	**13.31**	**12.62**	**11.92**
	$n = \infty$	15.2	14.4	15.6	12.8	12.0	11.2
$k_0 = 20\%$	$n = 1$	19.6	19.2	18.8	18.4	18.1	17.7
	$n = 2$	**19.45**	**18.97**	**18.45**	**17.93**	**17.37**	**16.86**
	$n = 3$	**19.41**	**18.82**	**18.23**	**17.64**	**17.05**	**16.45**
	$n = 5$	**19.35**	**18.69**	**18.03**	**17.36**	**16.70**	**16.03**
	$n = 10$	**19.27**	**18.54**	**17.80**	**17.05**	**16.30**	**15.54**
	$n = \infty$	19.0	18.0	17.0	16.0	15.0	14.0
$k_0 = 24\%$	$n = 1$	23.6	23.2	22.8	22.4	22.0	21.6
	$n = 2$	**23.46**	**22.94**	**22.37**	**21.80**	**21.30**	**20.75**
	$n = 3$	**23.39**	**22.77**	**22.15**	**21.54**	**20.91**	**20.29**
	$n = 5$	**23.31**	**22.61**	**21.91**	**21.21**	**20.51**	**19.80**
	$n = 10$	**23.21**	**22.40**	**21.60**	**20.78**	**19.96**	**19.13**
	$n = \infty$	22.8	21.6	20.4	19.2	18.0	16.8

3. The relative difference between 1-year and 2-year projects increases when the equity cost k_0 decreases. At the same time, the relative difference between 2-year project and perpetuity MM project increases with the equity cost k_0.

We can also show in Table 5.4 and Fig. 5.5 the dependence of the WACC on leverage level L for $n = 1$, $n = 3$, and $n = \infty$.

From Table 5.4 and Fig. 5.5, it is obviously that WACC has a maximum for one-year company and decreases with the age (lifetime) of the company, reaching the minimum in the Modigliani–Miller perpetuity case. (Note, however, that this not always be so via the effect of "golden age" of the company (see Chaps. 18 and 19)).

Table 5.2 Dependence of the differences $\Delta_1 = \text{WACC}_1 - \text{WACC}_\infty$ (first line), $\Delta_2 = \text{WACC}_1 - \text{WACC}_2$ [second line (bulk)], and their ratio $r = \Delta_1/\Delta_2$ (third line) on debt share w_d for different values of equity cost k_0

	$w_d = 10\%$	20%	30%	40%	50%	60%
$k_0 = 10\%$	0.20	0.30	0.4	0.60	0.7	0.8
	0.19	**0.25**	**0.31**	**0.47**	**0.56**	**0.64**
	1.05	1.2	1.29	1.28	1.25	1.25
$k_0 = 12\%$	0.2	0.5	0.7	0.9	1.2	1.4
	0.09	**0.28**	**0.36**	**0.43**	**0.6**	**0.71**
	2.22	1.76	1.94	2.09	2	1.97
$k_0 = 16\%$	0.4	0.8	1.3	1.7	2.1	2.5
	0.08	**0.21**	**0.4**	**0.52**	**0.63**	**0.74**
	5.0	3.81	3.25	3.27	3.33	3.38
$k_0 = 20\%$	0.6	1.2	1.8	2.4	3.1	3.7
	0.15	**0.23**	**0.35**	**0.47**	**0.73**	**0.84**
	4.0	5.22	5.14	5.11	4.25	4.4
$k_0 = 24\%$	0.8	1.6	2.4	5.2	4.0	4.8
	0.14	**0.26**	**0.43**	**0.6**	**0.7**	**0.85**
	5.7	6.15	5.58	5.33	5.71	5.65

Table 5.3 Average (by debt share w_d) values of ratios $\bar{r} = \langle \Delta_1/\Delta_2 \rangle$ for $k_0 = 10$; 12; 16; 20; and 24%

k_0	10%	12%	16%	20%	24%
$\bar{r} =< \Delta_1/\Delta_2 >$	1.22	2.00	3.67	4.69	5.69

5.3 Brusov–Filatova–Orekhova Theorem

5.3.1 Case of Absence of Corporate Taxes

Modigliani–Miller theory in the case of absence of corporate taxes gives the following results for the dependence of WACC and equity cost k_e on leverage:

1.

$$V_0 = V_L; \quad \text{CF}/k_0 = \text{CF}/\text{WACC}, \quad \text{and thus WACC} = k_0. \tag{5.14}$$

2. $\text{WACC} = w_e \cdot k_e + w_d \cdot k_d$, and thus

$$k_e = \frac{\text{WACC} - w_d \cdot k_d}{w_e} = \frac{k_0 - \frac{L}{1+L} k_d}{\frac{1}{1+L}} = k_0 + L(k_0 - k_d). \tag{5.15}$$

For the finite lifetime (finite age) companies, Modigliani–Miller theorem about equality of value of financially independent and financially dependent companies

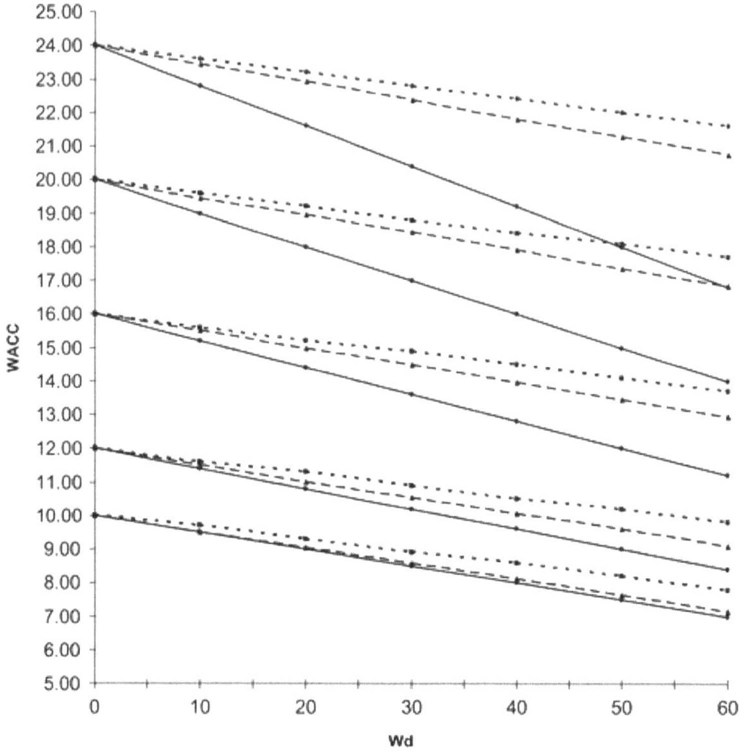

Fig. 5.1 The dependence of the WACC on debt share w_d for companies with different lifetimes for different cost of equity, k_0 (from Table 5.1)

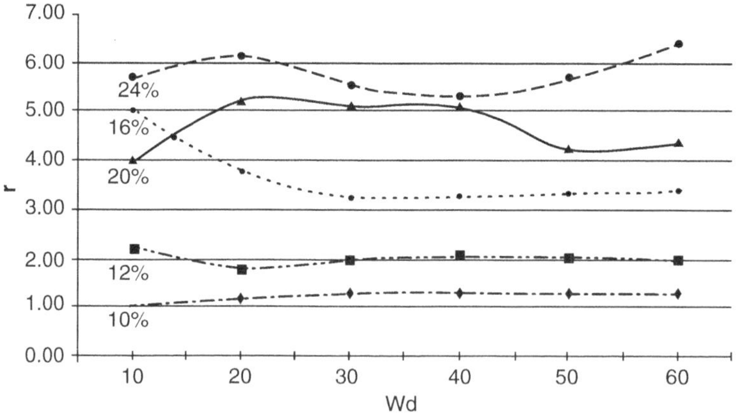

Fig. 5.2 Dependence of the ratio $r = \Delta_1/\Delta_2$ of differences $\Delta_1 = \text{WACC}_1 - \text{WACC}_\infty$ and $\Delta_2 = \text{WACC}_1 - \text{WACC}_2$ on debt share w_d for different values of equity cost k_0 (from Table 5.2)

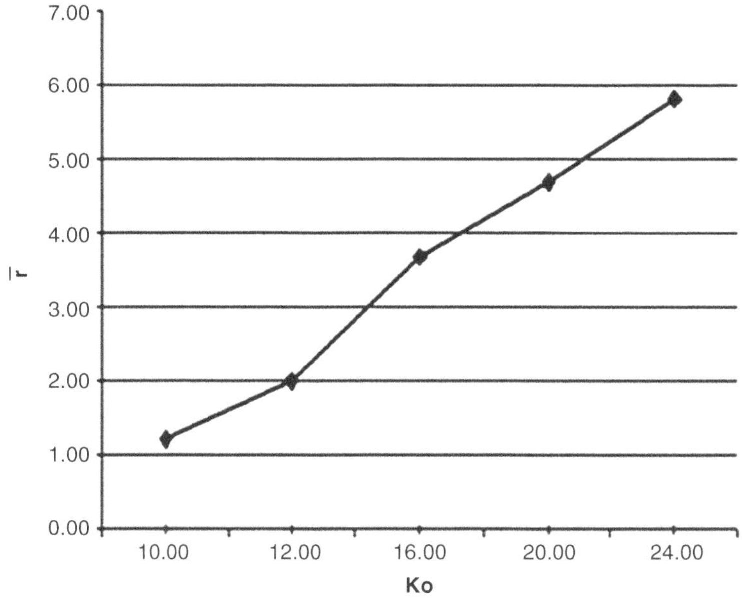

Fig. 5.3 Dependence of the average values of ratio $\overline{r} = \langle \Delta_1 / \Delta_2 \rangle$ on the equity cost, k_0

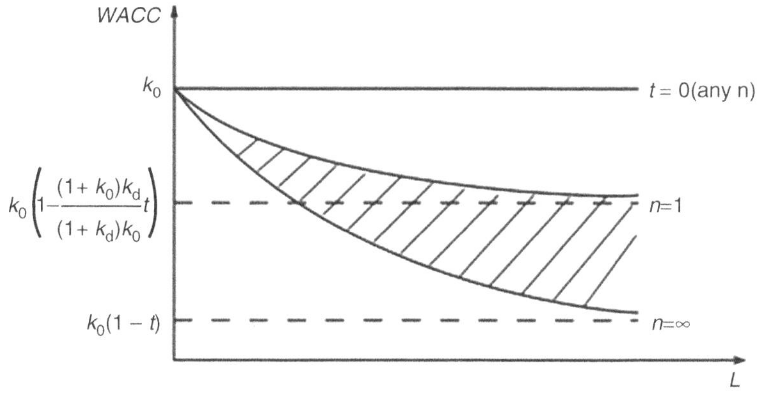

Fig. 5.4 The dependence of the WACC on leverage in the absence of corporate taxes [the horizontal line ($t = 0$)], as well as in the presence of corporate taxes [for 1-year ($n = 1$) and perpetuity companies ($n = \infty$)]. Curves for the WACC of companies with an intermediate lifetime (age) ($1 < n < \infty$) lie within the shaded region

($V_0 = V_L$) has the following view (Brusov and Filatova 2011; Brusov et al. 2011a, b, c, 2012a, b, 2013a, b, 2014a, b):

Table 5.4 The dependence of the WACC on leverage level L for $n = 1$, $n = 3$, and $n = \infty$

L	K_o	K_d	t	W_d	WACC $n = 1$	WACC $n = 3$ (%)	WACC (MM) (%)
0	0.2	0.1	0.2	0.00	20.00	20.00	20.00
1	0.2	0.1	0.2	0.50	18.91	18.41	18.00
2	0.2	0.1	0.2	0.67	18.55	17.87	17.33
3	0.2	0.1	0.2	0.75	18.36	17.61	17.00
4	0.2	0.1	0.2	0.80	18.25	17.44	16.80
5	0.2	0.1	0.2	0.83	18.18	17.34	16.67
6	0.2	0.1	0.2	0.86	18.13	17.26	16.57
7	0.2	0.1	0.2	0.88	18.09	17.20	16.50
8	0.2	0.1	0.2	0.89	18.06	17.16	16.44
9	0.2	0.1	0.2	0.90	18.04	17.12	16.40
10	0.2	0.1	0.2	0.91	18.02	17.09	16.36

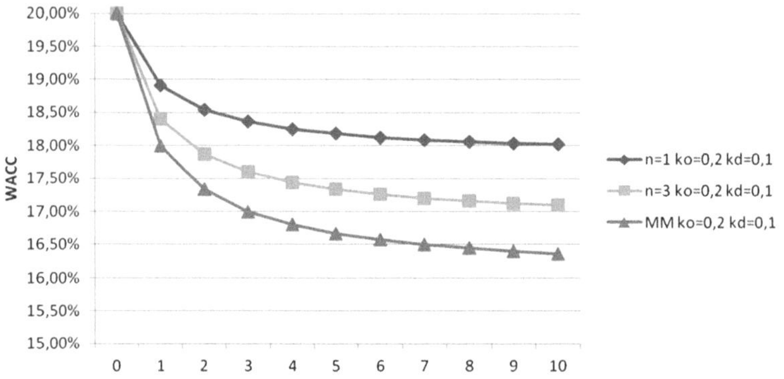

Fig. 5.5 Dependence of WACC on leverage level for $n = 1$, $n = 3$, and $n = \infty$

$$V_0 = V_L;$$

$$\mathrm{CF} \cdot \frac{[1 - (1 + k_0)^{-n}]}{k_0} = \mathrm{CF} \cdot \frac{[1 - (1 + \mathrm{WACC})^{-n}]}{\mathrm{WACC}}. \tag{5.16}$$

Using this relation, we prove an important Brusov–Filatova–Orekhova theorem:

Under the absence of corporate taxes, the equity cost of the company, k_e, as well as its weighted average cost of capital, WACC, does not depend on the lifetime (age) of the company and is equal, respectively, to

$$k_e = k_0 + L(k_0 - k_d); \quad \mathrm{WACC} = k_0. \tag{5.17}$$

Let us consider first the 1- and 2-year companies

(a) For 1-year company, one has from (5.15)

$$\frac{1-(1+k_0)^{-1}}{k_0}=\frac{1-(1+\mathrm{WACC})^{-1}}{\mathrm{WACC}}, \tag{5.18}$$

and thus

$$\frac{1}{1+k_0}=\frac{1}{1+\mathrm{WACC}}. \tag{5.19}$$

Hence

$$\mathrm{WACC}=k_0. \tag{5.20}$$

The formula for equity cost $k_e = k_0 + L(k_0 - k_d)$ now obtained by substituting WACC $= k_0$ into (5.14).

(b) For 2-year company, one has from (5.15)

$$\frac{\left[1-(1+k_0)^{-2}\right]}{k_0}=\frac{\left[1-(1+\mathrm{WACC})^{-2}\right]}{\mathrm{WACC}},$$

and thus

$$\frac{2+k_0}{(1+k_0)^2}=\frac{2+\mathrm{WACC}}{(1+\mathrm{WACC})^2}. \tag{5.21}$$

Denoting $\alpha=\frac{2+k_0}{(1+k_0)^2}$, we get the following quadratic equation for WACC:

$$\alpha\cdot\mathrm{WACC}^2+(2\alpha-1)\cdot\mathrm{WACC}+(\alpha-2)=0. \tag{5.22}$$

It has two solutions

$$\mathrm{WACC}_{1,2}=\frac{1-2\alpha\pm\sqrt{4\alpha+1}}{2\alpha}. \tag{5.23}$$

Substituting $\alpha=\frac{2+k_0}{(1+k_0)^2}$, we get.

$$\mathrm{WACC}_{1,2}=\frac{\left(k_0^2-3\right)\pm(k_0+3)(1+k_0)}{2(2+k_0)}. \tag{5.24}$$

$$\mathrm{WACC}_1 = k_0; \quad \mathrm{WACC}_2 = -\frac{2k_0 + 3}{k_0 + 2} < 0. \tag{5.25}$$

The second root is negative, but the weighted average cost of capital can only be positive, so only one value remains

$$\mathrm{WACC}_1 = k_0.$$

(c) For company with arbitrary lifetime, n, Brusov–Filatova–Orekhova formula (5.15) gives

$$\frac{1-(1+k_0)^{-n}}{k_0} = \frac{1-(1+\mathrm{WACC})^{-n}}{\mathrm{WACC}}. \tag{5.26}$$

For a fixed k_0, (Eq. 5.25) is an equation of $(n + 1)$-degree relative to WACC. It has $n + 1$ roots (in general complex). One of the roots, as a direct substitution shows, is always $\mathrm{WACC} = k_0$.. Investigation of the remaining roots is difficult and not a part of our problem.

The formula for equity cost $k_e = k_0 + L(k_0 - k_d)$ is now obtained by substituting $\mathrm{WACC} = k_0$ into (Eq. 5.14).

Thus, we have proved the Brusov–Filatova–Orekhova theorem.

5.3.2 *Case of the Presence of Corporate Taxes*

Modigliani–Miller theory in the case of presence of corporate taxes gives the following results for dependence of WACC and equity cost k_e on leverage:

1. WACC

$$V_L = V_0 + Dt; D = w_d V_L; \tag{5.27}$$

$$\mathrm{CF}/\mathrm{WACC} = \mathrm{CF}/k_0 + Dt = \mathrm{CF}/k_0 + w_d t \mathrm{CF}/\mathrm{WACC}, \tag{5.28}$$

$$\frac{1 - w_d t}{\mathrm{WACC}} = \frac{1}{k_0}; \tag{5.29}$$

$$\mathrm{WACC} = k_0(1 - w_d t) = k_0\left(1 - \frac{L}{1+L}t\right). \tag{5.30}$$

Thus, WACC decreases with leverage from k_0 [in the absence of debt financing ($L = 0$)] up to $k_0(1 - t)$ (at $L = \infty$).

2. The equity cost k_e

$$\mathrm{WACC} = k_0(1 - w_d t) = w_e \cdot k_e + w_d \cdot k_d(1 - t);$$

and thus

$$k_e = \frac{\mathrm{WACC} - w_d \cdot k_d \cdot (1 - t)}{w_e} = \frac{k_0(1 - w_d t) - \frac{L}{1 + L} k_d(1 - t)}{\frac{1}{1 + L}} = k_0 + L(k_0 - k_d)(1 - t). \tag{5.31}$$

5.4 From Modigliani–Miller to General Theory of Capital Cost and Capital Structure

Let us consider, how the weighted average cost of capital, WACC, and the cost of equity capital, k_e, will be changed when taking into account the finite age of the company.

(a) 1-year company

From (5.7), one has

$$\frac{1 - (1 + \mathrm{WACC})^{-n}}{\mathrm{WACC}} = \frac{1 - (1 + k_0)^{-n}}{k_0[1 - w_d t(1 - (1 + k_d)^{-n})]}. \tag{5.32}$$

For 1-year company, we get

$$\frac{1 - (1 + \mathrm{WACC})^{-1}}{\mathrm{WACC}} = \frac{1 - (1 + k_0)^{-1}}{k_0\left[1 - w_d t\left(1 - (1 + k_d)^{-1}\right)\right]} \tag{5.33}$$

From (Eq. 5.33), we obtain the well-known Myers formula (Eq. 5.8), which is the particular case of Brusov–Filatova–Orekhova formula (Eq. 5.7).

$$\mathrm{WACC} = k_0 - \frac{1 + k_0}{1 + k_d} k_d w_d t.$$

Thus

$$\mathrm{WACC} = k_0\left(1 - \frac{(1 + k_0) \cdot k_\mathrm{d}}{(1 + k_\mathrm{d}) \cdot k_0} \cdot \frac{L}{1 + L}t\right). \tag{5.34}$$

Thus, WACC decreases with leverage from k_0 [in the absence of debt financing $(L = 0)$] up to $k_0\left(1 - \frac{(1+k_0)\cdot k_\mathrm{d}}{(1+k_\mathrm{d})\cdot k_0}t\right)$ (at $L = \infty$)..

Equating the right part of Eq. (5.34) to general expression for WACC

$$WACC = w_\mathrm{e} \cdot k_\mathrm{e} + w_\mathrm{d} \cdot k_\mathrm{d}(1 - t), \tag{5.35}$$

one gets

$$k_0 - \frac{1 + k_0}{1 + k_\mathrm{d}}k_\mathrm{d}w_\mathrm{d}t = w_\mathrm{e} \cdot k_\mathrm{e} + w_\mathrm{d} \cdot k_\mathrm{d}(1 - t). \tag{5.36}$$

Thus,

$$\begin{aligned} k_\mathrm{e} &= \frac{1}{w_\mathrm{e}}\left[k_0 - \frac{1 + k_0}{1 + k_\mathrm{d}}k_\mathrm{d}w_\mathrm{d}t - k_\mathrm{d}w_\mathrm{d}(1 - t)\right] \\ &= (1 + L)k_0 - L\frac{k_\mathrm{d}}{1 + k_\mathrm{d}}[(1 + k_0)t + (1 + k_\mathrm{d})(1 - t)] \\ &= k_0 + L(k_0 - k_\mathrm{d})\left(1 - \frac{k_\mathrm{d}}{1 + k_\mathrm{d}}t\right). \end{aligned}$$

$$k_\mathrm{e} = k_0 + L(k_0 - k_\mathrm{d})\left(1 - \frac{k_\mathrm{d}}{1 + k_\mathrm{d}}t\right). \tag{5.37}$$

So we see that in the case of 1-year company, the perpetuity limit

$k_\mathrm{e} = k_0 + L(k_0 - k_\mathrm{d})(1 - t)$ is replaced by (Eq. 5.37).

Difference is due to different values of the tax shield for a 1-year company and perpetuity one (Fig. 5.6).

Let us investigate the question of the tax shield value for companies with different lifetime (age) in more detail.

5.4.1 Tax Shield

General expression for the tax shield for n-year company has the form (Brusov–Filatova–Orekhova)

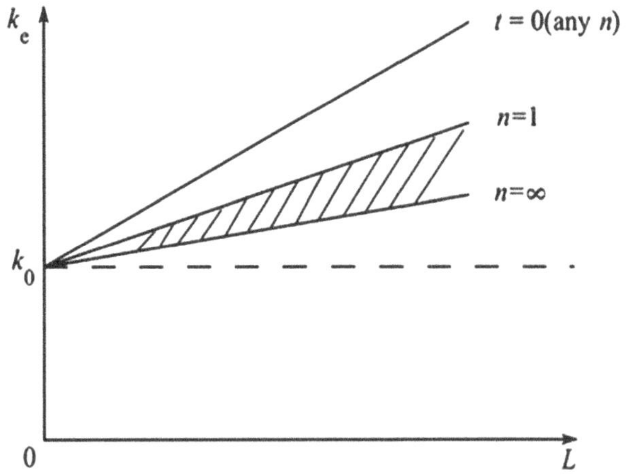

Fig. 5.6 Dependence of the equity cost, k_e, on leverage in the absence of corporate taxes [the upper line ($t = 0$)], as well as in the presence of corporate taxes [for 1-year ($n = 1$) and perpetuity companies ($n = \infty$)]. Dependences of the cost of equity capital of companies, k_e, of an intermediate age ($1 < n < \infty$) lie within the shaded region

$$\mathrm{TS} = \sum_{i=1}^{n} \frac{k_d Dt}{(1+k_d)^i} = \frac{k_d Dt\left[1-(1+k_d)^{-n}\right]}{(1+k_d)\left(1-(1+k_d)^{-1}\right)} = Dt\left[1-(1+k_d)^{-n}\right]. \quad (5.38)$$

1. In perpetuity limit ($n \to \infty$), tax shield is equal to $\mathrm{TS}_\infty = Dt$, which leads to the so-called effect of the tax shield associated with the appearance of a factor $(1 - t)$ in the equity cost $k_e = k_0 + L(k_0 - k_d)(1 - t)$.
2. For the 1-year company, tax shield value is equal to

$$\mathrm{TS}_1 = Dt\left(1-(1+k_d)^{-1}\right) = Dtk_d/(1+k_d). \quad (5.39)$$

This leads to appearance of a factor $\left(1-\frac{k_d}{1+k_d}t\right)$ in the equity cost (Eq. 5.36) $k_e = k_0 + L(k_0 - k_d)\left(1-\frac{k_d}{1+k_d}t\right)$.

3. Tax shield for a 2-year company is equal to

$$\mathrm{TS}_2 = Dt\left(1-(1+k_d)^{-2}\right) = Dtk_d(2+k_d)/(1+k_d)^2 \quad (5.40)$$

and if the analogy with 1-year company remains, then factor $(1 - t)$ in the Modigliani–Miller theory would be replaced by the factor

$$\left(1-\frac{k_d(2+k_d)}{(1+k_d)^2}t\right). \quad (5.41)$$

However, due to a nonlinear relation between WACC and k_0 and k_d in Brusov–Filatova–Orekhova formula (Eqs. 5.9, 5.10, and 5.11) for 2-year company (and companies of bigger age), such a simple analogy is no longer observed, and the calculations become more complex.

5.5 BFO Theory in the Case, When the Company Ceased to Exist at the Time Moment *n* (BFO-2 Theory)

From the output of the BFO formula, it follows that developed ideology is applied to companies which have reached the age of n-years and continue to exist on the market, while the theory of MM is only applicable to infinitely old (perpetuity) companies. In other words, BFO is applicable for the most interesting case of companies that reached the age of n-years and continue to exist on the market, and allows us to analyze the financial condition of the operating companies.

However, the BFO theory also allows us to examine the financial status of the companies which ceased to exist, i.e., of those for which n means not age, but a lifetime, i.e., the time of existence. A lot of schemes of termination of activities of the company can exist: bankruptcy, merger, acquisition, etc. Below we consider one of those schemes, when the value of the debt capital D becomes zero at the time of termination of activity of company n: in this case, the BFO theory requires minimal upgrades, shown below.

From the formula for the capitalization of the company (5.1), it is easy to get an estimation for the "residual capitalization" of the company, discounted to the time moment k:

$$V_k = \sum_{t=k+1}^{n} \frac{\mathrm{CF}}{(1+\mathrm{WACC})^t} = \frac{\mathrm{CF}}{\mathrm{WACC}}\left[1-(1+\mathrm{WACC})^{-(n-k)}\right]. \tag{5.42}$$

Using the formula

$$V_k = w_\mathrm{d} D, \tag{5.43}$$

we obtain an expression for the tax shield for n-years subject to the termination of the activities of the company at the moment n:

$$\begin{aligned} TS_n &= tk_\mathrm{d}w_\mathrm{d}\sum_{k=1}^{n}\frac{V_{k-1}}{(1+k_\mathrm{d})^k} = \frac{tk_\mathrm{d}w_\mathrm{d}CF}{\mathrm{WACC}}\sum_{k=1}^{n}\frac{1-(1+\mathrm{WACC})^{-(n-k+1)}}{(1+k_\mathrm{d})^k} = \\ &= \frac{tk_\mathrm{d}w_\mathrm{d}}{\mathrm{WACC}}\left[\frac{1-(1+k_\mathrm{d})^{-n}}{k_\mathrm{d}} - \frac{(1+k_\mathrm{d})^{-n}-(1+\mathrm{WACC})^{-n}}{\mathrm{WACC}-k_\mathrm{d}}\right]. \end{aligned} \tag{5.44}$$

Substituting this expression into Eq. (5.3)

$$V_L = V_0 + (TS)_n$$

one gets the equation (let us call it BFO-2)

$$\frac{1-(1+\mathrm{WACC})^{-n}}{\mathrm{WACC}} = \frac{1-(1+k_0)^{-n}}{k_0} + \frac{tk_\mathrm{d}w_\mathrm{d}}{\mathrm{WACC}} \times \left[\frac{1-(1+k_\mathrm{d})^{-n}}{k_\mathrm{d}} - \frac{(1+k_\mathrm{d})^{-n}-(1+\mathrm{WACC})^{-n}}{\mathrm{WACC}-k_\mathrm{d}}\right], \tag{5.45}$$

from which one can find the WACC for companies with arbitrary lifetime n, provided that the company ceases to function at the time moment n.

Below in the monograph, we investigate the companies that have reached the age of n-years and continue to exist on the market, i.e., we will use formula BFO (5.7), but in this paragraph we present some results obtained from the formula BFO-2 (5.45).

5.5.1 Application of Formula BFO-2

Formula BFO-2 (5.45) in MS Excel takes a following form:

$$\left(\left(1-(1+C4)^{(-H4)}\right)/C4\right) - \left(\left(\left(1-(1+D4)^{(-H4)}\right)/D4\right) + (((G4*E4*F4)/C4)*\left(\left(1-(1+E4)^{(-H4)}\right)/E4\right) - \left(\left((1+E4)^{(-H4)}-(1+C4)^{(-H4)}\right)/(C4-E4)\right)\right)\right) = 0. \tag{5.46}$$

Using it we get the following results for dependence of WACC on leverage level L, lifetime n, and on tax on profit rate t (Figs. 5.7, 5.8, and 5.9).

5.5.2 Comparison of Results Obtained from Formulas BFO and BFO-2

Let us compare results obtained from formulas BFO and BFO-2 (Figs. 5.10, 5.11, 5.12, and 5.13).

Comparison of results obtained from formulas BFO and BFO-2 shows that WACC values (at the same values of other parameters) turn out to be higher for the companies which ceased to exist at the time moment n, than for companies which have reached the age of n-years and continue to exist on the market. In other words,

Fig. 5.7 The dependence of the WACC on leverage level L for $n = 3$ and $n = 5$; $k_0 = 0.2$; $k_d = 0.15$

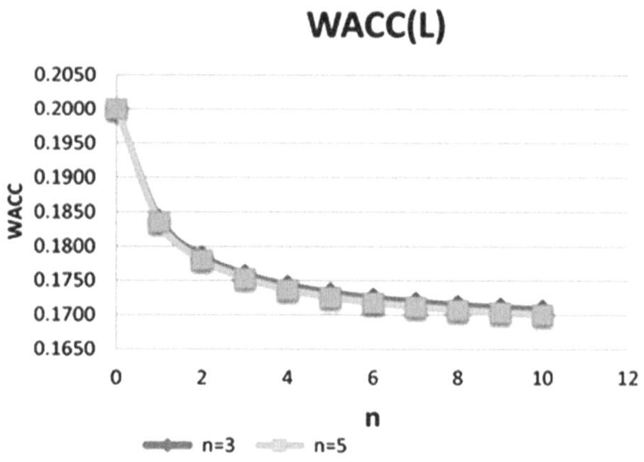

Fig. 5.8 The dependence of the WACC on lifetime n at different leverage level L

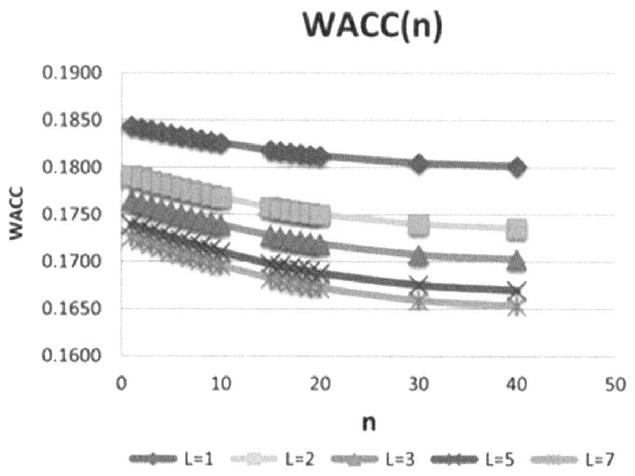

Fig. 5.9 The dependence of the WACC on tax on profit rate t for $n = 3$ and $n = 5$; $k_0 = 0.2$; $k_d = 0.15$

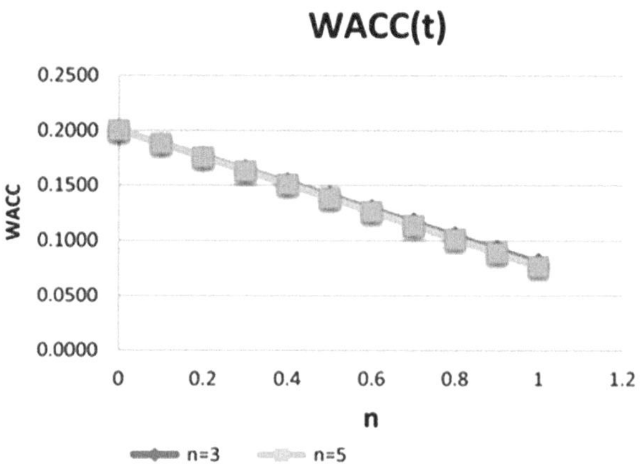

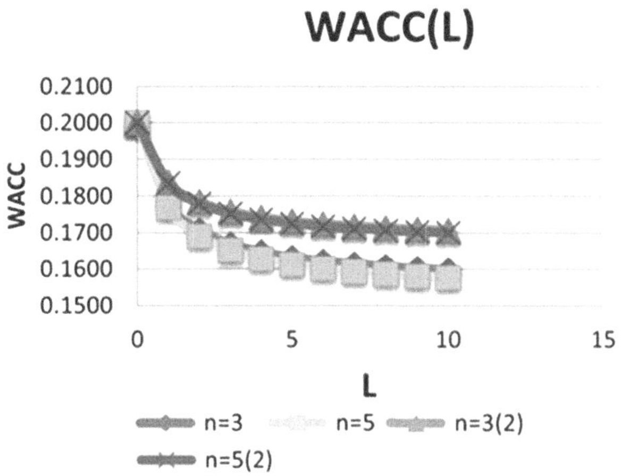

Fig. 5.10 Comparison of the dependence of the WACC on leverage level L for $n = 3$ and $n = 5$ from formulas BFO and BFO-2

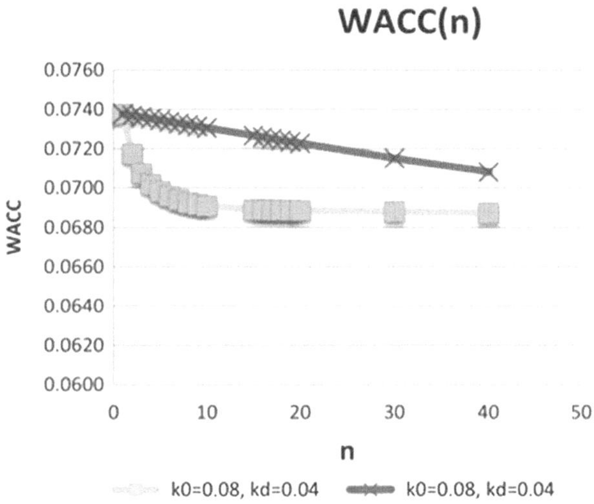

Fig. 5.11 Comparison of the dependence of the WACC on lifetime n from formulas BFO (*lower curve*) and BFO-2 (*upper curve*); $k_0 = 0.08$; $k_d = 0.04$

the companies which ceased to exist at the time moment n can attract a capital at higher rate, than for companies which have reached the age of n-years and continue to exist on the market.

We will develop the detailed investigation of the companies which ceased to exist at the time moment n (described by formula BFO-2) somewhere also and in this monograph we will limit ourselves by consideration of the companies which have reached the age of n-years and continue to exist on the market (described by formula BFO).

Conclusions In this chapter, an important step toward a general theory of capital cost and capital structure of the company has been done. For this, perpetuity theory of Nobel Prize winners Modigliani and Miller, which was until recently (until 2008)

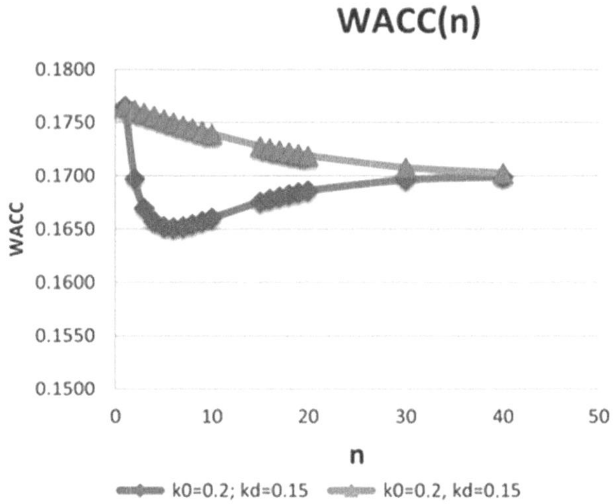

Fig. 5.12 Comparison of the dependence of the WACC on lifetime *n* from formulas BFO (*lower curve*) and BFO-2 (*upper curve*); $k_0 = 0.2$; $k_d = 0.15$; $L = 3$

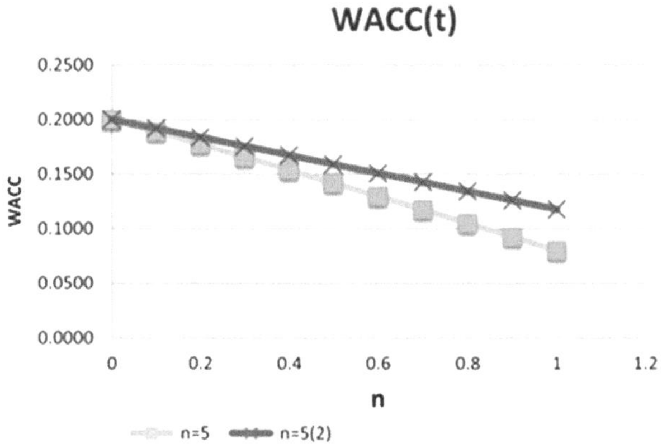

Fig. 5.13 Comparison of the dependence of the WACC on tax on profit rate *t* from formulas BFO (*lower curve*) and BFO-2 (*upper curve*); $k_0 = 0.2$; $k_d = 0.15$; $n = 5$

the main and the basic theory of capital cost and capital structure of companies, has been extended to the case of companies of arbitrary age and of companies with an arbitrary lifetime, as well as for projects of arbitrary duration.

We show that taking into account the finite age of the company or the finite lifetime of the company in the presence of corporate taxes leads to a change in the equity cost of the company, k_e, as well as in its weighted average cost, WACC, and company capitalization, V.

Thus, we have removed one of the most serious limitations of the theory of Modigliani–Miller, connected with the assumption of perpetuity of the companies. The effect of leverage on the cost of equity capital, k_e, of the company of an arbitrary age or with arbitrary lifetime and its weighted average cost, WACC, is investigated. We give a rigorous proof of an important Brusov–Filatova–Orekhova theorem that in the absence of corporate tax, equity cost of companies, k_e, as well as its weighted average cost, WACC, does not depend on the lifetime (age) of the company.

Table 5.5 Comparison of results, obtained within the Modigliani–Miller theory and within the general Brusov–Filatova–Orekhova theory

Financial parameter	Modigliani–Miller (MM) results	Brusov–Filatova–Orekhova (BFO) results
Capitalization of financially independent company	$V_0 = \mathrm{CF}/k_0$	$V_0 = \frac{\mathrm{CF}}{k_0}\left[1-(1+k_0)^{-n}\right]$
Capitalization of leverage (financially dependent) company	$V = \mathrm{CF}/\mathrm{WACC}$	$V = \frac{\mathrm{CF}}{\mathrm{WACC}}\left[1-(1+\mathrm{WACC})^{-n}\right]$
Tax shield	$(TS)_\infty = DT$	BFO-1: $TS_n = DT[1-(1+k_d)^{-n}]$
		BFO-2: $\mathrm{TS}_n = \frac{T \cdot k_d \cdot w_d}{\mathrm{WACC}}\left[\frac{1-(1+k_d)^{-n}}{k_d} - \frac{(1+k_d)^{-n}-(1+\mathrm{WACC})^{-n}}{\mathrm{WACC}-k_d}\right]$
Modigliani–Miller theorem with taxes	$V = V_0 + DT$	$V = V_0 + DT[1-(1+k_d)^{-n}]$
Weighted average cost of capital, WACC	$\mathrm{WACC} = k_0(1-w_d t)$	BFO-1: $\frac{1-(1+\mathrm{WACC})^{-n}}{\mathrm{WACC}} = \frac{1-(1+k_0)^{-n}}{k_0[1-\omega_d T(1-(1+k_d)^{-n})]}$
		BFO-2: $\frac{1-(1+\mathrm{WACC})^{-n}}{\mathrm{WACC}} = \frac{1-(1+k_0)^{-n}}{k_0} + \frac{Tk_d w_d}{\mathrm{WACC}} \cdot \left[\frac{1-(1+k_d)^{-n}}{k_d} - \frac{(1+k_d)^{-n}-(1+\mathrm{WACC})^{-n}}{\mathrm{WACC}-k_d}\right]$
Equity cost, k_e	$k_e = k_0 + L(k_0-k_d)(1-t)$	$k_e = (1+L)\cdot \mathrm{WACC} - k_d L(1-T)$

We summarize the difference in results obtained within the modern Brusov–Filatova–Orekhova theory and within the classical Modigliani–Miller one in Table 5.5.

The first four formulas from the right-hand column are sometimes used in practice, but there are several significant nuances. First, these formulas do not take account of the residual value of the company, and only take into account the operating flows, and this must be borne in mind. Second, these formulas contain the weighted average cost of capital of the company, WACC. If it is estimated within the traditional approach or the theory of Modigliani–Miller, it gives a lower WACC value, than the real value, and, therefore, overestimates the capitalization of both financially dependent and financially independent companies. Therefore, in order to assess a company's capitalization by the first two formulas, one needs to use Brusov–Filatova–Orekhova formulas for weighted average cost of capital, WACC, and equity cost, k_e.

To calculate the equity cost in BFO approximation (last line in Table 5.5), one first needs to use Brusov–Filatova–Orekhova formula for weighted average cost of capital, WACC (Brusov and Filatova 2011; Brusov et al. 2011a, b, c, 2012a, b, 2013a, b, 2014a, b; Filatova et al. 2008, Brusov (2018a, b), Brusov et al. (2015, 2018a, b, c, d, e, f, g, 2019, 2020), Filatova et al. (2018a, b)).

References

Brusov P (2018a) Editorial: introduction on special issue on the banking system and financial markets of Russia and other countries: problems and prospects. J Rev Glob Econ 7:i–vi. SCOPUS

Brusov P (2018b) Editorial. J Rev Glob Econ 7:i–v, SCOPUS

Brusov PN, Filatova TV (2011a) From Modigliani–Miller to general theory of capital cost and capital structure of the company. Finance Credit 435:2–8

Brusov P, Filatova T, Orehova N, Brusova A (2011a) Weighted average cost of capital in the theory of Modigliani–Miller, modified for a finite life-time company. Appl Financ Econ 21(11):815–824

Brusov P, Filatova T, Orehova N et al (2011b) From Modigliani–Miller to general theory of capital cost and capital structure of the company. Res J Econ Bus ICT 2:16–21

Brusov P, Filatova T, Orehova N et al (2011c) Influence of debt financing on the effectiveness of the investment project within the Modigliani–Miller theory. Res J Econ Bus ICT (UK) 2:11–15

Brusov P, Filatova T, Eskindarov M, Orehova N (2012a) Influence of debt financing on the effectiveness of the finite duration investment project. Appl Financ Econ 22(13):1043–1052

Brusov P, Filatova T, Eskindarov M, Orehova N (2012b) Hidden global causes of the global financial crisis. J Rev Global Econ 1:106–111

Brusov P, Filatova P, Orekhova N (2013a) Absence of an optimal capital structure in the famous tradeoff theory! J Rev Global Econ 2:94–116

Brusov P, Filatova T, Orehova N (2013h) A qualitatively new effect in corporative finance: abnormal dependence of cost of equity of company on leverage. J Rev Global Econ 2:183–193

Brusov P, Filatova P, Orekhova N (2014a) Mechanism of formation of the company optimal capital structure, different from suggested by trade off theory. Cogent Econ Finance 2:1–13. https://doi.org/10.1080/23322039.2014.946150

Brusov P, Filatova T, Orehova N (2014b) Inflation in Brusov–Filatova–Orekhova theory and in its perpetuity limit—Modigliani–Miller theory. J Rev Global Econ 3:175–185
Brusov P, Filatova T, Orekhova N, Eskindarov M (2015) Modern corporate finance, investments and taxation. Springer International Publishing, Switzerland. p 373. Monograph. SCOPUS. https://www.springer.com/gp/book/9783319147314
Brusov P, Filatova T, Orekhova N, Eskindarov M (2018a), Modern corporate finance, investments, taxation and ratings. Springer Nature Publishing. Switzerland, p 571. Monograph
Brusov PN, Filatova TV, Orekhova NP, Kulik VL (2018b) Rating: new approach. J Rev Glob Econ 7:37–62. SCOPUS. https://doi.org/10.6000/1929-7092.2018.07.05
Brusov PN, Filatova TV, Orekhova NP, Kulik VL (2018c) A "golden age" of the companies: conditions of its existence. J Rev Glob Econ 7:88–103. SCOPUS. https://doi.org/10.6000/1929-7092.2018.07.07
Brusov PN, Filatova TV, Orekhova NP, Kulik VL (2018d) Rating methodology: new look and new horizons. J Rev Glob Econ 7:63–87. SCOPUS. https://doi.org/10.6000/1929-7092.2018.07.06
Brusov PN, Filatova TV, Orekhova NP, Kulik VL, Weil I (2018e) New meaningful effects in modern capital structure theory. J Rev Glob Econ 7:104–122. SCOPUS. https://doi.org/10.6000/1929-7092.2018.07.08
Brusov P, Filatova T, Orekhova N, Kulik V, Weil I, Brailov A (2018f) The impact of the central bank key rate and commercial banks credit rates on creating and maintaining of a favorable investment climate in the country. J Rev Glob Econ 7:360–376. SCOPUS. https://doi.org/10.6000/1929-7092.2018.07.31
Brusov PN, Filatova TV, Orekhova NP (2018g) Modern corporate finance and investments, monograph. Knorus Publishing House, Moscow, p 517
Brusov PN, Filatova TV, Orekhova NP, Kulik VL, Weil I (2019) Ratings of the investment projects of arbitrary durations: new methodology. J Rev Glob Econ 8:437–448. SCOPUS. https://doi.org/10.6000/1929-7092.2019.08.37
Brusov PN, Filatova TV, Orekhova NP, Kulik VL, Chang S-I, Lin YCG (2020) Modification of the Modigliani–Miller theory for the case of advance payments of tax on profit. J Rev Glob Econ 9:257–268
Filatova T, Orehova N, Brusova A (2008) Weighted average cost of capital in the theory of Modigliani–Miller, modified for a finite lifetime company. Bull FU 48:68–77
Filatova TV, Brusov PN, Orekhova NP, Kulik VL (2018a) Ratings of the long-term projects: new approach. J Rev Glob Econ 7:645–661. SCOPUS. https://doi.org/10.6000/1929-7092.2018.07.59
Filatova TV, Brusov PN, Orekhova NP, Kulik VL (2018b) Ratings of the long-term projects: new approach. J Rev Glob Econ 7:645–661. SCOPUS. https://doi.org/10.6000/1929-7092.2018.07.59
Modigliani F, Miller M (1958) The cost of capital, corporate finance, and the theory of investment. Am Econ Rev 48:261–297
Modigliani F, Miller M (1963) Corporate income taxes and the cost of capital: a correction. Am Econ Rev 53:147–175
Modigliani F, Miller M (1966) Some estimates of the cost of capital to the electric utility industry 1954–1957. Am Econ Rev 56:333–391
Myers S (2001) Capital structure. J Econ Perspect 15(2):81–102

Part II
Ratings and Rating Methodologies of Non-financial Issuers

Chapter 6
Application of the Modigliani–Miller Theory in Rating Methodology

6.1 Introduction

Rating agencies play a very important role in economics. Their analysis of issuer's state and generated credit ratings of issuers help investors make reasonable investment decision, as well as help issuers with good enough ratings get credits on lower rates.

But from time to time we hear about scandals involving rating agencies and their credit ratings: let us just remind the situation with sovereign rating of the USA in 2011 and of the Russia in 2015.

Were these ratings objective? And how objectively credit ratings could be issued in principle?

To answer this question, we need to understand how rating agencies (RA) consider, evaluate, and analyze. But this is the secret behind the seven seals: rating agencies stood to the death, but did not reveal their secrets, even under the threat of multibillion-dollar sanctions.

Thus, rating agencies represent some "black boxes," the information about which is almost completely absent.

6.2 The Closeness of the Rating Agencies

The closeness of the rating agencies is caused by multiple causes.

1. The desire to preserve their "know-how." Rating agencies get big enough money for generated ratings (mostly from issuers) to replicate its methodology.
2. On the other hand, closeness of rating agencies is caused by the desire to avoid public discussion of the ratings with anyone, including the issuer. It is a very

P. Brusov et al., *Ratings*, Contributions to Finance and Accounting,
https://doi.org/10.1007/978-3-030-56243-4_6

convenient position—rating agency "a priori" avoids any criticism of generated ratings.
3. The absence of any external control and external analysis of the methodologies results in the fact that shortcomings of methodologies are not subjected to serious critical analysis and stored long enough.

The illustration of the closeness of rating agencies is the behavior of the S&P (Standard & Poor's) Director after a decline in the sovereign rating of USA, who left his position but has not opened the methodology used.

But even in this situation, some analysis of the activities and findings of the rating agencies, based on knowledge and understanding of existing methods of evaluation, is still possible. Rating agencies cannot use methods other than developed up to now by leading economists and financiers.

6.3 The Use of Discounting in the Rating

One of the major flaws of all existing rating methodologies is a failure or a very narrow use of discounting. But even in those rare cases where it is used, it is not quite correct, since the discount rate when discounting financial flows is chosen incorrectly.

The need to take into account the time factor in terms of discounting is obvious, because it is associated with the time value of money. The financial part of the rating is based on a comparison of generated income with the value of the debt and the interest payable. Because income and disbursement of debt and interest are separated in time, the use of discounting when comparing revenues with the value of debt and interest is absolutely necessary for assigning credit ratings for issuers.

This raises the question about the value of discount rate. This question has always been one of the major and extremely difficult in many areas of finance: corporate finance and investment; it is particularly important in business valuation, where a slight change in the discount rate leads to a significant change in the assessment of company capitalization, which is used by unscrupulous appraisers for artificial bankruptcy of the company. And the value of discount rate is extremely essential as well in rating.

6.4 Incorporation of Parameters, Using in Ratings, into Perpetuity Limit of Modern Theory of Capital Structure by Brusov–Filatova–Orekhova

In quantification of the creditworthiness of the issuers the crucial role belongs to the so-called financial "ratios," which constitute direct and inverse ratios of various generated cash flows to debt values and interest ones. We could mention such ratios as DCF/Debt, FFO/Debt, CFO/Debt, FOCF/Debt, *FFO*/cash interest, EBITDA/interest, Interests/EBITDA, Debt/EBITDA, and some others.

We incorporate these rating parameters (financial "ratios") into the modern theory of capital structure—BFO theory (into its perpetuity limit) (Brusov et al. 2018d). The importance of such incorporation, which has been done by us for the first time, is in using this theory as a powerful tool when discounting financial flows using the correct discounting rate in rating. Only this theory allows us to valuate adequately the weighted average cost of capital WACC and equity cost of capital k_e used when discounting financial flows.

The use of the tools of well-developed theories in rating opens completely new horizons in the rating industry, which could go from mainly the use of qualitative methods of the evaluation of the creditworthiness of issuers to a predominantly quantitative evaluation method that will certainly enhance the quality and correctness of the rating.

Currently, rating agencies just directly use financial ratios, while the new methodology will allow (knowing the values of these "relations" (and parameter k_0)) us to determine the correct values of discount rates (WACC and k_e) that should be used when discounting the various financial flows, both in terms of their timing and forecasting.

This has required the modification of the BFO theory (and its perpetuity limit—Modigliani–Miller theory) (Brusov 2018a, b; Brusov et al. 2018a, b, c, e, f, g, 2019, 2020; Filatova et al. 2008, 2018a, b; Modigliani and Miller 1966), as the concept of "leverage" as the ratio of debt value to the equity value used in financial management substantially differs from the concept of "leverage" in the rating, where it is understood as the direct and inverse ratio of the debt value to the generated cash flow values (income, profit, etc.). The authors introduced some additional ratios, allowing us to more fully characterize the issuer's ability to repay debts and to pay interest thereon.

Thus, the bridge is building between the discount rates (WACC, k_e) used when discounting financial flows and "ratios" in the rating methodology. The algorithm for finding the discount rates for given ratio values is developed.

6.5 Models

Two kinds of models of the evaluation of the creditworthiness of issuers, taking into account the discounting of financial flows, could be used in rating: one-period model and multi-period model.

6.5.1 *One-Period Model*

One-period model is described by the following formula (see Fig. 6.1):

Fig. 6.1 One-period model

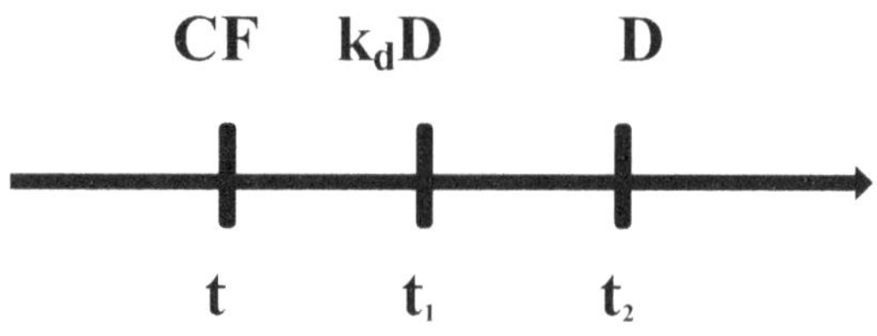

$$CF(1+i)^{t_2-t} \geq D + k_d D(1+i)^{t_2-t_1}$$
$$CF(1+i)^{t_2-t} \geq D\left[1 + k_d(1+i)^{t_2-t_1}\right] \quad (6.1)$$

Here CF is the value of income for period, D is debt value, t, t_1, t_2 the moments of income, payment of interest, and payment of debt, respectively, i is the discount rate, k_d is credit rate, and $k_d D$ is interest on credit.

6.5.2 *Multi-Period Model*

One-period model of the evaluation of the creditworthiness of issuers, taking into account the discounting of financial flows, could be generalized for more interesting multi-period case.

Multi-period model is described by the following formula:

$$\sum_j CF_j(1+i_j)^{t_{2j}-t_j} \geq \sum_j D_j\left[1 + k_{dj}(1+i_j)^{t_{2j}-t_{1j}}\right] \quad (6.2)$$

Here CF_j is income for j-st period, D_j is debt value in j-st period, t_j, t_{1j}, t_{2j} the moments of income, payment of interests, and payment of debt, respectively, in j-st period, i_j is the discount rate in j-st period, and k_{dj} is credit rate in j-st period.

There are several options to work with these models:

1. One can check the creditworthiness of the issuer, knowing parameters CF_j, D_j, t_j, t_{1j}, t_{2j}, k_{dj} and defining discount rate i by the method described below.
2. When D_j, t_j, t_{1j}, t_{2j}, k_{dj} are preset, one can determine which income CF_j the issuer would require to ensure its creditworthiness.
3. When D_j, t_j, t_{1j}, t_{2j}, k_{dj} are preset, one can define an acceptable level of debt financing (including the credit value D_j and credit rates k_{dj}) when issuer retains its creditworthiness.

6.6 Theory of Incorporation of Parameters, Using in Ratings, into Perpetuity Limit of Modern Theory of Capital Structure by Brusov–Filatova–Orekhova

For the first time we incorporate below the parameters, used in ratings, into perpetuity limit of the modern theory of capital structure by Brusov–Filatova–Orekhova (BFO theory).

We will consider two kinds of ratios: coverage ratios and leverage ratios.

Let us start from the coverage ratios.

6.6.1 *Coverage Ratios*

We will consider three kinds of coverage ratios: coverage ratios of debt, coverage ratios of interest on the credit, and coverage ratios of debt and interest on the credit.

6.6.1.1 Coverage Ratios of Debt

$$Here\ i_1 = CF/D \tag{6.3}$$

Modigliani–Miller theorem for the case with corporate taxes (Modigliani and Miller 1958, 1963) shows that capitalization of leveraged company, V_L, is equal to the capitalization of unleveraged company, V_0, plus tax shield for perpetuity time, Dt,

$$V_L = V_0 + Dt. \tag{6.4}$$

Substituting the expressions for both capitalizations, one has

$$\frac{CF}{\text{WACC}} = \frac{CF}{k_0} + Dt$$

Dividing both parts by D, one gets

$$\begin{aligned} \frac{i_1}{\text{WACC}} &= \frac{i_1}{k_0} + t \\ \text{WACC} &= \frac{i_1 k_0}{i_1 + tk_0} \end{aligned} \tag{6.5}$$

This ratio (i_1) can be used to assess the following parameters used in rating, DCF/Debt, FFO/Debt, CFO/Debt, FOCF/Debt, and some others. We will use the last formula to build a curve of dependence WACC(i_1).

6.6.1.2 Coverage Ratios of Interest on the Credit

$$\text{Here } i_2 = CF/k_\text{d}D \tag{6.6}$$

Using the Modigliani–Miller theorem for the case with corporate taxes

$$V_L = V_0 + Dt,$$

we derive the expression for WACC(i_2)

$$\begin{aligned} \frac{CF}{\text{WACC}} &= \frac{CF}{k_0} + Dt \\ \frac{i_2}{\text{WACC}} &= \frac{i_2}{k_0} + \frac{i_2}{k_\text{d}} \\ \text{WACC} &= \frac{i_2 k_0 k_\text{d}}{i_2 k_\text{d} + t k_0} \end{aligned} \tag{6.7}$$

This ratio (i_2) can be used to assess the following parameters, used in rating, *FFO/* cash interest, EBITDA/interest, and some others. We will use the last formula to build a curve of dependence WACC(i_2).

6.6.1.3 Coverage Ratios of Debt and Interest on the Credit (New Ratios)

Let us consider the coverage ratios of debt and interest on the credit simultaneously: this is new ratio, introduced by us for the first time here.

$$\text{Here } i_3 = \frac{CF}{D(1 + k_\text{d})} \tag{6.8}$$

Using as above the Modigliani–Miller theorem for the case with corporate taxes

$$V_L = V_0 + Dt$$

one gets the expression for WACC(i_3)

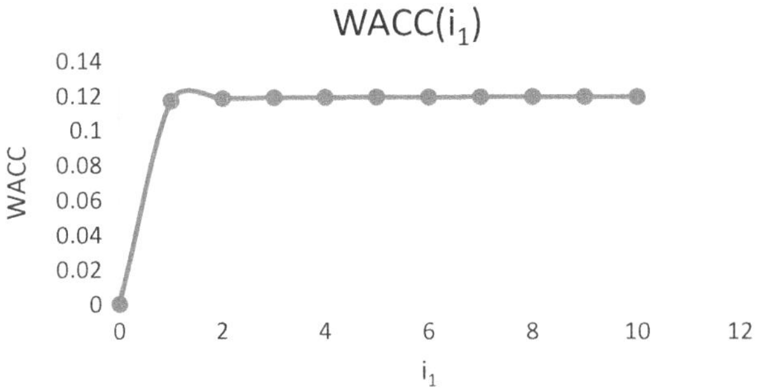

Fig. 6.2 The dependence of company's weighted average cost of capital (WACC) on the coverage ratio on debt i_1

$$\begin{aligned}\frac{CF}{\text{WACC}} &= \frac{CF}{k_0} + Dt\\ \frac{i_3}{\text{WACC}} &= \frac{i_3}{k_0} + \frac{t}{1 + k_d}\\ \text{WACC} &= \frac{i_3 k_0 (1 + k_d)}{i_3(1 + k_d) + tk_0}\end{aligned} \tag{6.9}$$

This ratio (i_3) can be used to assess the following parameters used in rating, FFO/Debt + interest, EBITDA/Debt + interest, and some others. We will use the last formula to build a curve of dependence WACC(i_3).

Let us analyze the dependence of company's weighted average cost of capital (WACC) on the coverage ratios on debt i_1, on interest on the credit i_2, and on coverage ratios on debt and interest on the credit with the following data: $k_0 = 12\%$; $k_d = 6\%$; $t = 20\%$; i_j run from 0 up to 10.

The dependence of company's weighted average cost of capital (WACC) on the coverage ratio on interest on the credit i_2 is presented in Fig. 6.3.

The dependence of company's weighted average cost of capital (WACC) on the coverage ratio on debt and interest on the credit i_2 is presented in Fig. 6.4.

The dependence of company's weighted average cost of capital (WACC) on the coverage ratio on debt i_1, on interest on the credit i_2, and on debt and interest on the credit i_3 is presented in Fig. 6.5.

It is seen from Figs. 6.2, 6.3, 6.4 and 6.5 that WACC(i_j) is increasing function on i_j with saturation around i_j value of order 1 for ratios i_1 and i_3 and of order 4 or 5 for ratios i_2. At saturation WACC reaches the value k_0 (equity value at zero leverage level). This means that for high values of i_j one can choose k_0 as a discount rate with a good accuracy. Thus, the role of parameter k_0 increases drastically. The method of determination of parameter k_0 has been developed by Anastasiya Brusova [Brusova A (2011)]. So, parameter k_0 is the discount rate for the limit case of high values of i_j (see, however, below more detailed consideration).

It is clear from Figs. 6.2, 6.3, 6.4 and 6.5 that the case of low values of i_j requires more detailed consideration. Let us consider the situation with low values of i_j which seems to be the case of the most interest.

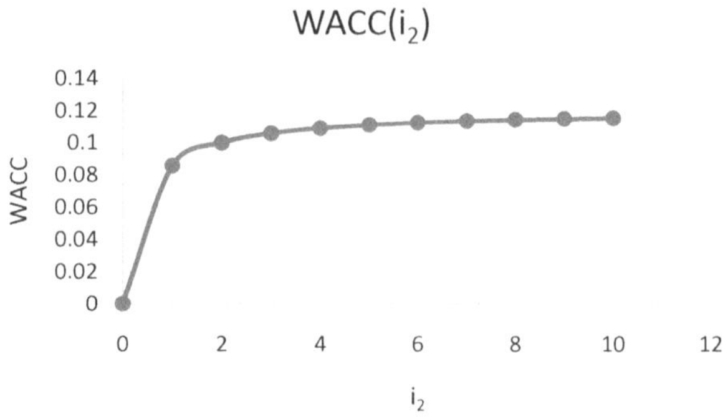

Fig. 6.3 The dependence of company's weighted average cost of capital (WACC) on the coverage ratio on interest on the credit i_2

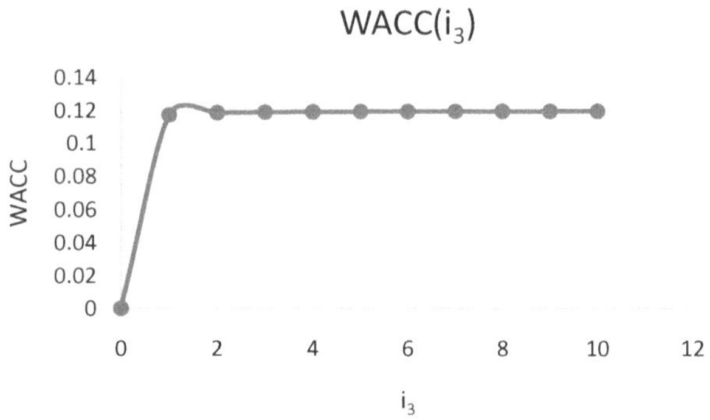

Fig. 6.4 The dependence of company's weighted average cost of capital (WACC) on the coverage ratio on debt and interest on the credit i_3

6.6.2 More Detailed Consideration

Below we consider the case of low values of i_j with more details. i_j will vary from zero up to 1 with all other parameters being the same (Figs. 6.6, 6.7, 6.8 and 6.9).

More detailed consideration leads us to the following conclusions:

1. In the case of coverage ratio on debt and interest on the credit i_3 WACC goes to saturation very fast: with accuracy of 20% at $i_3 = 0.15$ and with accuracy of 5% at $i_3 = 0.5$.
2. In the case of coverage ratio on debt i_1, WACC practically linearly increases with parameter i_1 and goes to saturation at $i_1 = 0.1$.
3. In the case of coverage ratio on interest on the credit i_2 WACC increases with parameter i_2 much more slowly than in two previous cases and goes to saturation at high values of i_2: with accuracy of 10% at $i_2 = 4$.

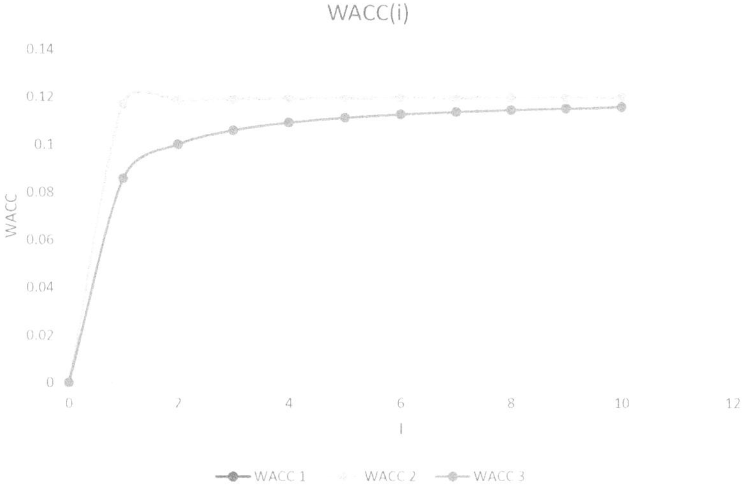

Fig. 6.5 The dependence of company's weighted average cost of capital (WACC) on the coverage ratio on debt i_1, on interest on the credit i_2, and on debt and interest on the credit i_3

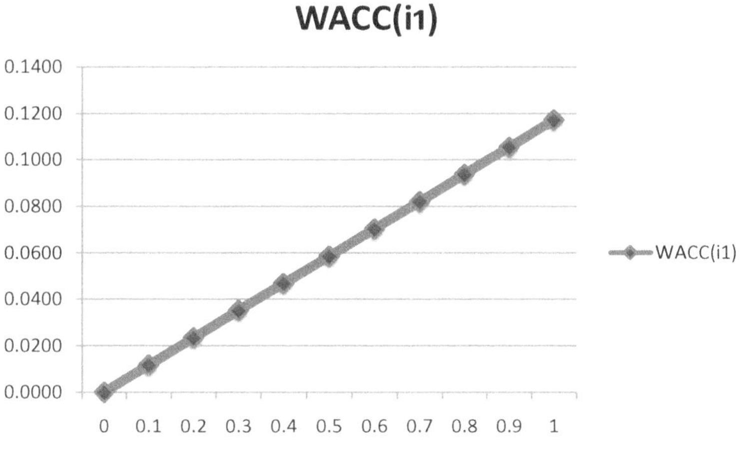

Fig. 6.6 The dependence of company's weighted average cost of capital (WACC) on the coverage ratio on debt and interest on the credit i_1

6.6.3 Leverage Ratios

Let us consider now the leverage ratios. We will consider three kinds of leverage ratios: leverage ratios of debt, leverage ratios of interest on the credit, and leverage ratios of debt and interest on the credit.

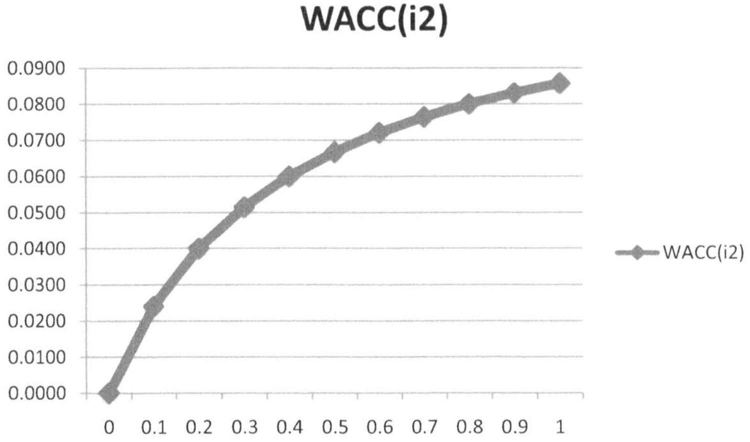

Fig. 6.7 The dependence of company's weighted average cost of capital (WACC) on the coverage ratio on debt and interest on the credit i_2

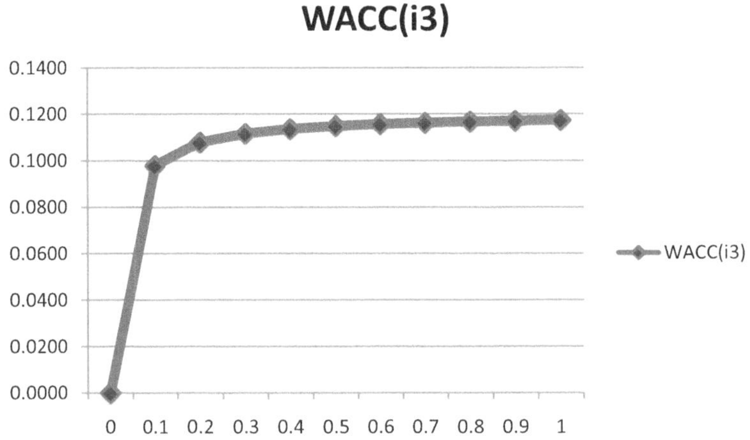

Fig. 6.8 The dependence of company's weighted average cost of capital (WACC) on the coverage ratio on debt and interest on the credit i_3

6.6.3.1 Leverage Ratios for Debt

$$\text{Here } l_1 = D/CF \tag{6.10}$$

As above for coverage ratios using the Modigliani–Miller theorem for the case with corporate taxes

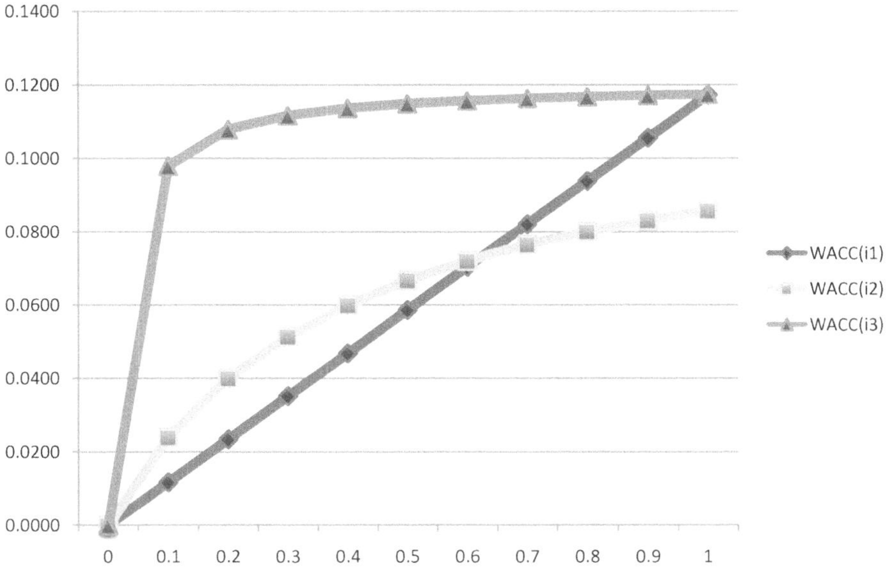

Fig. 6.9 The dependence of company's weighted average cost of capital (WACC) on the coverage ratio on debt i_1, on interest on the credit i_2, and on debt and interest on the credit i_3

$$V_L = V_0 + Dt,$$

we derive the expression for WACC(l_1)

$$\begin{aligned}
\frac{CF}{\mathrm{WACC}} &= \frac{CF}{k_0} + Dt \\
\frac{1}{\mathrm{WACC}} &= \frac{1}{k_0} + l_1 t \\
\mathrm{WACC} &= \frac{k_0}{1 + t l_1 k_0}
\end{aligned} \tag{6.11}$$

This ratio (l_1) can be used to assess the following parameters used in rating, Debt/EBITDA and some others. We will use the last formula to build a curve of dependence WACC(l_1).

6.6.3.2 Leverage Ratios for Interest on Credit

$$\text{Here } l_2 = k_{\mathrm{d}} D / CF \tag{6.12}$$

Using again the Modigliani–Miller theorem for the case with corporate taxes

$$V_L = V_0 + Dt,$$

we derive the expression for WACC(l_2)

$$\begin{aligned}\frac{CF}{\text{WACC}} &= \frac{CF}{k_0} + Dt \\ \frac{1}{\text{WACC}} &= \frac{1}{k_0} + \frac{l_2 t}{k_\text{d}} \\ \text{WACC} &= \frac{k_0 k_\text{d}}{k_\text{d} + t l_2 k_0}\end{aligned} \tag{6.13}$$

This ratio (l_2) can be used to assess the following parameters used in rating, Interests/EBITDA and some others. We will use the last formula to build a curve of dependence WACC(l_2).

6.6.3.3 Leverage Ratios for Debt and Interest on Credit

$$\text{Here} \quad l_3 = D(1 + k_\text{d})/CF \tag{6.14}$$

Using the Modigliani–Miller theorem for the case with corporate taxes

$$V_L = V_0 + Dt,$$

we derive the expression for WACC(l_3)

$$\begin{aligned}\frac{CF}{\text{WACC}} &= \frac{CF}{k_0} + Dt \\ \frac{1}{\text{WACC}} &= \frac{1}{k_0} + \frac{l_3 t}{1 + k_\text{d}} \\ \text{WACC} &= \frac{k_0(1 + k_\text{d})}{1 + k_\text{d} + t l_3 k_0}\end{aligned} \tag{6.15}$$

This ratio (l_3) can be used to assess the following parameters used in rating, Debt +interest/FFO, Debt+interest/EBIT, Debt+interest/EBITDA(R), and some others. We will use the last formula to build a curve of dependence WACC(l_3).

Let us analyze the dependence of company's weighted average cost of capital (WACC) on the leverage ratios with the following data: $k_0 = 12\%$; $k_\text{d} = 6\%$; $t = 20\%$; l_i runs from 0 up to 10.

The dependence of company's weighted average cost of capital (WACC) on the leverage ratio on debt l_1 is presented in Fig. 6.10.

The dependence of company's weighted average cost of capital (WACC) on the leverage ratio on interest on credit l_2 is presented in Fig. 6.11.

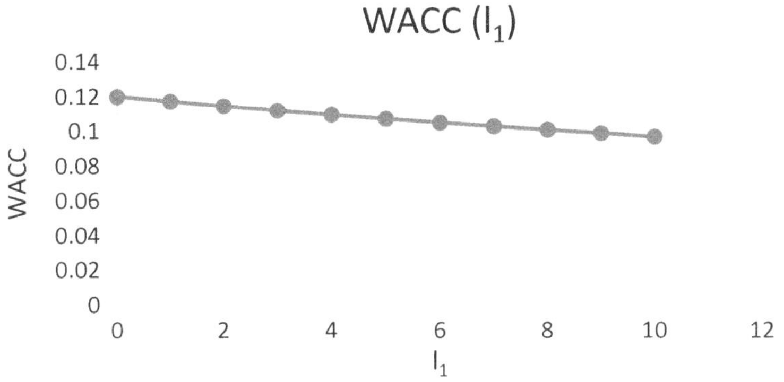

Fig. 6.10 The dependence of company's weighted average cost of capital (WACC) on the leverage ratio on debt l_1

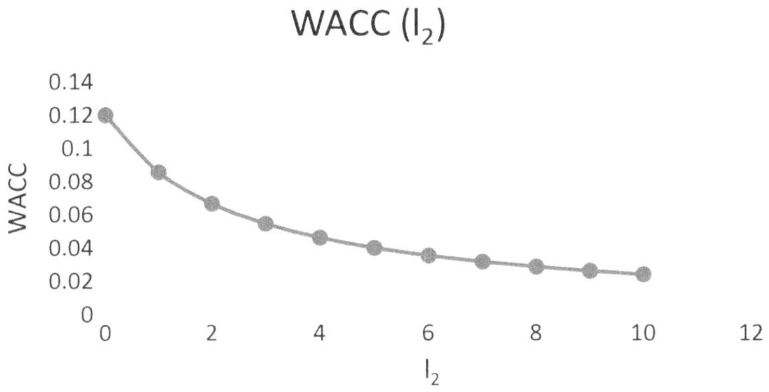

Fig. 6.11 The dependence of company's weighted average cost of capital (WACC) on the leverage ratio on interest on credit l_2

The dependence of company's weighted average cost of capital (WACC) on the leverage ratio on debt and interest on credit l_3 is presented in Fig. 6.12.

The dependence of company's weighted average cost of capital (WACC) on the leverage ratio on debt, l_1, on interest on credit, l_2, and on debt and interest on credit, l_3, simultaneously is presented in Fig. 6.13.

Analysis of the dependences of company's weighted average cost of capital (WACC) on the leverage ratio on debt, l_1, on interest on credit, l_2, and on debt and interest on credit, l_3, shows the following: for all leverage ratios weighted average cost of capital (WACC) decreases with leverage ratios. For leverage ratio on debt l_1 and leverage ratio on debt and interest on credit l_3, WACC decreases very similarly and practically linearly from $k_0 = 12\%$ at $l_{1,3} = 0$ up to 9.7% at $l_{1,3} = 10$. For leverage ratio on interest on credit l_2, WACC decreases nonlinearly and much faster from $k_0 = 12\%$ at $l_2 = 0$ up to 2.4% at $l_2 = 10$.

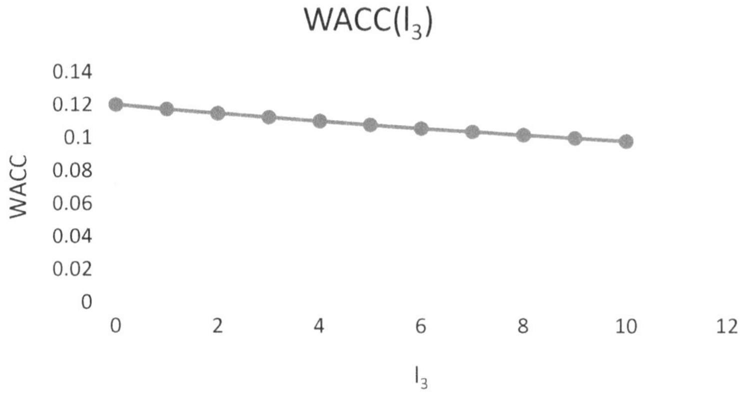

Fig. 6.12 The dependence of company's weighted average cost of capital (WACC) on the leverage ratio on debt and interest on credit l_3

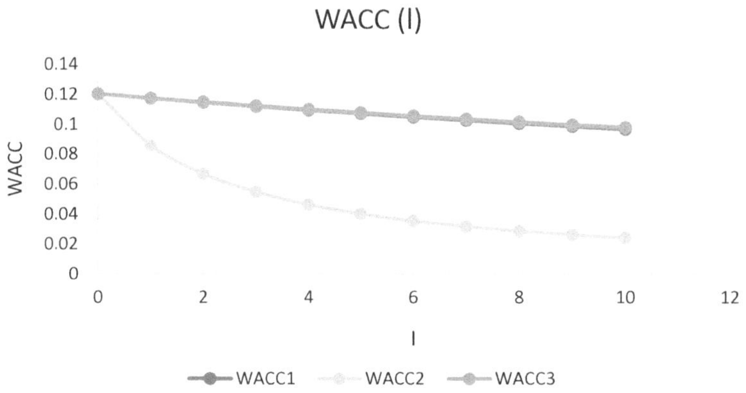

Fig. 6.13 The dependence of company's weighted average cost of capital (WACC) on the leverage ratio on debt, l_1, on interest on credit, l_2, and on debt and on interest on credit, l_3, simultaneously

6.7 Equity Cost

Equity cost plays a very important role in economy and finance because it is the essence of the dividend policy of companies, which should be accounted in rating. A modern approach to the dividend policy of companies, based on the real value of their equity capital cost, compared to its efficiency of planned investment is suggested in the article (Brusov et al. 2018b). This allows us to return to the economic essence of dividends, as the payment to shareholders for the use of equity capital.

Equity cost k_e determines the economically reasonable dividend value. Rating agencies will be able to compare payable dividend value with economically

Table 6.1 The dependence of company's weighted average cost of capital (WACC) on the coverage ratio on debt i_1

t	i_1	k_0	k_d	WACC
0.2	0	0.12	0.06	0
0.2	1	0.12	0.06	0.1171875
0.2	2	0.12	0.06	0.1185771
0.2	3	0.12	0.06	0.1190476
0.2	4	0.12	0.06	0.1192843
0.2	5	0.12	0.06	0.1194268
0.2	6	0.12	0.06	0.1195219
0.2	7	0.12	0.06	0.11959
0.2	8	0.12	0.06	0.1196411
0.2	9	0.12	0.06	0.1196809
0.2	10	0.12	0.06	0.1197127

Table 6.2 The dependence of company's weighted average cost of capital (WACC) on the coverage ratio on debt i_2

t	i_2	k_0	k_d	WACC
0.2	0	0.12	0.06	0
0.2	1	0.12	0.06	0.085714
0.2	2	0.12	0.06	0.1
0.2	3	0.12	0.06	0.105882
0.2	4	0.12	0.06	0.109091
0.2	5	0.12	0.06	0.111111
0.2	6	0.12	0.06	0.1125
0.2	7	0.12	0.06	0.113514
0.2	8	0.12	0.06	0.114286
0.2	9	0.12	0.06	0.114894
0.2	10	0.12	0.06	0.115385

Table 6.3 The dependence of company's weighted average cost of capital (WACC) on the coverage ratio on debt i_3

t	i_3	k_0	k_d	WACC
0.2	0	0.12	0.06	0
0.2	1	0.12	0.06	0.1173432
0.2	2	0.12	0.06	0.1186567
0.2	3	0.12	0.06	0.1191011
0.2	4	0.12	0.06	0.1193246
0.2	5	0.12	0.06	0.1194591
0.2	6	0.12	0.06	0.1195489
0.2	7	0.12	0.06	0.1196131
0.2	8	0.12	0.06	0.1196613
0.2	9	0.12	0.06	0.1196989
0.2	10	0.12	0.06	0.1197289

reasonable dividend level and make conclusion about the adequacy of the dividend policy of companies and its influence on company's credit rating.

For finding the dependence of equity cost k_e on coverage ratios and leverage ratios, we consider consistently the dependence of equity cost k_e on ratios i_1, i_2, i_3, l_1, l_2, l_3, using the following formula, which couples weighted average cost of capital

Table 6.4 The dependence of company's weighted average cost of capital (WACC) on the coverage ratio on debt i_1

i_1	K_o	K_d	t	WACC(i_1)
0	0.12	0.06	0.2	0.0000
0.1	0.12	0.06	0.2	0.0117
0.2	0.12	0.06	0.2	0.0234
0.3	0.12	0.06	0.2	0.0352
0.4	0.12	0.06	0.2	0.0469
0.5	0.12	0.06	0.2	0.0586
0.6	0.12	0.06	0.2	0.0703
0.7	0.12	0.06	0.2	0.0820
0.8	0.12	0.06	0.2	0.0938
0.9	0.12	0.06	0.2	0.1055
1	0.12	0.06	0.2	0.1172

Table 6.5 The dependence of company's weighted average cost of capital (WACC) on the coverage ratio on debt i_1

i_2	K_o	K_d	t	WACC(i_2)
0	0.12	0.06	0.2	0.0000
0.1	0.12	0.06	0.2	0.0240
0.2	0.12	0.06	0.2	0.0400
0.3	0.12	0.06	0.2	0.0514
0.4	0.12	0.06	0.2	0.0600
0.5	0.12	0.06	0.2	0.0667
0.6	0.12	0.06	0.2	0.0720
0.7	0.12	0.06	0.2	0.0764
0.8	0.12	0.06	0.2	0.0800
0.9	0.12	0.06	0.2	0.0831
1	0.12	0.06	0.2	0.0857

Table 6.6 The dependence of company's weighted average cost of capital (WACC) on the coverage ratio on debt i_3

i_3	K_o	K_d	t	WACC(i_3)
0	0.12	0.06	0.2	0.0000
0.1	0.12	0.06	0.2	0.0978
0.2	0.12	0.06	0.2	0.1078
0.3	0.12	0.06	0.2	0.1116
0.4	0.12	0.06	0.2	0.1136
0.5	0.12	0.06	0.2	0.1148
0.6	0.12	0.06	0.2	0.1156
0.7	0.12	0.06	0.2	0.1162
0.8	0.12	0.06	0.2	0.1167
0.9	0.12	0.06	0.2	0.1171
1	0.12	0.06	0.2	0.1173

Table 6.7 The dependence of company's weighted average cost of capital (WACC) on the coverage ratio on debt l_1

t	l_1	k_0	k_d	WACC
0.2	0	0.12	0.06	0.12
0.2	1	0.12	0.06	0.117188
0.2	2	0.12	0.06	0.114504
0.2	3	0.12	0.06	0.11194
0.2	4	0.12	0.06	0.109489
0.2	5	0.12	0.06	0.107143
0.2	6	0.12	0.06	0.104895
0.2	7	0.12	0.06	0.10274
0.2	8	0.12	0.06	0.100671
0.2	9	0.12	0.06	0.098684
0.2	10	0.12	0.06	0.096774

Table 6.8 The dependence of company's weighted average cost of capital (WACC) on the coverage ratio on debt l_2

t	l_2	k_0	k_d	WACC
0.2	0	0.12	0.06	0.12
0.2	1	0.12	0.06	0.085714
0.2	2	0.12	0.06	0.066667
0.2	3	0.12	0.06	0.054545
0.2	4	0.12	0.06	0.046154
0.2	5	0.12	0.06	0.04
0.2	6	0.12	0.06	0.035294
0.2	7	0.12	0.06	0.031579
0.2	8	0.12	0.06	0.028571
0.2	9	0.12	0.06	0.026087
0.2	10	0.12	0.06	0.024

Table 6.9 The dependence of company's weighted average cost of capital (WACC) on the coverage ratio on debt l_3

t	l_3	k_0	k_d	WACC
0.2	0	0.12	0.06	0.12
0.2	1	0.12	0.06	0.117353
0.2	2	0.12	0.06	0.114819
0.2	3	0.12	0.06	0.112393
0.2	4	0.12	0.06	0.110068
0.2	5	0.12	0.06	0.107836
0.2	6	0.12	0.06	0.105693
0.2	7	0.12	0.06	0.103634
0.2	8	0.12	0.06	0.101654
0.2	9	0.12	0.06	0.099747
0.2	10	0.12	0.06	0.097911

WACC (calculated by us above: see Tables 6.1, 6.2, 6.3, 6.4, 6.5, 6.6, 6.7, 6.8 and 6.9) and equity cost k_e

$$k_e = \mathrm{WACC}(1 + L) - Lk_d(1 - t). \tag{6.16}$$

6.7.1 *The Dependence of Equity cost* k_e *on Coverage Ratios* i_1, i_2, i_3

Let us study the dependence of equity cost k_e on coverage ratios i_1, i_2, i_3 for the same set of parameters as used above and for leverage levels $L = 1$ and $L = 2$ (Tables 6.10, 6.11 and 6.12).

1. $L = 1$

2. $L = 2$

Table 6.10 The dependence of equity cost k_e on coverage ratio i_1 at leverage level $L = 1$

L	i_1	WACC(i_1)	K_d	t	K_e
1	0	0.00000	0.06	0.2	–0.0480
1	1	0.11719	0.06	0.2	0.1864
1	2	0.11858	0.06	0.2	0.1892
1	3	0.11905	0.06	0.2	0.1901
1	4	0.11928	0.06	0.2	0.1906
1	5	0.11943	0.06	0.2	0.1909
1	6	0.11952	0.06	0.2	0.1910
1	7	0.11959	0.06	0.2	0.1912
1	8	0.11964	0.06	0.2	0.1913
1	9	0.11968	0.06	0.2	0.1914
1	10	0.11971	0.06	0.2	0.1914

Table 6.11 The dependence of equity cost k_e on coverage ratio i_1 at leverage level $L = 2$

L	i_1	WACC(i_1)	K_d	t	K_e
2	0	0.00000	0.06	0.2	–0.0960
2	1	0.11719	0.06	0.2	0.2556
2	2	0.11858	0.06	0.2	0.2597
2	3	0.11905	0.06	0.2	0.2611
2	4	0.11928	0.06	0.2	0.2619
2	5	0.11943	0.06	0.2	0.2623
2	6	0.11952	0.06	0.2	0.2626
2	7	0.11959	0.06	0.2	0.2628
2	8	0.11964	0.06	0.2	0.2629
2	9	0.11968	0.06	0.2	0.2630
2	10	0.11971	0.06	0.2	0.2631

Table 6.12 The dependence of equity cost k_e on coverage ratio i_2 at leverage level $L = 1$

L	i_2	WACC(i_2)	K_d	t	K_e
1	0	0.00000	0.06	0.2	–0.0480
1	1	0.11734	0.06	0.2	0.1867
1	2	0.11866	0.06	0.2	0.1893
1	3	0.11910	0.06	0.2	0.1902
1	4	0.11932	0.06	0.2	0.1906
1	5	0.11946	0.06	0.2	0.1909
1	6	0.11955	0.06	0.2	0.1911
1	7	0.11961	0.06	0.2	0.1912
1	8	0.11966	0.06	0.2	0.1913
1	9	0.11970	0.06	0.2	0.1914
1	10	0.11973	0.06	0.2	0.1915

Table 6.13 The dependence of equity cost k_e on coverage ratio i_2 at leverage level $L = 2$

L	i_2	WACC(i_2)	K_d	t	K_e
2	0	0.00000	0.06	0.2	–0.0960
2	1	0.11734	0.06	0.2	0.2560
2	2	0.11866	0.06	0.2	0.2600
2	3	0.11910	0.06	0.2	0.2613
2	4	0.11932	0.06	0.2	0.2620
2	5	0.11946	0.06	0.2	0.2624
2	6	0.11955	0.06	0.2	0.2626
2	7	0.11961	0.06	0.2	0.2628
2	8	0.11966	0.06	0.2	0.2630
2	9	0.11970	0.06	0.2	0.2631
2	10	0.11973	0.06	0.2	0.2632

Table 6.14 The dependence of equity cost k_e on coverage ratio i_3 at leverage level $L = 1$

L	i_3	WACC(i_3)	K_d	t	K_e
1	0	0.00000	0.06	0.2	–0.0480
1	1	0.08571	0.06	0.2	0.1234
1	2	0.10000	0.06	0.2	0.1520
1	3	0.10588	0.06	0.2	0.1638
1	4	0.10909	0.06	0.2	0.1702
1	5	0.11111	0.06	0.2	0.1742
1	6	0.11250	0.06	0.2	0.1770
1	7	0.11351	0.06	0.2	0.1790
1	8	0.11429	0.06	0.2	0.1806
1	9	0.11489	0.06	0.2	0.1818
1	10	0.11538	0.06	0.2	0.1828

We could make some conclusions, based on Tables 6.13, 6.14 and 6.15 and Figs. 6.14, 6.15 and 6.16. In all three cases, equity cost k_e increases with coverage ratios and goes to saturation at high values of coverage ratios. Saturation values increase with leverage level from 19% at $L = 1$ up to value above 26% at $L = 2$. Note

Table 6.15 The dependence of equity cost k_e on coverage ratio i_3 at leverage level $L = 2$

L	i_3	WACC(i_3)	K_d	t	K_e
2	0	0.00000	0.06	0.2	–0.0960
2	1	0.08571	0.06	0.2	0.1611
2	2	0.10000	0.06	0.2	0.2040
2	3	0.10588	0.06	0.2	0.2216
2	4	0.10909	0.06	0.2	0.2313
2	5	0.11111	0.06	0.2	0.2373
2	6	0.11250	0.06	0.2	0.2415
2	7	0.11351	0.06	0.2	0.2445
2	8	0.11429	0.06	0.2	0.2469
2	9	0.11489	0.06	0.2	0.2487
2	10	0.11538	0.06	0.2	0.2502

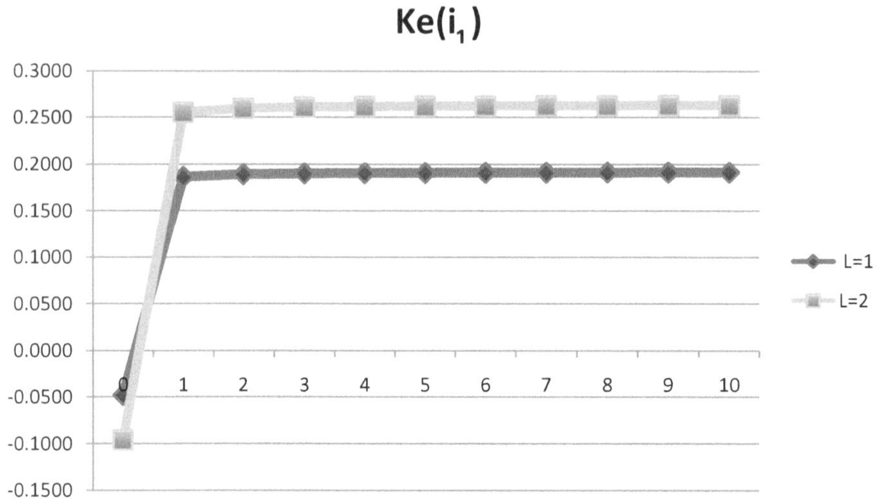

Fig. 6.14 The dependence of equity cost k_e on coverage ratio i_1 at two leverage level values $L = 1$ and $L = 2$

that for coverage ratios i_1 and i_2 the saturation takes place at values $i_{1,2}$ of order unit, while for coverage ratio i_3 the saturation takes place at much higher i_3 values of order 6 or 7.

Equity cost k_e should be used as discount rate for unleveraged (financially independent) companies. For coverage ratios i_1 and i_2 saturation values of equity cost k_e could be used as discount rate above unit, while for coverage ratio i_3 saturation values of equity cost k_e could be used as discount rate at i_3 value above 6 or 7.

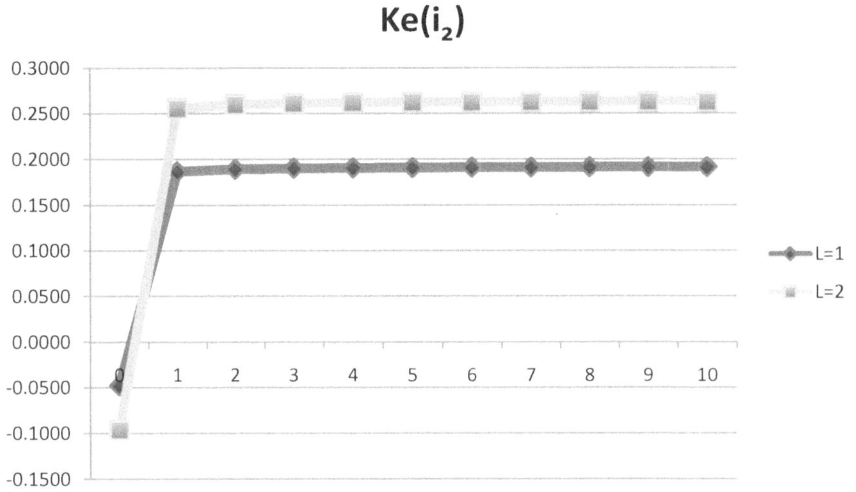

Fig. 6.15 The dependence of equity cost k_e on coverage ratio i_2 at two leverage level values $L = 1$ and $L = 2$

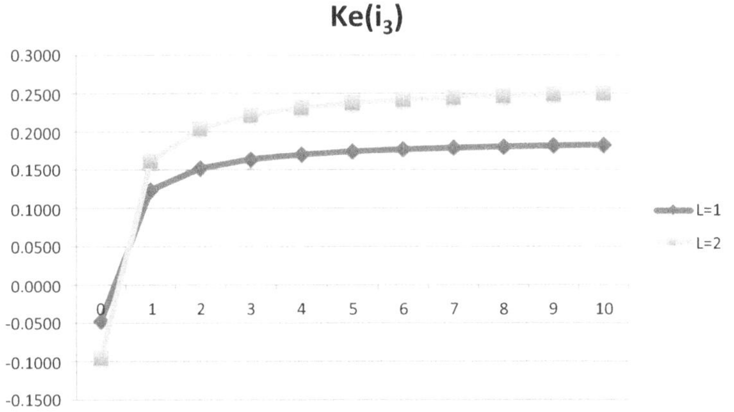

Fig. 6.16 The dependence of equity cost k_e on coverage ratio i_3 at two leverage level values $L = 1$ and $L = 2$

6.7.2 *The Dependence of Equity Cost* k_e *on Leverage Ratios* l_1, l_2, l_3

We study below the dependence of equity cost k_e on leverage ratios l_1, l_2, l_3 for the same set of parameters as used above and for leverage levels $L = 1$ and $L = 2$.

Table 6.16 The dependence of equity cost k_e on leverage ratio l_1 at leverage level $L = 1$

L	l_1	WACC(l_1)	K_d	t	K_e
1	0	0.12000	0.06	0.2	0.1920
1	1	0.11719	0.06	0.2	0.1864
1	2	0.11450	0.06	0.2	0.1810
1	3	0.11194	0.06	0.2	0.1759
1	4	0.10949	0.06	0.2	0.1710
1	5	0.10714	0.06	0.2	0.1663
1	6	0.10490	0.06	0.2	0.1618
1	7	0.10274	0.06	0.2	0.1575
1	8	0.10067	0.06	0.2	0.1533
1	9	0.09868	0.06	0.2	0.1494
1	10	0.09677	0.06	0.2	0.1455

Table 6.17 The dependence of equity cost k_e on leverage ratio l_1 at leverage level $L = 2$

L	l_1	WACC(l_1)	K_d	t	K_e
2	0	0.12000	0.06	0.2	0.2640
2	1	0.11719	0.06	0.2	0.2556
2	2	0.11450	0.06	0.2	0.2475
2	3	0.11194	0.06	0.2	0.2398
2	4	0.10949	0.06	0.2	0.2325
2	5	0.10714	0.06	0.2	0.2254
2	6	0.10490	0.06	0.2	0.2187
2	7	0.10274	0.06	0.2	0.2122
2	8	0.10067	0.06	0.2	0.2060
2	9	0.09868	0.06	0.2	0.2001
2	10	0.09677	0.06	0.2	0.1943

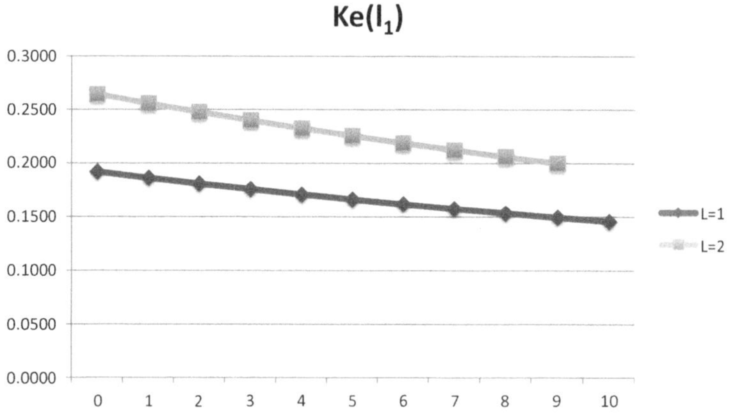

Fig. 6.17 The dependence of equity cost k_e on leverage ratio l_1 at two leverage level values $L = 1$ and $L = 2$

Table 6.18 The dependence of equity cost k_e on leverage ratio l_2 at leverage level $L = 1$

L	l_2	WACC(l_2)	K_d	t	K_e
1	0	0.12000	0.06	0.2	0.1920
1	1	0.08571	0.06	0.2	0.1234
1	2	0.06667	0.06	0.2	0.0853
1	3	0.05455	0.06	0.2	0.0611
1	4	0.04615	0.06	0.2	0.0443
1	5	0.04000	0.06	0.2	0.0320
1	6	0.03529	0.06	0.2	0.0226
1	7	0.03158	0.06	0.2	0.0152
1	8	0.02857	0.06	0.2	0.0091
1	9	0.02609	0.06	0.2	0.0042
1	10	0.02400	0.06	0.2	0.0000

Table 6.19 The dependence of equity cost k_e on leverage ratio l_2 at leverage level $L = 2$

L	l_2	WACC(l_2)	K_d	t	K_e
2	0	0.12000	0.06	0.2	0.2640
2	1	0.08571	0.06	0.2	0.1611
2	2	0.06667	0.06	0.2	0.1040
2	3	0.05455	0.06	0.2	0.0676
2	4	0.04615	0.06	0.2	0.0425
2	5	0.04000	0.06	0.2	0.0240
2	6	0.03529	0.06	0.2	0.0099
2	7	0.03158	0.06	0.2	–0.0013
2	8	0.02857	0.06	0.2	–0.0103
2	9	0.02609	0.06	0.2	–0.0177
2	10	0.02400	0.06	0.2	–0.0240

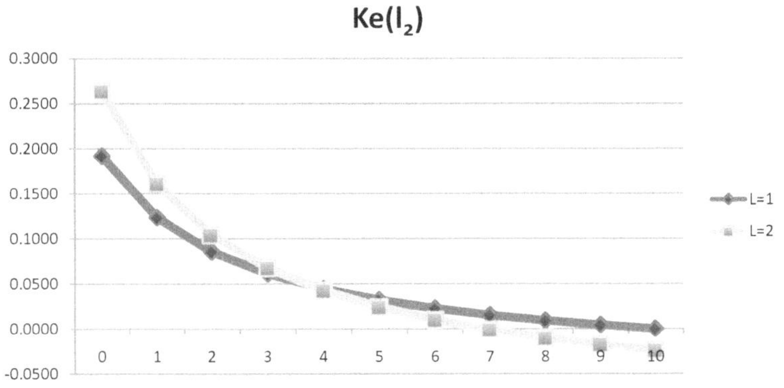

Fig. 6.18 The dependence of equity cost k_e on leverage ratio l_2 at two leverage level values $L = 1$ and $L = 2$

6.7.3 The Dependence of Equity Cost k_e on Leverage Ratio l_1

1. $\boldsymbol{L = 1}$ (Table 6.16)

2. $\boldsymbol{L = 2}$ (Table 6.17 and Fig. 6.17)

6.7.4 The Dependence of Equity Cost k_e on Leverage Ratios l_2

1. $\boldsymbol{L = 1}$ (Table 6.18 and Fig. 6.18)

2. $\boldsymbol{L = 2}$ (Table 6.19)

6.7.5 The Dependence of Equity Cost k_e on Leverage Ratios l_3

1. $\boldsymbol{L = 1}$ (Table 6.20 and Fig. 6.19)

Table 6.20 The dependence of equity cost k_e on leverage ratio l_2 at leverage level $L = 1$

L	l_3	WACC(l_3)	K_d	t	K_e
1	0	0.12000	0.06	0.2	0.1920
1	1	0.11735	0.06	0.2	0.1867
1	2	0.11482	0.06	0.2	0.1816
1	3	0.11239	0.06	0.2	0.1768
1	4	0.11007	0.06	0.2	0.1721
1	5	0.10784	0.06	0.2	0.1677
1	6	0.10569	0.06	0.2	0.1634
1	7	0.10363	0.06	0.2	0.1593
1	8	0.10165	0.06	0.2	0.1553
1	9	0.09975	0.06	0.2	0.1515
1	10	0.09791	0.06	0.2	0.1478

Table 6.21 The dependence of equity cost k_e on leverage ratio l_2 at leverage level $L = 2$

L	l_3	WACC(l_3)	K_d	t	K_e
2	0	0.12000	0.06	0.2	0.2640
2	1	0.11735	0.06	0.2	0.2561
2	2	0.11482	0.06	0.2	0.2485
2	3	0.11239	0.06	0.2	0.2412
2	4	0.11007	0.06	0.2	0.2342
2	5	0.10784	0.06	0.2	0.2275
2	6	0.10569	0.06	0.2	0.2211
2	7	0.10363	0.06	0.2	0.2149
2	8	0.10165	0.06	0.2	0.2090
2	9	0.09975	0.06	0.2	0.2032
2	10	0.09791	0.06	0.2	0.1977

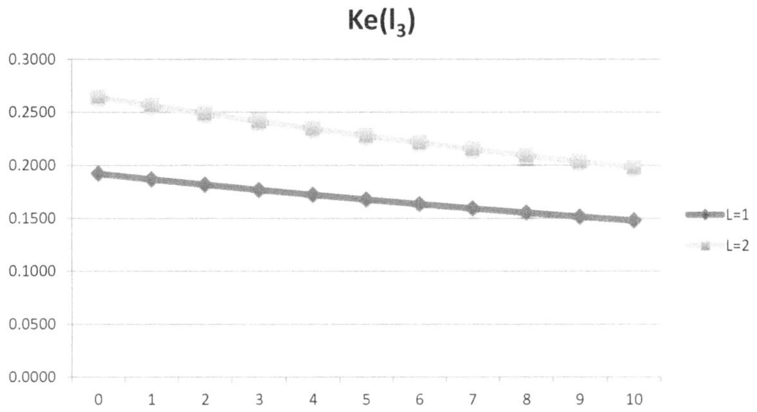

Fig. 6.19 The dependence of equity cost k_e on leverage ratio l_3 at two leverage level values $L = 1$ and $L = 2$

2. $\boldsymbol{L = 2}$ (Table 6.21 and Fig. 6.19)

6.8 How to Evaluate the Discount Rate?

Let us discuss now the algorithm of valuation of the discount rate, if we know one or a few ratios (coverage or leverage ones). The developed above method allows us to estimate discount rate with the best accuracy characteristic for used theory of capital structure (perpetuity limit).

6.8.1 *Using One Ratio*

If one knows one ratio (coverage or leverage one) the algorithm of valuation of the discount rate is as follows:

- Determination of the parameter k_0.
- Knowing k_0, k_d, and t, one builds the curve of dependence WACC(i) or WACC(l).
- Then, using the known value of coverage ratio (i_0) or leverage ratio (l_0), one finds the value WACC(i_0) or WACC(l_0), which represents the discount rate.

6.8.2 *Using a Few Ratios*

If we know say m values of coverage ratios (i_j) and n values of leverage ratios (l_k)

- We find by the above algorithm m values of WACC(i_j) and n values of WACC(l_k) first.

– Then we find the average value of WACC by the following formula:

$$\mathrm{WACC_{av}} = \frac{1}{m+n}\left[\sum_{j=1}^{m}\mathrm{WACC}(i_j) + \sum_{k=1}^{n}\mathrm{WACC}(l_k)\right].$$

This value $\mathrm{WACC_{av}}$ should be used when discounting the financial flows in rating.

6.9 Influence of Leverage Level

We discuss also the interplay between rating ratios and leverage level which can be quite important in rating.

6.9.1 The Dependence of Equity Cost k_e on Leverage Level at Two Coverage Ratio Values $i_j = 1$ and $i_j = 2$

1. $i_1 = 1$

2. $i_1 = 2$

1. $i_2 = 1$

2. $i_2 = 2$

1. $i_3 = 1$

2. $i_3 = 2$

It is seen from Tables 6.22, 6.23, 6.24, 6.25, 6.26, 6.27 and Figs. 6.20, 6.21 and 6.22 that equity cost k_e increases practically linearly with leverage level for all coverage

Table 6.22 The dependence of equity cost k_e on leverage level L at coverage ratio $i_1 = 1$

L	WACC($i_1 = 1$)	K_d	t	K_e
0	0.11719	0.06	0.2	0.1172
1	0.11719	0.06	0.2	0.1864
2	0.11719	0.06	0.2	0.2556
3	0.11719	0.06	0.2	0.3248
4	0.11719	0.06	0.2	0.3939
5	0.11719	0.06	0.2	0.4631
6	0.11719	0.06	0.2	0.5323
7	0.11719	0.06	0.2	0.6015
8	0.11719	0.06	0.2	0.6707
9	0.11719	0.06	0.2	0.7399
10	0.11719	0.06	0.2	0.8091

Table 6.23 The dependence of equity cost k_e on leverage level L at coverage ratio $i_1 = 2$

L	WACC($i_1 = 2$)	K_d	t	K_e
0	0.11858	0.06	0.2	0.1186
1	0.11858	0.06	0.2	0.1892
2	0.11858	0.06	0.2	0.2597
3	0.11858	0.06	0.2	0.3303
4	0.11858	0.06	0.2	0.4009
5	0.11858	0.06	0.2	0.4715
6	0.11858	0.06	0.2	0.5420
7	0.11858	0.06	0.2	0.6126
8	0.11858	0.06	0.2	0.6832
9	0.11858	0.06	0.2	0.7538
10	0.11858	0.06	0.2	0.8243

Table 6.24 The dependence of equity cost k_e on leverage level L at coverage ratio $i_2 = 1$

L	WACC($i_2 = 1$)	K_d	t	K_e
0	0.11734	0.06	0.2	0.1173
1	0.11734	0.06	0.2	0.1867
2	0.11734	0.06	0.2	0.2560
3	0.11734	0.06	0.2	0.3254
4	0.11734	0.06	0.2	0.3947
5	0.11734	0.06	0.2	0.4641
6	0.11734	0.06	0.2	0.5334
7	0.11734	0.06	0.2	0.6027
8	0.11734	0.06	0.2	0.6721
9	0.11734	0.06	0.2	0.7414
10	0.11734	0.06	0.2	0.8108

Table 6.25 The dependence of equity cost k_e on leverage level L at coverage ratio $i_2 = 2$

L	WACC($i_2 = 2$)	K_d	t	K_e
0	0.11866	0.06	0.2	0.1187
1	0.11866	0.06	0.2	0.1893
2	0.11866	0.06	0.2	0.2600
3	0.11866	0.06	0.2	0.3306
4	0.11866	0.06	0.2	0.4013
5	0.11866	0.06	0.2	0.4719
6	0.11866	0.06	0.2	0.5426
7	0.11866	0.06	0.2	0.6133
8	0.11866	0.06	0.2	0.6839
9	0.11866	0.06	0.2	0.7546
10	0.11866	0.06	0.2	0.8252

ratios i_1, i_2, i_3. For each of two coverage ratios i_1, i_2, curves k_e (L) for two values of i_j (1 and 2) practically coincide. For coverage ratio i_3 curve k_e (L) for value of $i_3 = 2$ lies above one for $i_3 = 1$ and angle of inclination for value of $i_3 = 2$ is bigger.

Table 6.26 The dependence of equity cost k_e on leverage level L at coverage ratio $i_3 = 1$

L	WACC($i_3 = 1$)	K_d	t	K_e
0	0.08571	0.06	0.2	0.0857
1	0.08571	0.06	0.2	0.1234
2	0.08571	0.06	0.2	0.1611
3	0.08571	0.06	0.2	0.1989
4	0.08571	0.06	0.2	0.2366
5	0.08571	0.06	0.2	0.2743
6	0.08571	0.06	0.2	0.3120
7	0.08571	0.06	0.2	0.3497
8	0.08571	0.06	0.2	0.3874
9	0.08571	0.06	0.2	0.4251
10	0.08571	0.06	0.2	0.4629

Table 6.27 The dependence of equity cost k_e on leverage level L at coverage ratio $i_3 = 2$

L	WACC($i_3 = 2$)	K_d	t	K_e
0	0.10000	0.06	0.2	0.1000
1	0.10000	0.06	0.2	0.1520
2	0.10000	0.06	0.2	0.2040
3	0.10000	0.06	0.2	0.2560
4	0.10000	0.06	0.2	0.3080
5	0.10000	0.06	0.2	0.3600
6	0.10000	0.06	0.2	0.4120
7	0.10000	0.06	0.2	0.4640
8	0.10000	0.06	0.2	0.5160
9	0.10000	0.06	0.2	0.5680
10	0.10000	0.06	0.2	0.6200

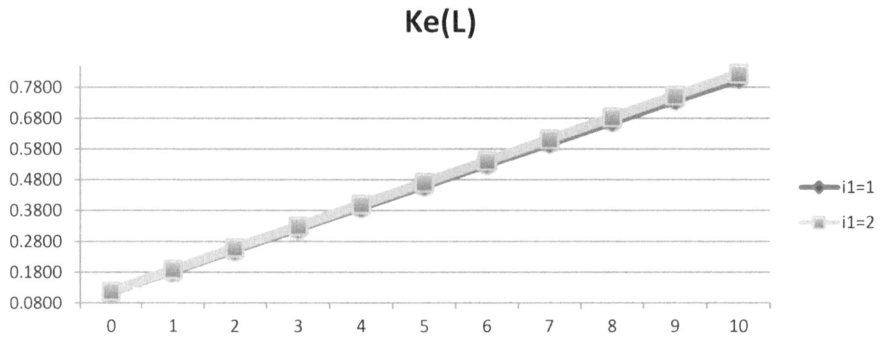

Fig. 6.20 The dependence of equity cost k_e on leverage level at two coverage ratio values $i_1 = 1$ and $i_1 = 2$

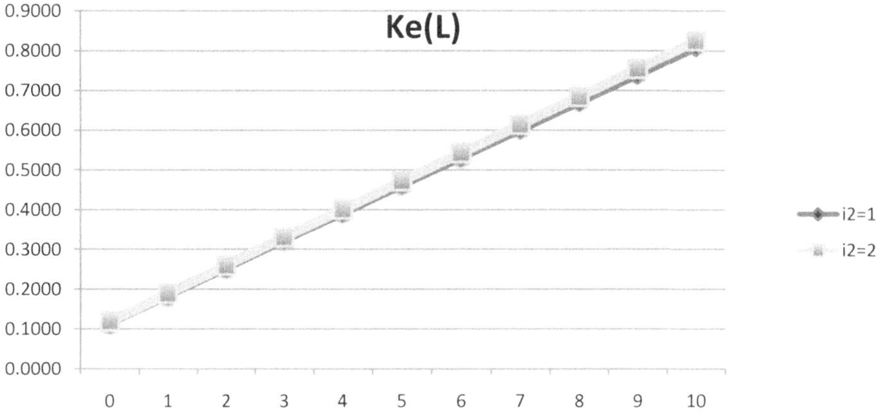

Fig. 6.21 The dependence of equity cost k_e on leverage level at two coverage ratio values $i_2 = 1$ and $i_2 = 2$

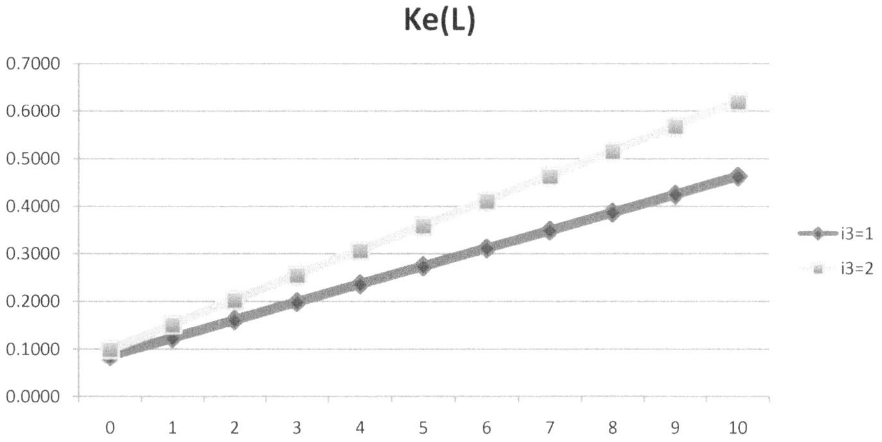

Fig. 6.22 The dependence of equity cost k_e on leverage level at two coverage ratio values $i_3 = 1$ and $i_3 = 2$

6.10 The Dependence of Equity Cost k_e on Leverage Level at Two Leverage Ratio Values $l_j = 1$ and $l_j = 2$

Let us now study the dependence of equity cost k_e on leverage level at two leverage ratio values $l_j = 1$ and $l_j = 2$ for leverage ratios l_1, l_2, l_3.

1. $\mathbf{l_1 = 1}$

2. $\mathbf{l_1 = 2}$

1. $\boldsymbol{l_2 = 1}$

2. $\boldsymbol{l_2 = 2}$

1. $\boldsymbol{l_3 = 1}$

2. $\boldsymbol{l_3 = 2}$

It is seen from Tables 6.28, 6.29, 6.30, 6.31, 6.32 and 6.33 and Figs. 6.23, 6.24 and 6.25 that equity cost k_e increases practically linearly with leverage level for all leverage ratios l_1, l_2, l_3. For each of two leverage ratios l_1, l_3, curves k_e (L) for two values of l_j (1 and 2) practically coincide. For leverage ratio l_2 curve k_e (L) for value of $l_3 = 1$ lies above one for $l_3 = 2$ and angle of inclination for value of $l_3 = 1$ is bigger.

Table 6.28 The dependence of equity cost k_e on leverage level L at leverage ratio $l_1 = 1$

L	WACC($l_1 = 1$)	K_d	t	K_e
0	0.11719	0.06	0.2	0.1172
1	0.11719	0.06	0.2	0.1864
2	0.11719	0.06	0.2	0.2556
3	0.11719	0.06	0.2	0.3248
4	0.11719	0.06	0.2	0.3939
5	0.11719	0.06	0.2	0.4631
6	0.11719	0.06	0.2	0.5323
7	0.11719	0.06	0.2	0.6015
8	0.11719	0.06	0.2	0.6707
9	0.11719	0.06	0.2	0.7399
10	0.11719	0.06	0.2	0.8091

Table 6.29 The dependence of equity cost k_e on leverage level L at leverage ratio $l_1 = 2$

L	WACC($l_1 = 2$)	K_d	t	K_e
0	0.11450	0.06	0.2	0.1145
1	0.11450	0.06	0.2	0.1810
2	0.11450	0.06	0.2	0.2475
3	0.11450	0.06	0.2	0.3140
4	0.11450	0.06	0.2	0.3805
5	0.11450	0.06	0.2	0.4470
6	0.11450	0.06	0.2	0.5135
7	0.11450	0.06	0.2	0.5800
8	0.11450	0.06	0.2	0.6465
9	0.11450	0.06	0.2	0.7130
10	0.11450	0.06	0.2	0.7795

Table 6.30 The dependence of equity cost k_e on leverage level L at leverage ratio $l_2 = 1$

L	WACC($l_2 = 1$)	K_d	t	K_e
0	0.08571	0.06	0.2	0.0857
1	0.08571	0.06	0.2	0.1234
2	0.08571	0.06	0.2	0.1611
3	0.08571	0.06	0.2	0.1989
4	0.08571	0.06	0.2	0.2366
5	0.08571	0.06	0.2	0.2743
6	0.08571	0.06	0.2	0.3120
7	0.08571	0.06	0.2	0.3497
8	0.08571	0.06	0.2	0.3874
9	0.08571	0.06	0.2	0.4251
10	0.08571	0.06	0.2	0.4629

Table 6.31 The dependence of equity cost k_e on leverage level L at leverage ratio $l_2 = 2$

L	WACC($l_2 = 2$)	K_d	t	K_e
0	0.06667	0.06	0.2	0.0667
1	0.06667	0.06	0.2	0.0853
2	0.06667	0.06	0.2	0.1040
3	0.06667	0.06	0.2	0.1227
4	0.06667	0.06	0.2	0.1413
5	0.06667	0.06	0.2	0.1600
6	0.06667	0.06	0.2	0.1787
7	0.06667	0.06	0.2	0.1973
8	0.06667	0.06	0.2	0.2160
9	0.06667	0.06	0.2	0.2347
10	0.06667	0.06	0.2	0.2533

Table 6.32 The dependence of equity cost k_e on leverage level L at leverage ratio $l_3 = 1$

L	WACC($l_3 = 1$)	K_d	t	K_e
0	0.11735	0.06	0.2	0.1174
1	0.11735	0.06	0.2	0.1867
2	0.11735	0.06	0.2	0.2561
3	0.11735	0.06	0.2	0.3254
4	0.11735	0.06	0.2	0.3948
5	0.11735	0.06	0.2	0.4641
6	0.11735	0.06	0.2	0.5335
7	0.11735	0.06	0.2	0.6028
8	0.11735	0.06	0.2	0.6722
9	0.11735	0.06	0.2	0.7415
10	0.11735	0.06	0.2	0.8109

Table 6.33 The dependence of equity cost k_e on leverage level L at leverage ratio $l_3 = 2$

L	WACC($l_3 = 2$)	K_d	t	K_e
0	0.11482	0.06	0.2	0.1148
1	0.11482	0.06	0.2	0.1816
2	0.11482	0.06	0.2	0.2485
3	0.11482	0.06	0.2	0.3153
4	0.11482	0.06	0.2	0.3821
5	0.11482	0.06	0.2	0.4489
6	0.11482	0.06	0.2	0.5157
7	0.11482	0.06	0.2	0.5826
8	0.11482	0.06	0.2	0.6494
9	0.11482	0.06	0.2	0.7162
10	0.11482	0.06	0.2	0.7830

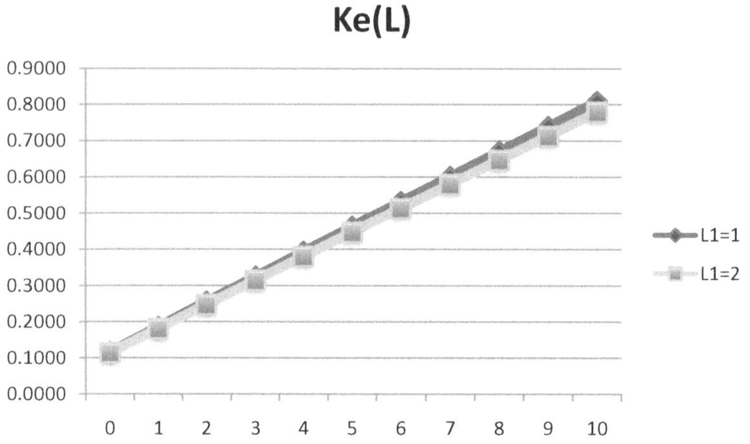

Fig. 6.23 The dependence of equity cost k_e on leverage level at two leverage ratio values $l_1 = 1$ and $l_1 = 2$

6.11 Conclusion

Chapters 6–8 and 11–13 suggest a new approach to rating methodology. This chapter as and the next two (Chaps. 7 and 8) are devoted to rating of non-financial issuers, while Chapters 11–13 are devoted to long-term project rating, as well as to rating of arbitrary projects. The key factors of a new approach are (1) the adequate use of discounting of financial flows virtually not used in existing rating methodologies and (2) the incorporation of rating parameters (financial "ratios") into the modern theory of capital structure BFO (and its perpetuity limit). This on the one hand allows us to use the powerful tool of this theory in the rating, and on the other hand, it ensures the correct discount rates when discounting financial flows. Two models for accounting of discounting of financial flows—one-period and multi-period—are discussed. An algorithm of valuation of correct discount rate, taking

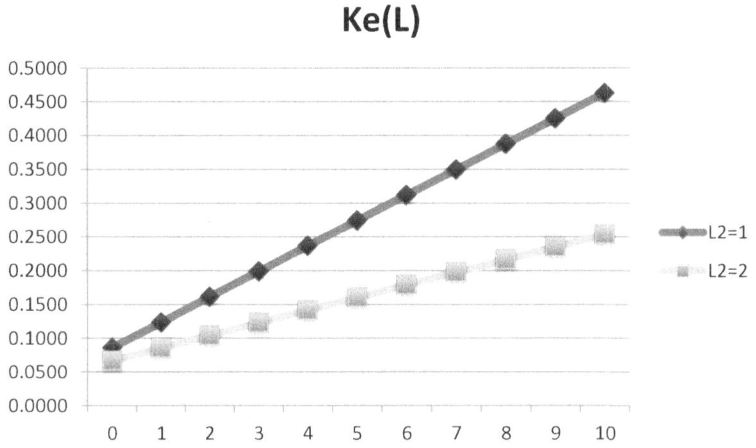

Fig. 6.24 The dependence of equity cost k_e on leverage level at two leverage ratio values $l_2 = 1$ and $l_2 = 2$

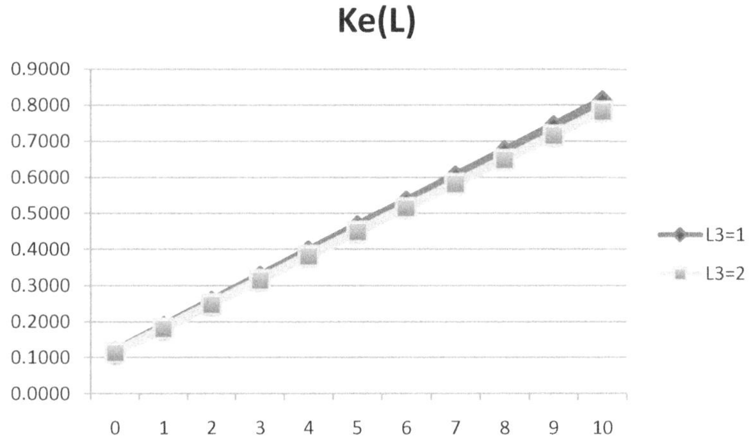

Fig. 6.25 The dependence of equity cost k_e on leverage level at two leverage ratio values $l_3 = 1$ and $l_3 = 2$

into account rating ratios, is suggested. We also discuss the interplay between rating ratios and leverage level which can be quite important in rating. All these create a new base for rating methodologies.

References

Brusov P (2018a) Editorial: introduction on special issue on the Banking System and financial markets of Russia and other countries: problems and prospects. J Rev Glob Econ 7:1–6. SCOPUS

Brusov P (2018b) Editorial. J Rev Glob Econ 7:1–5. SCOPUS

Brusov P, Filatova T, Orekhova N, Eskindarov M (2015) Modern corporate finance, investments and taxation. Springer International Publishing, Berlin, p 373, monograph, SCOPUS, https://www.springer.com/gp/book/9783319147314

Brusov P, Filatova T, Orekhova N, Eskindarov M (2018a) Modern corporate finance, investments, taxation and ratings. Springer Nature Publishing, Berlin, p 571, monograph

Brusov PN, Filatova TV, Orekhova NP, Kulik VL (2018b) Rating: new approach. J Rev Glob Econ 7:37–62. https://doi.org/10.6000/1929-7092.2018.07.05. SCOPUS

Brusov PN, Filatova TV, Orekhova NP, Kulik VL (2018c) A "golden age" of the companies: conditions of its existence. J Rev Glob Econ 7:88–103. https://doi.org/10.6000/1929-7092.2018.07.07. SCOPUS

Brusov PN, Filatova TV, Orekhova NP, Kulik VL (2018d) Rating methodology: new look and new horizons. J Rev Glob Econ 7:63–87. https://doi.org/10.6000/1929-7092.2018.07.06. SCOPUS

Brusov PN, Filatova TV, Orekhova NP, Kulik VL, Weil I (2018e) New meaningful effects in modern capital structure theory. J Rev Glob Econ 7:104–122. https://doi.org/10.6000/1929-7092.2018.07.08. SCOPUS

Brusov P, Filatova T, Orekhova N, Kulik V, Weil I, Brailov A (2018f) The impact of the central bank key rate and commercial banks credit rates on creating and maintaining of a favorable investment climate in the country. J Rev Glob Econ 7:360–376. https://doi.org/10.6000/1929-7092.2018.07.31. SCOPUS

Brusov PN, Filatova TV, Orekhova NP (2018g) Modern corporate finance and investments, monograph. Knorus Publishing House, Moscow, 517 p

Brusov PN, Filatova TV, Orekhova NP, Kulik VL, Weil I (2019) Ratings of the investment projects of arbitrary durations: new methodology. J Rev Glob Econ 8:437–448. https://doi.org/10.6000/1929-7092.2019.08.37. SCOPUS

Brusov PN, Filatova TV, Orekhova NP, Kulik VL, Chang S-I, Lin YCG (2020) Modification of the Modigliani–Miller theory for the case of advance payments of tax on profit. J Rev Glob Econ 9:257–268

Brusova A (2011) A comparison of the three methods of estimation of weighted average cost of capital and equity cost of company. Financ Anal Prob Sol 34(76):36–42

Filatova T, Orehova N, Brusova A (2008) Weighted average cost of capital in the theory of Modigliani–Miller, modified for a finite lifetime company. Bull FU 48:68–77

Filatova TV, Brusov PN, Orekhova NP, Kulik VL (2018a) Ratings of the long-term projects: new approach. J Rev Glob Econ 7:645–661. https://doi.org/10.6000/1929-7092.2018.07.59. SCOPUS

Filatova TV, Brusov PN, Orekhova NP, Kulik VL (2018b) Ratings of the long-term projects: new approach. J Rev Glob Econ 7:645–661. https://doi.org/10.6000/1929-7092.2018.07.59. SCOPUS

Modigliani F, Miller M (1966) Some estimates of the cost of capital to the electric utility industry 1954–1957. Am Econ Rev 56:333–391

Modigliani F, Miller M (1958) The cost of capital, corporate finance, and the theory of investment. Am Econ Rev 48:261–297

Modigliani F, Miller M (1963) Corporate income taxes and the cost of capital: a correction. Am Econ Rev 53:147–175

Chapter 7
Application of the Modigliani–Miller Theory, Modified for the Case of Advance Payments of Tax on Profit, in Rating Methodologies

7.1 Introduction

In our previous papers (Brusov and Filatova (2011), Brusov et al. (2011a, b, c, 2012a, b, 2013a, b, 2014a, b) Brusov et al. 2018e, g, 2019, 2020), we have applied the theory of Nobel Prize winners Modigliani and Miller, which is the perpetuity limit of the general theory of capital cost and capital structure—Brusov–Filatova–Orekhova (BFO) theory (Brusov et al. 2011, 2014, 2015, 2018e, g)—for rating needs. It has become a very important step in developing a qualitatively new rating methodology.

Recently, we have generalized the Modigliani and Miller theory (Modigliani and Miller 1958, 1963, 1966) for a more realistic method of tax on profit payments: for the case of advance payments of tax on profit, which is widely used in practice (Brusov et al. 2020). Modigliani–Miller theory considers these tax payments as annuity-immediate, while in practice these payments are made in advance and thus should be considered as annuity-due.

We have shown that this generalization leads to some important consequences, which change seriously all the main statements by Modigliani and Miller (Modigliani and Miller 1958, 1963, 1966). These consequences are the following: WACC depends on debt cost k_d, WACC turns out to be lower than in the case of classical Modigliani–Miller theory, and thus company capitalization becomes higher than in the ordinary Modigliani–Miller theory. We show that equity dependence on leverage level L is still linear, but the tilt angle with respect to the L-axis turns out to be smaller: this could lead to the modification of the dividend policy of the company.

In this chapter, we use the modified Modigliani–Miller theory (MMM theory) and apply it for rating methodologies needs. A serious modification of MMM theory in order to use it in rating procedure is required. The financial "ratios" (main rating parameters) were introduced into MMM theory. The necessity of an appropriate use of financial flows discounting in rating methodologies is discussed. The dependence

P. Brusov et al., *Ratings*, Contributions to Finance and Accounting,
https://doi.org/10.1007/978-3-030-56243-4_7

of the weighted average cost of capital (WACC), which plays the role of discount rate, on coverage and leverage ratios is analyzed.

Obtained results make it possible to use the power of this theory in the rating and create a new basis for rating methodologies; in other words, this allows us to develop a new approach to methodology of rating, requiring a serious modification of existing rating methodologies.

7.2 Modified Modigliani–Miller Theory

Let us shortly discuss some main points of modified Modigliani–Miller theory (MMM) and its features (see Chap. 4), which are different from those of the "classical" Modigliani–Miller theory (Brusov et al. 2020).

7.2.1 *Tax Shield*

To calculate tax shield TS in the case of advance tax payments, one should use annuity-due

$$\begin{aligned} TS &= k_d Dt + \frac{k_d Dt}{(1+k_d)} + \frac{k_d Dt}{(1+k_d)^2} + \cdots = \frac{k_d Dt}{\left(1-(1+k_d)^{-1}\right)} \\ &= Dt(1+k_d) \end{aligned} \tag{7.1}$$

This expression is different from the case of the classical Modigliani–Miller theory (which used annuity-immediate).

$$TS = \frac{k_d Dt}{(1+k_d)} + \frac{k_d Dt}{(1+k_d)^2} + \cdots = \frac{k_d Dt}{(1+k_d)\left(1-(1+k_d)^{-1}\right)} = Dt \tag{7.2}$$

Thus, in the former case tax shield TS is bigger by multiplier $(1+k_d)$. This is connected with the time value of money: money today is more expensive than money tomorrow due to the possibility of their alternative investment.

7.2.2 *The Weighted Average Cost of Capital (WACC)*

For WACC in MMM theory, we have the following formula:

$$\text{WACC} = k_0(1 - w_d t(1+k_d)) \tag{7.3}$$

At $L \to \infty$

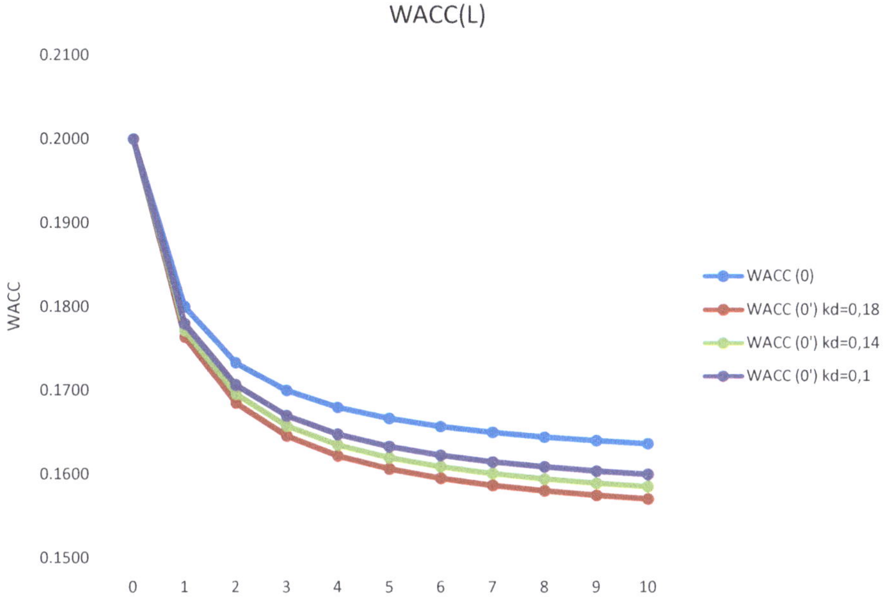

Fig. 7.1 Dependence of WACC on leverage level L: in the "classical" Modigliani–Miller theory (curve WACC(0)) and—in the modified Modigliani–Miller theory (MMM theory) at different values of debt cost: kd=0.18; kd=0.14; kd=0.1 (curves WACC(0'))

$$\mathrm{WACC} = k_0(1 - t(1 + k_d)) \tag{7.4}$$

This expression is different from that of the classical Modigliani–Miller theory

$$\mathrm{WACC} = k_0(1 - w_d t) \tag{7.5}$$

At $L \to \infty$ WACC $= k_0(1 - t)$.

From these expressions, it is seen that WACC decreases with L, achieving lower value WACC $= k_0(1 - t(1 + k_d))$ at $L \to \infty$ in the considered case comparing with the classical Modigliani–Miller theory WACC $= k_0(1 - t)$.

This also means that company capitalization becomes higher than in the ordinary Modigliani–Miller theory.

Let us compare the dependence of the weighted average cost of capital, WACC, on leverage level in the "classical" Modigliani–Miller theory (MM theory) and in the modified Modigliani–Miller theory (MMM theory). Study of such dependence is very important, because the weighted average cost of capital, WACC, plays the role of discount rate in operating financial flows discounting as well as of financial flows in rating methodologies. WACC's value determines as well the capitalization of the company $V =$ CF/WACC.

From Fig. 7.1, it is seen that WACC in MMM theory turns out to be lower than in the case of classical Modigliani–Miller theory and thus company capitalization becomes higher than in the ordinary Modigliani–Miller theory. It is seen that WACC decreases with debt cost k_d.

In the paper of Brusov et al. (2020) we study as well the equity cost dependence on leverage level L and show that it is still linear, but the tilt angle with respect to the L-axis turns out to be smaller in MMM theory $tg\alpha = (k_0 - k_d)(1 - t) - k_0 k_d t$, than in the classical Modigliani–Miller theory $tg\alpha = (k_0 - k_d)(1 - t)$. This could lead to the modification of the dividend policy of the company, because the equity cost is economically sound value of dividends. Thus, the company could decrease the value of dividends, which they should pay to shareholders.

Correct accounting of the method of tax on profit payments demonstrates that shortcomings of Modigliani–Miller theory are serious, than everybody suggested: the underestimation of WACC really turns out to be bigger, as well as the overestimation of the capitalization of the company. This means that systematic risks arising from the use of modified Modigliani–Miller theory (MMM theory) (which is more correct than the "classical" one) in practice are higher than it was suggested by the "classical" version of this theory.

Because the advance payments of tax on profit are widely used in practice, modified Modigliani–Miller theory (MMM theory) should be used instead of the classical version of this theory (MM theory). And below we apply the modified Modigliani–Miller theory for rating needs.

7.3 Application of Modified of Modigliani–Miller Theory for Rating Needs

The financial "ratios" constitute direct and inverse ratios of various generated cash flows to debt and interest values and play quite a significant role in the quantification of the creditworthiness of the issuers. The examples of such ratios are the following: DCF/Debt, FFO/Debt, CFO/Debt, FOCF/Debt, FFO/cash interest, EBITDA/interest, Interests/EBITDA, Debt/EBITDA, and some others.

We introduce these financial "ratios" into the modified perpetuity limit of modern theory of capital structure—BFO theory ((MMM theory), which is valid for companies of arbitrary age. This is quite important because it allows us to use this theory as a powerful tool when discounting financial flows using the correct discounting rate in rating.

This has required the modification of the perpetuity limit of the BFO theory—Modified Modigliani–Miller theory (MMM theory). The need of modification is connected to the fact that the concept of "leverage" as the ratio of debt value to the equity value used in financial management substantially differs from the concept of "leverage" in the rating, where it is understood as the ratio of the debt value to the generated cash flow values (income, profit, etc.).

Developed by us recently (Brusov et al. 2020) the modified Modigliani–Miller theory (MMM theory) with corporate taxes (Modigliani and Miller 1966) shows that capitalization of financially dependent (leveraged) company, V_L, is equal to the capitalization of financially independent (unleveraged) company, V_0, increased by the size of the tax shield for perpetuity time, $Dt(1 + k_d)$,

$$V_L = V_0 + Dt(1 + k_d) \tag{7.6}$$

Substituting the expressions for both capitalizations, one has

$$\frac{\mathrm{CF}}{\mathrm{WACC}} = \frac{\mathrm{CF}}{k_0} + Dt(1 + k_d) \tag{7.7}$$

Let us now introduce the parameters, using in ratings (ratios), into the modified Modigliani–Miller theory (MMM theory), which represents a perpetuity limit of modern theory of capital structure by Brusov–Filatova–Orekhova theory (BFO theory) (Brusov 2018a, b; Brusov et al. 2015, 2018a, b, c, e, f, g, 2019, 2020; Filatova et al. 2008; Modigliani and Miller 1966; Myers 2001).

Two kinds of financial ratios will be considered: coverage ratios and leverage ratios.

We will start from the coverage ratios.

7.3.1 *Coverage Ratios*

We will consider three kinds of coverage ratios: coverage ratio of debt, coverage ratio of interest on the credit, and coverage ratio of debt and interest on the credit.

7.3.1.1 Coverage Ratios of Debt

Let us consider first the coverage ratios of debt $i_1 = \mathrm{CF}/D$.

Dividing both parts of Eq. (7.7) by D, one gets

$$\begin{aligned} \frac{i_1}{\mathrm{WACC}} &= \frac{i_1}{k_0} + t(1 + k_d) \\ \frac{i_1}{\mathrm{WACC}} &= \frac{i_1 + k_0 t(1 + k_d)}{k_0} \\ \mathrm{WACC} &= \frac{i_1 k_0}{i_1 + t k_0(1 + k_d)} \end{aligned} \tag{7.8}$$

The coverage ratio of debt $i_1 = \mathrm{CF}/D$ could be used for the assessment of the following rating ratios: DCF/Debt, FFO/Debt, CFO/Debt, FOCF/Debt, and some others. Formula (7.8) will be used to find a dependence $\mathrm{WACC}(i_1)$.

7.3.1.2 Coverage Ratios of Interest on the Credit

Consider now coverage ratio of interest on the credit $i_2 = \mathrm{CF}/k_dD$.

Using the Modified Modigliani–Miller theory (MMM theory) for the case with corporate taxes

$$V_L = V_0 + Dt(1 + k_d),$$

and dividing both the parts by k_dD, one could derive the expression for dependence $\mathrm{WACC}(i_2)$

$$\begin{aligned} \frac{\mathrm{CF}}{\mathrm{WACC}} &= \frac{\mathrm{CF}}{k_0} + Dt(1 + k_d) \\ \frac{i_2}{\mathrm{WACC}} &= \frac{i_2}{k_0} + \frac{t(1 + k_d)}{k_d} \\ \mathrm{WACC} &= \frac{i_2 k_0 k_d}{i_2 k_d + t k_0 (1 + k_d)} \end{aligned} \tag{7.9}$$

This ratio (i_2) could be used for the assessment of the following parameters, used in rating, FFO/cash interest, EBITDA/interest, and some others. Formula (7.9) will be used to find a dependence $\mathrm{WACC}(i_2)$.

7.3.1.3 Coverage Ratios of Debt and Interest on the Credit

Below we consider the coverage ratios of debt and interest on the credit simultaneously $i_3 = \frac{\mathrm{CF}}{D(1+k_d)}$. This is a new value, introduced by us here for the first time. Using the modified Modigliani–Miller theory (MMM theory) for the case with corporate taxes

$$V_L = V_0 + Dt(1 + k_d)$$

and dividing both the parts by $(1 + k_d)D$, we get the dependence $\mathrm{WACC}(i_3)$

$$\begin{aligned} \frac{\mathrm{CF}}{\mathrm{WACC}} &= \frac{\mathrm{CF}}{k_0} + Dt(1 + k_d) \\ \frac{i_3}{\mathrm{WACC}} &= \frac{i_3}{k_0} + \frac{t}{k_d} \\ \mathrm{WACC} &= \frac{i_3 k_0 k_d}{i_3 k_d + t k_0} \end{aligned} \tag{7.10}$$

This ratio (i_3) could be used for the assessment of the following rating ratios: FFO/Debt + interest, EBITDA/Debt + interest, and some others. Formula (7.10) will be used to find a dependence $\mathrm{WACC}(i_3)$.

7.3.2 Dependence of WACC on Leverage Ratios of Debt in the "Classical" Modigliani–Miller Theory (MM theory) and Modified Modigliani–Miller Theory (MMM Theory)

Below we study the dependences of WACC on leverage ratios of debt in the "classical" Modigliani–Miller theory (MM theory) and modified Modigliani–Miller theory (MMM theory). We use Microsoft Excel, and the following parameters: equity cost at $L = 0$ $k0 = 0.2$; tax on profit rate $t = 0.2$; debt cost k_d =0.1;0.14;0.18; leverage ratios of debt l_1=0;1;2;3;4;5;6;7;8;9;10 (Tables 7.1, 7.2, 7.3 and 7.4).

Let us analyze the dependence of company's weighted average cost of capital (WACC) on the coverage ratios on debt i_1. It is seen from Fig. 7.2 that the weighted average cost of capital, WACC, increases with coverage ratio of debt for both versions of the Modigliani–Miller theory: for the "classical" Modigliani–Miller theory (MM theory) as well as for the modified Modigliani–Miller theory (MMM theory). WACC increases very rapidly as L increases from L = 0 to L = 1 and then

Table 7.1 Dependence of WACC on coverage ratios of debt in the "classical" Modigliani–Miller theory

ko	i_1	*t*	WACC
0.2	0	0.2	0.0000
0.2	1	0.2	0.1923
0.2	2	0.2	0.1961
0.2	3	0.2	0.1974
0.2	4	0.2	0.1980
0.2	5	0.2	0.1984
0.2	6	0.2	0.1987
0.2	7	0.2	0.1989
0.2	8	0.2	0.1990
0.2	9	0.2	0.1991
0.2	10	0.2	0.1992

Table 7.2 Dependence of WACC on coverage ratios of debt in the modified Modigliani–Miller theory (MMM theory) at $kd = 0.18$

ko	*i*1	*t*	*kd*	WACC
0.2	0	0.2	0.18	0.0000
0.2	1	0.2	0.18	0.1910
0.2	2	0.2	0.18	0.1954
0.2	3	0.2	0.18	0.1969
0.2	4	0.2	0.18	0.1977
0.2	5	0.2	0.18	0.1981
0.2	6	0.2	0.18	0.1984
0.2	7	0.2	0.18	0.1987
0.2	8	0.2	0.18	0.1988
0.2	9	0.2	0.18	0.1990
0.2	10	0.2	0.18	0.1991

Table 7.3 Dependence of WACC on coverage ratios of debt in the modified Modigliani–Miller theory (MMM theory) at $kd = 0.14$

ko	*i*1	*t*	*kd*	WACC
0.2	0	0.2	0.14	0.0000
0.2	1	0.2	0.14	0.1913
0.2	2	0.2	0.14	0.1955
0.2	3	0.2	0.14	0.1970
0.2	4	0.2	0.14	0.1977
0.2	5	0.2	0.14	0.1982
0.2	6	0.2	0.14	0.1985
0.2	7	0.2	0.14	0.1987
0.2	8	0.2	0.14	0.1989
0.2	9	0.2	0.14	0.1990
0.2	10	0.2	0.14	0.1991

Table 7.4 Dependence of WACC on coverage ratios of debt in the modified Modigliani–Miller theory (MMM theory) at $kd = 0.1$

ko	*i*1	*t*	*kd*	WACC
0.2	0	0.2	0.1	0.0000
0.2	1	0.2	0.1	0.1916
0.2	2	0.2	0.1	0.1957
0.2	3	0.2	0.1	0.1971
0.2	4	0.2	0.1	0.1978
0.2	5	0.2	0.1	0.1983
0.2	6	0.2	0.1	0.1985
0.2	7	0.2	0.1	0.1988
0.2	8	0.2	0.1	0.1989
0.2	9	0.2	0.1	0.1990
0.2	10	0.2	0.1	0.1991

comes to saturation very fast (after L = 3 WACC changes very weakly). At saturation WACC reaches the value k_0 (equity cost at zero leverage level). This means that for high values of i_j one can choose k_0 as a discount rate with a good accuracy. Thus, the role of parameter k_0 increases drastically. The method of determination of parameter k_0 has been developed by Anastasiya Brusova (2011). So, parameter k_0 is the discount rate for limit case of high values of i_1.

We observe that results for both versions of Modigliani–Miller theory are very closed: only from tables it is seen that the curve of dependence of WACC on leverage ratios of debt in the "classical" Modigliani–Miller theory (curve WACC (2)) lies a little bit above all dependences of WACC on coverage ratio of debt in the modified Modigliani–Miller theory. The WACC values are practically independent on k_d. As we will see below, the situation is quite different in the case of leverage ratios, where the influence of k_d on dependences of WACC on leverage ratios is significant.

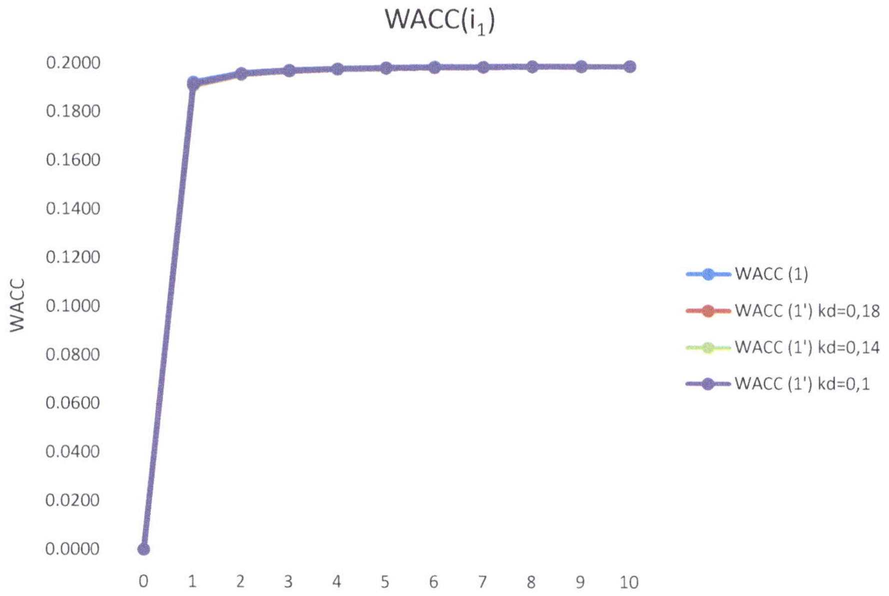

Fig 7.2 Dependence of WACC on coverage ratios of debt in the "classical" Modigliani–Miller theory (curve WACC(1)) and in the modified Modigliani–Miller theory (MMM theory) (curves WACC(1')) at $kd = 0.1;0.14;0.18$

7.3.3 Leverage Ratios

We will consider now the leverage ratios. Three kinds of leverage ratios will be considered: leverage ratios of debt, leverage ratios of interest on the credit, and leverage ratios of debt and interest on the credit.

7.3.3.1 Leverage Ratios for Debt

Here

$$l_1 = D/\mathrm{CF} \tag{7.11}$$

As above for coverage ratios using the modified Modigliani–Miller theorem for the case with corporate taxes, one has

$$V_L = V_0 + Dt(1 + k_d)$$

and dividing both the parts by CF, we derive the expression for WACC(l_1)

$$\begin{aligned}\frac{\mathrm{CF}}{\mathrm{WACC}} &= \frac{\mathrm{CF}}{k_0} + Dt(1+k_d)\\ \frac{1}{\mathrm{WACC}} &= \frac{1}{k_0} + l_1 t(1+k_d)\\ \mathrm{WACC} &= \frac{k_0}{1+tl_1 k_0(1+k_d)}\end{aligned} \tag{7.12}$$

This ratio (l_1) can be used to assess the following parameters used in rating, Debt/EBITDA and some others. We will use the last formula to build a curve of dependence WACC(l_1).

7.3.3.2 Leverage Ratios for Interest on Credit

Here

$$l_2 = k_d D/\mathrm{CF} \tag{7.13}$$

We use again the modified Modigliani–Miller theory (MMM theory) for the case with corporate taxes

$$V_L = V_0 + Dt(1+k_d),$$

and dividing both the parts by CF/k_d, we derive the expression for WACC(l_2)

$$\begin{aligned}\frac{\mathrm{CF}}{\mathrm{WACC}} &= \frac{\mathrm{CF}}{k_0} + Dt(1+k_d)\\ \frac{1}{\mathrm{WACC}} &= \frac{1}{k_0} + \frac{l_2 t(1+k_d)}{k_d}\\ \mathrm{WACC} &= \frac{k_0 k_d}{k_d + tl_2 k_0(1+k_d)}\end{aligned} \tag{7.14}$$

This ratio (l_2) can be used to assess the following parameters used in rating, Interests/EBITDA and some others. We will use the last formula to build a curve of dependence WACC(l_2).

7.3.3.3 Leverage Ratios for Debt and Interest on Credit

Here

$$l_3 = D(1+k_d)\mathrm{CF} \tag{7.15}$$

Using the modified Modigliani–Miller theory (MMM theory) for the case with corporate taxes

$$V_L = V_0 + Dt(1 + k_d),$$

and dividing both the parts by CF/(1 + k_d), we derive the expression for WACC(l_3)

$$\begin{aligned} \frac{\text{CF}}{\text{WACC}} &= \frac{\text{CF}}{k_0} + Dt(1 + k_d) \\ \frac{1}{\text{WACC}} &= \frac{1}{k_0} + l_3 t \\ \text{WACC} &= \frac{k_0}{1 + t l_3 k_0} \end{aligned} \tag{7.16}$$

This ratio (l_3) can be used to assess the following parameters used in rating, Debt + interest/FFO, Debt + interest/EBIT, Debt + interest/EBITDA(R), and some others. We will use the last formula to build a curve of dependence WACC(l_3).

7.3.3.4 Dependence of WACC on Leverage Ratios of Debt in the “Classical” Modigliani–Miller Theory (MM Theory) and Modified Modigliani–Miller Theory (MMM Theory)

Below we study the dependences of WACC on leverage ratios of debt in the “classical” Modigliani–Miller theory (MM theory) and modified Modigliani–Miller theory (MMM theory). We use Microsoft Excel, and the following parameters: equity cost at L = 0 $k0$ = 0.2; tax on profit rate t = 0.2; debt cost k_d =0.1;0.14;0.18; leverage ratios of debt l_1 = 0;1;2;3;4;5;6;7;8;9;10 (Tables 7.5, 7.6, 7.7 and 7.8).

Analysis of the dependences of company’s weighted average cost of capital (WACC) on the leverage ratio on debt, l_1, shows the following: (see Fig. 7.3) the

Table 7.5 Dependence of WACC on leverage ratios of debt in the “classical” Modigliani–Miller theory

ko	l_1	t	WACC
0.2	0	0.2	0.2000
0.2	1	0.2	0.1923
0.2	2	0.2	0.1852
0.2	3	0.2	0.1786
0.2	4	0.2	0.1724
0.2	5	0.2	0.1667
0.2	6	0.2	0.1613
0.2	7	0.2	0.1563
0.2	8	0.2	0.1515
0.2	9	0.2	0.1471
0.2	10	0.2	0.1429

Table 7.6 Dependence of WACC on leverage ratios of debt in the modified Modigliani–Miller theory (MMM theory) at $kd = 0.18$

ko	l_1	t	kd	WACC
0.2	0	0.2	0.18	0.2000
0.2	1	0.2	0.18	0.1910
0.2	2	0.2	0.18	0.1827
0.2	3	0.2	0.18	0.1752
0.2	4	0.2	0.18	0.1682
0.2	5	0.2	0.18	0.1618
0.2	6	0.2	0.18	0.1559
0.2	7	0.2	0.18	0.1503
0.2	8	0.2	0.18	0.1452
0.2	9	0.2	0.18	0.1404
0.2	10	0.2	0.18	0.1359

Table 7.7 Dependence of WACC on leverage ratios of debt in the modified Modigliani–Miller theory (MMM theory) at $kd = 0.14$

ko	l_1	t	kd	WACC
0.2	0	0.2	0.14	0.2000
0.2	1	0.2	0.14	0.1913
0.2	2	0.2	0.14	0.1833
0.2	3	0.2	0.14	0.1759
0.2	4	0.2	0.14	0.1691
0.2	5	0.2	0.14	0.1629
0.2	6	0.2	0.14	0.1570
0.2	7	0.2	0.14	0.1516
0.2	8	0.2	0.14	0.1465
0.2	9	0.2	0.14	0.1418
0.2	10	0.2	0.14	0.1374

Table 7.8 Dependence of WACC on leverage ratios of debt in the modified Modigliani–Miller theory (MMM theory) at $kd = 0.1$

ko	l_1	t	kd	WACC
0.2	0	0.2	0.1	0.2000
0.2	1	0.2	0.1	0.1916
0.2	2	0.2	0.1	0.1838
0.2	3	0.2	0.1	0.1767
0.2	4	0.2	0.1	0.1701
0.2	5	0.2	0.1	0.1639
0.2	6	0.2	0.1	0.1582
0.2	7	0.2	0.1	0.1529
0.2	8	0.2	0.1	0.1479
0.2	9	0.2	0.1	0.1433
0.2	10	0.2	0.1	0.1389

weighted average cost of capital, WACC, decreases with leverage ratios for both versions of Modigliani–Miller theory: for the "classical" Modigliani–Miller theory (MM theory) as well as for the modified Modigliani–Miller theory (MMM theory). But we observe that the curve of dependence of WACC on leverage ratios of debt in

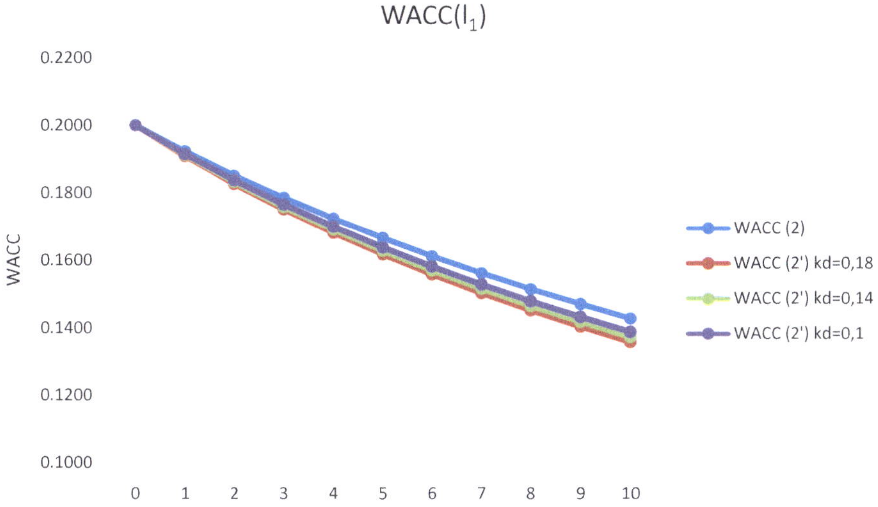

Fig. 7.3 Dependence of WACC on leverage ratios of debt in the "classical" Modigliani–Miller theory (curve WACC(2)) and in the modified Modigliani–Miller theory (MMM theory) (curves WACC(2')) at $kd = 0.1;0.14;0.18$

the "classical" Modigliani–Miller theory (curve WACC(2)) lies above all dependences of WACC on leverage ratios of debt in the modified Modigliani–Miller theory. The WACC values decreases with k_d. So we are observing the influence of k_d on dependences of WACC on leverage ratios. This effect is absent in the "classical" Modigliani–Miller theory. Thus, the use of the modified Modigliani–Miller theory (MMM theory) leads to more correct valuation of the weighted average cost of capital (WACC), which plays the role of discount rate in financial flows discounting in rating methodologies. Obtained results will help improve the existing rating methodologies.

7.4 Discussions

In this chapter, we use the modified Modigliani–Miller theory (MMM theory) and apply it for rating methodologies needs. The financial "ratios" (main rating parameters) were introduced into MMM theory. The dependence of the weighted average cost of capital (WACC), which plays the role of discount rate in financial flows discounting in rating methodologies, on coverage and leverage ratios is analyzed. Obtained results will help improve the existing rating methodologies.

The analysis of the dependence of company's weighted average cost of capital (WACC) on the coverage ratios on debt i_1 shows that WACC increases with coverage ratio of debt for both versions of the Modigliani–Miller theory: for the "classical" Modigliani–Miller theory (MM theory) as well as for the modified

Modigliani–Miller theory (MMM theory). WACC increases very rapidly as L increases from L = 0 to L = 1 and then comes to saturation very fast (after L = 3 WACC changes very weakly). At saturation, WACC reaches the value k_0 (equity cost at zero leverage level). This means that for high values of i_j one can choose k_0 as a discount rate with a good accuracy. Thus, the role of parameter k_0 increases drastically. The method of determination of parameter k_0 has been developed by Anastasiya Brusova (2011). So, parameter k_0 is the discount rate for the limit case of high values of i_1.

We observe that results for both versions of Modigliani–Miller theory are very closed: only from tables it is seen that curve of dependence of WACC on leverage ratios of debt in the "classical" Modigliani–Miller theory lies a little bit above all dependences of WACC on coverage ratio of debt in the modified Modigliani–Miller theory. The WACC values are practically independent of k_d. The situation is quite different in the case of leverage ratios, where the influence of k_d on dependences of WACC on leverage ratios is significant.

Analysis of the dependences of company's weighted average cost of capital (WACC) on the leverage ratio on debt, l_1, shows that WACC decreases with leverage ratios for both versions of the Modigliani–Miller theory: for the "classical" Modigliani–Miller theory (MM theory) as well as for the modified Modigliani–Miller theory (MMM theory). We observe that curve of dependence of WACC on leverage ratios of debt in the "classical" Modigliani–Miller theory lies above all dependences of WACC on leverage ratios of debt in the modified Modigliani–Miller theory. The WACC values decreases with k_d. So we are observing the influence of k_d on dependences of WACC on leverage ratios. This effect is absent in the "classical" Modigliani–Miller theory. Thus, the use of the modified Modigliani–Miller theory (MMM theory) leads to more correct valuation of the weighted average cost of capital (WACC), which plays the role of discount rate in financial flows discounting in rating methodologies. Obtained results will help improve the existing rating methodologies, which are used for the valuation of the creditworthiness of companies.

Correct accounting of the method of tax on profit payments demonstrates that shortcomings of the Modigliani–Miller theory are serious, than thought: the underestimation of WACC really turns out to be bigger, as well as the overestimation of the capitalization of the company. This means that systematic risks arising from the use of the modified Modigliani–Miller theory (MMM theory) (which is more correct than the "classical" one) in practice are higher than it was suggested by the "classical" version of this theory.

References

Brusov P (2018a) Editorial: introduction on special issue on the Banking System and financial markets of Russia and other countries: problems and prospects. J Rev Global Econ 7:i–vi. SCOPUS

Brusov P (2018b) Editorial. J Rev Global Econ 7:i–v. SCOPUS
Brusov PN, Filatova TV (2011b) From Modigliani–Miller to general theory of capital cost and capital structure of the company. Finance Credit 435:2–8
Brusov PN, Filatova TV, Orekhova NP (2018d) Modern corporate finance and investments, monograph. Knorus Publishing House, Moscow, 517 p
Brusov P, Filatova T, Orehova N, Brusova A (2011a) Weighted average cost of capital in the theory of Modigliani–Miller, modified for a finite life–time company. Appl Financ Econ 21(11):815–824
Brusov P, Filatova T, Orehova N et al (2011b) From Modigliani–Miller to general theory of capital cost and capital structure of the company. Res J Econ Bus ICT 2:16–21
Brusov P, Filatova T, Orehova N et al (2011c) Influence of debt financing on the effectiveness of the investment project within the Modigliani–Miller theory. Res J Econ Bus ICT (UK) 2:11–15
Brusov P, Filatova T, Eskindarov M, Orehova N (2012a) Influence of debt financing on the effectiveness of the finite duration investment project. Appl Financ Econ 22(13):1043–1052
Brusov P, Filatova T, Eskindarov M, Orehova N (2012b) Hidden global causes of the global financial crisis. J Rev Global Econ 1:106–111
Brusov P, Filatova P, Orekhova N (2013a) Absence of an optimal capital structure in the famous tradeoff theory! J Rev Global Econ 2:94–116
Brusov P, Filatova T, Orehova N (2013b) A qualitatively new effect in corporative finance: abnormal dependence of cost of equity of company on leverage. J Rev Global Econ 2:183–193
Brusov P, Filatova P, Orekhova N (2014a) Mechanism of formation of the company optimal capital structure, different from suggested by trade off theory. Cogent Econ Finance 2:1–13. https://doi.org/10.1080/23322039.2014.946150
Brusov P, Filatova T, Orehova N (2014b) Inflation in Brusov–Filatova–Orekhova theory and in its perpetuity limit—Modigliani–Miller theory. J Rev Global Econ 3:175–185
Brusov P, Filatova T, Orekhova N, Eskindarov M (2015) Modern corporate finance, investments and taxation. Springer International Publishing, Switzerland, 373 p. monograph. SCOPUS. https://www.springer.com/gp/book/9783319147314
Brusov P, Filatova T, Orekhova N, Eskindarov M (2018c) Modern corporate finance, investments, taxation and ratings. Springer Nature Publishing, Switzerland, 571 p. monograph
Brusov PN, Filatova TV, Orekhova NP, Kulik VL (2018e) Rating: new approach. J Rev Global Econ 7:37–62. SCOPUS. https://doi.org/10.6000/1929-7092.2018.07.05
Brusov PN, Filatova TV, Orekhova NP, Kulik VL (2018f) A "golden age" of the companies: conditions of its existence. J Rev Global Econ 7:88–103. SCOPUS. https://doi.org/10.6000/1929-7092.2018.07.07
Brusov PN, Filatova TV, Orekhova NP, Kulik VL (2018g) Rating methodology: new look and new horizons. J Rev Global Econ 7:63–87. SCOPUS. https://doi.org/10.6000/1929-7092.2018.07.06
Brusov PN, Filatova TV, Orekhova NP, Kulik VL, Weil I (2018b) New meaningful effects in modern capital structure theory. J Rev Global Econ 7:104–122. SCOPUS. https://doi.org/10.6000/1929-7092.2018.07.08
Brusov PN, Filatova TV, Orekhova NP, Kulik VL, Weil I (2019) Ratings of the investment projects of arbitrary durations: new methodology. J Rev Global Econ 8:437–448. SCOPUS. https://doi.org/10.6000/1929-7092.2019.08.37
Brusov PN, Filatova TV, Orekhova NP, Kulik VL, Chang S-I, Lin YCG (2020) Modification of the Modigliani–Miller theory for the case of advance payments of tax on profit. J Rev Global Econ 9:257–268
Brusov P, Filatova T, Orekhova N, Kulik V, Weil I, Brailov A (2018a) The impact of the central bank key rate and commercial banks credit rates on creating and maintaining of a favorable investment climate in the country. J Rev Global Econ 7:360–376. SCOPUS. https://doi.org/10.6000/1929-7092.2018.07.31
Brusova A (2011) A comparison of the three methods of estimation of weighted average cost of capital and equity cost of company. Financ Anal Prob Sol 34(76):36–42

Filatova T, Orehova N, Brusova A (2008) Weighted average cost of capital in the theory of Modigliani–Miller, modified for a finite life–time company. Bull FU 48:68–77
Modigliani F, Miller M (1958) The cost of capital, corporate finance, and the theory of investment. Am Econ Rev 48:261–297
Modigliani F, Miller M (1963) Corporate income taxes and the cost of capital: a correction. Am Econ Rev 53:147–175
Modigliani F, Miller M (1966) Some estimates of the cost of capital to the electric utility industry 1954 1957. Am Econ Rev 56:333–391
Myers S (2001) Capital structure. J Econ Perspect 15(2):81–102

Chapter 8
Application of Brusov–Filatova–Orekhova Theory (BFO Theory) in Rating Methodology

8.1 Introduction

In Chaps. 6 and 7, we have offered fundamentally new approach to rating methodology, which includes adequate application of discounting of financial flows virtually not used in existing rating methodologies. The incorporation of rating parameters (financial "ratios") into the perpetuity limit of modern theory of capital structure by Brusov–Filatova–Orekhova (BFO) theory has been done: it requires a modification of perpetuity limit of the BFO theory for rating needs. Two models (one-period and multi-period) for accounting of discounting of financial flows were discussed. An algorithm of valuation of discount rate, taking into account rating ratios, has been suggested. We also discuss the interplay between rating ratios and leverage level which can be quite important in rating.

As we have discussed in a number of works (Brusov and Filatova 2011; Brusov 2018a, b; Brusov et al. 2011a, b, c, 2012a, b, 2013a, b, 2014a, b; 2015, 2018a, e, f, g, 2019, 2020; Filatova et al. 2008, 2018) perpetuity limit of the BFO theory—Modigliani–Miller theory (Modigliani and Miller 1958, 1963, 1966; Myers 2001)—underestimated the assessment of the attracting capital cost and therefore overestimated the assessment of the capitalization of the company. Besides, the time factor, which is very important, does not exist in the perpetuity limit. And therefore in this limit there is no concept of the age of the company, and their lifetime is infinite (perpetuity).

In this chapter, the generalization of the approach for the case of modern theory of capital structure and capital cost by Brusov–Filatova–Orekhova (BFO theory) for companies and corporations of arbitrary age, i.e., for general case of the BFO theory, has been done (Brusov et al. 2018c).

This has required the modification of the BFO theory for the rating needs (much more complicated than in the case of perpetuity limit—Modigliani–Miller theory), as the concept of "leverage" as the ratio of debt value to the equity value used in

P. Brusov et al., *Ratings*, Contributions to Finance and Accounting,
https://doi.org/10.1007/978-3-030-56243-4_8

financial management substantially differs from the concept of "leverage" in the rating, where it is understood as the direct and inverse ratio of the debt value to the generated cash flow values (income, profit, etc.). We introduce here some additional ratios, allowing us to more fully characterize the issuer's ability to repay debts and to pay interest thereon.

As we have mentioned in the previous chapter, the bridge is building between the discount rates (WACC, *ke*) used when discounting financial flows and "ratios" in the rating methodology. The algorithm for finding the discount rates for given ratio values is developed.

Application of the BFO theory modified for rating purposes allows us to adequately produce the discounting of financial flows by using the correct discount rates when discounting the magnitude of rating ratios and to take into account the time factor missing in perpetuity limit and being important, i.e., to take into account the company age (in BFO-I theory) or the company lifetime (in the BFO-II theory).

8.1.1 Modification of the BFO Theory for Companies and Corporations of Arbitrary Age for the Purposes of Ranking

We will conduct below the modification of the BFO theory for companies and corporations of arbitrary age for the purposes of ranking, which proved much more difficult than modification of its (BFO theory) perpetuity limit.

As it turned out, the use of the famous formula BFO

$$\frac{[1-(1+\mathrm{WACC})^{-n}]}{\mathrm{WACC}}=\frac{[1-(1+k_0)^{-n}]}{k_0[1-\omega_d T(1-(1+k_d)^{-n})]} \tag{8.1}$$

is not possible, since it no longer includes cash flows CF and debt value D, and the leverage level $L = D/S$ (in the same sense as it is used in financial management) is included only through the share of leveraged $w_d = L/(L + 1)$.

For the modification of the general theory of BFO for ranking purposes, one must return to the initial assumptions under the derivation of the BFO formula.

The Modigliani–Miller theorem in the case of existing corporate taxes, generalized by us for the case of finite company age, states that the capitalization of leveraged company (using debt financing), V_L, is equal to the capitalization of non-leveraged company (which does not use debt financing), V_0, increased by the amount of the tax shield for the finite period of time, TS_n,

$$V_L = V_0 + \mathrm{TS}_n. \tag{8.2}$$

where

the capitalization of leveraged company V_L

$$= \frac{\mathrm{CF}}{\mathrm{WACC}}\left(1-(1+\mathrm{WACC})^{-n}\right); \tag{8.3}$$

the capitalization of non-leveraged company

$$V_0 = \frac{\mathrm{CF}}{k_0}\left(1-(1+k_0)^{-n}\right); \tag{8.4}$$

and the tax shield for the period of n-years

$$\mathrm{TS}_n = tD\left(1-(1+k_\mathrm{d})^{-n}\right). \tag{8.5}$$

Substituting Eqs. (8.3–8.5) into Eq. (8.2), we obtain Eq. (8.6), which will be used by us in the future to modify the BFO theory for the needs of the ranking.

$$\frac{\mathrm{CF} * \left(1-(1+\mathrm{WACC})^{-n}\right)}{\mathrm{WACC}} = \frac{\mathrm{CF}}{K_0} * \left(1-(1+k_0)^{-n}\right) + t * D * \left(1-(1+k_\mathrm{d})^{-n}\right) \tag{8.6}$$

Below we fulfill the incorporation of rating parameters (financial "ratios") into the modern theory of capital structure (Brusov–Filatova–Orekhova (BFO) theory).

As we have noted in a previous papers (Brusov et al. 2018b, d), in quantification of the creditworthiness of the issuers the crucial role belongs to the so-called financial "ratios," which constitute direct and inverse ratios of various generated cash flows to debt values and interest ones. We could mention such ratios as DCF/Debt, FFO/Debt, CFO/Debt, FOCF/Debt, *FFO*/cashinterest, EBITDA/interest, Interests/EBITDA, Debt/EBITDA, and some others.

Let us consider two kinds of rating ratios: coverage ratios and leverage ratios.

8.1.1.1 Coverage Ratios

We start from the coverage ratios and will consider three kinds of coverage ratios: coverage ratios of debt, coverage ratios of interest on the credit, and coverage ratios of debt and interest on the credit. Note that the last type of ratios has been introduced by us for the first time for a more complete valuation of the issuer's ability to repay debts and to pay interest thereon.

8.1.1.2 Coverage Ratios of Debt

Here $i_1 = \mathrm{CF}/D$

Let us consider the coverage ratios of debt first.

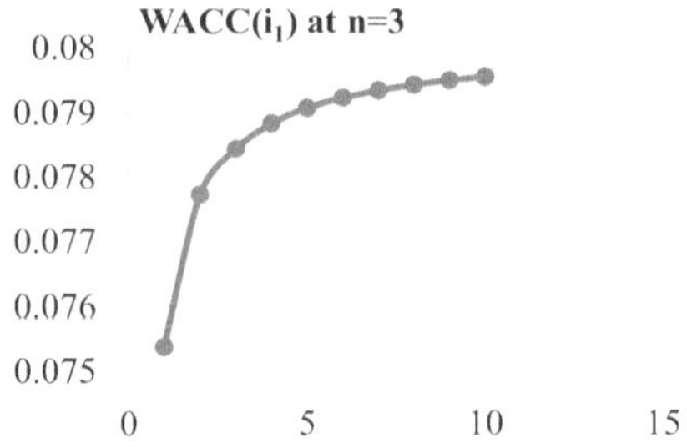

Fig. 8.1 The dependence of company's weighted average cost of capital (WACC) on the coverage ratio on debt i_1 at $n = 3$

Dividing both the parts of formula (8.6) by the value of the debt D, enter the debt coverage ratio into the general BFO theory

$$i_1 = \mathrm{CF}/D \tag{8.7}$$

$$i_1 * \left(\frac{1-(1+\mathrm{WACC})^{-n}}{\mathrm{WACC} = i_1 * \left(\frac{1-(1+k_0)^{-n}}{k_0 + t*(1-(1+k_\mathrm{d})^{-n})}\right.}\right. \tag{8.8}$$

$$i_1 * A = i_1 * B + t * C \tag{8.9}$$

$$A = \left(\frac{1-(1+\mathrm{WACC})^{-n}}{\mathrm{WACC};}\right. \tag{8.10}$$

$$B = \left(\frac{1-(1+k_0)^{-n}}{k_0;}\right. \tag{8.11}$$

$$C = (1-(1+k_\mathrm{d})^{-n}); \tag{8.12}$$

This ratio (i_1) can be used to assess the following parameters used in rating, DCF/Debt, FFO/Debt, CFO/Debt, FOCF/Debt, and some others. We will use formula (8.8) to study the dependence WACC(i_1) and to build a curve of this dependence.

Let us analyze the dependence of the weighted average cost of capital (WACC) on debt coverage ratio i_1. We consider the case $k_0 = 8\%$; $k_\mathrm{d} = 4\%$; $t = 20\%$; i_1 is changed from 1 up to 10, for two company ages $n = 3$ and $n = 5$.

The dependence of company's weighted average cost of capital (WACC) on the coverage ratio on debt i_1 is shown in Figs. 8.1 and 8.2.

8.1.1.3 The Coverage Ratio on Interest on the Credit

Let us analyze now the dependence of company's weighted average cost of capital (WACC) on the coverage ratio on interest on the credit i_2.

Dividing both the parts of formula (8.6) by the value of the interest on the credit $k_\mathrm{d}D$, enter the coverage ratio on interest on the credit i_2 into the general BFO theory

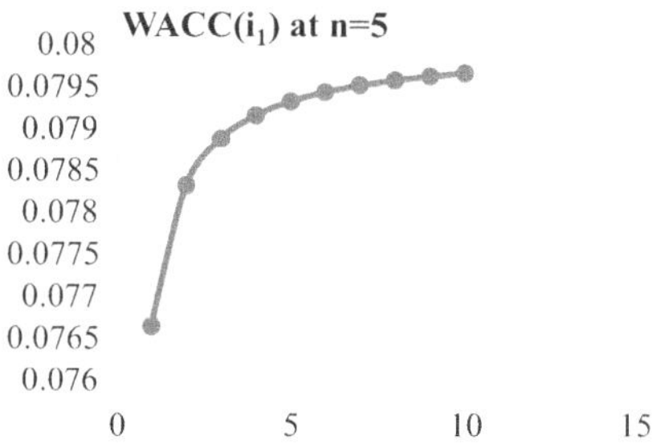

Fig. 8.2 The dependence of company's weighted average cost of capital (WACC) on the coverage ratio on debt i_1 at $n = 5$

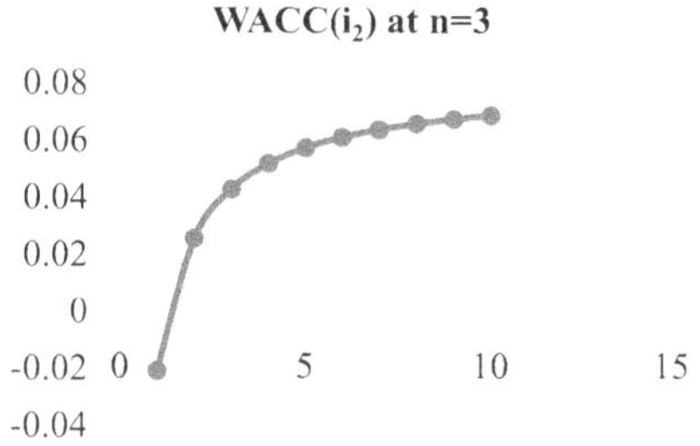

Fig. 8.3 The dependence of company's weighted average cost of capital (WACC) on the coverage ratio on interest on the credit i_2 at company age $n = 3$

$$i_2 * \left(\frac{1-(1+\mathrm{WACC})^{-n}}{\mathrm{WACC} = i_2 * \left(\frac{1-(1+k_0)^{-n}}{k_0 + \frac{t*(1-(1+k_d)^{-n})}{k_d}} \right.} \right.$$

Here

$$\frac{\mathrm{CF}}{D * k_d} = i_2$$

$$i_2 * A = i_2 * B + \frac{t * C}{k_d}$$

The dependences of company's weighted average cost of capital (WACC) on the coverage ratio on interest on the credit i_2 at company ages $n = 3$ and $n = 5$ are shown in Figs. 8.3 and 8.4.

This ratio (i_2) can be used to assess the following parameters, used in rating, *FFO/* cashinterest, EBITDA/interest, and some others. We will use the last formula to build a curve of dependence WACC(i_2).

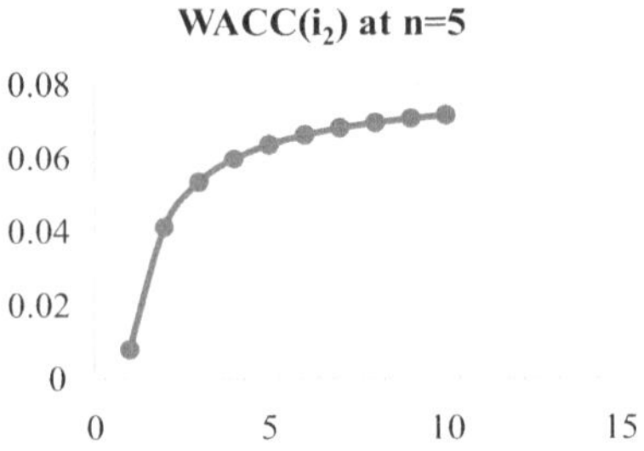

Fig. 8.4 The dependence of company's weighted average cost of capital (WACC) on the coverage ratio on interest on the credit i_2 at company age $n = 5$

8.1.1.4 Coverage Ratios of Debt and Interest on the Credit (New Ratios)

Let us now study the dependence of the company's weighted average cost of capital (WACC) on the coverage ratios of debt and interest on the credit simultaneously i_3: this is new ratio, introduced by us for the first time here for a more complete description of the issuer's ability to repay debts and to pay interest thereon.

Dividing both the parts of the formula (8.6) by the value of the debt and interest on the credit $(1 + k_d)D$, enter the coverage ratio on debt and interest on the credit i_3 into the general BFO theory

$$\frac{\mathrm{CF}}{D*(1+k_\mathrm{d})}=i_3$$

$$i_3*A=i_3*B+\frac{t*C}{1+k_\mathrm{d}}$$

$$i_3*\left(\frac{1-(1+\mathrm{WACC})^{-n}}{\mathrm{WACC}=i_3*\left(\frac{1-(1+k_0)^{-n}}{k_0+\frac{t*\left(1-(1+k_\mathrm{d})^{-n}\right)}{1+k_\mathrm{d}}}\right.}\right.$$

The dependences of company weighted average cost of capital (WACC) on the coverage ratio on debt and interest on the credit i_3 at company ages $n = 3$ and $n = 5$ are shown in Figs. 8.5 and 8.6.

8.1.1.5 All Three Coverage Ratios Together

Consolidated data of dependence of WACC on i_1, i_2, i_3, at company ages $n = 3$ and $i = 5$ are shown in Figs. 8.7 and 8.8.

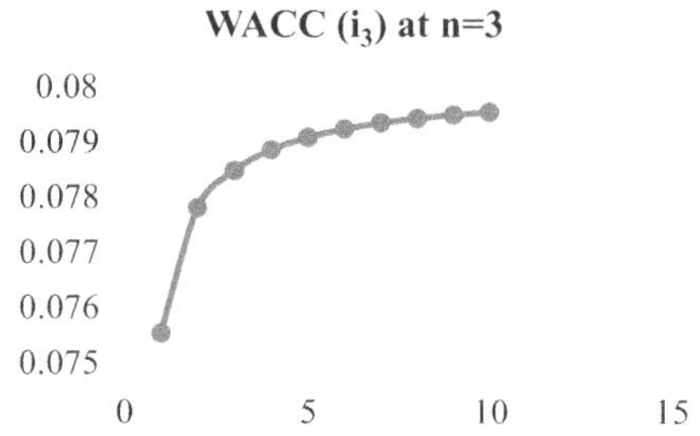

Fig. 8.5 The dependence of company's weighted average cost of capital (WACC) on the coverage ratio on debt and interest on the credit i_3 at company age $n = 3$

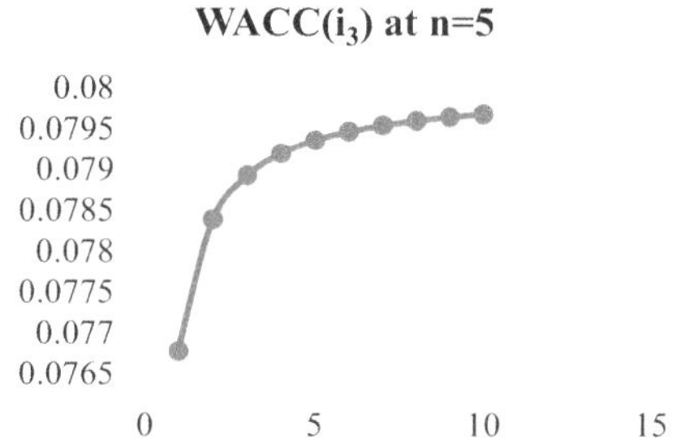

Fig. 8.6 The dependence of company's weighted average cost of capital (WACC) on the coverage ratio on debt and interest on the credit i_2 at company age $n = 5$

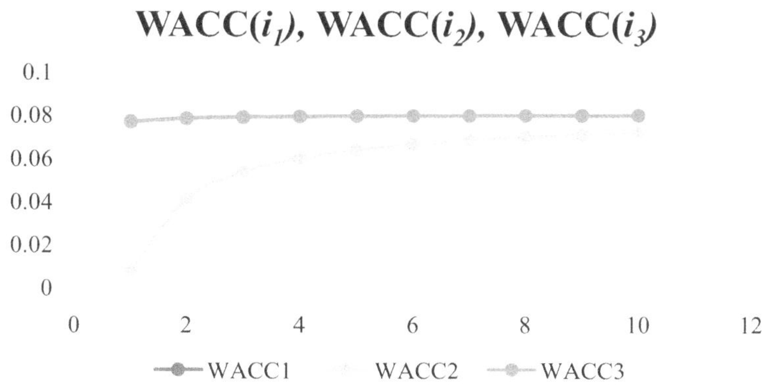

Fig. 8.7 Consolidated data of dependence of WACC on i_1, i_2, i_3, at company age $n = 3$

The analysis of Tables 8.1, 8.2, 8.3, 8.4, 8.5, 8.6, and 8.7 and Figs. 8.1, 8.2, 8.3, 8.4, 8.5, 8.6, 8.7, and 8.8 as well as conclusions will be made at the end of the next paragraph.

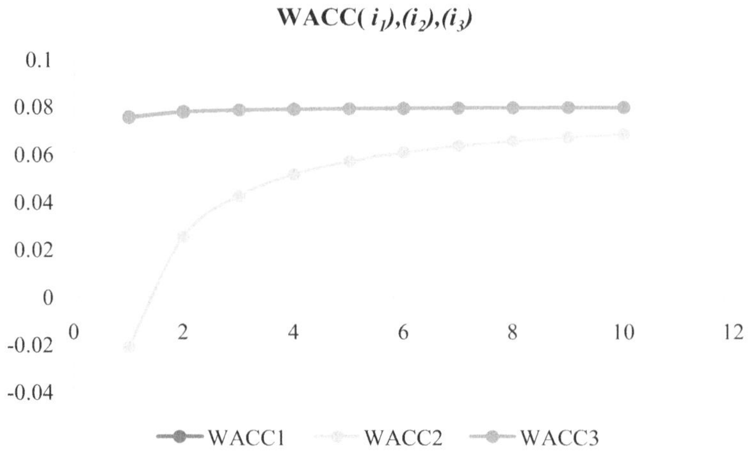

Fig. 8.8 Consolidated data of dependence of WACC on i_1, i_2, i_3, at company age $n = 5$

Table 8.1 The dependence of the weighted average cost of capital (WACC) on debt coverage ratio i_1 for company age $n = 3$

t	k_0	k_d	i_1	WACC
0.2	0.08	0.04	1	0.075356711
0.2	0.08	0.04	2	0.077705469
0.2	0.08	0.04	3	0.078412717
0.2	0.08	0.04	4	0.078808879
0.2	0.08	0.04	5	0.079046807
0.2	0.08	0.04	6	0.079205521
0.2	0.08	0.04	7	0.079318935
0.2	0.08	0.04	8	0.079404022
0.2	0.08	0.04	9	0.079470216
0.2	0.08	0.04	10	0.07952318

Table 8.2 The dependence of the weighted average cost of capital (WACC) on debt coverage ratio i_1 for company age $n = 5$

t	k_0	k_d	i_1	WACC
0.2	0.08	0.04	1	0.07663868
0.2	0.08	0.04	2	0.0783126
0.2	0.08	0.04	3	0.0788732
0.2	0.08	0.04	4	0.079154
0.2	0.08	0.04	5	0.07932264
0.2	0.08	0.04	6	0.07943518
0.2	0.08	0.04	7	0.0795156
0.2	0.08	0.04	8	0.07957594
0.2	0.08	0.04	9	0.07962287
0.2	0.08	0.04	10	0.07966043

Table 8.3 The dependence of the weighted average cost of capital (WACC) on interest on the credit coverage ratio i_2 for company age $n = 3$

t	k_0	k_d	i_2	WACC
0.2	0.08	0.04	1	−0.021238089
0.2	0.08	0.04	2	0.02529016
0.2	0.08	0.04	3	0.042483465
0.2	0.08	0.04	4	0.051456351
0.2	0.08	0.04	5	0.056965593
0.2	0.08	0.04	6	0.060692181
0.2	0.08	0.04	7	0.063380861
0.2	0.08	0.04	8	0.065412245
0.2	0.08	0.04	9	0.067001115
0.2	0.08	0.04	10	0.068277865

Table 8.4 The dependence of the weighted average cost of capital (WACC) on interest on the credit coverage ratio i_2 for company age $n = 5$

t	k_0	k_d	i_2	WACC
0.2	0.08	0.04	1	0.00793717
0.2	0.08	0.04	2	0.04111354
0.2	0.08	0.04	3	0.0533843
0.2	0.08	0.04	4	0.05974575
0.2	0.08	0.04	5	0.06365738
0.2	0.08	0.04	6	0.06630611
0.2	0.08	0.04	7	0.06821315
0.2	0.08	0.04	8	0.06966377
0.2	0.08	0.04	9	0.07078076
0.2	0.08	0.04	10	0.07168658

Table 8.5 The dependence of the weighted average cost of capital (WACC) on debt and interest on the credit coverage ratio i_3 for company age $n = 3$

t	k_0	k_d	i_3	WACC
0.2	0.08	0.04	1	0.075536724
0.2	0.08	0.04	2	0.077796177
0.2	0.08	0.04	3	0.078473634
0.2	0.08	0.04	4	0.078854621
0.2	0.08	0.04	5	0.079083426
0.2	0.08	0.04	6	0.079236052
0.2	0.08	0.04	7	0.079345114
0.2	0.08	0.04	8	0.079426934
0.2	0.08	0.04	9	0.079490586
0.2	0.08	0.04	10	0.079541516

8.1.2 Coverage Ratios (Different Capital Cost Values)

Let us analyze the dependence of company weighted average cost of capital (WACC) of coverage ratios (i_1, i_2, i_3), for different capital cost values $k_0 = 14\%$, $k_d = 8\%$.

Here as before $t = 20\%$, $n = 3$; 5, the value of coverage ratios i is in the range from 1 to 10.

Table 8.6 The dependence of the weighted average cost of capital (WACC) on debt and interest on the credit coverage ratio i_3 for company age $n = 5$

t	k_0	k_d	i_3	WACC
0.2	0.08	0.04	1	0.07676703
0.2	0.08	0.04	2	0.07837722
0.2	0.08	0.04	3	0.07891638
0.2	0.08	0.04	4	0.07918642
0.2	0.08	0.04	5	0.07934861
0.2	0.08	0.04	6	0.07945683
0.2	0.08	0.04	7	0.07953417
0.2	0.08	0.04	8	0.07959218
0.2	0.08	0.04	9	0.07963732
0.2	0.08	0.04	10	0.07967343

Table 8.7 The dependence of the weighted average cost of capital (WACC) on debt coverage ratio i_1 for company age $n = 3$

i_1	t	k_0	k_d	WACC	n	BFO
1	0.2	0.14	0.08	0.1298	3	0.00
2	0.2	0.14	0.08	0.1347	3	0.00
3	0.2	0.14	0.08	0.1365	3	0.00
4	0.2	0.14	0.08	0.1374	3	0.00
5	0.2	0.14	0.08	0.1379	3	0.00
6	0.2	0.14	0.08	0.1382	3	0.00
7	0.2	0.14	0.08	0.1385	3	0.00
8	0.2	0.14	0.08	0.1387	3	0.00
9	0.2	0.14	0.08	0.1388	3	0.00
10	0.2	0.14	0.08	0.1389	3	0.00

8.1.2.1 Coverage Ratios of Debt

As we have derived above the dependence of the weighted average cost of capital (WACC) on debt coverage ratio (i_1) in the BFO theory is described by the following formula:

$$i_1 * \frac{(1-(1+\mathrm{WACC})^{-n})}{\mathrm{WACC}} - i_1 * \frac{(1-(1+K_0)^{-n})}{K_0} - t * [1-(1+K_d)^{-n}] = 0,$$

Here $i_1 = \frac{CF}{D}$.

By using it we get the following results, representing in Table 8.8 and Fig. 8.9 for company age $n = 3$ and in Table 8.9 and Fig. 8.10 for company age $n = 5$.

8.1.2.2 The Coverage Ratio on Interest on the Credit

As we have derived above the dependence of the weighted average cost of capital (WACC) on interests on credit coverage ratio (i_2) in the BFO theory is described by the following formula:

Table 8.8 The dependence of the weighted average cost of capital (WACC) on debt coverage ratio i_1 for company age $n = 5$

i_1	t	K_0	K_d	WACC	n	BFO
1	0.2	0.14	0.08	0.1324	5	0.00
2	0.2	0.14	0.08	0.1362	5	0.00
3	0.2	0.14	0.08	0.1374	5	0.00
4	0.2	0.14	0.08	0.1381	5	0.00
5	0.2	0.14	0.08	0.1385	5	0.00
6	0.2	0.14	0.08	0.1387	5	0.00
7	0.2	0.14	0.08	0.1389	5	0.00
8	0.2	0.14	0.08	0.1390	5	0.00
9	0.2	0.14	0.08	0.1391	5	0.00
10	0.2	0.14	0.08	0.1392	5	0.00

Table 8.9 The dependence of the weighted average cost of capital (WACC) on interests on credit coverage ratio i_2 for company age $n = 3$

i_2	t	K_0	K_d	WACC	n	BFO
1	0.2	0.14	0.08	0.0285	3	0.00
2	0.2	0.14	0.08	0.0795	3	0.00
3	0.2	0.14	0.08	0.0985	3	0.00
4	0.2	0.14	0.08	0.1084	3	0.00
5	0.2	0.14	0.08	0.1145	3	0.00
6	0.2	0.14	0.08	0.1186	3	0.00
7	0.2	0.14	0.08	0.1216	3	0.00
8	0.2	0.14	0.08	0.1238	3	0.00
9	0.2	0.14	0.08	0.1256	3	0.00
10	0.2	0.14	0.08	0.1270	3	0.00

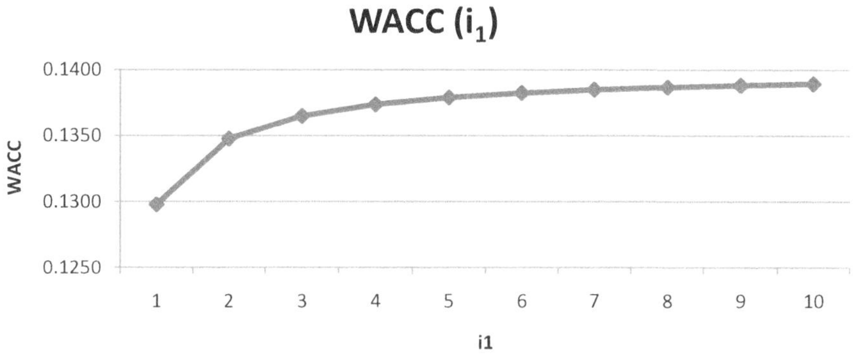

Fig. 8.9 The dependence of the weighted average cost of capital WACC on debt coverage ratio i_1 at company age $n = 3$

$$i_2 * \frac{\left(1-(1+\mathrm{WACC})^{-n}\right)}{\mathrm{WACC}} - i_2 * \frac{\left(1-(1+K_0)^{-n}\right)}{K_0} - \frac{\left(t*\left[1-(1+K_d)^{-n}\right]\right)}{K_d} = 0$$

Here $i_2 = \frac{\mathrm{CF}}{K_d * D}$.

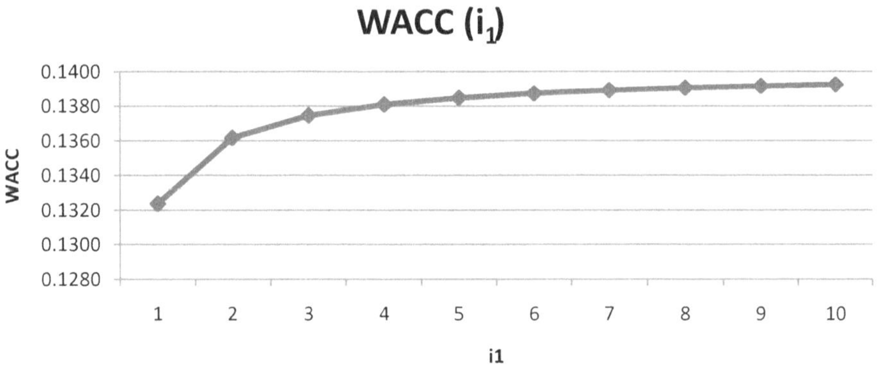

Fig. 8.10 The dependence of the weighted average cost of capital WACC on debt coverage ratio i_1 at company age $n = 5$

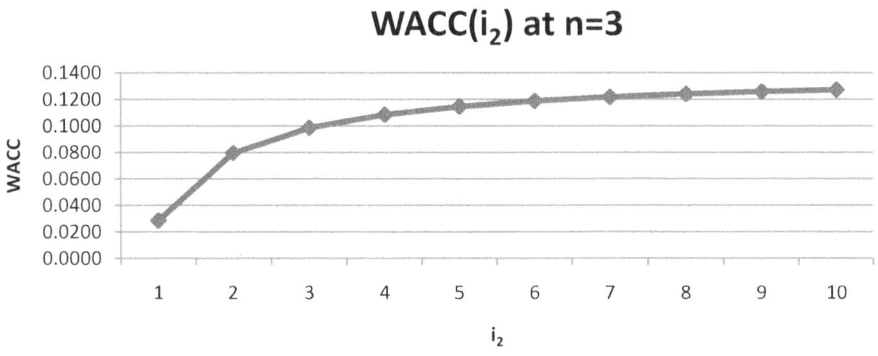

Fig. 8.11 The dependence of the weighted average cost of capital (WACC) on interests on credit coverage ratio (i_2) at company age $n = 3$

Table 8.10 The dependence of the weighted average cost of capital (WACC) on interests on credit coverage ratio i_2 for company age $n = 5$

i_2	t	k_0	k_d	WACC	n	BFO
1	0.2	0.14	0.08	0.0583	5	0.00
2	0.2	0.14	0.08	0.0957	5	0.00
3	0.2	0.14	0.08	0.1096	5	0.00
4	0.2	0.14	0.08	0.1169	5	0.00
5	0.2	0.14	0.08	0.1213	5	0.00
6	0.2	0.14	0.08	0.1244	5	0.00
7	0.2	0.14	0.08	0.1265	5	0.00
8	0.2	0.14	0.08	0.1282	5	0.00
9	0.2	0.14	0.08	0.1295	5	0.00
10	0.2	0.14	0.08	0.1305	5	0.00

Table 8.11 The dependence of the weighted average cost of capital (WACC) on debt and interests on credit coverage ratio i_2 for company age $n = 3$

i_3	t	K_0	K_d	WACC	n	BFO
1	0.2	0.14	0.08	0.1303	3	0.00
2	0.2	0.14	0.08	0.1351	3	0.00
3	0.2	0.14	0.08	0.1367	3	0.00
4	0.2	0.14	0.08	0.1376	3	0.00
5	0.2	0.14	0.08	0.1380	3	0.00
6	0.2	0.14	0.08	0.1384	3	0.00
7	0.2	0.14	0.08	0.1386	3	0.00
8	0.2	0.14	0.08	0.1388	3	0.00
9	0.2	0.14	0.08	0.1389	3	0.00
10	0.2	0.14	0.08	0.1390	3	0.00

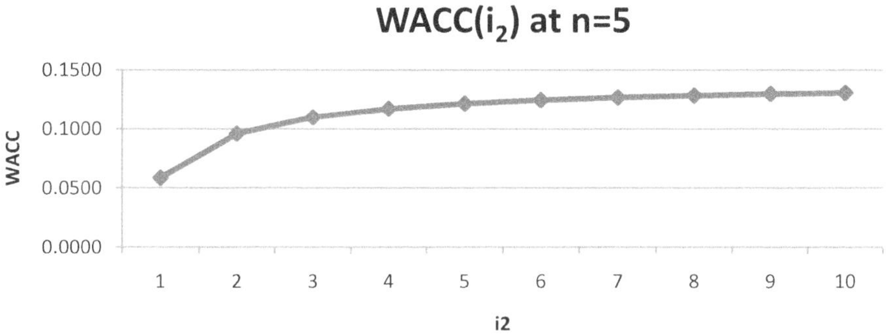

Fig. 8.12 The dependence of the weighted average cost of capital (WACC) on interests on credit leverage ratio (i_2) at company age $n = 5$

By using it we get the following results, representing in Table 8.10 and Fig. 8.11 for company age $n = 3$ and in Table 8.11 and Fig. 8.12 for company age $n = 5$.

8.1.2.3 Coverage Ratios of Debt and Interest on the Credit (New Ratios)

As we have derived above the dependence of the weighted average cost of capital (WACC) on debt and interests on credit coverage ratio (i_3) in the BFO theory is described by the following formula:

$$i_3 * \frac{(1-(1+\mathrm{WACC})^{-n})}{\mathrm{WACC}} - i_3 * \frac{(1-(1+K_0)^{-n})}{K_0} - \frac{t * [1-(1+K_d)^{-n}]}{(K_d+1)} = 0,$$

Here $i_3 = \frac{\mathrm{CF}}{(K_d+1)*D}$.

By using it we get the following results, representing in Table 8.12 and Fig. 8.13 for company age $n = 3$ and in Table 8.13 and Fig. 8.14 for company age $n = 5$.

Table 8.12 The dependence of the weighted average cost of capital (WACC) on debt and interests on credit coverage ratio i_2 for company age $n = 5$

i_3	t	K_0	K_d	WACC	n	BFO
1	0.2	0.14	0.08	0.1329	5	0.00
2	0.2	0.14	0.08	0.1364	5	0.00
3	0.2	0.14	0.08	0.1376	5	0.00
4	0.2	0.14	0.08	0.1382	5	0.00
5	0.2	0.14	0.08	0.1386	5	0.00
6	0.2	0.14	0.08	0.1388	5	0.00
7	0.2	0.14	0.08	0.1390	5	0.00
8	0.2	0.14	0.08	0.1391	5	0.00
9	0.2	0.14	0.08	0.1392	5	0.00
10	0.2	0.14	0.08	0.1393	5	0.00

Table 8.13 The dependence of the weighted average cost of capital (WACC) on debt leverage ratio l_1 for company age $n = 3$

l_1	t	k_0	k_d	WACC(l_1)	n	BFO
0	0.2	0.1	0.06	0.1000	3	0.00
1	0.2	0.1	0.06	0.0928	3	0.00
2	0.2	0.1	0.06	0.0857	3	0.00
3	0.2	0.1	0.06	0.0787	3	0.00
4	0.2	0.1	0.06	0.0720	3	0.00
5	0.2	0.1	0.06	0.0654	3	0.00
6	0.2	0.1	0.06	0.0587	3	0.00
7	0.2	0.1	0.06	0.0523	3	0.00
8	0.2	0.1	0.06	0.0461	3	0.00
9	0.2	0.1	0.06	0.0399	3	0.00
10	0.2	0.1	0.06	0.0339	3	0.00

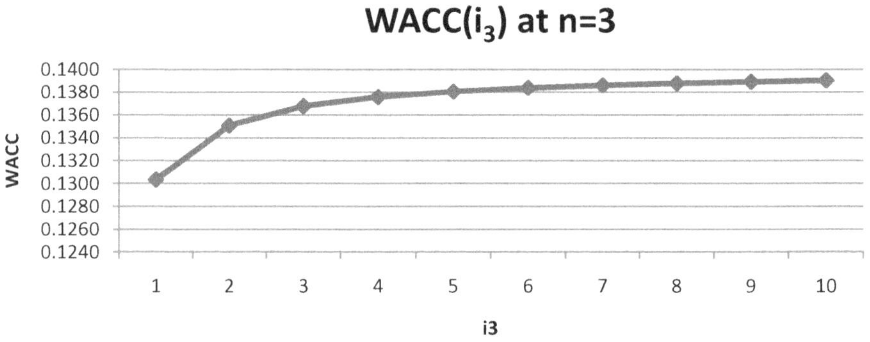

Fig. 8.13 The dependence of the weighted average cost of capital (WACC) on debt and interests on credit leverage ratio (i_3) at company age $n = 3$

8.1.2.4 Analysis and Conclusions

It is seen from Tables 8.1, 8.2, 8.3, 8.4, 8.5, 8.6, 8.7, 8.8, 8.9, 8.10, 8.11, 8.12, and 8.13 and Figs. 8.1, 8.2, 8.3, 8.4, 8.5, 8.6, 8.7, 8.8, 8.9, 8.10, 8.11, 8.12, 8.13, 8.14,

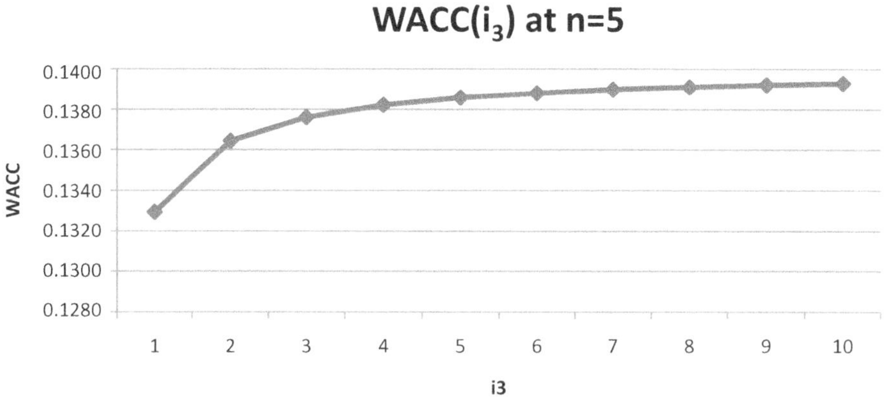

Fig. 8.14 The dependence of the weighted average cost of capital (WACC) on debt and interests on credit leverage ratio (i_3) at company age $n = 5$

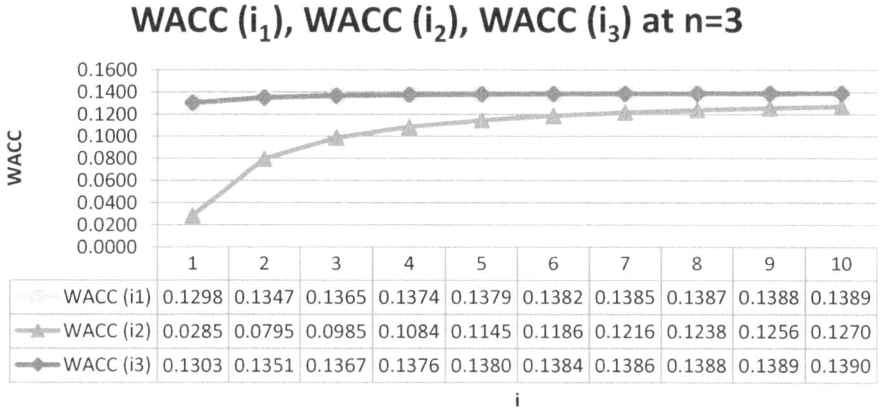

	1	2	3	4	5	6	7	8	9	10
WACC (i1)	0.1298	0.1347	0.1365	0.1374	0.1379	0.1382	0.1385	0.1387	0.1388	0.1389
WACC (i2)	0.0285	0.0795	0.0985	0.1084	0.1145	0.1186	0.1216	0.1238	0.1256	0.1270
WACC (i3)	0.1303	0.1351	0.1367	0.1376	0.1380	0.1384	0.1386	0.1388	0.1389	0.1390

Fig. 8.15 Consolidated data of dependence of WACC on i_1, i_2, i_3, at company age $n = 3$

8.15, and 8.16 that WACC(i_j) is an increasing function of i_j with saturation WACC $= k_0$ at high values of i_j. Note that this saturation for companies of finite age is a little bit more gradual than in the case of perpetuity companies: in the latter case, the saturation takes place around i_j value of order 1 for ratios i_1 and i_3 and of order 4 or 5 for ratios i_2. In the case of perpetuity as well as companies of finite age at saturation WACC reaches the value k_0 (equity value at zero leverage level). This means that for high values of i_j one can choose k_0 as a discount rate with a very good accuracy in the perpetuity case and with a little bit less accuracy in the general case (companies of arbitrary ages). Thus, the role of parameter k_0 increases drastically. The method of determination of parameter k_0 has been developed by Anastasiya Brusova (Brusova 2011). So, parameter k_0 is the discount rate for the case of high

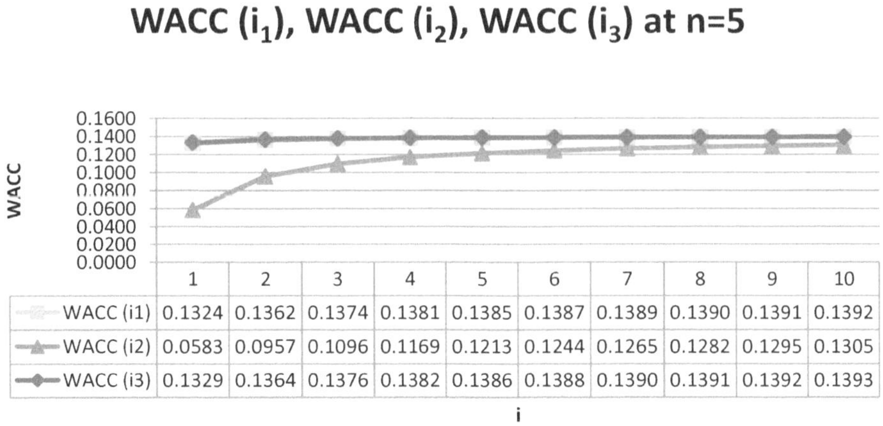

	1	2	3	4	5	6	7	8	9	10
WACC (i1)	0.1324	0.1362	0.1374	0.1381	0.1385	0.1387	0.1389	0.1390	0.1391	0.1392
WACC (i2)	0.0583	0.0957	0.1096	0.1169	0.1213	0.1244	0.1265	0.1282	0.1295	0.1305
WACC (i3)	0.1329	0.1364	0.1376	0.1382	0.1386	0.1388	0.1390	0.1391	0.1392	0.1393

Fig. 8.16 Consolidated data of dependence of WACC on i_1, i_2, i_3, at company age $n = 5$

values of i_j. For ratio i_2 in the general as well as in the perpetuity case the saturation of WACC(i_2) takes place at higher values of i_2.

In contrast to perpetuity case within the BFO theory one could make calculations for companies of arbitrary age because a factor of time is present in this theory. Our calculations show that curve WACC(i_j) for company of higher age lies above this curve for younger company. And with the increase of i_j value the WACC values for different company ages n become closer to each other.

Note that curves WACC(i_1) and WACC(i_3) are very close to each other at small enough credit rates, but difference between them will become bigger at higher values of credit rates.

Curve WACC(i_2) turns out to be different enough from WACC(i_1) and curves WACC(i_3).

8.1.3 Leverage Ratios

8.1.3.1 Leverage Ratios for Debt

We will analyze the dependence of company weighted average cost of capital (WACC) on leverage ratios (l_1, l_2, l_3). We will make calculation for capital costs $k_0 = 10\%$, $k_d = 6\%$, $t = 20\%$, $n = 3$; 5, l values range from 0 to 10.

Dividing both the parts of formula (8.6) by the income value for one period CF, we enter the leverage ratios l_1 for debt into the general BFO theory

Table 8.14 The dependence of the weighted average cost of capital (WACC) on debt leverage ratio l_1 for company age $n = 5$

l_1	t	k_0	k_d	WACC(l_1)	n	BFO
0	0.2	0.1	0.06	0.1000	5	0.00
1	0.2	0.1	0.06	0.0948	5	0.00
2	0.2	0.1	0.06	0.0898	5	0.00
3	0.2	0.1	0.06	0.0848	5	0.00
4	0.2	0.1	0.06	0.0799	5	0.00
5	0.2	0.1	0.06	0.0752	5	0.00
6	0.2	0.1	0.06	0.0705	5	0.00
7	0.2	0.1	0.06	0.0660	5	0.00
8	0.2	0.1	0.06	0.0615	5	0.00
9	0.2	0.1	0.06	0.0571	5	0.00
10	0.2	0.1	0.06	0.0528	5	0.00

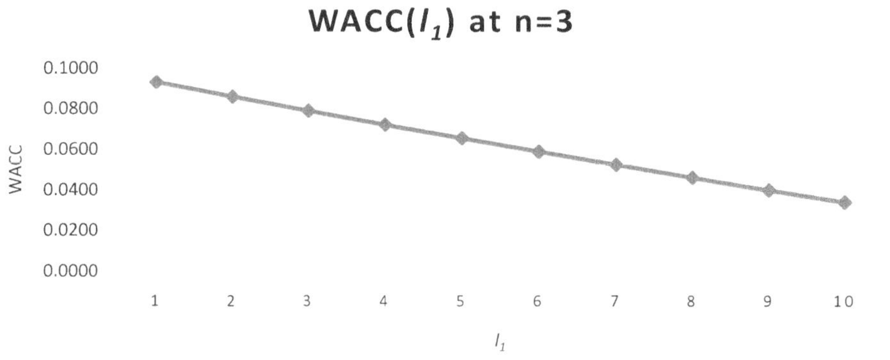

Fig. 8.17 The dependence of company weighted average cost of capital (WACC) on debt leverage ratio l_1 at $n = 3$

$$\frac{(1-(1+\mathrm{WACC})^{-n})}{\mathrm{WACC}} - \frac{(1-(1+K_0)^{-n})}{K_0} - t*[1-(1+K_d)^{-n}]*l_1 = 0,$$

Here $l_1 = \frac{D}{\mathrm{CF}}$.

Note that here WACC is the weighted average cost of capital of the company, l_1—the leverage ratios l_1 for debt, t is the tax on profit rate for organizations ($t = 20\%$), k_0—equity cost of financially independent company, k_d is the debt capital cost, n is the company age, CF—income value for one period, and D—debt capital value.

The ratio (l_2) can be used to assess the following parameters used in rating, Interests/EBITDA, and some others.

By using the above equation we get the following results, representing in Table 8.14 and Fig. 8.17 for company age $n = 3$ and in Table 8.15 and Fig. 8.18 for company age $n = 5$.

Table 8.15 The dependence of the weighted average cost of capital (WACC) on interests on credit leverage ratio l_2 for company age $n = 3$

l_2	t	k_0	k_d	WACC(l_2)	n	BFO
0	0.2	0.1	0.06	0.0998	3	0.00
1	0.2	0.1	0.06	−0.0036	3	0.00
2	0.2	0.1	0.06	−0.0804	3	0.00
3	0.2	0.1	0.06	−0.1403	3	0.00
4	0.2	0.1	0.06	−0.1888	3	0.00
5	0.2	0.1	0.06	−0.2289	3	0.00
6	0.2	0.1	0.06	−0.2629	3	0.00
7	0.2	0.1	0.06	−0.2922	3	0.00
8	0.2	0.1	0.06	−0.3178	3	0.00
9	0.2	0.1	0.06	−0.3404	3	0.00
10	0.2	0.1	0.06	−0.3605	3	0.00

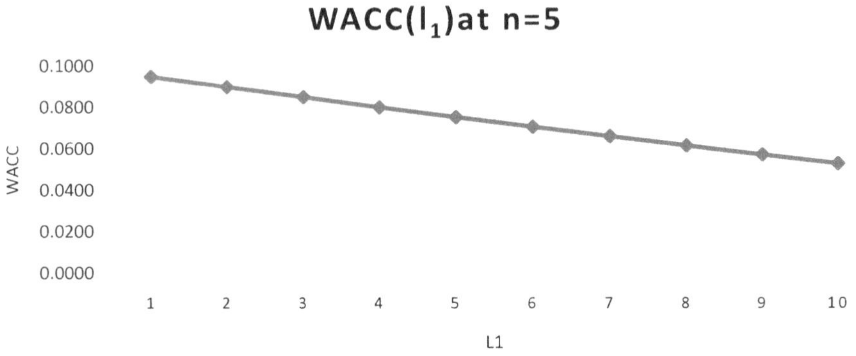

Fig. 8.18 The dependence of company weighted average cost of capital WACC on debt leverage ratio at $n = 5$

8.1.3.2 Leverage Ratios for Interest on Credit

The dependence of company weighted average cost of capital (WACC) on leverage ratios on interests on credit l_2 is described within the BFO theory by the following formula:

$$\frac{(1-(1+\mathrm{WACC})^{-n})}{\mathrm{WACC}}-\frac{(1-(1+K_0)^{-n})}{K_0}-\frac{(t*l_2*[1-(1+K_d)^{-n}])}{K_d}=0,$$

Here $l_2 = \frac{K_d * D}{\mathrm{CF}}$.

Using it, we find the dependence WACC(l_2) at company ages $n = 3$ and $n = 5$.

This ratio l_2 can be used to assess the following parameters used in rating, Interests/EBITDA, and some others.

The dependence of company weighted average cost of capital (WACC) on leverage ratios on debt and interests on credit l_3 is described within the BFO theory by the following formula:

$$\frac{(1-(1+\mathrm{WACC})^{-n})}{\mathrm{WACC}}-\frac{(1-(1+K_0)^{-n})}{K_0}-\frac{t*l_3*[1-(1+K_\mathrm{d})^{-n}]}{(K_\mathrm{d}+1)}=0,$$

Here $l_3=\frac{(K_\mathrm{d}+1)*D}{\mathrm{CF}}$.

The ratio l_3 can be used to assess the following parameters used in rating, Debt + interest/FFO, Debt + interest/EBIT, Debt + interest/EBITDA(R), and some others.

Using it, we find the dependence WACC(l_3) at company ages $n=3$ and $n=5$.

Below we represent the consolidated data of dependence of WACC on l_1, l_2, l_3, at company ages $n=3$ and $n=5$.

8.1.4 Leverage Ratios (Different Capital Costs)

8.1.4.1 Leverage Ratios for Debt

Below we analyze the dependence of company weighted average cost of capital (WACC) on leverage ratios l_1, l_2, l_3, at capital costs values $k_0=12\%$, $k_\mathrm{d}=6\%$.

As before $t=20\%$, company age $n=3$; 5, leverage ratios values range from 0 to 10.

The dependence of company weighted average cost of capital (WACC) on leverage ratios on debt l_1 is described within the BFO theory by the following formula:

$$\frac{(1-(1+\mathrm{WACC})^{-n})}{\mathrm{WACC}}-\frac{(1-(1+k_0)^{-n})}{k_0}-t*c*l_1=0.$$

Here $l_1=\frac{D}{\mathrm{CF.}}$

Using it, we find the dependence WACC(l_1) at company ages $n=3$ and $n=5$.

8.1.4.2 Leverage Ratios for Interests on Credit

The dependence of company weighted average cost of capital (WACC) on leverage ratios on interests on credit l_2 is described within the BFO theory by the following formula:

$$\frac{(1-(1+\mathrm{WACC})^{-n})}{\mathrm{WACC}}-\frac{(1-(1+K_0)^{-n})}{k_0}-\frac{t*l_2*(1-(1+k_\mathrm{d})^{-n})}{k_\mathrm{d}}=0$$

Here $l_2=\frac{D*k_\mathrm{d}}{\mathrm{CF}}$

Using it, we find the dependence WACC(l_2) at company ages $n=3$ and $n=5$.

8.1.4.3 Leverage Ratios for Debt and Interests on Credit

The dependence of company weighted average cost of capital (WACC) on leverage ratios on debt and interests on credit l_3 is described within the BFO theory by the following formula:

$$\frac{(1-(1+\mathrm{WACC})^{-n})}{\mathrm{WACC}}-\frac{(1-(1+K_0)^{-n})}{K_0}-\frac{t*l_3*(1-(1+k_\mathrm{d})^{-n})}{1+K_\mathrm{d}}=0$$

Here $l_3=\frac{D(1+k_\mathrm{d})}{\mathrm{CF}}$.

Using it, we find the dependence WACC(l_3) at company ages $n=3$ and $n=5$.

8.1.4.4 Analysis and Conclusions

It is seen from Tables 8.14, 8.15, 8.16, 8.17, 8.18, 8.19, 8.20, 8.21, 8.22, 8.23, and 8.24 and Figs. 8.17, 8.18, 8.19, 8.20, 8.21, 8.22, 8.23, 8.24, 8.25, 8.26, 8.27, 8.28,

Table 8.16 The dependence of the weighted average cost of capital (WACC) on interests on credit leverage ratio l_2 for company age $n=5$

l_2	t	k_0	k_d	WACC(l_2)	n	BFO
0	0.2	0.1	0.06	0.1000	5	0.00
1	0.2	0.1	0.06	0.0259	5	0.00
2	0.2	0.1	0.06	−0.0296	5	0.00
3	0.2	0.1	0.06	−0.0732	5	0.00
4	0.2	0.1	0.06	−0.1089	5	0.00
5	0.2	0.1	0.06	−0.1388	5	0.00
6	0.2	0.1	0.06	−0.1643	5	0.00
7	0.2	0.1	0.06	−0.1865	5	0.00
8	0.2	0.1	0.06	−0.2061	5	0.00
9	0.2	0.1	0.06	−0.2235	5	0.00
10	0.2	0.1	0.06	−0.2391	5	0.00

Table 8.17 The dependence of the weighted average cost of capital (WACC) on debt and interests on credit leverage ratio l_2 for company age $n=3$

l_3	t	k_0	k_d	WACC(l_3)	n	BFO
0	0.2	0.1	0.06	0.1000	3	0.00
1	0.2	0.1	0.06	0.0930	3	0.00
2	0.2	0.1	0.06	0.0864	3	0.00
3	0.2	0.1	0.06	0.0798	3	0.00
4	0.2	0.1	0.06	0.0734	3	0.00
5	0.2	0.1	0.06	0.0671	3	0.00
6	0.2	0.1	0.06	0.0608	3	0.00
7	0.2	0.1	0.06	0.0548	3	0.00
8	0.2	0.1	0.06	0.0489	3	0.00
9	0.2	0.1	0.06	0.0430	3	0.00
10	0.2	0.1	0.06	0.0371	3	0.00

Table 8.18 The dependence of the weighted average cost of capital (WACC) on debt and interests on credit leverage ratio l_2 for company age $n = 5$

l_3	t	k_0	k_d	WACC(l_3)	n	BFO
0	0.2	0.1	0.06	0.1000	5	0.00
1	0.2	0.1	0.06	0.0951	5	0.00
2	0.2	0.1	0.06	0.0903	5	0.00
3	0.2	0.1	0.06	0.0856	5	0.00
4	0.2	0.1	0.06	0.0810	5	0.00
5	0.2	0.1	0.06	0.0765	5	0.00
6	0.2	0.1	0.06	0.0721	5	0.00
7	0.2	0.1	0.06	0.0678	5	0.00
8	0.2	0.1	0.06	0.0635	5	0.00
9	0.2	0.1	0.06	0.0593	5	0.00
10	0.2	0.1	0.06	0.0552	5	0.00

Table 8.19 The dependence of the weighted average cost of capital (WACC) on debt leverage ratio l_1 for company age $n = 3$

l_1	k_0	k_d	n	t	WACC	BFO
0	0.12	0.06	3	0.2	0.119997	0.00
1	0.12	0.06	3	0.2	0.112294	0.00
2	0.12	0.06	3	0.2	0.104774	0.00
3	0.12	0.06	3	0.2	0.097444	0.00
4	0.12	0.06	3	0.2	0.090128	0.00
5	0.12	0.06	3	0.2	0.083078	0.00
6	0.12	0.06	3	0.2	0.076332	0.00
7	0.12	0.06	3	0.2	0.06959	0.00
8	0.12	0.06	3	0.2	0.062962	0.00
9	0.12	0.06	3	0.2	0.056492	0.00
10	0.12	0.06	3	0.2	0.050163	0.00

Table 8.20 The dependence of the weighted average cost of capital (WACC) on debt leverage ratio l_1 for company age $n = 5$

l_1	k_0	k_d	n	t	WACC	BFO
0	0.12	0.06	5	0.2	0.119994	0.00
1	0.12	0.06	5	0.2	0.114311	0.00
2	0.12	0.06	5	0.2	0.108927	0.00
3	0.12	0.06	5	0.2	0.103556	0.00
4	0.12	0.06	5	0.2	0.098332	0.00
5	0.12	0.06	5	0.2	0.093123	0.00
6	0.12	0.06	5	0.2	0.088164	0.00
7	0.12	0.06	5	0.2	0.083265	0.00
8	0.12	0.06	5	0.2	0.078452	0.00
9	0.12	0.06	5	0.2	0.073744	0.00
10	0.12	0.06	5	0.2	0.069	0.00

8.29, 8.30, 8.31, and 8.32 that WACC(l_j) is a decreasing function of l_j. WACC decreases from value of k_0 (equity value at zero leverage level) practically linearly for WACC(l_1) and WACC(l_3) and with higher speed for WACC(l_2). In contrast to the perpetuity case within the BFO theory, one could make calculations for

Table 8.21 The dependence of the weighted average cost of capital (WACC) on interests on credit leverage ratio l_2 for company age $n = 3$

l_2	k_0	k_d	n	t	WACC	BFO
0	0.12	0.06	3	0.2	0.119997	0.00
1	0.12	0.06	3	0.2	0.010838	0.00
2	0.12	0.06	3	0.2	−0.06941	0.00
3	0.12	0.06	3	0.2	−0.13171	0.00
4	0.12	0.06	3	0.2	−0.18169	0.00
5	0.12	0.06	3	0.2	−0.22298	0.00
6	0.12	0.06	3	0.2	−0.25785	0.00
7	0.12	0.06	3	0.2	−0.28784	0.00
8	0.12	0.06	3	0.2	−0.31392	0.00
9	0.12	0.06	3	0.2	−0.33692	0.00
10	0.12	0.06	3	0.2	−0.35745	0.00

Table 8.22 The dependence of the weighted average cost of capital (WACC) on interests on credit leverage ratio l_2 for company age $n = 5$

l_2	k_0	k_d	n_1	t	WACC	BFO
0	0.12	0.06	5	0.2	0.119994	0.00
1	0.12	0.06	5	0.2	0.040367	0.00
2	0.12	0.06	5	0.2	−0.01846	0.00
3	0.12	0.06	5	0.2	−0.06439	0.00
4	0.12	0.06	5	0.2	−0.10159	0.00
5	0.12	0.06	5	0.2	−0.13262	0.00
6	0.12	0.06	5	0.2	−0.15899	0.00
7	0.12	0.06	5	0.2	−0.18185	0.00
8	0.12	0.06	5	0.2	−0.20194	0.00
9	0.12	0.06	5	0.2	−0.21978	0.00
10	0.12	0.06	5	0.2	−0.23578	0.00

Table 8.23 The dependence of the weighted average cost of capital (WACC) on debt and interests on credit leverage ratio l_3 for company age $n = 3$

l_3	k_0	k_d	n	t	WACC	BFO
0	0.12	0.06	3	0.2	0.119997	0.00
1	0.12	0.06	3	0.2	0.112716	0.00
2	0.12	0.06	3	0.2	0.105604	0.00
3	0.12	0.06	3	0.2	0.098686	0.00
4	0.12	0.06	3	0.2	0.091785	0.00
5	0.12	0.06	3	0.2	0.085114	0.00
6	0.12	0.06	3	0.2	0.078654	0.00
7	0.12	0.06	3	0.2	0.072249	0.00
8	0.12	0.06	3	0.2	0.065828	0.00
9	0.12	0.06	3	0.2	0.059771	0.00
10	0.12	0.06	3	0.2	0.053729	0.00

companies of arbitrary age because a factor of time is present in this theory. Our calculations show that curve WACC(l_i) for company of higher age lies above this curve for younger company.

Table 8.24 The dependence of the weighted average cost of capital (WACC) on debt and interests on credit leverage ratio l_3 for company age $n = 5$

l_3	k_0	k_d	n	t	WACC	BFO
0	0.12	0.06	5	0.2	0.119994	0.00
1	0.12	0.06	5	0.2	0.114614	0.00
2	0.12	0.06	5	0.2	0.10954	0.00
3	0.12	0.06	5	0.2	0.104444	0.00
4	0.12	0.06	5	0.2	0.099512	0.00
5	0.12	0.06	5	0.2	0.094598	0.00
6	0.12	0.06	5	0.2	0.08988	0.00
7	0.12	0.06	5	0.2	0.0852	0.00
8	0.12	0.06	5	0.2	0.080618	0.00
9	0.12	0.06	5	0.2	0.076129	0.00
10	0.12	0.06	5	0.2	0.071733	0.00

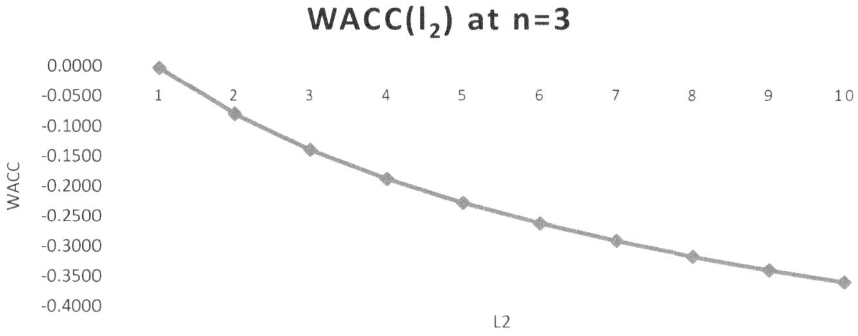

Fig. 8.19 The dependence of company weighted average cost of capital (WACC) on leverage ratio of interests on credit at company age $n = 3$

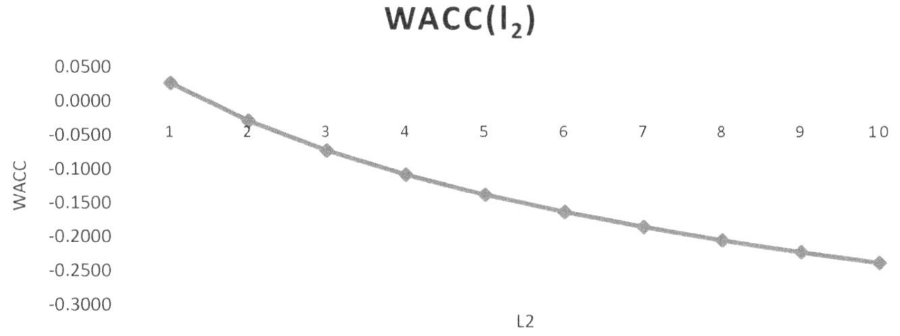

Fig. 8.20 The dependence of company weighted average cost of capital (WACC) on leverage ratio of interests on credit at company age $n = 3$

Note that curves WACC(l_1) and WACC(l_3) are very close to each other at small enough credit rates, but difference between them will become bigger at higher values of credit rates.

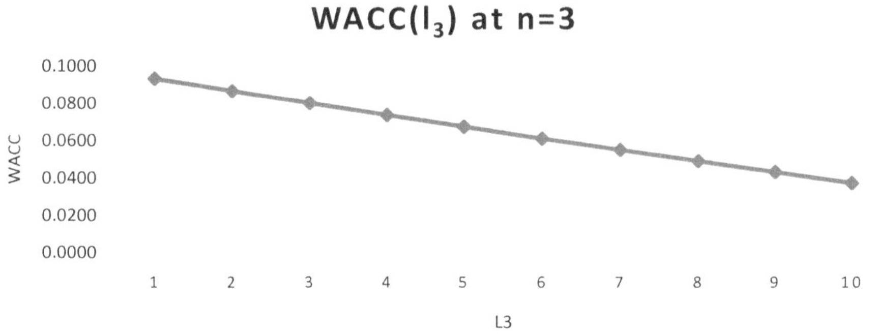

Fig. 8.21 The dependence of company weighted average cost of capital (WACC) on leverage ratio on debt and interests on credit at company age $n = 3$

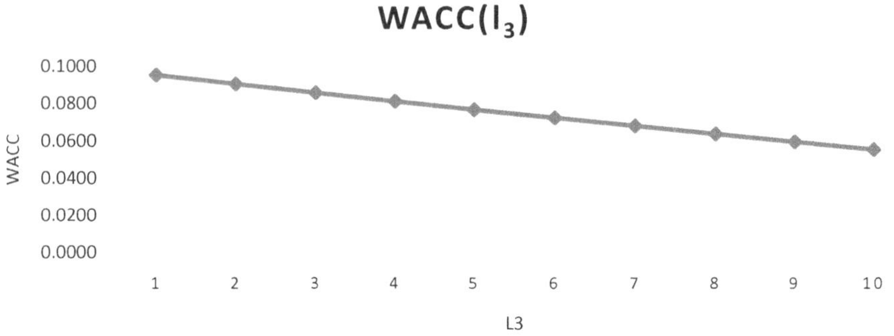

Fig. 8.22 The dependence of company weighted average cost of capital (WACC) on leverage ratio of debt and interests on credit at company age $n = 5$

Curve WACC(l_2) turns out to be different enough from WACC(l_1) and curves WACC(l_3).

8.2 Conclusions

In this chapter, further development of a new approach to rating methodology has been done. We have generalized it for the general case of modern theory of capital structure (Brusov–Filatova–Orekhova (BFO) theory): for companies of arbitrary age. A serious modification of the BFO theory in order to use it in rating procedure is required. It allows us to apply obtained results for real economics, where all companies have finite lifetime, introduce a factor of time into theory, estimate the creditworthiness of companies of arbitrary age (or arbitrary lifetime), introduce discounting of the financial flows, using the correct discount rate, etc. This allows us to use the powerful tools of the BFO theory in the rating. All these create a new base for rating methodologies.

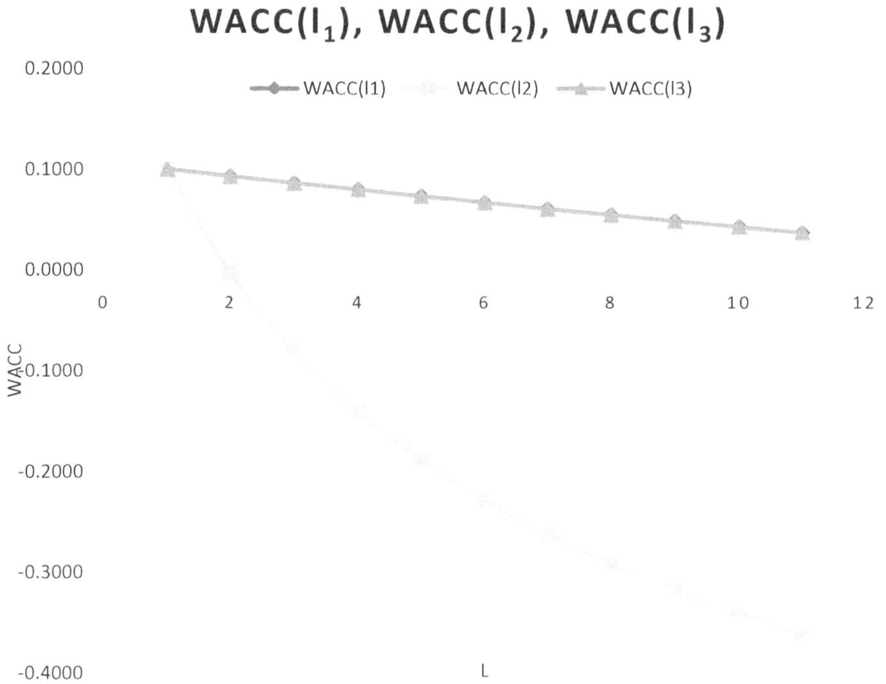

Fig. 8.23 Consolidated data of dependence of WACC on l_1, l_2, l_3, at company age $n = 3$

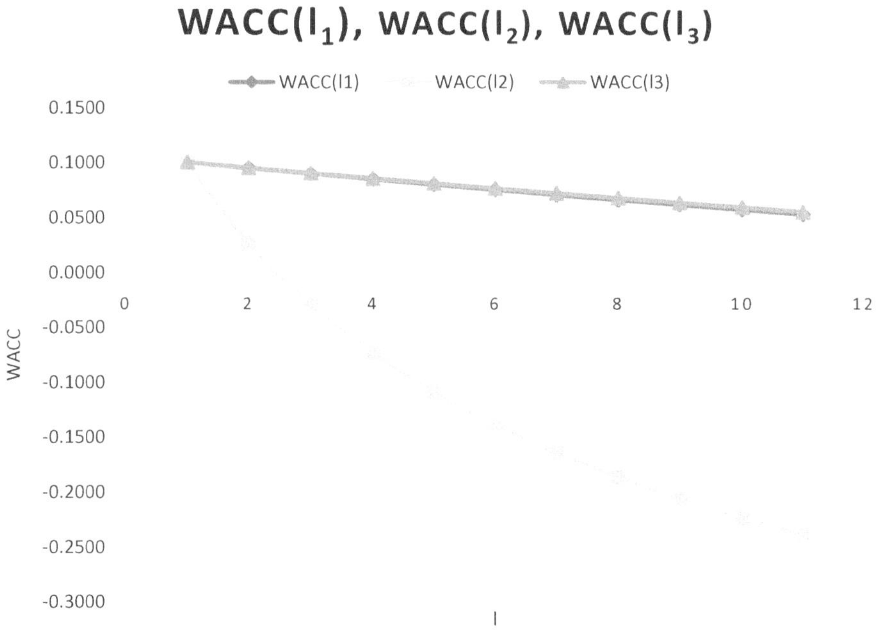

Fig. 8.24 Consolidated data of dependence of WACC on l_1, l_2, l_3, at company age $n = 5$

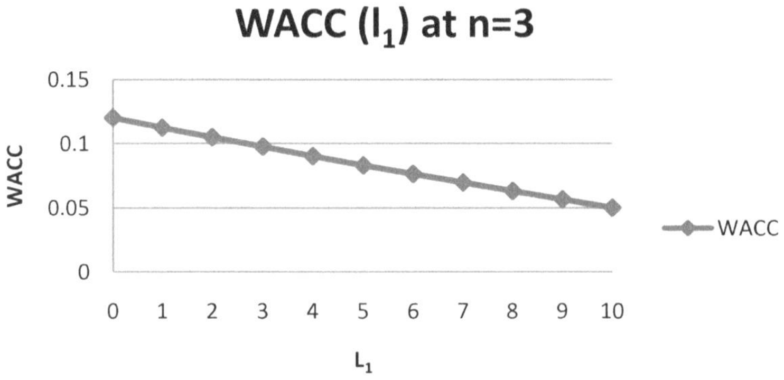

Fig. 8.25 The dependence of company weighted average cost of capital (WACC) on leverage ratio of debt l_1 at company age $n = 3$

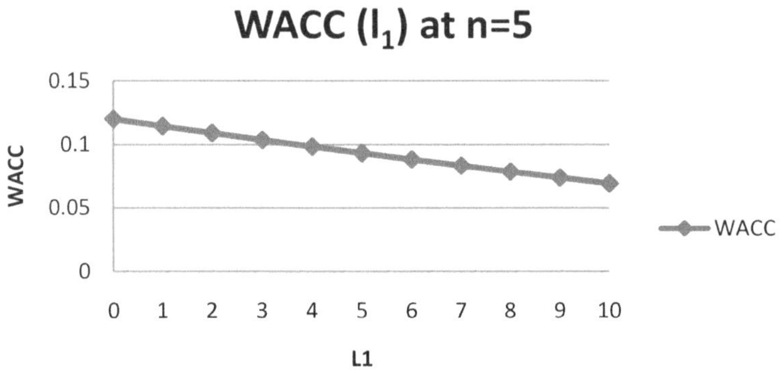

Fig. 8.26 The dependence of company weighted average cost of capital (WACC) on leverage ratio of debt at company age $n = 3$

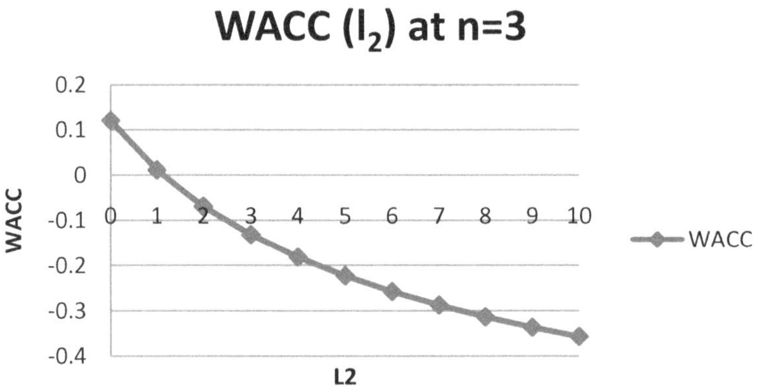

Fig. 8.27 The dependence of company weighted average cost of capital (WACC) on leverage ratio of interests on credit at company age $n = 3$

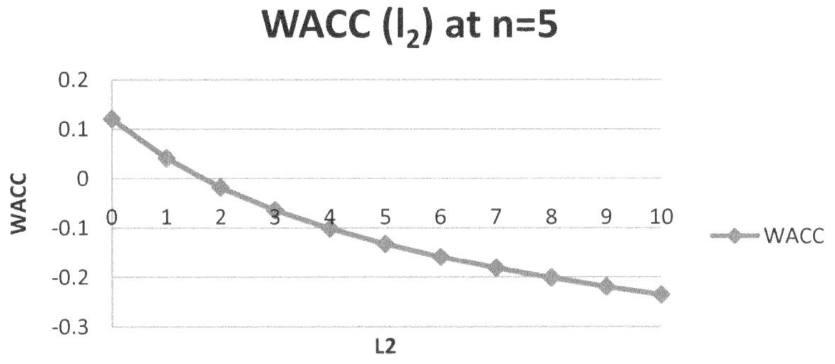

Fig. 8.28 The dependence of company weighted average cost of capital (WACC) on leverage ratio of interests on credit at company age $n = 5$

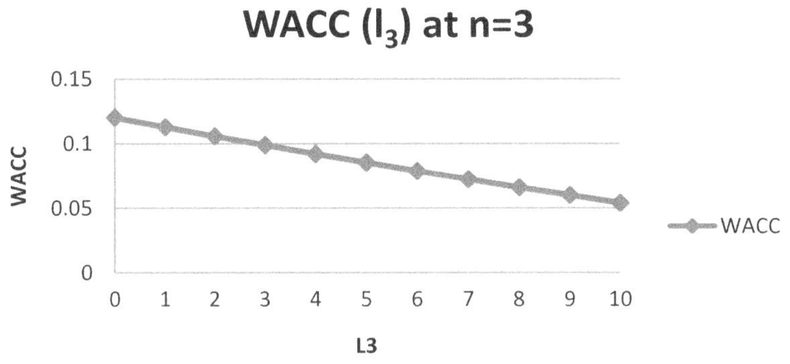

Fig. 8.29 The dependence of company weighted average cost of capital (WACC) on leverage ratio of debt and interests on credit at company age $n = 3$

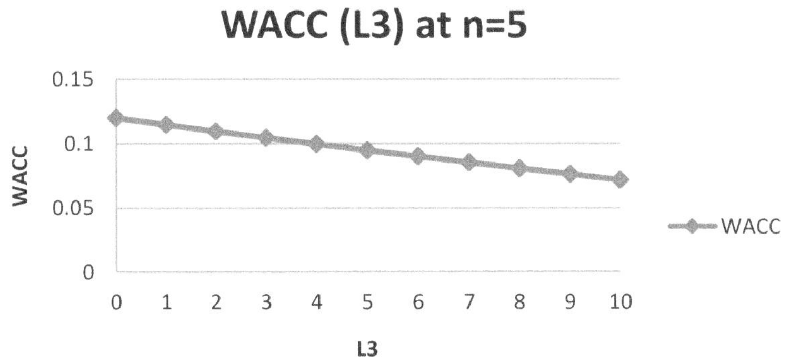

Fig. 8.30 The dependence of company weighted average cost of capital (WACC) on leverage ratio of debt and interests on credit at company age $n = 5$

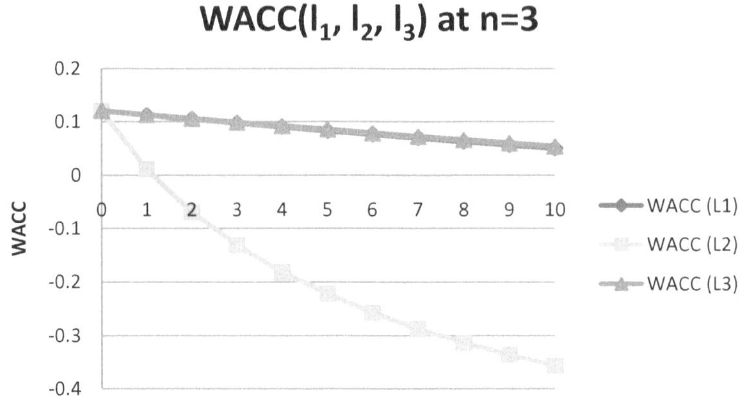

Fig. 8.31 Consolidated data of dependence of WACC on l_1, l_2, l_3, at company age $n = 3$

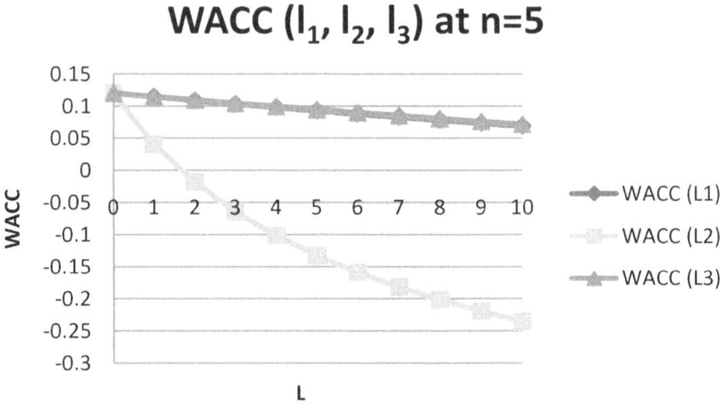

Fig. 8.32 Consolidated data of dependence of WACC on l_1, l_2, l_3, at company age $n = 5$

References

Brusov P (2018a) Editorial: introduction on special issue on the banking system and financial markets of Russia and other countries: problems and prospects. J Rev Glob Econ 7:i–vi, SCOPUS

Brusov P (2018b) Editorial. J Rev Glob Econ 7:i–v, SCOPUS

Brusov PN, Filatova TV (2011) From Modigliani–Miller to general theory of capital cost and capital structure of the company. Finance Credit 435:2–8

Brusov P, Filatova T, Orehova N, Brusova A (2011a) Weighted average cost of capital in the theory of Modigliani–Miller, modified for a finite life–time company. Appl Financ Econ 21(11):815–824

Brusov P, Filatova T, Orehova N et al (2011b) From Modigliani–Miller to general theory of capital cost and capital structure of the company. Res J Econ Bus ICT 2:16–21

Brusov P, Filatova T, Orehova N et al (2011c) Influence of debt financing on the effectiveness of the investment project within the Modigliani–Miller theory. Res J Econ Bus ICT (UK) 2:11–15

Brusov P, Filatova T, Eskindarov M, Orehova N (2012a) Influence of debt financing on the effectiveness of the finite duration investment project. Appl Financ Econ 22(13):1043–1052

Brusov P, Filatova T, Eskindarov M, Orehova N (2012b) Hidden global causes of the global financial crisis. J Rev Global Econ 1:106–111

Brusov P, Filatova P, Orekhova N (2013a) Absence of an optimal capital structure in the famous tradeoff theory! J Rev Global Econ 2:94–116

Brusov P, Filatova T, Orehova N (2013b) A qualitatively new effect in corporative finance: abnormal dependence of cost of equity of company on leverage. J Rev Global Econ 2:183–193

Brusov P, Filatova P, Orekhova N (2014a) Mechanism of formation of the company optimal capital structure, different from suggested by trade off theory. Cogent Econ Finance 2:1–13. https://doi.org/10.1080/23322039.2014.946150

Brusov P, Filatova T, Orehova N (2014b) Inflation in Brusov–Filatova–Orekhova theory and in its perpetuity limit—Modigliani–Miller theory. J Rev Global Econ 3:175–185

Brusov P, Filatova T, Orekhova N, Eskindarov M (2015) Modern corporate finance, investments and taxation, Springer International Publishing, Switzerland, p 373. Monograph, SCOPUS. https://www.springer.com/gp/book/9783319147314

Brusov P, Filatova T, Orekhova N, Eskindarov M (2018a) Modern corporate finance, investments, taxation and ratings, Springer Nature Publishing, Switzerland, p 571. Monograph

Brusov PN, Filatova TV, Orekhova NP, Kulik VL (2018b) Rating: new approach. J Rev Glob Econ 7:37–62. SCOPUS. https://doi.org/10.6000/1929-7092.2018.07.05

Brusov PN, Filatova TV, Orekhova NP, Kulik VL (2018c) A "golden age" of the companies: conditions of its existence. J Rev Glob Econ 7:88–103. SCOPUS. https://doi.org/10.6000/1929-7092.2018.07.07

Brusov PN, Filatova TV, Orekhova NP, Kulik VL (2018d) Rating methodology: new look and new horizons. J Rev Glob Econ 7:63–87. SCOPUS. https://doi.org/10.6000/1929-7092.2018.07.06

Brusov PN, Filatova TV, Orekhova NP, Kulik VL, Weil I (2018e) New meaningful effects in modern capital structure theory. J Rev Glob Econ 7:104–122. SCOPUS. https://doi.org/10.6000/1929-7092.2018.07.08

Brusov P, Filatova T, Orekhova N, Kulik V, Weil I, Brailov A (2018f) The impact of the central bank key rate and commercial banks credit rates on creating and maintaining of a favorable investment climate in the country. J Rev Glob Econ 7:360–376. SCOPUS. https://doi.org/10.6000/1929-7092.2018.07.31

Brusov PN, Filatova TV, Orekhova NP (2018g) Modern corporate finance and investments, monograph. Knorus Publishing House, Moscow, p 517

Brusov PN, Filatova TV, Orekhova NP, Kulik VL, Weil I (2019) Ratings of the investment projects of arbitrary durations: new methodology. J Rev Glob Econ 8:437–448. SCOPUS. https://doi.org/10.6000/1929-7092.2019.08.37

Brusov PN, Filatova TV, Orekhova NP, Kulik VL, Chang S-I, Lin YCG (2020) Modification of the Modigliani–Miller theory for the case of advance payments of tax on profit. J Rev Glob Econ 9:257–268

Brusova A (2011) A comparison of the three methods of estimation of weighted average cost of capital and equity cost of company. Financ Anal Prob Sol 34(76):36–42

Filatova T, Orehova N, Brusova A (2008) Weighted average cost of capital in the theory of Modigliani–Miller, modified for a finite lifetime company. Bull FU 48:68–77

Filatova TV, Brusov PN, Orekhova NP, Kulik VL (2018) Ratings of the long-term projects: new approach. J Rev Glob Econ 7:645–661, SCOPUS. https://doi.org/10.6000/1929-7092.2018.07.59

Modigliani F, Miller M (1958) The cost of capital, corporate finance, and the theory of investment. Am Econ Rev 48:261–297

Modigliani F, Miller M (1963) Corporate income taxes and the cost of capital: a correction. Am Econ Rev 53:147–175
Modigliani F, Miller M (1966) Some estimates of the cost of capital to the electric utility industry 1954–1957. Am Econ Rev 56:333–391
Myers S (2001) Capital structure. J Econ Perspect 15(2):81–102

Part III
Project Ratings

Chapter 9
Investment Models with Debt Repayment at the End of the Project and their Application

In this and the next chapter, we describe the modern investment models, created by the authors and well tested in the real economy. These models are used by us for investigating different problems of investments, such as influence of debt financing, leverage level, taxing, project duration, method of financing, and some other parameters on the efficiency of investments and other problems. But we use them in Chaps. 11–13 for modification of methodology of project ratings. In this chapter, we consider the investment models with debt repayment at the end of the project and their application, while in Chap. 10 we consider the investment models with uniform debt repayment and their application.

9.1 Investment Models

The effectiveness of the investment project is considered from two perspectives: the owners of equity and debt and the equity holders only. For each of these cases, NPV is calculated in two ways: with the division of credit and investment flows (and thus discounting of the payments using two different rates) and without such a division (in this case, both flows are discounted using the same rate, at which WACC can be, obviously, chosen). For each of the four situations, two cases are considered: (1) a constant value of equity S and (2) a constant value of the total invested capital $I = S + D$ (D is value of debt funds).

As it was stated above, the effectiveness of the investment project is considered from two perspectives: the owners of equity and debt and the equity holders only. In the first case, the interest and duty paid by owners of equity (negative flows) returned to the project because they are exactly equal to the flow (positive), obtained by owners of debt capital. The only effect of leverage in this case is the effect of the tax shield, generated from tax relief: interest on the loan is entirely included in the cost

P. Brusov et al., *Ratings*, Contributions to Finance and Accounting,
https://doi.org/10.1007/978-3-030-56243-4_9

and thus reduces the tax base. After-tax flow of capital for each period in this case is equal to

$$\mathrm{NOI}(1-t)+k_{\mathrm{d}}Dt \tag{9.1}$$

and the value of investments at the initial time moment $T = 0$ is equal to $-I = -S - D$.

Here, NOI stands for net operating income (before taxes).

In the second case, investments at the initial time moment $T = 0$ are equal to $-S$ and the flow of capital for the period (in addition to the tax shields $k_{\mathrm{d}}\,Dt$ it includes a payment of interest on a loan $-k_{\mathrm{d}}D$):

$$(\mathrm{NOI}-k_{\mathrm{d}}D)(1-t). \tag{9.2}$$

Here, for simplicity, we suppose that interest on the loan will be paid in equal shares $k_{\mathrm{d}}\,D$ during all periods. Note that principal repayment is made at the end of the last period.

Some variety of repayment of long-term loans will be considered below (see in Chap. 14).

We will consider two different ways of discounting:

1. Operating and financial flows are not separated and both are discounted, using the general rate (at which, obviously, the weighted average cost of capital (WACC) can be selected). In this case for perpetuity projects, the Modigliani–Miller formula (Modigliani and Miller 1958, 1963, 1966) for WACC will be used and for projects of finite (arbitrary) duration Brusov–Filatova–Orekhova formula (Brusov and Filatova 2011; Brusov et al. 2011a, b, c, 2012a, b, 2013a, b, 2014a, b; Filatova et al. 2008; Brusova 2011, Brusov (2018a, b), Brusov et al. (2015, 2018a, b, c, d, e, f, g, 2019, 2020), Filatova et al. (2018a, b)).
2. Operating and financial flows are separated and are discounted at different rates: the operating flow at the rate which is equal to the equity cost k_{e}, depending on leverage, and credit flow at the rate which is equal to the debt cost k_{d}, which until fairly large values of leverage remain constant and start to grow only at high values of leverage L, when there is a danger of bankruptcy.

Note that loan capital is the least risky, because interest on credit is paid after taxes in the first place. Therefore, the cost of credit will always be less than the equity cost, whether of ordinary or of preference shares $k_{\mathrm{e}} > k_{\mathrm{d}}$; $k_{\mathrm{p}} > k_{\mathrm{d}}$. Here k_{e} and k_{p} are the equity cost of ordinary and that of preference shares respectively.

9.2 The Effectiveness of the Investment Project from the Perspective of the Equity Holders Only

9.2.1 With the Division of Credit and Investment Flows

9.2.1.1 Projects of Finite (Arbitrary) Duration

In this case, the expression for NPV has the form

$$\begin{aligned}\mathrm{NPV} &= -S + \sum_{i=1}^{n} \frac{\mathrm{NOI}(1-t)}{(1+k_e)^i} + \sum_{i=1}^{n} \frac{-k_d D(1-t)}{(1+k_d)^i} - \frac{D}{(1+k_d)^n} \\ &= -S + \frac{\mathrm{NOI}(1-t)}{k_e}\left(1 - \frac{1}{(1+k_e)^n}\right) - D(1-t)\left(1 - \frac{1}{(1+k_d)^n}\right) - \frac{D}{(1+k_d)^n}.\end{aligned} \tag{9.3}$$

The last term in the first line, discounted (present) value of credit, extinguished a one-off payment at the end of the last period n.

Below we will look at two cases:

1. A constant value of the invested capital $I = S + D$ (D—debt value).
2. A constant value of equity capital S.

We will start with the first case.

9.2.1.2 At a Constant Value of the Invested Capital (I = const)

In the case of a constant value of the invested capital (I = const), taking into account $D = IL/(1 + L)$, $S = I/(1 + L)$, one gets

$$\begin{aligned}\mathrm{NPV} = &-\frac{I}{1+L}\left[1 + L\left((1-t)\left(1 - \frac{1}{(1+k_d)^n}\right) + \frac{1}{(1+k_d)^n}\right)\right] \\ &+ \frac{\mathrm{NOI}(1-t)}{k_e}\left(1 - \frac{1}{(1+k_e)^n}\right).\end{aligned} \tag{9.4}$$

9.2.1.3 For 1-Year Project

Substituting into Eq. (9.4) $n = 1$, one gets for NPV

$$\mathrm{NPV} = -\frac{I}{1+L}\left[1 + L\left(\frac{1+k_{\mathrm{d}}(1-t)}{(1+k_{\mathrm{d}})}\right)\right] + \frac{\mathrm{NOI}(1-t)}{1+k_{\mathrm{e}}}. \tag{9.5}$$

9.2.1.4 At a Constant Value of Equity Capital (S = const)

Accounting that in the case $S =$ const NOI is proportional to the invested capital, $\mathrm{NOI} = \beta I = \beta S(1 + L)$, we get

$$\mathrm{NPV} = -S\left[1 + L\left((1-t)\left(1 - \frac{1}{(1+k_{\mathrm{d}})^n}\right) + \frac{1}{(1+k_{\mathrm{d}})^n}\right)\right] + \frac{\beta S(1+L)(1-t)}{k_{\mathrm{e}}}\left(1 - \frac{1}{(1+k_{\mathrm{e}})^n}\right). \tag{9.6}$$

9.2.1.5 For 1-Year Project

Substituting into Eq. (9.6) $n = 1$, one gets for NPV

$$\mathrm{NPV} = -S\left(1 + L\left(\frac{1+k_{\mathrm{d}}(1-t)}{1+k_{\mathrm{d}}}\right)\right) + \frac{\beta S(1+L)(1-t)}{1+k_{\mathrm{e}}}. \tag{9.7}$$

9.3 Without Flows Separation

In this case operating and financial flows are not separated and are discounted, using the general rate (at which, obviously, WACC can be selected).

The credit reimbursable at the end of the project (at the end of the period (n)) can be discounted either at the same rate WACC or at the debt cost rate k_{d}. Now we choose a uniform rate and the first option.

$$\begin{aligned}\mathrm{NPV} &= -S + \sum_{i=1}^{n}\frac{\mathrm{NOI}(1-t) - k_{\mathrm{d}}D(1-t)}{(1+\mathrm{WACC})^i} - \frac{D}{(1+\mathrm{WACC})^n}\\ &= -S + \frac{\mathrm{NOI}(1-t) - k_{\mathrm{d}}D(1-t)}{\mathrm{WACC}}\left(1 - \frac{1}{(1+\mathrm{WACC})^n}\right) - \frac{D}{(1+\mathrm{WACC})^n}.\end{aligned} \tag{9.8}$$

At a Constant Value of the Invested Capital (I = const)

In the case of a constant value of the invested capital (I = const), taking into account $D = IL/(1 + L)$, $S = I/(1 + L)$, one gets

$$\text{NPV} = -\frac{I}{1+L}\left[1 + L\frac{k_{\text{d}}(1-t)}{\text{WACC}}\left(1 - \frac{1}{(1+\text{WACC})^n}\right) + \frac{L}{(1+\text{WACC})^n}\right] + \frac{\text{NOI}(1-t)}{\text{WACC}}\left(1 - \frac{1}{(1+\text{WACC})^n}\right). \tag{9.9}$$

For 1-Year Project

Substituting into Eq. (9.9) $n = 1$, one gets for NPV

$$\text{NPV} = -\frac{I}{1+L}\left[1 + L\frac{1 + k_{\text{d}}(1-t)}{1+\text{WACC}}\right] + \frac{\text{NOI}(1-t)}{1+\text{WACC}}. \tag{9.10}$$

At a Constant Value of Equity Capital (S = const)

Accounting that in the case S = const NOI is proportional to the invested capital, I, $\text{NOI} = \beta I = \beta S(1 + L)$, and substituting $D = LS$, we get

$$\text{NPV} = -S + \frac{\text{NOI}(1-t) - k_{\text{d}}D(1-t)}{\text{WACC}}\left(1 - \frac{1}{(1+\text{WACC})^n}\right) - \frac{D}{(1+\text{WACC})^n}, \tag{9.11}$$

$$\text{NPV} = -S\left[1 + \frac{Lk_{\text{d}}(1-t)}{\text{WACC}}\left(1 - \frac{1}{(1+\text{WACC})^n}\right) + \frac{L}{(1+\text{WACC})^n}\right] + \frac{\beta S(1+L)(1-t)}{\text{WACC}}\left(1 - \frac{1}{(1+\text{WACC})^n}\right). \tag{9.12}$$

For 1-Year Project

Substituting into Eq. (9.12) $n = 1$, one gets for NPV

$$\text{NPV} = -S\left[1 + \frac{Lk_{\text{d}}(1-t)}{\text{WACC}}\left(1 - \frac{1}{(1+\text{WACC})^n}\right) + \frac{L}{(1+\text{WACC})^n}\right] + \frac{\beta S(1+L)(1-t)}{\text{WACC}}\left(1 - \frac{1}{(1+\text{WACC})^n}\right).$$

$$\text{NPV} = -S + \frac{\text{NOI}(1-t) - k_{\text{d}}D(1-t) - D}{1+\text{WACC}}. \tag{9.13}$$

Substituting $D = LS$, $\text{NOI} = \beta I = \beta S(1 + L)$, we get

$$\mathrm{NPV} = -S\left[1 + \frac{L(k_{\mathrm{d}}(1-t)-1)}{1+\mathrm{WACC}}\right] + \frac{\beta S(1+L)(1-t)}{1+\mathrm{WACC}}. \tag{9.14}$$

9.4 Modigliani–Miller Limit (Perpetuity Projects)

9.4.1 With Flows Separation

In perpetuity limit (Modigliani–Miller limit) (turning to the limit $n \to \infty$ in the relevant equations), we have

$$\mathrm{NPV} = -S + \frac{\mathrm{NOI}(1-t)}{k_{\mathrm{e}}} - D(1-t). \tag{9.15}$$

9.4.1.1 At a Constant Value of the Invested Capital (I = const)

At a constant value of the invested capital (I = const), accounting $D = IL/(1+L)$, $S = I/(1+L)$, we get

$$\mathrm{NPV} = -\frac{I}{1+L}(1+L(1-t)) + \frac{\mathrm{NOI}(1-t)}{k_{\mathrm{e}}}. \tag{9.16}$$

$$\mathrm{NPV} = -\frac{I}{1+L}(1+L(1-t)) + \frac{\mathrm{NOI}(1-t)}{k_0 + (k_0 - k_{\mathrm{d}})L(1-t)}. \tag{9.17}$$

In order to obtain Eqs. (9.17) from (9.16), we used the Modigliani–Miller formula (Modigliani and Miller 1963) for equity cost k_{e} for perpetuity projects:

$$k_{\mathrm{e}} = k_0 + (k_0 - k_{\mathrm{d}})L(1-t). \tag{9.18}$$

9.4.1.2 At a Constant Value of Equity Capital (S = const)

Accounting $D = LS$, we get in perpetuity limit ($n \to \infty$) (Modigliani–Miller limit)

$$\mathrm{NPV} = -S(1+L(1-t)) + \frac{\beta S(1+L)(1-t)}{k_0 + (k_0 - k_{\mathrm{d}})Lt}. \tag{9.19}$$

9.4.2 *Without Flows Separation*

In perpetuity limit ($n \to \infty$) (Modigliani–Miller limit) (turning to the limit $n \to \infty$ in the relevant equations), we have

$$\mathrm{NPV} = -S + \frac{\mathrm{NOI}(1-t) - k_\mathrm{d} D(1-t)}{\mathrm{WACC}}. \tag{9.20}$$

9.4.2.1 At a Constant Value of the Invested Capital (I = const)

At a constant value of the invested capital (I = const), accounting $D = IL/(1+L)$, $S = I/(1+L)$, we get

$$\begin{aligned}\mathrm{NPV} &= -I \cdot \frac{1}{1+L} + \frac{\mathrm{NOI}(1-t) - I\frac{L}{1+L}k_\mathrm{d}(1-t)}{\mathrm{WACC}} \\ &= -I \cdot \frac{1}{1+L}\left[1 + \frac{Lk_\mathrm{d}(1-t)}{k_0(1-Lt/(1+L))}\right] + \frac{\mathrm{NOI}(1-t)}{k_0(1-Lt/(1+L))}.\end{aligned} \tag{9.21}$$

9.4.2.2 At a Constant Value of Equity Capital (S = const)

$$\mathrm{NPV} = -S + \frac{\mathrm{NOI}(1-t) - k_\mathrm{d} D(1-t)}{\mathrm{WACC}} \tag{9.22}$$

Substituting $D = LS$, we get

$$\begin{aligned}\mathrm{NPV} &= -S\left[1 + \frac{Lk_\mathrm{d}(1-t)}{\mathrm{WACC}}\right] + \frac{\mathrm{NOI}(1-t)}{\mathrm{WACC}} \\ &= -S\left[1 + \frac{Lk_\mathrm{d}(1-t)}{k_0(1-Lt/(1+L))}\right] + \frac{\beta S(1+L)(1-t)}{k_0(1-Lt/(1+L))}.\end{aligned} \tag{9.23}$$

9.5 The Effectiveness of the Investment Project from the Perspective of the Owners of Equity and Debt

9.5.1 *With Flows Separation*

9.5.1.1 Projects of Arbitrary (Finite) Duration

In this case, operating and financial flows are separated and are discounted, using different rates: the operating flow at the rate equal to the equity cost k_e, depending on leverage, and credit flow at the rate equal to the debt cost k_d, which until fairly large values of leverage remain constant and start to grow only at high values of leverage L, when there is a danger of bankruptcy.

$$\begin{aligned}\text{NPV} &= -I + \sum_{i=1}^{n} \frac{\text{NOI}(1-t)}{(1+k_e)^i} + \sum_{i=1}^{n} \frac{k_d D t}{(1+k_d)^i} \\ &= -I + \frac{\text{NOI}(1-t)}{k_e}\left(1 - \frac{1}{(1+k_e)^n}\right) + Dt\left(1 - \frac{1}{(1+k_d)^n}\right).\end{aligned} \tag{9.24}$$

Below we will consider two cases:

1. At a constant value of the invested capital ($I = S + D$ (D is the debt value).
2. At a constant value of equity capital S.

We will start with the first case.

9.5.1.2 At a Constant Value of the Invested Capital (I = const)

At a constant value of the invested capital (I = const), accounting $D = IL/(1 + L)$, $S = I/(1 + L)$, we get

$$\begin{aligned}\text{NPV} &= -I + \frac{\text{NOI}(1-t)}{k_e}\left(1 - \frac{1}{(1+k_e)^n}\right) + \frac{ILt}{1+L}\left(1 - \frac{1}{(1+k_d)^n}\right) \\ &= -I\left[1 - \frac{Lt}{1+L}\left(1 - \frac{1}{(1+k_d)^n}\right)\right] + \frac{\text{NOI}(1-t)}{k_e}\left(1 - \frac{1}{(1+k_e)^n}\right).\end{aligned} \tag{9.25}$$

9.5.1.3 At a Constant Value of Equity Capital (S = const)

Accounting $D = LS$, $I = S(1 + L)$, we get

$$\mathrm{NPV} = -S - LS + \frac{\mathrm{NOI}(1-t)}{k_{\mathrm{e}}}\left(1 - \frac{1}{(1+k_{\mathrm{e}})^n}\right) + Dt\left(1 - \frac{1}{(1+k_{\mathrm{d}})^n}\right). \quad (9.26)$$

Accounting that in the case $S = \text{const}$ NOI is not a constant, but is proportional to the invested capital, $\mathrm{NOI} = \beta I = \beta S(1 + L)$, we get

$$\mathrm{NPV} = -S\left[1 + L - tL\left(1 - \frac{1}{(1+k_{\mathrm{d}})^n}\right)\right] + \frac{\beta S(1+L)(1-t)}{k_{\mathrm{e}}} \times \left(1 - \frac{1}{(1+k_{\mathrm{e}})^n}\right). \quad (9.27)$$

9.5.1.4 For 1-Year Project

$$\mathrm{NPV} = -S\left[1 + L - tL\frac{k_{\mathrm{d}}}{1+k_{\mathrm{d}}}\right] + \frac{\beta S(1+L)(1-t)}{1+k_{\mathrm{e}}}. \quad (9.28)$$

9.5.2 *Without Flows Separation*

In this case, operating and financial flows are not separated and both are discounted, using the general rate (at which, obviously, WACC can be selected):

$$\begin{aligned}\mathrm{NPV} &= -I + \sum_{i=1}^{n} \frac{\mathrm{NOI}(1-t) + k_{\mathrm{d}}Dt}{(1+\mathrm{WACC})^i} \\ &= -I + \frac{\mathrm{NOI}(1-t) + k_{\mathrm{d}}Dt}{\mathrm{WACC}}\left(1 - \frac{1}{(1+\mathrm{WACC})^n}\right).\end{aligned} \quad (9.29)$$

9.5.2.1 At a Constant Value of the Invested Capital (I = const)

At a constant value of the invested capital ($I = \text{const}$), we have

$$\mathrm{NPV} = -I + \frac{\mathrm{NOI}(1-t) + k_{\mathrm{d}}Dt}{\mathrm{WACC}}\left(1 - \frac{1}{(1+\mathrm{WACC})^n}\right).$$

Accounting $D = IL/(1 + L)$, $S = I/(1 + L)$, we get

$$\begin{aligned}\mathrm{NPV}=&-I\left[1-\frac{k_d t\frac{L}{1+L}}{k_0\left(1-\gamma\frac{L}{1+L}t\right)}\left(1-\frac{1}{\left(1+k_0\left(1-\gamma\frac{L}{1+L}t\right)\right)^n}\right)\right]\\&+\frac{\mathrm{NOI}(1-t)}{k_0\left(1-\gamma\frac{L}{1+L}t\right)}\left(1-\frac{1}{\left(1+k_0\left(1-\gamma\frac{L}{1+L}t\right)\right)^n}\right).\end{aligned}\qquad(9.30)$$

9.5.2.2 For 1-Year Project

Substituting into Eq. (9.30) $n=1$, one gets for NPV

$$\mathrm{NPV}=-I\left[1-\frac{k_d t\frac{L}{1+L}}{1+\mathrm{WACC}}\right]+\frac{\mathrm{NOI}(1-t)}{1+\mathrm{WACC}}.\qquad(9.31)$$

9.5.2.3 At a Constant Value of Equity Capital (S = const)

$$\begin{aligned}\mathrm{NPV}&=-I+\frac{\mathrm{NOI}(1-t)+k_d Dt}{\mathrm{WACC}}\left(1-\frac{1}{(1+\mathrm{WACC})^n}\right)\\&=-S\left[1+L-\frac{k_d Lt}{\mathrm{WACC}}\left(1-\frac{1}{(1+\mathrm{WACC})^n}\right)\right]\\&+\frac{\beta S(1+L)(1-t)}{\mathrm{WACC}}\left(1-\frac{1}{(1+\mathrm{WACC})^n}\right).\end{aligned}\qquad(9.32)$$

9.5.2.4 For 1-Year Project

$$\begin{aligned}\mathrm{NPV}&=-I+\frac{\mathrm{NOI}(1-t)+k_d Dt}{1+\mathrm{WACC}}\\&=-S\left[1+L-\frac{k_d Lt}{1+\mathrm{WACC}}\right]+\frac{\mathrm{NOI}(1-t)}{1+\mathrm{WACC}}.\end{aligned}\qquad(9.33)$$

9.6 Modigliani–Miller Limit

9.6.1 With Flows Separation

In perpetuity limit ($n \to \infty$) (Modigliani–Miller limit), we have

$$\mathrm{NPV} = -I + \frac{\mathrm{NOI}(1-t)}{k_e} + Dt. \tag{9.34}$$

At a constant value of the invested capital ($I = \mathrm{const}$), accounting $D = IL/(1+L)$, we have

$$\mathrm{NPV} = -I\left(1 - t\frac{L}{1+L}\right) + \frac{\mathrm{NOI}(1-t)}{k_e}. \tag{9.35}$$

For equity cost k_e and WACC in Modigliani–Miller theory, we have consequently

$$k_e = k_0 + (k_0 - k_d)L(1-t), \tag{9.36}$$

$$\mathrm{WACC} = k_0(1 - w_d t) = k_0(1 - Lt/(1+L)). \tag{9.37}$$

Substituting Eq. (9.36) into (9.37), we get

$$\mathrm{NPV} = -I\left(1 - t\frac{L}{1+L}\right) + \frac{\mathrm{NOI}(1-t)}{k_0 + (k_0 - k_d)L(1-t)}. \tag{9.38}$$

9.6.1.1 At a Constant Value of Equity Capital (S = const)

Accounting $D = LS$, $I = S(1+L)$, in perpetuity limit ($n \to \infty$) (Modigliani–Miller limit), we have

$$\mathrm{NPV} = -S(1 + L(1-t)) + \frac{\mathrm{NOI}(1-t)}{k_0 + (k_0 - k_d)Lt}. \tag{9.39}$$

Note that in the case $S = \mathrm{const}$ NOI is not a constant, but is proportional to the invested capital, $\mathrm{NOI} = \beta I = \beta S(1+L)$.

In this case, Eq. (9.38) is replaced by

$$\mathrm{NPV} = -S(1 + L(1-t)) + \frac{\beta S(1+L)(1-t)}{k_0 + (k_0 - k_d)Lt}, \tag{9.40}$$

9.6.2 *Without Flows Separation*

In perpetuity limit ($n \to \infty$) (Modigliani–Miller limit), we have

$$\mathrm{NPV} = -I + \frac{\mathrm{NOI}(1-t) + k_{\mathrm{d}}Dt}{\mathrm{WACC}}. \tag{9.41}$$

At a constant value of the invested capital ($I = \mathrm{const}$), we have

$$\begin{aligned} \mathrm{NPV} &= -I + \frac{\mathrm{NOI}(1-t) + k_{\mathrm{d}}Dt}{\mathrm{WACC}} \\ &= -I\left(1 - \frac{k_{\mathrm{d}}t\frac{L}{1+L}}{k_0\left(1 - \frac{L}{1+L}t\right)}\right) + \frac{\mathrm{NOI}(1-t)}{k_0\left(1 - \frac{L}{1+L}t\right)}. \end{aligned} \tag{9.42}$$

9.6.2.1 At a Constant Value of Equity Capital (S = const)

In perpetuity limit ($n \to \infty$) (Modigliani–Miller limit), we have

$$\mathrm{NPV} = -S\left[1 + L - \frac{k_{\mathrm{d}}Lt}{\mathrm{WACC}}\right] + \frac{\mathrm{NOI}(1-t)}{\mathrm{WACC}}. \tag{9.43}$$

$$\mathrm{NPV} = -S\left[1 + L - \frac{k_{\mathrm{d}}Lt}{k_0\left(1 - \frac{L}{1+L}t\right)}\right] + \frac{\beta S(1+L)(1-t)}{k_0\left(1 - \frac{L}{1+L}t\right)}. \tag{9.44}$$

References

Brusov P (2018a) Editorial: introduction on special issue on the banking system and financial markets of Russia and other countries: problems and prospects. J Rev Glob Econ 7:1–6. SCOPUS

Brusov P (2018b) Editorial. J Rev Glob Econ 7:1–5. SCOPUS

Brusov PN, Filatova TV (2011) From Modigliani–Miller to general theory of capital cost and capital structure of the company. Finance Credit 435:2–8

Brusov P, Filatova T, Orehova N, Brusova A (2011a) Weighted average cost of capital in the theory of Modigliani–Miller, modified for a finite life-time company. Appl Financ Econ 21(11):815–824

Brusov P, Filatova T, Orehova N et al (2011b) From Modigliani–Miller to general theory of capital cost and capital structure of the company. Res J Econ Bus ICT 2:16–21

Brusov P, Filatova T, Orehova N et al (2011c) Influence of debt financing on the effectiveness of the investment project within the Modigliani–Miller theory. Res J Econ Bus ICT (UK) 2:11–15

Brusov P, Filatova T, Eskindarov M, Orehova N (2012a) Influence of debt financing on the effectiveness of the finite duration investment project. Appl Financ Econ 22(13):1043–1052
Brusov P, Filatova T, Eskindarov M, Orehova N (2012b) Hidden global causes of the global financial crisis. J Rev Global Econ 1:106–111
Brusov P, Filatova P, Orekhova N (2013a) Absence of an optimal capital structure in the famous tradeoff theory! J Rev Global Econ 2:94–116
Brusov P, Filatova T, Orehova N (2013b) A qualitatively new effect in corporative finance: abnormal dependence of cost of equity of company on leverage. J Rev Global Econ 2:183–193
Brusov P, Filatova P, Orekhova N (2014a) Mechanism of formation of the company optimal capital structure, different from suggested by trade off theory. Cogent Econ Finance 2:1–13. https://doi.org/10.1080/23322039.2014.946150
Brusov P, Filatova T, Orehova N (2014b) Inflation in Brusov–Filatova–Orekhova theory and in its perpetuity limit—Modigliani–Miller theory. J Rev Global Econ 3:175–185
Brusov P, Filatova T, Orekhova N, Eskindarov M (2015) Modern corporate finance, investments and taxation. Springer International Publishing, Berlin, p 373. monograph, SCOPUS, https://www.springer.com/gp/book/9783319147314
Brusov P, Filatova T, Orekhova N, Eskindarov M (2018a) Modern corporate finance, investments, taxation and ratings. Springer Nature Publishing, Berlin, p 571, monograph
Brusov PN, Filatova TV, Orekhova NP, Kulik VL (2018b) Rating: new approach. J Rev Glob Econ 7:37–62. SCOPUS. https://doi.org/10.6000/1929-7092.2018.07.05
Brusov PN, Filatova TV, Orekhova NP, Kulik VL (2018c) A "golden age" of the companies: conditions of its existence. J Rev Glob Econ 7:88–103. SCOPUS. https://doi.org/10.6000/1929-7092.2018.07.07
Brusov PN, Filatova TV, Orekhova NP, Kulik VL (2018d) Rating methodology: new look and new horizons. J Rev Glob Econ 7:63–87. SCOPUS. https://doi.org/10.6000/1929-7092.2018.07.06
Brusov PN, Filatova TV, Orekhova NP, Kulik VL, Weil I (2018e) New meaningful effects in modern capital structure theory. J Rev Glob Econ 7:104–122. SCOPUS. https://doi.org/10.6000/1929-7092.2018.07.08
Brusov P, Filatova T, Orekhova N, Kulik V, Weil I, Brailov A (2018f) The impact of the central bank key rate and commercial banks credit rates on creating and maintaining of a favorable investment climate in the country. J Rev Glob Econ 7:360–376. SCOPUS. https://doi.org/10.6000/1929-7092.2018.07.31
Brusov PN, Filatova TV, Orekhova NP (2018g) Modern corporate finance and investments, monograph. Knorus Publishing House, Moscow, p 517
Brusov PN, Filatova TV, Orekhova NP, Kulik VL, Weil I (2019) Ratings of the investment projects of arbitrary durations: new methodology. J Rev Glob Econ 8:437–448. SCOPUS. https://doi.org/10.6000/1929-7092.2019.08.37
Brusov PN, Filatova TV, Orekhova NP, Kulik VL, Chang S-I, Lin YCG (2020) Modification of the Modigliani–Miller theory for the case of advance payments of tax on profit. J Rev Glob Econ 9:257–268
Brusova A (2011) A comparison of the three methods of estimation of weighted average cost of capital and equity cost of company. Financ Anal Prob Sol 34(76):36–42
Filatova T, Orekhova N, Brusova A (2008) Weighted average cost of capital in the theory of Modigliani–Miller, modified for a finite life–time company. Bull FU 48:68–77
Filatova TV, Brusov PN, Orekhova NP, Kulik VL (2018a) Ratings of the long-term projects: new approach. J Rev Glob Econ. SCOPUS 7:645–661. https://doi.org/10.6000/1929-7092.2018.07.59
Filatova TV, Brusov PN, Orekhova NP, Kulik VL (2018b) Ratings of the long-term projects: new approach. J Rev Glob Econ 7:645–661., SCOPUS. https://doi.org/10.6000/1929-7092.2018.07.59
Modigliani F, Miller M (1966) Some estimates of the cost of capital to the electric utility industry 1954–1957. Am Econ Rev 56:333–391
Modigliani F, Miller M (1958) The cost of capital, corporate finance, and the theory of investment. Am Econ Rev 48:261–297
Modigliani F, Miller M (1963) Corporate income taxes and the cost of capital: a correction. Am Econ Rev 53:147–175

Chapter 10
Investment Models with Uniform Debt Repayment and Their Application

In previous chapters, we have established investment models with debt repayment at the end of the project, well proven in the analysis of real investment projects. In practice, however, a scheme of uniform debt repayment during the duration of the project is more extended. In this chapter, we describe new investment models with uniform debt repayment during the duration of the investment project, quite adequately describing real investment projects. Within these models, it is possible, in particular, to analyze the dependence of effectiveness of investment projects on debt financing and taxation. We will work on the modern theory of capital cost and capital structure developed by Brusov–Filatova–Orekhova as well as on perpetuity limit (Modigliani and Miller 1958, 1963, 1966).

In Chap. 13, we consider the application of the investment models with uniform debt repayment to rating methodology.

10.1 Investment Models with Uniform Debt Repayment

As in the case of debt repayment at the end of the project, the effectiveness of the investment project is considered from two perspectives: the owners of equity and debt and the equity holders only. In the first case, the interest and duty paid by owners of equity (negative flows) returned to the project because they are exactly equal to the flow (positive), obtained by owners of debt capital. The only effect of leverage in this case is the effect of tax shield, generated from tax relief: interest on the loan is entirely included in the net cost and, thus, reduces the tax base. For each of these cases, NPV is calculated in two ways: with the division of credit and investment flows (and thus discounting the payments, using two different rates) and without such a division (in this case, both flows are discounted at the same rate at which, obviously, WACC can be chosen). For each of the four situations, two cases

P. Brusov et al., *Ratings*, Contributions to Finance and Accounting,
https://doi.org/10.1007/978-3-030-56243-4_10

Table 10.1 The sequence of debt and interest values and credit values

Period number	1	2	3	...	n
Debt	D	$D \cdot \frac{n-1}{n}$	$D \cdot \frac{n-2}{n}$	...	$D \cdot \frac{1}{n}$
Interest	$k_d D$	$k_d D \cdot \frac{n-1}{n}$	$k_d D \cdot \frac{n-2}{n}$	...	$k_d D \cdot \frac{1}{n}$

are considered: (1) a constant value of equity S and (2) a constant value of the total invested capital $I = S + D$ (D is value of debt funds).

The main debt repayment occurs evenly (by equal parts) at the end of each period, and the remaining debt at the end of each period is an arithmetic progression with the difference $-D/n$

$$\left\{D, D - \frac{D}{n}, D - \frac{2D}{n}, \ldots, \frac{D}{n}\right\} = \left\{D, D\left(\frac{n-1}{n}\right), D\left(\frac{n-2}{n}\right), \ldots, \frac{D}{n}\right\} \tag{10.1}$$

Interest constitutes a sequence:

$$\left\{k_d D, k_d D\left(\frac{n-1}{n}\right), k_d D\left(\frac{n-2}{n}\right), \ldots, k_d \frac{D}{n}\right\}. \tag{10.2}$$

In the case of consideration from the point of view of equity owners and debt owners, the after-tax flow of capital for each period is equal to

$$\mathrm{NOI}(1 - t) + k_d D_i t, \tag{10.3}$$

where

$$D_i = D\frac{n - (i - 1)}{n}, \tag{10.4}$$

and investments at time moment $T = 0$ are equal to $-I = -S - D$. Here NOI stands for net operating income (before tax).

In the second case (from the point of view of equity owners only), investments at the initial moment $T = 0$ are equal to $-S$, and the flow of capital for the ith period (apart from tax shields $k_d Dt$ it includes payment of interest on the loan $-k_d D_i$) is equal to

$$(\mathrm{NOI} - k_d D_i)(1 - t) - \frac{D_i}{n}. \tag{10.5}$$

We suppose that the interest on the loan and the loans itself are paid in tranches $k_d Di$ and $D \cdot \frac{n-i}{n}$ consequently during all the ith periods. We cite in Table 10.1 the sequence of debt and interest values and credit values.

As in the case of debt repayment at the end of the project, we will consider two different ways of discounting:

1. Operating and financial flows are not separated and both are discounted, using the general rate (at which, obviously, the weighted average cost of capital (WACC) can be selected). For perpetuity projects, the Modigliani–Miller formula (Modigliani and Miller 1963) for WACC will be used and for projects of finite duration Brusov–Filatova–Orekhova formula for WACC (Brusov and Filatova 2011; Brusov et al. 2011a, b, c, 2012a, b, 2013a, b, 2014a, b; Filatova et al. 2008).
2. Operating and financial flows are separated and are discounted at different rates: the operating flow at the rate equal to the equity cost k_e, depending on leverage, and credit flow at the rate equal to the debt cost k_d, which until fairly large values of leverage remain constant and start to grow only at high values of leverage L, when there is a danger of bankruptcy.

Note once again that loan capital is the least risky, because interest on credit is paid after tax in the first place. Therefore, the cost of credit will always be less than the equity cost, whether of ordinary or of preference shares $k_e > k_d$; $k_p > k_d$. Here k_e and k_p are equity cost of ordinary or that of preference shares consequently.

One can show that the present value of interest can be calculated by using the following formula, which we have been able to derive:

$$\frac{1}{a}+\frac{2}{a^2}+\frac{3}{a^3}+\cdots+\frac{n}{a^n}=\frac{a(1-a^{-n})}{(a-1)^2}-\frac{n}{(a-1)a^n}. \tag{10.6}$$

Here $a = 1 + i$.

We will use this formula in the further calculations.

10.2 The Effectiveness of the Investment Project from the Perspective of the Equity Holders Only

10.2.1 With the Division of Credit and Investment Flows

To obtain an expression for NPV, the discounted flow values for one period, given by formulas (Eq. 10.3) and (Eq. 10.5), must be summed, using our obtained formula (Eq. 10.6), in which $a = 1 + i$, where i is the discount rate. Its accurate assessment is one of the most important advantages of BFO theory (Brusov–Filatova–Orekhova) (Brusov and Filatova 2011; Brusov et al. 2011a, b, c, 2012a, b, 2013a, b, 2014a, b; Filatova et al. 2008) over its perpetuity limit—Modigliani–Miller theory (Modigliani and Miller 1958, 1963, 1966).

In this case, the expression for NPV has the form

$$\begin{aligned}\mathrm{NPV} &= -S + \sum_{i=1}^{n} \frac{\mathrm{NOI}(1-t)}{(1+k_{\mathrm{e}})^{i}} + \sum_{i=1}^{n} \frac{-k_{\mathrm{d}} D \frac{n+1-i}{n}(1-t) - \frac{D}{n}}{(1+k_{\mathrm{d}})^{i}} \\ &= -S + \frac{\mathrm{NOI}(1-t)(1-(1+k_{\mathrm{e}})^{-n})}{k_{\mathrm{e}}} \\ &\quad - \left(\frac{D}{n} + k_{\mathrm{d}} D \frac{n+1}{n}(1-t)\right) \frac{1-(1+k_{\mathrm{d}})^{-n}}{k_{\mathrm{d}}} \\ &\quad + k_{\mathrm{d}} \frac{D}{n}(1-t) \left\{ \frac{(1+k_{\mathrm{d}})[1-(1+k_{\mathrm{d}})^{-n}]}{k_{\mathrm{d}}^{2}} - \frac{n}{k_{\mathrm{d}}(1+k_{\mathrm{d}})^{n}} \right\}\end{aligned} \tag{10.7}$$

In perpetuity limit (let us call it Modigliani–Miller limit), one has

$$\mathrm{NPV} = -S + \frac{\mathrm{NOI}(1-t)}{k_{\mathrm{e}}} - D(1-t). \tag{10.8}$$

10.2.2 Without Flows Separation

In this case, operating and financial flows are not separated and are discounted, using the general rate (at which, obviously, WACC can be selected).

The main debt repayment, which occurs evenly (by equal parts) at the end of each period, can be discounted either at the same rate WACC or at the debt cost rate k_{d}. Now we choose a uniform rate and the first option.

We still consider the effectiveness of the investment project from the perspective of the equity holders only.

$$\begin{aligned}NPV &= -S + \sum_{i=1}^{n} \frac{NOI(1-t) - k_d D \frac{n+1-i}{n}(1-t) - \frac{D}{n}}{(1+WACC)^{i}} = \\ &= -S + \frac{NOI(1-t) - \frac{D}{n} - k_d D \frac{n+1}{n}(1-t)}{WACC} \cdot \\ &\quad \cdot \left(1 - \frac{1}{(1+WACC)^{n}}\right) + \\ &\quad + \frac{k_d D}{n}(1-t) \left\{ \frac{(1+WACC)[1-(1+WACC)^{-n}]}{WACC^{2}} - \right. \\ &\quad \left. - \frac{n}{WACC(1+WACC)^{n}} \right\}\end{aligned} \tag{10.9}$$

In perpetuity limit (Modigliani–Miller limit) (turning to the limit $n \to \infty$ in the relevant equations), we have

$$\mathrm{NPV} = -S + \frac{\mathrm{NOI}(1-t) - k_{\mathrm{d}}D(1-t)}{\mathrm{WACC}}. \tag{10.10}$$

Note that formula (10.10) as well as other formulas for perpetuity limit (10.12) and (10.14) could be applied for analyzing the effectiveness of the long-term investment projects.

10.3 The Effectiveness of the Investment Project from the Perspective of the Owners of Equity and Debt

10.3.1 With Flows Separation

Projects of Arbitrary (Finite) Duration

In the case of consideration from the perspective of the owners of equity and debt

$$\begin{aligned}
\mathrm{NPV} &= -I + \sum_{i=1}^{n} \frac{\mathrm{NOI}(1-t)}{(1+k_{\mathrm{e}})^{i}} + \sum_{i=1}^{n} \frac{k_{\mathrm{d}} D \frac{n+1-i}{n} t}{(1+k_{\mathrm{d}})^{i}} \\
&= -I + \frac{\mathrm{NOI}(1-t)(1-(1+k_{\mathrm{e}})^{-n})}{k_{\mathrm{e}}} \\
&\quad + D\frac{n+1}{n} t \cdot [1-(1+k_{\mathrm{d}})^{-n}] \\
&\quad - k_{\mathrm{d}} \frac{D}{n} t \left\{ \frac{(1+k_{\mathrm{d}})[1-(1+k_{\mathrm{d}})^{-n}]}{k_{\mathrm{d}}^{2}} - \frac{n}{k_{\mathrm{d}}(1+k_{\mathrm{d}})^{n}} \right\}
\end{aligned} \tag{10.11}$$

In perpetuity limit (Modigliani–Miller limit) (turning to the limit $n \to \infty$ in the relevant equations), we have

$$\mathrm{NOI} = -I + \frac{\mathrm{NOI}(1-t)}{k_{\mathrm{e}}} + Dt. \tag{10.12}$$

10.3.2 Without Flows Separation

We still consider the effectiveness of the investment project from the perspective of the owners of equity and debt.

$$\begin{aligned}\mathrm{NPV} &= -I+\sum_{i=1}^{n}\frac{\mathrm{NOI}(1-t)+k_{\mathrm{d}}D\frac{n+1-i}{n}t}{(1+\mathrm{WACC})^{i}}\\ &= -I+\frac{\mathrm{NOI}(1-t)+k_{\mathrm{d}}D\frac{n+1}{n}t}{\mathrm{WACC}}\left(1-\frac{1}{(1+\mathrm{WACC})^{n}}\right)\\ &\quad -\frac{k_{\mathrm{d}}D}{n}t\left\{\frac{(1+\mathrm{WACC})\left[1-(1+\mathrm{WACC})^{-n}\right]}{\mathrm{WACC}^{2}}-\frac{n}{\mathrm{WACC}(1+\mathrm{WACC})^{n}}\right\}\end{aligned} \tag{10.13}$$

In perpetuity limit (Modigliani–Miller limit) (turning to the limit $n \to \infty$ in the relevant equations), we have

$$\mathrm{NPV} = -I + \frac{\mathrm{NOI}(1-t) + k_{\mathrm{d}}Dt}{\mathrm{WACC}}. \tag{10.14}$$

10.4 Example of the Application of the Derived Formulas

As an example of application of the obtained formulas, let us take a look at the dependence of the NPV of project on the leverage level at three values of the tax on profit rates in the case of consideration from the perspective of the equity holders only without flows separation on operating and finance ones.

We use formula (Eq. 10.10) and the next parameters values

$$\mathrm{NOI} = 800;\ \ S = 500;\ \ k_0 = 22\ \%;\ \ k_{\mathrm{d}} = 19\ \%;\ \ T = 15\ \%;\ \ 20\%;\ \ 25\ \%.$$

Making the calculations in Excel, we get the data, which are shown in Fig. 10.1.

From the calculations and Fig. 10.1, one can make the following conclusions:

1. With growth of the tax on profit rate, the NPV of the project decreases and our model makes it possible to estimate the percent of decrease of NPV with the growth of tax on profit rate, for example, 1%.

   It should be noted that the possibility of such evaluations is unique.
2. The effect of taxation on the NPV significantly depends on the leverage level:

   With its increase, the impact of changing of tax on profit rate is greatly reduced. This is valid for increasing the tax on profit rate and for its reduction.
3. At tax on profit rates 20% (as in Russia) and 25%, there is an optimum in NPV dependence on leverage. Investors should take into account the invested capital structure: in this case, they may, without special effort (only changing this structure), obtain (sometimes very substantial) gains in NPV. Note that at tax

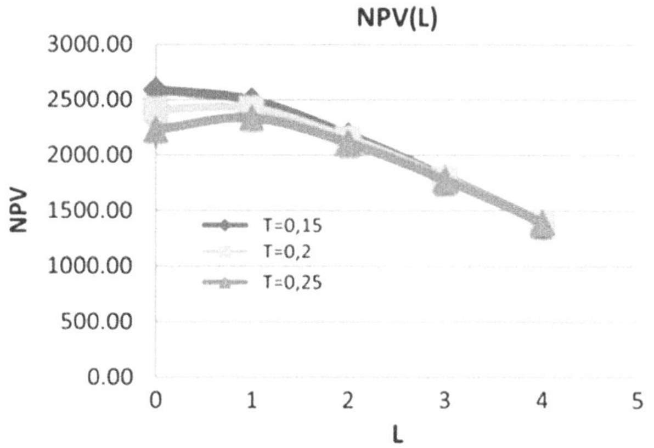

Fig. 10.1 Dependence of NPV of the project on the leverage level at three values of the tax on profit rates NOI = 800; $S = 500$; $k_0 = 22\ \%$; $k_d = 19\ \%$; $T = 15\ \%$; $20\ \%$; $25\ \%$

on profit rate 15%, there is no optimum in NPV dependence on leverage: NPV descends monotonically with leverage.

10.5 Conclusions

New investment models with uniform debt repayment during the duration of the project, quite adequately describing real investment projects, are described. Within these models, it is possible, in particular, to analyze the dependence of effectiveness of investment projects on debt financing and taxation. We work on the modern theory of capital cost and capital structure developed by Brusov–Filatova–Orekhova as well as on perpetuity limit—Modigliani-Miller (MM theory) (Brusov 2018a, b; Brusov et al. 2015, 2018a, b, c, d, e, f, g, 2019, 2020; Filatova et al. 2018).

As in the case of debt repayment at the end of the project, the effectiveness of the investment project is considered from two perspectives: the owners of equity and debt and the equity holders only. For each of these cases, NPV is calculated in two ways: with the division of credit and investment flows (and thus discounting the payments, using two different rates) and without such a division (in this case, both flows are discounted at the same rate at which, obviously, WACC can be chosen). For each of the four situations, two cases are considered: (1) a constant value of equity S and (2) a constant value of the total invested capital $I = S + D$ (D is value of debt funds).

As an example of application of the obtained formulas, the dependence of the NPV of project on the leverage level at three values of the tax on profit rate has been investigated in the case of consideration from the perspective of the equity holders only and without flows separation on operating and financial ones. It has been shown that the effect of taxation on the NPV significantly depends on the leverage level: with its increase, the impact of changing of tax on profit rates is greatly reduced. This is valid for increasing the tax on profit rate and for its reduction. The model allows us to investigate the dependence of effectiveness of the investment project on leverage level, on the tax on profit rate, on credit rate, on equity cost, etc.

References

Brusov PN, Filatova TV (2011) From Modigliani–Miller to general theory of capital cost and capital structure of the company. Finance Credit 435:2–8

Brusov P, Filatova T, Orehova N, Brusova A (2011a) Weighted average cost of capital in the theory of Modigliani–Miller, modified for a finite life–time company. Appl Financ Econ 21(11):815–824

Brusov P, Filatova T, Orehova N et al (2011b) From Modigliani–Miller to general theory of capital cost and capital structure of the company. Res J Econ Bus ICT 2:16–21

Brusov P, Filatova T, Orehova N et al (2011c) Influence of debt financing on the effectiveness of the investment project within the Modigliani–Miller theory. Res J Econ Bus ICT (UK) 2:11–15

Brusov P, Filatova T, Eskindarov M, Orehova N (2012a) Influence of debt financing on the effectiveness of the finite duration investment project. Appl Financ Econ 22(13):1043–1052

Brusov P, Filatova T, Eskindarov M, Orehova N (2012b) Hidden global causes of the global financial crisis. J Rev Global Econ 1:106–111

Brusov P, Filatova P, Orekhova N (2013a) Absence of an optimal capital structure in the famous tradeoff theory! J Rev Global Econ 2:94–116

Brusov P, Filatova T, Orehova N (2013b) A qualitatively new effect in corporative finance: abnormal dependence of cost of equity of company on leverage. J Rev Global Econ 2:183–193

Brusov P, Filatova P, Orekhova N (2014a) Mechanism of formation of the company optimal capital structure, different from suggested by trade off theory. Cogent Econ Finance 2:1–13. https://doi.org/10.1080/23322039.2014.946150

Brusov P, Filatova T, Orehova N (2014b) Inflation in Brusov–Filatova–Orekhova theory and in its perpetuity limit—Modigliani–Miller theory. J Rev Global Econ 3:175–185

Brusov P (2018a) Editorial. Introduction on special issue on the banking system and financial markets of Russia and other countries: problems and prospects. J Rev Global Econ 7:i–vi

Brusov P (2018b) Editorial. J Rev Global Econ 7:i–v

Brusov P, Filatova T, Orekhova N, Eskindarov M (2015) Modern corporate finance, investments and taxation. Springer International Publishing, Cham, 373p. https://www.springer.com/gp/book/9783319147314

Brusov PN, Filatova TV, Orekhova NP, Kulik VL, Weil I (2018a) New meaningful effects in modern capital structure theory. J Rev Global Econ 7:104–122. https://doi.org/10.6000/1929-7092.2018.07.08

Brusov P, Filatova T, Orekhova N, Kulik V, Weil I, Brailov A (2018b) The impact of the central bank key rate and commercial banks credit rates on creating and maintaining of a favorable investment climate in the country. J Rev Global Econ 7:360–376. https://doi.org/10.6000/1929-7092.2018.07.31

Brusov P, Filatova T, Orekhova N, Eskindarov M (2018c) Modern corporate finance, investments, taxation and ratings. Springer Nature Publishing, Cham, 571p

Brusov PN, Filatova TV, Orekhova NP, Kulik VL (2018d) Rating: new approach. J Rev Global Econ 7:37–62. https://doi.org/10.6000/1929-7092.2018.07.05

Brusov PN, Filatova TV, Orekhova NP, Kulik VL (2018e) A "golden age" of the companies: conditions of its existence. J Rev Global Econ 7:88–103. https://doi.org/10.6000/1929-7092.2018.07.07

Brusov PN, Filatova TV, Orekhova NP, Kulik VL (2018f) Rating methodology: new look and new horizons. J Rev Global Econ 7:63–87. https://doi.org/10.6000/1929-7092.2018.07.06

Brusov PN, Filatova TV, Orekhova NP (2018g) Modern corporate finance and investments, monograph. Knorus Publishing House, Moscow, 517p

Brusov PN, Filatova TV, Orekhova NP, Kulik VL, Weil I (2019) Ratings of the investment projects of arbitrary durations: new methodology. J Rev Global Econ 8:437–448. https://doi.org/10.6000/1929-7092.2019.08.37

Brusov PN, Filatova TV, Orekhova NP, Kulik VL, Chang S-I, Lin YCG (2020) Modification of the Modigliani–Miller theory for the case of advance payments of tax on profit. J Rev Global Econ 9:257–268

Filatova T, Orehova N, Brusova A (2008) Weighted average cost of capital in the theory of Modigliani–Miller, modified for a finite life-time company. Bull FU 48:68–77

Filatova TV, Brusov PN, Orekhova NP, Kulik VL (2018) Ratings of the long-term projects: new approach. J Rev Global Econ 7:645–661. https://doi.org/10.6000/1929-7092.2018.07.59

Modigliani F, Miller M (1958) The cost of capital, corporate finance, and the theory of investment. Am Econ Rev 48:261–297

Modigliani F, Miller M (1963) Corporate income taxes and the cost of capital: a correction. Am Econ Rev 53:147–175

Modigliani F, Miller M (1966) Some estimates of the cost of capital to the electric utility industry 1954–1957. Am Econ Rev 56:333–391

Chapter 11
A New Approach to Ratings of the Long-Term Projects

Rating agencies play a very important role in economics. Their analysis of issuer's state and generated credit ratings of issuers help investors make reasonable investment decision, as well as help issuers with good enough ratings get credits on lower rates.

The chapter continues to create a new approach to rating methodology: in addition to two papers, which have considered the creditworthiness of the non-finance issuers (Brusov et al. 2018c, d), we develop the new approach to project rating. We work within investment models, created by authors. One of them describes the effectiveness of investment project from the perspective of equity capital owners, while the other model describes the effectiveness of investment project from the perspective of equity capital and debt capital owners (Brusov 2018a, b); Brusov et al. (2015, 2018a, b, e, f, g, 2019, 2020); Filatova et al. (2018).

The important features of current consideration as well as in previous studies are (1) the adequate use of discounting of financial flows virtually not used in existing rating methodologies and (2) the incorporation of rating parameters (financial "ratios"), used in project rating, into considered modern investment models.

Analyzing within these investment models with incorporated rating parameters the dependence of NPV on rating parameters (financial "ratios") at different values of equity cost k_0, at different values of credit rates k_d, as well as at different values of leverage level L, we come to a very important conclusion that NPV (in units of NOI) (NPV/NOI) (as well as NPV (in units of D) (NPV/D)) depends only on equity cost k_0, on credit rates k_d, on leverage level L, as well as on one of the leverage ratios l_j (on one of the coverage ratios i_j) and does not depend on equity value S, debt value D, and NOI. This means that results on the dependence of NPV (in units of NOI) (NPV/NOI) on leverage ratios l_j (as well as on the dependence of NPV (in units of D) (NPV/D) on coverage ratios i_j) at different equity costs k_0, at different credit rates k_d, and at different leverage levels L carry the universal character: these dependencies remain valid for investment projects with any equity value S, debt value D, and NOI.

P. Brusov et al., *Ratings*, Contributions to Finance and Accounting,
https://doi.org/10.1007/978-3-030-56243-4_11

11.1 Investment Models

We work within investment models, created by authors. One of them describes the effectiveness of investment project from the perspective of equity capital owners, while the other model describes the effectiveness of investment project from the perspective of equity capital and debt capital owners.

In the former case, investments at the initial time moment $T = 0$ are equal to $-S$ and the flow of capital for the period (in addition to the tax shields $k_d Dt$ it includes a payment of interest on a loan $-k_d D$):

$$CF = (\text{NOI} - k_d D)(1 - t). \tag{11.1}$$

Here, for simplicity, we suppose that interest on the loan will be paid in equal shares $k_d D$ during all periods. Note that principal repayment is made at the end of the last period.

We will consider the case of discounting, when operating and financial flows are not separated and both are discounted, using the general rate (at which, obviously, the weighted average cost of capital (WACC) can be selected). In this case for long-term (perpetuity) projects, the Modigliani–Miller formula (Modigliani and Miller 1958, 1963, 1966) for WACC will be used and for projects of finite (arbitrary) duration Brusov–Filatova–Orekhova formula will be used (Brusov and Filatova 2011; Brusov et al. 2011a, b, c, 2012a, b, 2013a, b, 2014a, b; Filatova et al. 2008; Brusova 2011).

Note that debt capital is the least risky, because interest on credit is paid after taxes in the first place. Therefore, the cost of credit will always be less than the equity cost, whether of ordinary or of preference shares $k_e > k_d$; $k_p > k_d$. Here k_e and k_p is the equity cost of ordinary and of preference shares, respectively.

11.1.1 The Effectiveness of the Investment Project from the Perspective of the Equity Holders Only (Without Flows Separation)

In this case operating and financial flows are not separated and are discounted, using the general rate (at which, obviously, WACC can be selected).

The credit reimbursable at the end of the project (at the end of the period (n)) can be discounted either at the same rate WACC or at the debt cost rate k_d. Now we choose a uniform rate and the first option.

$$\mathrm{NPV} = -S + \sum_{i=1}^{n} \frac{\mathrm{NOI}(1-t) - k_{\mathrm{d}}D(1-t)}{(1+\mathrm{WACC})^i} - \frac{D}{(1+\mathrm{WACC})^n}$$
$$= -S + \frac{\mathrm{NOI}(1-t) - k_{\mathrm{d}}D(1-t)}{\mathrm{WACC}}\left(1 - \frac{1}{(1+\mathrm{WACC})^n}\right) - \frac{D}{(1+\mathrm{WACC})^n}. \tag{11.2}$$

At a Constant Value of Equity Capital (S = const)

Accounting that in the case $S = \text{const}$, NOI is proportional to the invested capital, I, $\mathrm{NOI} = \beta I = \beta S(1 + L)$ and substituting $D = LS$, we get

$$\mathrm{NPV} = -S + \frac{\mathrm{NOI}(1-t) - k_{\mathrm{d}}D(1-t)}{\mathrm{WACC}}\left(1 - \frac{1}{(1+\mathrm{WACC})^n}\right) - \frac{D}{(1+\mathrm{WACC})^n}, \tag{11.3}$$

$$\mathrm{NPV} = -S\left[1 + \frac{Lk_{\mathrm{d}}(1-t)}{\mathrm{WACC}}\left(1 - \frac{1}{(1+\mathrm{WACC})^n}\right) + \frac{L}{(1+\mathrm{WACC})^n}\right] + \frac{\beta S(1+L)(1-t)}{\mathrm{WACC}}\left(1 - \frac{1}{(1+\mathrm{WACC})^n}\right). \tag{11.4}$$

11.1.2 Modigliani–Miller Limit (Long-–term (Perpetuity) Projects)

In perpetuity limit ($n \to \infty$) (Modigliani–Miller limit) (turning to the limit $n \to \infty$ in the relevant equations), we have

$$\mathrm{NPV} = -S + \frac{\mathrm{NOI}(1-t) - k_{\mathrm{d}}D(1-t)}{\mathrm{WACC}}. \tag{11.5}$$

At a Constant Value of Equity Capital (S = const)

$$\mathrm{NPV} = -S + \frac{\mathrm{NOI}(1-t) - k_{\mathrm{d}}D(1-t)}{\mathrm{WACC}} \tag{11.6}$$

Substituting $D = LS$, we get

$$
\begin{aligned}
\mathrm{NPV} &= -S\left[1+\frac{Lk_{\mathrm{d}}(1-t)}{\mathrm{WACC}}\right]+\frac{\mathrm{NOI}(1-t)}{\mathrm{WACC}} \\
&= -S\left[1+\frac{Lk_{\mathrm{d}}(1-t)}{k_0(1-Lt/(1+L))}\right]+\frac{\beta S(1+L)(1-t)}{k_0(1-Lt/(1+L))}.
\end{aligned} \tag{11.7}
$$

In the last equation we substituted the perpetuity (Modigliani–Miller) formula for WACC

$$
\mathrm{WACC} = k_0\left(1-\frac{Lt}{1+L}\right). \tag{11.8}
$$

So, below we consider the long-term (perpetuity) projects and will use the following formula for calculations:

$$
\mathrm{NPV} = -S\left[1+\frac{Lk_d(1-t)}{k_0\left(1-\frac{Lt}{1+L}\right)}\right]+\frac{\beta S(1+L)(1-t)}{k_0\left(1-\frac{Lt}{1+L}\right)} \tag{11.9}
$$

11.2 Incorporation of Financial Coefficients, Used in Project Rating, into Modern Investment Models

Below we incorporate the financial coefficients, used in project rating, into modern investment models, created by authors. We will consider two kinds of financial coefficients: coverage ratios and leverage coefficients. In each group of financial coefficients, we incorporate three particular quantities.

For coverage ratios we incorporate: (1) coverage ratios of debt, $i_1 = \mathrm{NPV}/D$; (2) coverage ratios of interest on the credit $i_2 = \mathrm{NPV}/k_{\mathrm{d}}D$; and (3) coverage ratios of debt and interest on the credit $i_3 = (\mathrm{NPV})/(1 + k_{\mathrm{d}})D$.

For leverage ratios we incorporate: (1) leverage ratios of debt, $l_1 = D/\mathrm{NPV}$; (2) leverage ratios of interest on the credit $l_2 = k_{\mathrm{d}}D/\mathrm{NPV}$; and (3) leverage ratios of debt and interest on the credit $l_3 = (1 + k_{\mathrm{d}})D/(\mathrm{NPV})$.

11.2.1 Coverage Ratios

11.2.1.1 Coverage Ratios of Debt

Let us first incorporate the coverage ratios, used in project rating, into modern investment models, created by authors. Dividing both parts of eq. (11.9) by D, one gets

$$\frac{\mathrm{NPV}}{D} = -\frac{1}{L} - \frac{(k_{\mathrm{d}} - i_1)(1-t)}{k_0\left(1 - \frac{Lt}{1+L}\right)} \tag{11.10}$$

$$\text{Here} \quad i_1 = \frac{\mathrm{NPV}}{D} \tag{11.11}$$

11.2.1.2 Coverage Ratios of Interest on the Credit

Dividing both parts of eq. (11.9) by $k_{\mathrm{d}}D$, one gets

$$\frac{\mathrm{NPV}}{k_{\mathrm{d}}D} = -\frac{1}{Lk_{\mathrm{d}}} - \frac{(1 - i_2)(1-t)}{k_0\left(1 - \frac{Lt}{1+L}\right)} \tag{11.12}$$

$$\text{Here} \quad i_2 = \frac{\mathrm{NPV}}{k_{\mathrm{d}}D} \tag{11.13}$$

11.2.1.3 Coverage Ratios of Debt and Interest on the Credit

Dividing both parts of eq. (11.9) by $(1 + k_{\mathrm{d}})D$, one gets

$$\frac{\mathrm{NPV}}{(1+k_{\mathrm{d}})D} = -\frac{1}{L(1+k_{\mathrm{d}})} - \frac{[k_{\mathrm{d}} - i_3(1+k_{\mathrm{d}})](1-t)}{k_0\left(1 - \frac{Lt}{1+L}\right)} \tag{11.14}$$

$$\text{Here} \quad i_3 = \frac{\mathrm{NPV}}{(1+k_{\mathrm{d}})D} \tag{11.15}$$

Analyzing formulas (11.10), (11.12), and (11.14) we come to a very important conclusion that NPV (in units of D) (NPV/D) depends only on equity cost k_0, on credit rates k_{d}, on leverage level L, as well as on one of the coverage ratios i_j and does not depend on equity value S, debt value D, and NOI. This means that results on the dependence of NPV (in units of D) (NPV/D) on coverage ratios i_j at different equity costs k_0, at different credit rates k_{d}, and at different leverage levels L carry the universal character: these dependencies remain valid for investment projects with any equity value S, debt value D, and NOI.

11.2.2 Leverage Ratios

11.2.2.1 Leverage Ratios for Debt

Now let us incorporate the leverage ratios, used in project rating, into modern investment models, created by authors.

Dividing both parts of eq. (11.9) by NOI, one gets

$$\frac{\text{NPV}}{\text{NOI}} = \frac{-l_1}{L} + \frac{(1 - k_\text{d} l_1)(1 - t)}{k_0 \left(1 - \frac{Lt}{1+L}\right)} \tag{11.16}$$

$$\text{Here} \quad l_1 = \frac{D}{\text{NOI}} \tag{11.17}$$

11.2.2.2 Leverage Ratios for Interest on Credit

$$\frac{\text{NPV}}{\text{NOI}} = \frac{-l_2}{k_\text{d} L} + \frac{(1 - l_2)(1 - t)}{k_0 \left(1 - \frac{Lt}{1+L}\right)} \tag{11.18}$$

$$\text{Here} \quad l_2 = \frac{k_\text{d} D}{\text{NOI}} \tag{11.19}$$

11.2.2.3 Leverage Ratios for Debt and Interest on Credit

$$\frac{\text{NPV}}{\text{NOI}} = \frac{-l_3}{(1 + k_\text{d})L} + \frac{(1 + k_\text{d} - l_3 k_\text{d})(1 - t)}{(1 + k_\text{d}) k_0 \left(1 - \frac{Lt}{1+L}\right)} \tag{11.20}$$

$$\text{Here} \quad l_3 = \frac{(1 + k_\text{d}) D}{\text{NOI}}. \tag{11.21}$$

Analyzing formulas (11.16), (11.18), and (11.20) we come to a very important conclusion that NPV (in units of NOI) (NPV/NOI) depends only on equity cost k_0, on credit rates k_d, on leverage level L, as well as on one of the leverage ratios l_j and does not depend on equity value S, debt value D, and NOI. This means that results on the dependence of NPV (in units of NOI) (NPV/NOI) on leverage ratios l_j at different equity costs k_0, at different credit rates k_d, and at different leverage levels L carry the universal character: these dependencies remain valid for investment projects with any equity value S, debt value D, and NOI.

We investigate below the effectiveness of long-term investment projects studying the dependence of NPV on coverage ratios and on leverage ratios. We make calculations for coefficients i_1 and l_1. Calculations for the rest of coefficients (i_2, i_3 and l_2, l_3) could be made in a similar way.

We start from the calculations of the dependence of NPV on coverage ratios. We consider different values of equity costs k_0, of debt costs k_d, and of leverage level $L = D/S$. Here t is tax on profit rate, which in our calculations is equal to 20%.

11.3 Dependence of NPV on Coverage Ratios

11.3.1 Coverage Ratio on Debt

Below we calculate the dependence of NPV (in units of D)(NPV/D) on coverage ratio on debt i_1 at different equity costs k_0 (k_0 is equity cost at $L = 0$). We will make calculations for two leverage levels L ($L = 1$ and $L = 3$) and for different credit rates k_d.

For calculation within MM approximation we use the formula (11.10)

$$\frac{\text{NPV}}{D} = -\frac{1}{L} - \frac{(k_d - i_1)(1 - t)}{k_0 * \left(1 - \frac{Lt}{1+L}\right)}$$

11.3.1.1 The Dependence of NPV on Coverage Ratio on Debt i_1 at Equity Cost $k_0 = 24\%$

Below we investigate the dependence of NPV on coverage ratio on debt i_1 at different values of equity costs k_0, at different values of debt costs k_d at fixed value of equity cost, as well as at different values of leverage levels L.

Let us start our calculations from the case of equity cost $k_0 = 24\%$.

The results of calculations of the dependence of NPV on coverage ratio on debt i_1 at equity cost $k_0 = 24\%$, different values of debt costs k_d, and $L = 1$ are shown in Table 11.1.

The dependence of NPV (in units of D) on coverage ratio on debt i_1 at $k_0 = 24\%$, $k_d = 6\%$, 10%, 14%, and 20%, and $L = 1$ is illustrated in Fig.11.1.

Let us calculate the value of i_1 above which the investment project remains effective (NPV > 0).

k_d	0.20	0.14	0.1	0.06
i_1	0.48	0.42	0.38	0.32

Table 11.1 The dependence of NPV on coverage ratio on debt i_1 at equity cost $k_0 = 24\%$, $k_d = 6\%$, 10%, 14%, and 20%, and $L = 1$

i_1	L	k_0	t	NPV/D ($k_d = 0.2$)	NPV/D ($k_d = 0.14$)	NPV/D ($k_d = 0.1$)	NPV/D ($k_d = 0.06$)
0	1	0.24	0.2	−1.741	−1.519	−1.37	−1.222
1	1	0.24	0.2	1.963	2.185	2.333	2.481
2	1	0.24	0.2	5.667	5.889	6.037	6.185
3	1	0.24	0.2	9.37	9.593	9.741	9.889
4	1	0.24	0.2	13.07	13.3	13.44	13.59
5	1	0.24	0.2	16.78	17	17.15	17.3
6	1	0.24	0.2	20.48	20.7	20.85	21
7	1	0.24	0.2	24.19	24.41	24.56	24.7
8	1	0.24	0.2	27.89	28.11	28.26	28.41
9	1	0.24	0.2	31.59	31.81	31.96	32.11
10	1	0.24	0.2	35.3	35.52	35.67	35.81

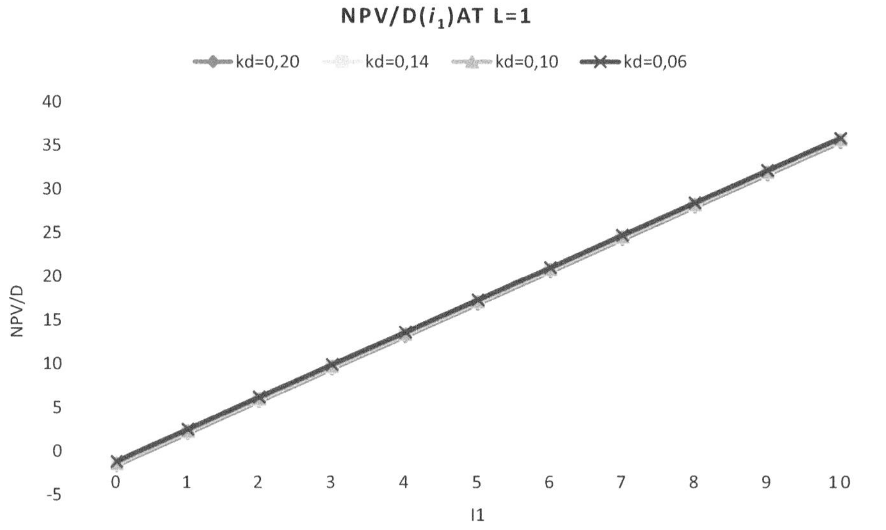

Fig. 11.1 The dependence of NPV(in units of D) on coverage ratio on debt i_1 at $k_0 = 24\%$, $k_d = 6\%$, 10%, 14%, and 20%, and $L = 1$

One can see from this table that the value of i_1 above which the investment project remains effective (NPV > 0) increases with credit rate k_d, which means that the effectiveness of the investment project as well as its creditworthiness decreases with credit rate k_d.

Let us calculate the dependence of NPV (in units of D) on coverage ratio on debt i_1 at $k_0 = 24\%$, $k_d = 6\%$, 10%, 14%, and 20%, and $L = 3$.

The dependence of NPV(in units of D) on coverage ratio on debt i_1 at $k_0 = 24\%$, $k_d = 6\%$, 10%, 14%, and 20%, and $L = 3$ is illustrated in Fig. 11.2.

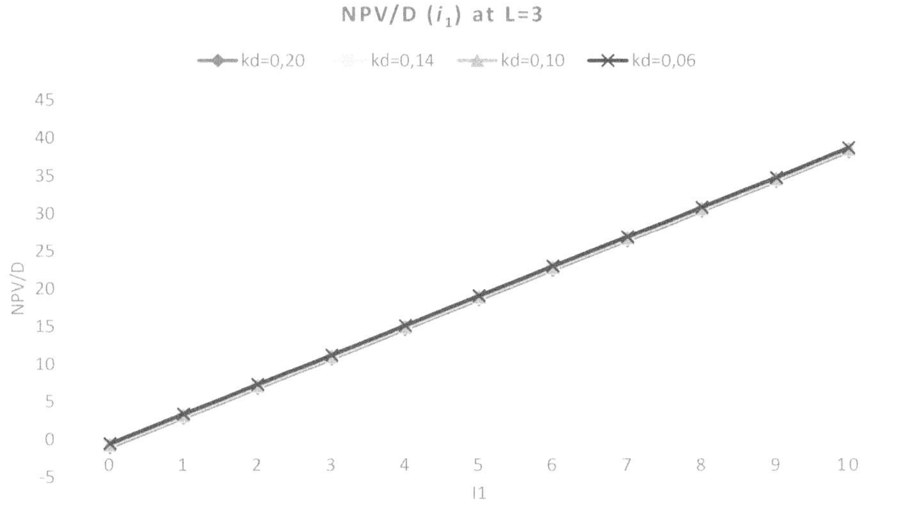

Fig. 11.2 The dependence of NPV(in units of D) on coverage ratio on debt i_1 at $k_0 = 24\%$, $k_d = 6\%$, 10%, 14%, and 20%, and $L = 3$

Let us calculate the value of l_1 above which the investment project remains effective (NPV > 0).

k_d	0.20	0.14	0.1	0.06
i_1	0.3	0.23	0.18	0.12

One can see from this Table that like the case of $L = 1$ the value of i_1 above which the investment project remains effective (NPV > 0) increases with credit rate k_d, which means that the effectiveness of the investment project as well as its creditworthiness decreases with credit rate k_d. Comparing the case of $L = 1$ one can see that at bigger leverage level ($L = 3$) the investment project becomes effective (NPV > 0) starting from smaller coverage ratio i_1, so bigger leverage level favors the effectiveness of the investment project as well as its creditworthiness.

We see from Tables 11.1 and 11.2 and Figs. 11.1 and 11.2 that (NPV/D) increases with i_1 and that (NPV/D) values turn out to be very close to each other at all i_1 values. It is seen as well that NPV increases with decreasing k_d. This means that the effectiveness of the investment project as well as its creditworthiness decreases with credit rate k_d.

Below we investigate the dependence of (NPV/D) on i_1 at different values of k_d in more detail and will show the ordering of (NPV/D)($i1$) curves at different values of k_d, as well as at different leverage levels L.

Table 11.2 The dependence of NPV on coverage ratio on debt i_1 at equity cost $k_0 = 24\%$, $k_d = 6\%$, 10%, 14%, and 20%, and $L = 3$

i_1	L	k_0	t	NPV/D ($k_d = 0.2$)	NPV/D ($k_d = 0.14$)	NPV/D ($k_d = 0.1$)	NPV/D ($k_d = 0.06$)
0	3	0.24	0.2	−1.118	−0.882	−0.725	−0.569
1	3	0.24	0.2	2.804	3.039	3.196	3.353
2	3	0.24	0.2	6.725	6.961	7.118	7.275
3	3	0.24	0.2	10.65	10.88	11.04	11.2
4	3	0.24	0.2	14.57	14.8	14.96	15.12
5	3	0.24	0.2	18.49	18.73	18.88	19.04
6	3	0.24	0.2	22.41	22.65	22.8	22.96
7	3	0.24	0.2	26.33	26.57	26.73	26.88
8	3	0.24	0.2	30.25	30.49	30.65	30.8
9	3	0.24	0.2	34.18	34.41	34.57	34.73
10	3	0.24	0.2	38.1	38.33	38.49	38.65

Table 11.3 The dependence of NPV(in units of D) on coverage ratio on debt i_1 at $k_0 = 12\%$, $k_d = 2\%$, 4%, 6%, 8%, and 10%, and $L = 1$

i_1	t	k_0	NPV/D ($k_d = 0.1$)	NPV/D ($k_d = 0.08$)	NPV/D ($k_d = 0.06$)	NPV/D ($k_d = 0.04$)	NPV/D ($k_d = 0.02$)
0	0.2	0.12	−1.741	−1.593	−1.444	−1.296	−1.148
1	0.2	0.12	5.667	5.815	5.963	6.111	6.259
2	0.2	0.12	13.074	13.222	13.370	13.519	13.667
3	0.2	0.12	20.481	20.630	20.778	20.926	21.074
4	0.2	0.12	27.889	28.037	28.185	28.333	28.481
5	0.2	0.12	35.296	35.444	35.593	35.741	35.889
6	0.2	0.12	42.704	42.852	43.000	43.148	43.296
7	0.2	0.12	50.111	50.259	50.407	50.556	50.704
8	0.2	0.12	57.519	57.667	57.815	57.963	58.111
9	0.2	0.12	64.926	65.074	65.222	65.370	65.519
10	0.2	0.12	72.333	72.481	72.630	72.778	72.926

11.3.1.2 The Dependence of NPV on Coverage Ratio on Debt i_1 at Equity Cost $k_0 = 12\%$

We study here the dependence of (NPV/D) on i_1 at fixed equity cost $k_0 = 12\%$ and at different values of k_d in more detail and will show the ordering of (NPV/D)($i1$) curves at different values of k_d, as well as at different leverage levels L.

The results of calculations of the dependence of NPV on coverage ratio on debt i_1 at equity cost $k_0 = 12\%$, different values of debt costs k_d, and $L = 1$ are shown in Table 11.3.

The results of calculations of the dependence of NPV on coverage ratio on debt i_1 at equity cost $k_0 = 12\%$, different values of debt costs k_d, and $L = 3$ are shown in Table 11.4.

Table 11.4 The dependence of NPV(in units of D) on coverage ratio on debt i_1 at $k_0 = 12\%$, $k_d = 2\%$, 4%, 6%, 8%, and 10%, and $L = 3$

i_1	t	k_0	NPV/D ($k_d = 0.1$)	NPV/D ($k_d = 0.08$)	NPV/D ($k_d = 0.06$)	NPV/D ($k_d = 0.04$)	NPV/D ($k_d = 0.02$)
0	0.2	0.12	−1.118	−0.961	−0.804	−0.647	−0.490
1	0.2	0.12	6.725	6.882	7.039	7.196	7.353
2	0.2	0.12	14.569	14.725	14.882	15.039	15.196
3	0.2	0.12	22.412	22.569	22.725	22.882	11.039
4	0.2	0.12	30.255	30.412	30.569	30.725	30.882
5	0.2	0.12	38.098	38.255	38.412	38.569	38.725
6	0.2	0.12	45.941	46.098	46.255	46.412	46.569
7	0.2	0.12	53.784	53.941	54.098	54.255	54.412
8	0.2	0.12	61.627	61.784	61.941	62.098	62.255
9	0.2	0.12	69.471	69.627	69.784	69.941	70.098
10	0.2	0.12	77.314	77.471	77.627	77.784	77.941

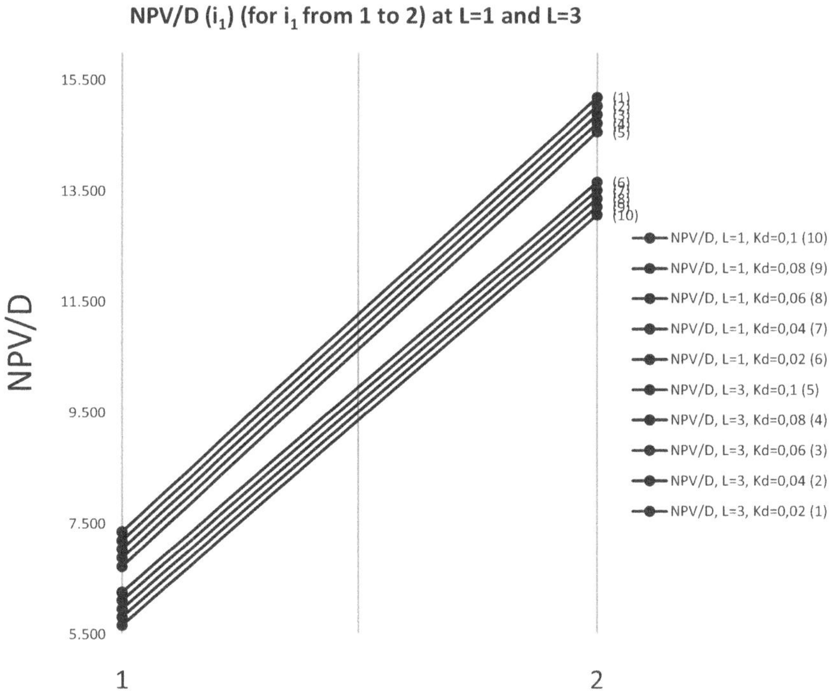

Fig. 11.3 The dependence of NPV(in units of D) on coverage ratio on debt i_1 at $k_0 = 12\%$, $k_d = 2\%$, 4%, 6%, 8%, and 10%, and $L = 1$ and $L = 3$

We see from Tables 11.3 and 11.4 that NPV (in units of D) (NPV/D) increases with i_1 and that (NPV/D) values turn out to be very close to each other at all i_1 values.

To show the difference in (NPV/D) values in more detail we show in Fig. 11.3 the dependence of (NPV/D) on parameter i_1 for range i_1 from 1 to 2.

One can see that all NPV (i_1) curves corresponding to $L = 3$ lie above the curves corresponding to $L = 1$. This means that NPV increases with L (with the increasing of the debt financing). At fixed value L NPV increases with decreasing the credit rate k_d. This means that the effectiveness of the investment project as well as its creditworthiness decreases with credit rate k_d.

Analyzing the obtained results, one should remember that NPV (in units of D) (NPV/D) depends only on equity cost k_0, on credit rates k_d, on leverage level L, as well as on one of the coverage ratios i_j and does not depend on equity value S, debt value D, and NOI. This means that obtained results on the dependence of NPV (in units of D) (NPV/D) on coverage ratios i_j at different equity costs k_0, at different credit rates k_d, and at different leverage levels L carry the universal character: these dependencies remain valid for investment projects with any equity value S, debt value D, and NOI.

11.4 Dependence of NPV on Leverage Ratios

11.4.1 Leverage Ratio of Debt

Below we calculate the dependence of NPV (in units of NOI) (NPV/NOI) on leverage ratio on debt l_1 at different equity costs k_0 (k_0 is equity cost at $L = 0$). We make calculations for two leverage levels L ($L = 1$ and $L = 3$) and for different credit rates k_d.

For calculation within MM approximation we use formula (11.19)

$$\frac{\text{NPV}}{\text{NOI}} = \frac{-l_1}{L} + \frac{(1 - K_d \times l_1)(1 - t)}{K_0 \times \left(1 - \frac{Lt}{1+L}\right)}.$$

11.4.1.1 The Dependence of NPV (in Units of NOI) (NPV/NOI) on Leverage Ratio on Debt l_1 at Equity Cost $k_0 = 0.12$

Results are shown in Tables 11.5 and 11.6 and in Figs. 11.4 and 11.5.

Based on the above calculations, we plot the dependences of (NPV/NOI) on leverage ratio on debt l_1 at different leverage levels L.

From Tables 11.5 and 11.6 and Figs. 11.4 and 11.5 one can come to the conclusion that the NPV(in units of NOI) (NPV/NOI) decreases with the increasing of the leverage ratio on debt l_1. With the increasing of the cost of debt capital k_d,

Table 11.5 The dependence of NPV (in units of NOI) (NPV/NOI) on leverage ratio on debt l_1 at equity cost $k_0 = 0.12$, $k_d = 4\%$, 6%, 8%, and 10%, and $L = 1$

l_1	0	1	2	3	4	5	6	7	8	9	10
$k_d = 0.10$	7.407	5.667	3.926	2.185	0.444	−1.296	−3.037	−4.778	−6.519	−8.259	−10
$k_d = 0.08$	7.407	5.815	4.222	2.63	1.037	−0.556	−2.148	−3.741	−5.333	−6.926	−8.519
$k_d = 0.06$	7.407	5.963	4.519	3.074	1.63	0.185	−1.259	−2.704	−4.148	−5.593	−7.037
$k_d = 0.04$	7.407	6.111	4.815	3.519	2.222	0.926	−0.37	−1.667	−2.963	−4.259	−5.556

Table 11.6 The dependence of NPV (in units of NOI) (NPV/NOI) on leverage ratio on debt l_1 at equity cost $k_0 = 0.12$, $k_d = 4\%$, 6%, 8%, and 10%, and $L = 3$

l_1	0	1	2	3	4	5	6	7	8	9	10
$k_d = 0.10$	7.843	6.725	5.608	4.49	3.373	2.255	1.137	0.02	−1.098	−2.216	−3.333
$k_d = 0.08$	7.843	6.882	5.922	4.961	4	3.039	2.078	1.118	0.157	−0.804	−1.765
$k_d = 0.06$	7.843	7.039	6.235	5.431	4.627	3.824	3.02	2.216	1.412	0.608	−0.196
$k_d = 0.04$	7.843	7.196	6.549	5.902	5.255	4.608	3.961	3.314	2.667	2.02	1.373

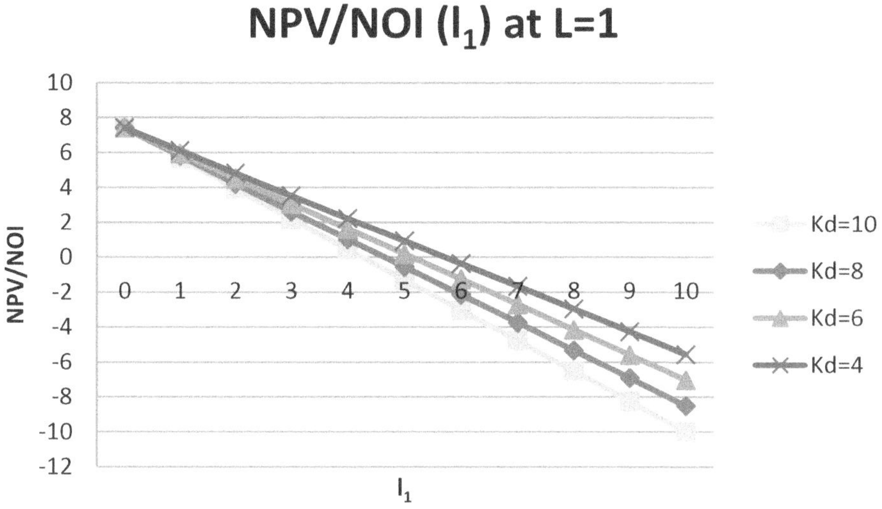

Fig. 11.4 The dependence of NPV(in units of D) on leverage ratio on debt l_1 at $k_0 = 12\%$, $k_d = 4\%$, 6%, 8%, and 10%, and $L = 1$

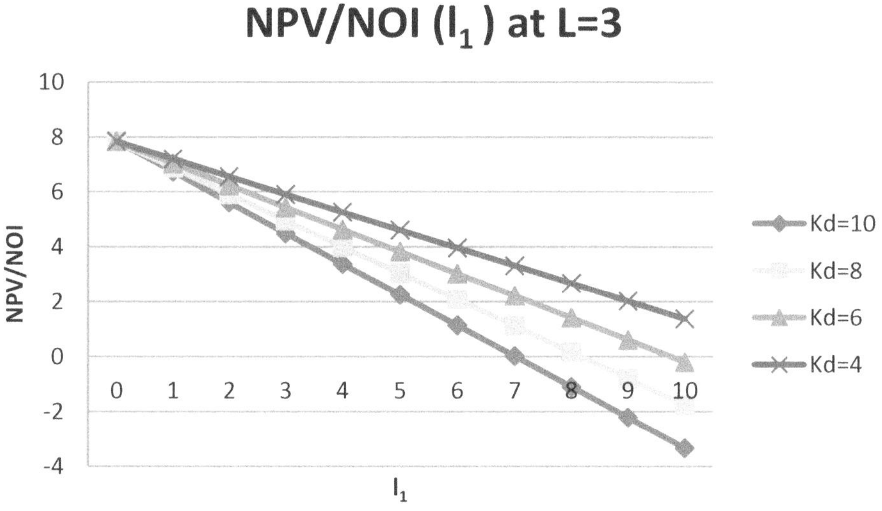

Fig. 11.5 The dependence of NPV(in units of D) on leverage ratio on debt l_1 at $k_0 = 12\%$, $k_d = 4\%$, 6%, 8%, and 10%, and $L = 3$

curves of the dependence of (NPV/NOI) (l_1), outgoing from a single point at a zero value of l_1, lie below (i.e., the rate of decrease (or negative slope of curves) grows). Note that while the dependences of NPV(in units of D) on coverage ratio on debt i_1 lie very close to each other (see above), the dependences of NPV(in units of NOI) on leverage ratio on debt l_1 are separated significantly more.

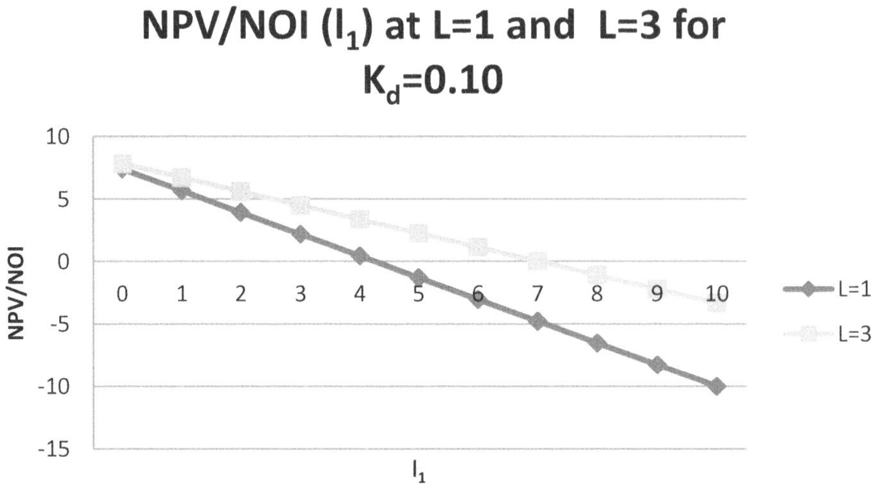

Fig. 11.6 The dependence of NPV(in units of NOI) on leverage ratio on debt l_1 at $k_0 = 12\%$, $k_d = 10\%$, and $L = 1$ and $L = 3$

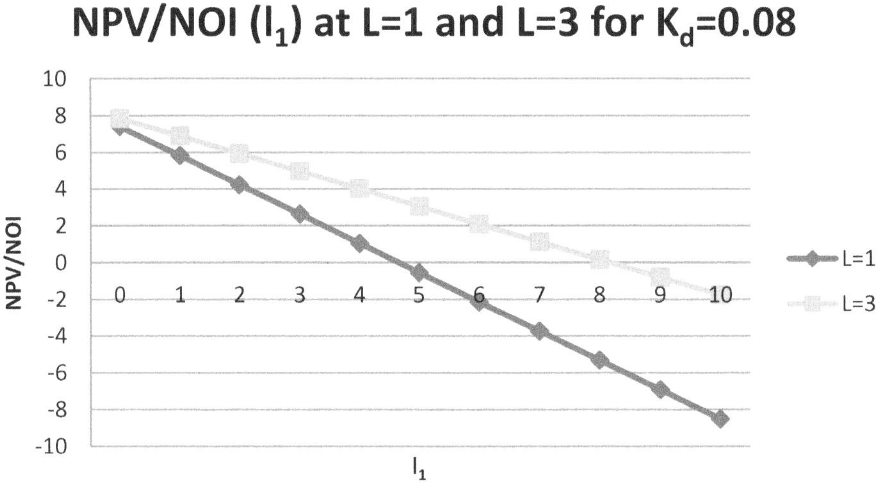

Fig. 11.7 The dependence of NPV(in units of NOI) on leverage ratio on debt l_1 at $k_0 = 12\%$, $k_d = 8\%$, and $L = 1$ and $L = 3$

Also, Figs. 11.6, 11.7, 11.8 and 11.9 of the (NPV/NOI) dependence on l_1 can be plotted for fixed values of the debt cost k_d and two values of the leverage level $L = 1$ and $L = 3$.

One can see that the rate of decrease of the ratio NPV/NOI decreases with the increasing of the leverage level L.

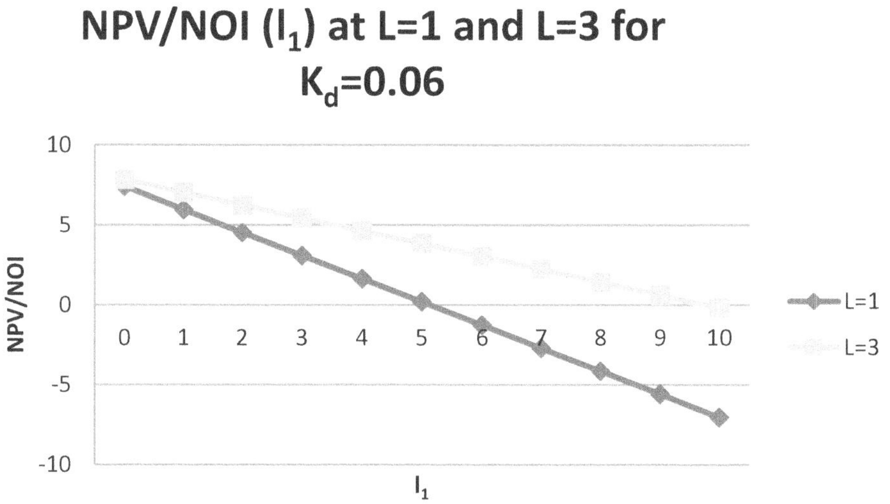

Fig. 11.8 The dependence of NPV(in units of NOI) on leverage ratio on debt l_1 at $k_0 = 12\%$, $k_d = 6\%$, and $L = 1$ and $L = 3$

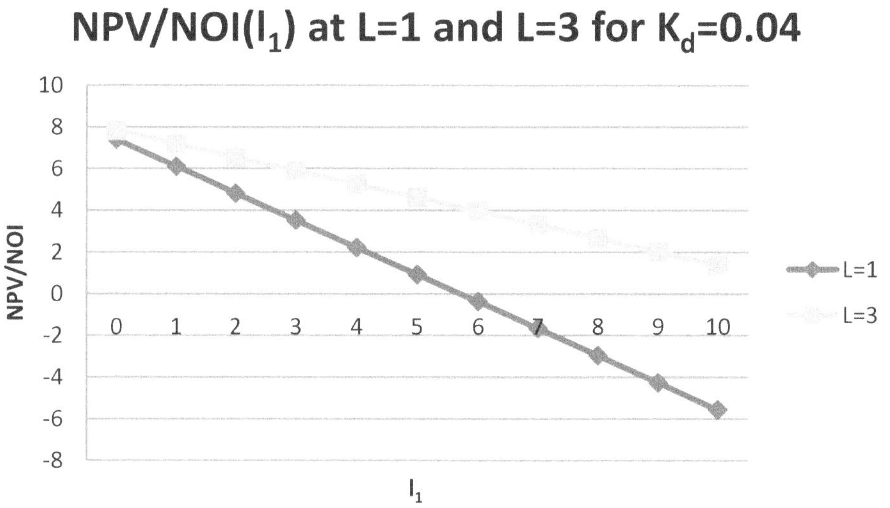

Fig. 11.9 The dependence of NPV(in units of NOI) on leverage ratio on debt l_1 at $k_0 = 12\%$, $k_d = 4\%$, and $L = 1$ and $L = 3$

11.4.1.2 The Dependence of NPV (in Units of NOI) (NPV/NOI) on Leverage Ratio on Debt l_1 at Equity Cost $k_0 = 0.14$

$$L = 1$$

$$L = 3$$

Based on the obtained data, we plot the dependences of NPV/NOI on l_1 at $k_0 = 14\%$, at different values of debt cost k_d, and at two different leverage levels $L = 1$ and $L = 3$ in Figs. 11.10 and 11.11.

From Tables 11.7 and 11.8 and Figs. 11.10 and 11.11, one can come to the conclusion that the NPV(in units of NOI) (NPV/NOI) decreases with the increasing of the leverage ratio on debt l_1. With the increasing of the cost of debt capital k_d, curves of the dependence of (NPV/NOI) (l_1), outgoing from a single point at a zero value of l_1, fall below (i.e., the rate of decrease grows) (Table 11.9).

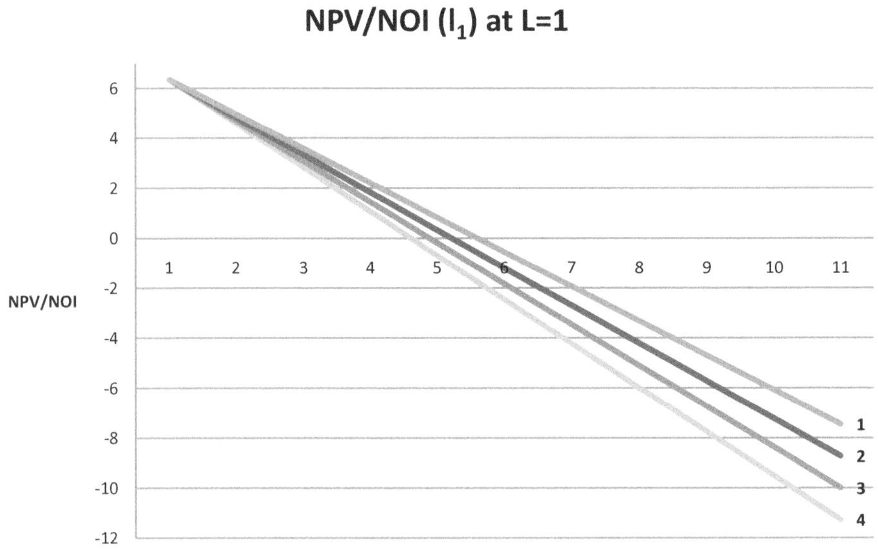

Fig. 11.10 The dependence of NPV(in units of NOI) on leverage ratio on debt l_1 at $k_0 = 14\%$, $k_d = 6\%$–(1),8%–(2), 10%–(3), and 12%–(4) at $L = 1$

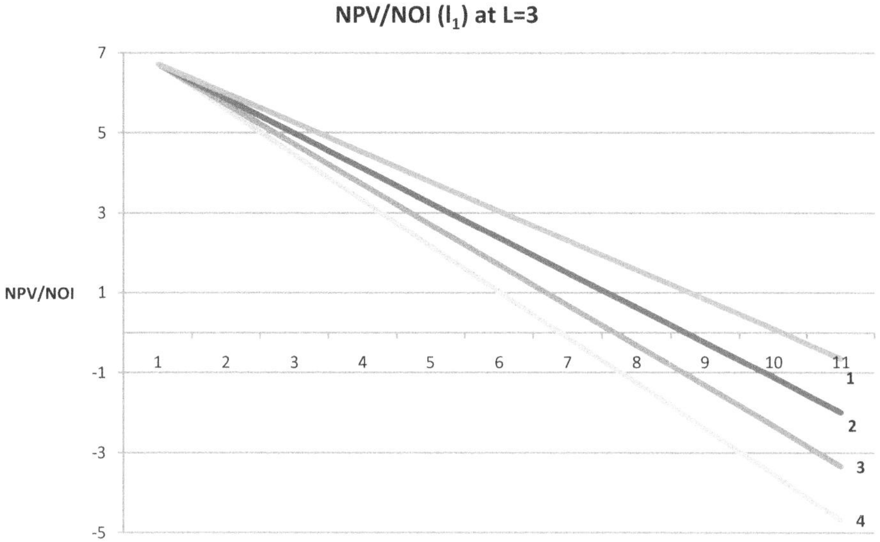

Fig. 11.11 The dependence of NPV(in units of NOI) on leverage ratio on debt l_1 at $k_0 = 14\%$, $k_d = 6\%$–(1), 8%–(2), 10%–(3), and 12%–(4) at $L = 3$

Table 11.7 The dependence of NPV (in units of NOI) (NPV/NOI) on leverage ratio on debt l_1 at equity cost $k_0 = 0.14$, $k_d = 6\%$, 8%, 10%, and 12%, and $L = 1$

l_1	L	k_0	t	NPV/NOI ($k_d = 0.12$)	NPV/NOI ($k_d = 0.1$)	NPV/NOI ($k_d = 0.08$)	NPV/NOI ($k_d = 0.06$)
0	1	0.14	0.2	6.349206349	6.349206349	6.349206349	6.349206349
1	1	0.14	0.2	4.587301587	4.714285714	4.841269841	4.968253968
2	1	0.14	0.2	2.825396825	3.079365079	3.333333333	3.587301587
3	1	0.14	0.2	1.063492063	1.444444444	1.825396825	2.206349206
4	1	0.14	0.2	−0.698412698	−0.19047619	0.317460317	0.825396825
5	1	0.14	0.2	−2.46031746	−1.825396825	−1.19047619	−0.555555556
6	1	0.14	0.2	−4.222222222	−3.46031746	−2.698412698	−1.936507937
7	1	0.14	0.2	−5.984126984	−5.095238095	−4.206349206	−3.317460317
8	1	0.14	0.2	−7.746031746	−6.73015873	−5.714285714	−4.698412698
9	1	0.14	0.2	−9.507936508	−8.365079365	−7.222222222	−6.079365079
10	1	0.14	0.2	−11.26984127	−10	−8.73015873	−7.46031746

11.4.1.3 The Dependence of NPV (in Units of NOI) (NPV/NOI) on Leverage Ratio on Debt l_1 at Equity Cost $k_0 = 0.26$

The formula of Modigliani and Miller in Excel will look like:

Table 11.8 The dependence of NPV (in units of NOI) (NPV/NOI) on leverage ratio on debt l_1 at equity cost $k_0 = 0.14$, $k_d = 6\%$, 8%, 10%, and 12%, and $L = 3$

l_1	L	k_0	t	NPV/NOI ($k_d = 0.12$)	NPV/NOI ($k_d = 0.1$)	NPV/NOI ($k_d = 0.08$)	NPV/NOI ($k_d = 0.06$)
0	3	0.14	0.2	6.722689	6.722689	6.722689	6.722689
1	3	0.14	0.2	5.582633	5.717087	5.851541	5.985994
2	3	0.14	0.2	4.442577	4.711485	4.980392	5.2493
3	3	0.14	0.2	3.302521	3.705882	4.109244	4.512605
4	3	0.14	0.2	2.162465	2.70028	3.238095	3.77591
5	3	0.14	0.2	1.022409	1.694678	2.366947	3.039216
6	3	0.14	0.2	−0.11765	0.689076	1.495798	2.302521
7	3	0.14	0.2	−1.2577	−0.31653	0.62465	1.565826
8	3	0.14	0.2	−2.39776	−1.32213	−0.2465	0.829132
9	3	0.14	0.2	−3.53782	−2.32773	−1.11765	0.092437
10	3	0.14	0.2	−4.67787	−3.33333	−1.9888	−0.64426

Table 11.9 The dependence of NPV (in units of NOI) (NPV/NOI) on leverage ratio on debt l_1 at equity cost $k_0 = 0.26$, $k_d = 22\%$, 16%, 10%, and 6%, and $L = 1$

l_1	NPV/NOI(l_1) ($K_d = 0.22$)	NPV/NOI(l_1) ($K_d = 0.16$)	NPV/NOI(l_1) ($K_d = 0.1$)	NPV/NOI(l_1) ($K_d = 0.06$)
0	3.418803419	3.4188034	3.41880342	3.4188034
1	1.666666667	1.8717949	2.07692308	2.2136752
2	−0.08547009	0.3247863	0.73504274	1.008547
3	−1.83760684	−1.2222222	−0.60683761	−0.196581
4	−3.58974359	−2.7692308	−1.94871795	−1.401709
5	−5.34188034	−4.3162393	−3.29059829	−2.606838
6	−7.09401709	−5.8632479	−4.63247863	−3.811966
7	−8.84615385	−7.4102564	−5.97435897	−5.017094
8	−10.5982906	−8.957265	−7.31623932	−6.222222
9	−12.3504274	−10.504274	−8.65811966	−7.42735
10	−14.1025641	−12.051282	−10	−8.632479

$$= (-\mathrm{A3}/\mathrm{C3}) + (((1 - (\mathrm{E3} \times \mathrm{A3})) \times (1 - \mathrm{B3}))/(\mathrm{D3} \times (1 - ((\mathrm{C3} \times \mathrm{B3})/(1 + \mathrm{C3})))))$$

Using this formula we calculate the dependence of NPV (in units of NOI) (NPV/NOI) on leverage ratio on debt l_1 at equity cost $k_0 = 0.26$, at different values of $k_d = 22\%$, 16%, 10%, and 6%, and at two values of leverage level $L = 1$ and $L = 3$.

Let us start from the case $L = 1$.

Let us calculate the value of l_1 below which the investment project remains effective (NPV > 0)

k_d	0.22	0.16	0.1	0.06
l_1	1.9	2.2	2.5	2.7

One can see from this Table that the value of l_1 below which the investment project remains effective (NPV > 0) decreases with credit rate k_d, which means that the effectiveness of the investment project as well as its creditworthiness decreases with credit rate k_d (Fig. 11.12 and Table 11.10).

Let us calculate the value of l_1 below which the investment project remains effective (NPV > 0)

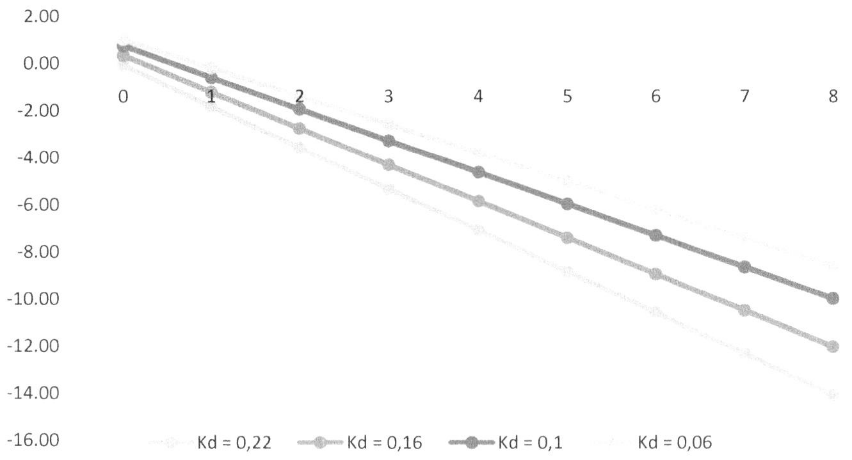

Fig. 11.12 The dependence of NPV (in units of NOI) (NPV/NOI) on leverage ratio on debt l_1 at equity cost $k_0 = 0.26$, $k_d = 22\%$, 16%, 10%, and 6%, and $L = 1$

Table 11.10 The dependence of NPV (in units of NOI) (NPV/NOI) on leverage ratio on debt l_1 at equity cost $k_0 = 0.26$, $k_d = 22\%$, 16%, 10%, and 6%, and $L = 3$

l_1	NPV/NOI(l_1) ($K_d = 0.22$)	NPV/NOI(l_1) ($K_d = 0.16$)	NPV/NOI(l_1) ($K_d = 0.1$)	NPV/NOI(l_1) ($K_d = 0.06$)
0	3.619909502	3.6199095	3.6199095	3.6199095
1	2.490196078	2.7073906	2.92458522	3.0693816
2	1.360482655	1.7948718	2.22926094	2.5188537
3	0.230769231	0.8823529	1.53393665	1.9683258
4	−0.89894419	−0.0301659	0.83861237	1.4177979
5	−2.02865762	−0.9426848	0.14328808	0.86727
6	−3.15837104	−1.8552036	−0.5520362	0.3167421
7	−4.28808446	−2.7677225	−1.24736048	−0.233786
8	−5.41779789	−3.6802413	−1.94268477	−0.784314
9	−6.54751131	−4.5927602	−2.63800905	−1.334842
10	−7.67722474	−5.505279	−3.33333333	−1.88537

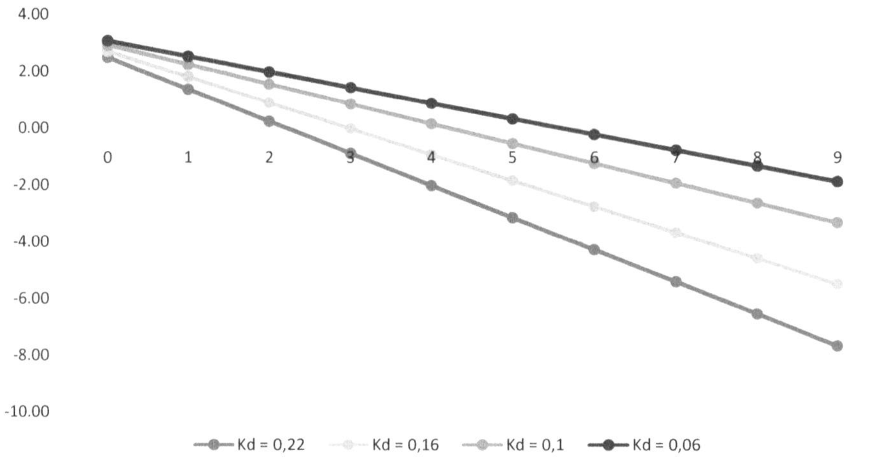

Fig. 11.13 The dependence of NPV (in units of NOI) (NPV/NOI) on leverage ratio on debt l_1 at equity cost $k_0 = 0.26$, $k_d = 22\%$, 16%, 10%, and 6%, and $L = 3$

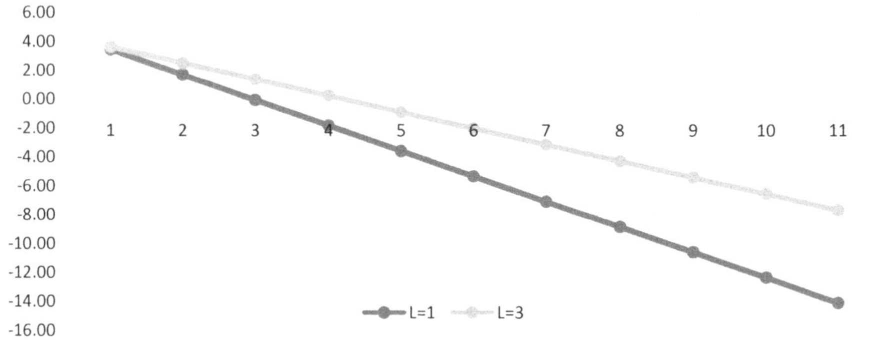

Fig. 11.14 The dependence of NPV (in units of NOI) (NPV/NOI) on leverage ratio on debt l_1 at equity cost $k_0 = 0.26$, $k_d = 22$, and $L = 1$ and $L = 3$

k_d	0.22	0.16	0.1	0.06
l_1	3.85	4	5.6	6.6

One can see from this Table that like the case of $L = 1$ the value of l_1 below which the investment project remains effective (NPV > 0) decreases with credit rate k_d, which means that the effectiveness of the investment project as well as its creditworthiness decreases with credit rate k_d. Comparing the case of $L = 1$ one can see that at bigger leverage level ($L = 3$) the investment project remains effective (NPV > 0) until bigger leverage ratio l_1, so bigger leverage level favors the effectiveness of the investment project as well as its creditworthiness (Fig. 11.13).

Let us analyze also the dependence of NPV (in units of NOI) (NPV/NOI) on leverage ratio on debt l_1 at equity cost $k_0 = 0.26$ and each value of k_d at two leverage levels $L = 1$ and $L = 3$ (Fig. 11.14, 11.5, 11.6, and 11.7).

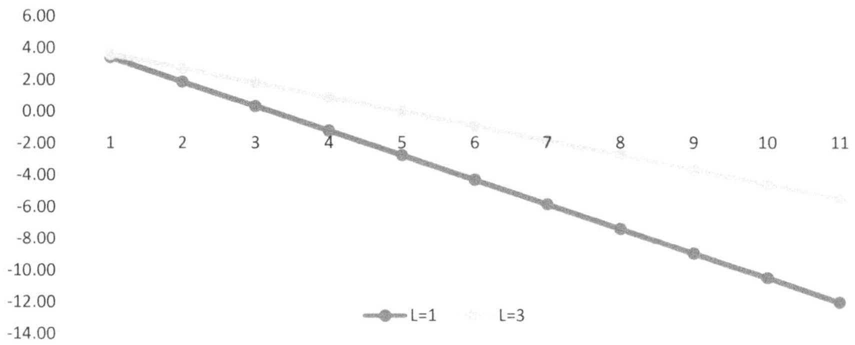

Fig. 11.15 The dependence of NPV (in units of NOI) (NPV/NOI) on leverage ratio on debt l_1 at equity cost $k_0 = 0.26$, $k_d = 16\%$, and $L = 1$ and $L = 3$

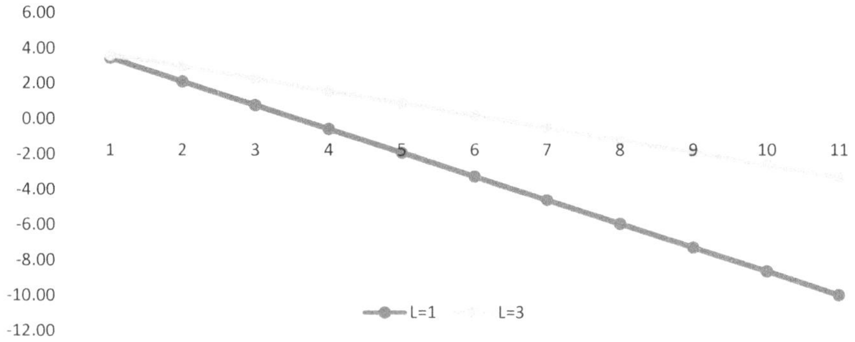

Fig. 11.16 The dependence of NPV (in units of NOI) (NPV/NOI) on leverage ratio on debt l_1 at equity cost $k_0 = 0.26$, $k_d = 10\%$, and $L = 1$ and $L = 3$

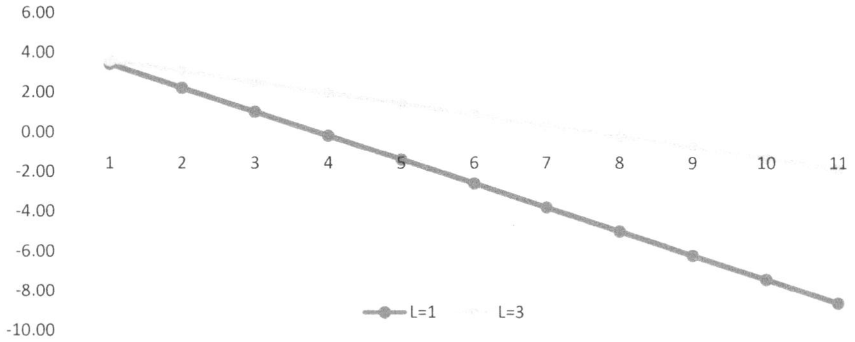

Fig. 11.17 The dependence of NPV (in units of NOI) (NPV/NOI) on leverage ratio on debt l_1 at equity cost $k_0 = 0.26$, $k_d = 6\%$, and $L = 1$ and $L = 3$

Studying the dependence of NPV (in units of NOI) (NPV/NOI) on leverage ratio on debt l_1 at equity cost $k_0 = 0.26$ and each value of k_d at two leverage levels $L = 1$ and $L = 3$ shows that the curve (NPV/NOI) (l_1) corresponding to bigger leverage level ($L = 3$) lies above the curve (NPV/NOI) (l_1) corresponding to smaller leverage level ($L = 1$). The curve (NPV/NOI) (l_1) corresponding to bigger leverage level ($L = 3$) has smaller (negative) slope. This means that debt financing of long-term projects favors the effectiveness of the investment project as well as its creditworthiness.

Analyzing the obtained results one should remember that NPV (in units of NOI) (NPV/NOI) depends only on equity cost k_0, on credit rates k_d, on leverage level L, as well as on one of the leverage ratios l_j and does not depend on equity value S, debt value D, and NOI. This means that obtained results on the dependence of NPV (in units of NOI) (NPV/NOI) on leverage ratios l_j at different equity costs k_0, at different credit rates k_d, and at different leverage levels L carry the universal character: these dependencies remain valid for investment projects with any equity value S, debt value D, and NOI.

11.5 Conclusions

This chapter continues to create a new approach to rating methodology: in addition to three previous chapters (Chaps. 6, 7 and 8), which have considered the creditworthiness of the non-finance issuers (Brusov et al. 2018c, d), we develop here a new approach to project rating. We work within investment models, created by authors. One of them describes the effectiveness of investment project from the perspective of equity capital owners, while the other model describes the effectiveness of investment project from the perspective of equity capital and debt capital owners.

The important features of current consideration as well as in previous studies are:

1. The adequate use of discounting of financial flows virtually not used in existing rating methodologies.
2. The incorporation of rating parameters (financial "ratios"), used in project rating, into considered modern investment models.

Analyzing within these investment models with incorporated rating parameters the dependence of NPV on rating parameters (financial "ratios") at different values of equity cost k_0, at different values of credit rates k_d, as well as at different values of on leverage level L, we come to a very important conclusion that NPV in units of NOI (NPV/NOI) (as well as NPV in units of D (NPV/D)) depends only on equity cost k_0, on credit rates k_d, on leverage level L, as well as on one of the leverage ratios l_j (on one of the coverage ratios i_j) and does not depend on equity value S, debt value D, and NOI. This means that obtained results on the dependence of NPV (in units of NOI) (NPV/NOI) on leverage ratios l_j (as well as on the dependence of NPV (in units of D) (NPV/D) on coverage ratios i_j) at different equity costs k_0, at different credit rates k_d, and at different leverage levels L carry the universal character: these dependencies remain valid for investment projects with any equity value S, debt value D, and NOI.

Calculations on dependence of NPV in units of D (NPV/D) on the coverage ratio on debt i_1 show that (NPV/D) increases with i_1 and that (NPV/D) values turn out to be very close to each other at all i_1 values. It is seen as well that NPV increases with decreasing k_d. This means that the effectiveness of the investment project as well as its creditworthiness decreases with credit rate k_d. One can see that all NPV (i_1) curves corresponding to $L = 3$ lie above the curves corresponding to $L = 1$. This means that NPV increases with leverage level L (with the increasing of debt financing). Thus, debt financing favors the effectiveness of the long-term project. At fixed value L NPV increases with the decreasing of the credit rate k_d.

It is shown the value of the coverage ratio on debt i_1 above which the investment project remains effective (NPV > 0) increases with credit rate k_d, which means that the effectiveness of the investment project as well as its creditworthiness decreases with credit rate k_d. Comparing the cases of $L = 1$ and $L = 3$, one can see that at bigger leverage level ($L = 3$) the investment project becomes effective (NPV > 0) starting from smaller coverage ratio i_1, so bigger leverage level favors the effectiveness of the investment project as well as its creditworthiness.

Calculations on dependence of NPV in units of NOI (NPV/NOI) on the leverage ratio on debt l_1 show that NPV in units of NOI decreases with the increasing of the leverage ratio on debt l_1. With the increasing of the cost of debt capital k_d, curves of the dependence of (NPV/NOI) (l_1), outgoing from a single point at a zero value of l_1, lie below (i.e., the rate of decrease (or negative slope of curves) grows). Note that while the dependences of NPV (in units of D) on coverage ratio on debt i_1 lie very close to each other, the dependences of NPV (in units of NOI) on leverage ratio on debt l_1 are separated significantly more.

One can see that the value of l_1 below which the investment project remains effective (NPV > 0) decreases with credit rate k_d, which means that the effectiveness of the investment project as well as its creditworthiness decreases with credit rate k_d.

Studying the dependence of NPV (in units of NOI) (NPV/NOI) on leverage ratio on debt l_1 at fixed equity cost k_0 and fixed credit rate k_d at two leverage levels $L = 1$ and $L = 3$, it was shown that the curve (NPV/NOI) (l_1) corresponding to bigger leverage level ($L = 3$) lies above the curve (NPV/NOI) (l_1) corresponding to smaller leverage level ($L = 1$). The curve (NPV/NOI) (l_1) corresponding to bigger leverage level ($L = 3$) has smaller (negative) slope. This means that debt financing of long-term projects favors the effectiveness of the investment project as well as its creditworthiness.

Investigations, conducted in this paper, create a new approach to rating methodology with respect to the long-term project rating. And this paper in combination with two of our previous papers on this topic (Brusov et al. 2018c, d) creates a new base for rating methodology on a whole.

In our future papers, we will consider rating methodology for investment projects of arbitrary duration.

References

Brusov PN, Filatova TV (2011) From Modigliani–Miller to general theory of capital cost and capital structure of the company. Finance Credit 435:2–8

Brusov P, Filatova T, Orehova N, Brusova A (2011a) Weighted average cost of capital in the theory of Modigliani–Miller, modified for a finite life–time company. Appl Financ Econ 21(11):815–824

Brusov P, Filatova T, Orehova N et al (2011b) From Modigliani–Miller to general theory of capital cost and capital structure of the company. Res J Econ Bus ICT 2:16–21

Brusov P, Filatova T, Orehova N et al (2011c) Influence of debt financing on the effectiveness of the investment project within the Modigliani–Miller theory. Res J Econ Bus ICT (UK) 2:11–15

Brusov P, Filatova T, Eskindarov M, Orehova N (2012a) Influence of debt financing on the effectiveness of the finite duration investment project. Appl Financ Econ 22(13):1043–1052

Brusov P, Filatova T, Eskindarov M, Orehova N (2012b) Hidden global causes of the global financial crisis. J Rev Global Econ 1:106–111

Brusov P, Filatova P, Orekhova N (2013a) Absence of an optimal capital structure in the famous tradeoff theory! J Rev Global Econ 2:94–116

Brusov P, Filatova T, Orehova N (2013b) A qualitatively new effect in corporative finance: abnormal dependence of cost of equity of company on leverage. J Rev Global Econ 2:183–193

Brusov P, Filatova P, Orekhova N (2014a) Mechanism of formation of the company optimal capital structure, different from suggested by trade off theory. Cogent Econ Finance 2:1–13. http://dx.doi.org/ 10.1080/23322039.2014.946150

Brusov P, Filatova T, Orehova N (2014b) Inflation in Brusov–mFilatova—Orekhova theory and in its perpetuity limit—Modigliani—Miller theory. J Rev Global Econ 3:175–185

Brusov P (2018a) Editorial: introduction on special issue on the banking system and financial markets of Russia and other countries: problems and prospects. J Rev Glob Econ 7:i–vi

Brusov P (2018b) Editorial. J Rev Glob Econ 7:i–v, SCOPUS

Brusov P, Filatova T, Orekhova N, Eskindarov M (2015) Modern corporate finance, investments and taxation, Springer International Publishing, Switzerland, p 373. Monograph, SCOPUS. https://www.springer.com/gp/book/9783319147314

Brusov PN, Filatova TV, Orekhova NP (2018a) Modern corporate finance and investments, monograph. Knorus Publishing House, Moscow, p 517

Brusov P, Filatova T, Orekhova N, Eskindarov M (2018b) Modern corporate finance, investments, taxation and ratings, Springer Nature Publishing, Switzerland, p 571. Monograph

Brusov PN, Filatova TV, Orekhova NP, Kulik VL (2018c) Rating: new approach. J Rev Glob Econ 7:37–62. SCOPUS. https://doi.org/10.6000/1929-7092.2018.07.05

Brusov PN, Filatova TV, Orekhova NP, Kulik VL (2018d) A "golden age" of the companies: conditions of its existence. J Rev Glob Econ 7:88–103. SCOPUS. https://doi.org/10.6000/1929-7092.2018.07.07

Brusov PN, Filatova TV, Orekhova NP, Kulik VL (2018e) Rating methodology: new look and new horizons. J Rev Glob Econ 7:63–87. SCOPUS. https://doi.org/10.6000/1929-7092.2018.07.06

Brusov PN, Filatova TV, Orekhova NP, Kulik VL, Weil I (2018f) New meaningful effects in modern capital structure theory. J Rev Glob Econ 7:104–122. SCOPUS. https://doi.org/10.6000/1929-7092.2018.07.08

Brusov P, Filatova T, Orekhova N, Kulik V, Weil I, Brailov A (2018g) The impact of the central bank key rate and commercial banks credit rates on creating and maintaining of a favorable investment climate in the country. J Rev Glob Econ 7:360–376. SCOPUS. https://doi.org/10.6000/1929-7092.2018.07.31

Brusov PN, Filatova TV, Orekhova NP, Kulik VL, Weil I (2019) Ratings of the investment projects of arbitrary durations: new methodology. J Rev Glob Econ 8:437–448. SCOPUS. https://doi.org/10.6000/1929-7092.2019.08.37

Brusov PN, Filatova TV, Orekhova NP, Kulik VL, Chang S-I, Lin YCG (2020) Modification of the Modigliani–Miller theory for the case of advance payments of tax on profit. J Rev Global Econ 9:257–268

Brusova A (2011) A comparison of the three methods of estimation of weighted average cost of capital and equity cost of company. Financ Anal Prob Sol 34(76):36–42

Filatova T, Orehova N, Brusova A (2008) Weighted average cost of capital in the theory of Modigliani–Miller, modified for a finite lifetime company. Bull FU 48:68–77

Filatova TV, Brusov PN, Orekhova NP, Kulik VL (2018) Ratings of the long–term projects: new approach. J Rev Glob Econ 7:645–661, SCOPUS. https://doi.org/10.6000/1929-7092.2018.07.59

Modigliani F, Miller M (1958) The cost of capital, corporate finance, and the theory of investment. Am Econ Rev 48:261–297

Modigliani F, Miller M (1963) Corporate income taxes and the cost of capital: a correction. Am Econ Rev 53:147–175

Modigliani F, Miller M (1966) Some estimates of the cost of capital to the electric utility industry 1954–1957. Am Econ Rev 56:333–391

Chapter 12
Ratings of the Investment Projects of Arbitrary Durations: New Methodology

In this chapter, we develop for the first time a new approach to ratings of the investment projects of arbitrary durations, applicable in particular to energy projects. The ratings of such energy projects as "Turkish stream" and "Nord stream-2," energy projects relating to clean, renewable, and sustainable energy, as well as relating to pricing carbon emissions, could be done using new rating methodologies. In our previous chapters, the new approach to the ratings of the long-term investment projects has been developed (Filatova et al. 2018). The important features of that consideration are the following: (1) The incorporation of rating parameters (financial "ratios"), used in project rating and playing a major role in it, into modern long-term investment models and (2) the adequate use of discounting of financial flows virtually not used in existing rating methodologies. Here, for the first time, we incorporate the rating parameters (financial "ratios"), used in project rating, into modern investment models, describing the investment projects of arbitrary durations. This was much more difficult task than in the case of the long-term investment projects, considered by us in previous chapters. We work within investment models, created by authors. One of them describes the effectiveness of investment project from the perspective of equity capital owners, while the other model describes the effectiveness of investment project from the perspective of equity capital and debt capital owners. New approach allows us to use the powerful instruments of modern theory of capital cost and capital structure (BFO theory) (Brusov et al. 2015, 2018; Brusov 2018a, b; Brusov et al. 2018f, g, 2019, 2020) and modern investment models, created by the authors and well tested in the real economy to evaluate investment project performance, including energy projects. In our calculations, we use Excel technique in two aspects: (1) we calculate WACC at different values of equity costs k_0, different values of debt costs k_d, and different values of leverage level $L = D/S$, using the famous BFO formula, and (2) we calculate the dependences of NPV on coverage ratios as well as leverage ratios at different values of equity costs k_0, different values of debt costs k_d, and different values of leverage level L.

P. Brusov et al., *Ratings*, Contributions to Finance and Accounting,
https://doi.org/10.1007/978-3-030-56243-4_12

12.1 Introduction

The investments play a very important role in economics and finance, wherein the role of energy projects in general and in particular relating to clean, renewable, and sustainable energy, as well as relating to pricing carbon emissions, is rapidly increasing.

In the conditions of limited financial resources, the selection of the most efficient projects from the point of view of investors becomes a very important task. Rating agencies are called upon to solve it.

Rating agencies play a very important role in economics. Their analysis of issuer's state and generated credit ratings of issuers and investment projects help investors make reasonable investment decision, as well as help issuer with good enough ratings get credits on lower rates etc.

But the methodologies of leading rating agencies, such as "the Big Three credit rating agencies" (Standard & Poor's (S&P), Moody's, and Fitch Group) as well as the Russian rating agency ACRA and all others, have a lot of shortcomings. A number of works by authors are devoted to eliminating some of these shortcomings (Brusov et al. 2018a, b, c, d, e).

Besides the fact that RA represent some "black boxes," the information about which is almost completely absent, there are some serious methodological and systematic errors in their activity. These errors and ways to overcome them have been discussed in a number of chapters (Brusov et al. 2018a, b, c, d, e), as well as in the monograph (Brusov et al. 2018).

The use of discounting in the rating. One of the major flaws of all existing rating methodologies is a failure or a very narrow use of discounting. But even in those rare cases where it is used, it is not quite correct, since the discount rate when discounting financial flows is chosen incorrectly.

As Brusov et al. (2018) have mentioned "the need to take into account the time factor in terms of discounting is obvious, because it is associated with the time value of money. The financial part of the rating is based on a comparison of generated income with the value of the debt and the interest payable. Because income and disbursement of debt and interest are separated in time, the use of discounting when comparing revenues with the value of debt and interest is absolutely necessary for assigning credit ratings for issuers."

This raises the question about the value of discount rate. This question has always been one of the major and extremely difficult in many areas of finance: corporate finance and investment; it is particularly important in business valuation, where a slight change in the discount rate leads to a significant change in the assessment of company capitalization, which is used by unscrupulous appraisers for artificial bankruptcy of the company. It is extremely essential as well in rating.

Incorporation of Financial "Ratios," used in Ratings, into Modern Investment Models In quantification of the creditworthiness of the issuers as well as in valuation of effectiveness of investment projects the crucial role belongs to the so-called financial "ratios," which constitute direct and inverse ratios of various generated cash flows to debt values and interest ones. We incorporate these financial "ratios" into the modern theory of capital structure, Brusov–Filatova–Orekhova (BFO) theory (Brusov et al. 2018), and as well into modern investment models, created by the authors.

Such incorporation, which has been done by us for the first time, is very important because one can use this theory as a powerful tool when discounting financial flows using the correct discounting rate in rating. Only this theory allows us to valuate adequately the weighted average cost of capital WACC and equity cost k_e used when discounting financial flows.

As Brusov et al. (2018) have mentioned the "use of the tools of well-developed theories in rating opens completely new horizons in the rating industry, which could be connected with transition from mainly the use of qualitative methods of the evaluation of the creditworthiness of issuers to a predominantly quantitative evaluation methods that will certainly enhance the quality and correctness of the rating."

Currently, RA just directly use financial ratios, while the new methodology will allow (knowing the values of these "relations" (and parameter k_0)) us to determine the correct values of discount rates (WACC and k_e) that should be used when discounting the various financial flows, both in terms of their timing and forecasting.

In relation to the rating of investment projects new methodology allows us to correctly determine the values of project NPV (both in units of D and in NOI), using modern investment models and correct discount rate.

As Brusov et al. (2018) mentioned "incorporation of financial 'ratios' has required the modification of the BFO theory (and its perpetuity limit—so-called Modigliani–Miller theory), as the concept of 'leverage' as the ratio of debt value to the equity value used in financial management substantially differs from the concept of 'leverage' in the rating, where it is understood as the direct and inverse ratio of the debt value to the generated cash flow values (income, revenue, etc.). The authors introduced some additional ratios, allowing us to more fully characterize the issuer's ability to repay debts and to pay interest thereon."

Thus, the bridge is building between the discount rates (WACC, k_e) used when discounting financial flows and "ratios" in the rating methodology.

The important features of current consideration as well as in previous studies are (1) the adequate use of discounting of financial flows virtually not used in existing rating methodologies and (2) the incorporation of rating parameters (financial "ratios"), used in project rating, into considered modern investment models.

12.2 Investment Models

We work within investment models, created by authors. One of them describes the effectiveness of investment project from the perspective of equity capital owners, while the other model describes the effectiveness of investment project from the perspective of equity capital and debt capital owners.

In the former case, investments at the initial time moment $T = 0$ are equal to $-S$ and the flow of capital for the period (in addition to the tax shields $k_d Dt$ it includes a payment of interest on a loan $-k_d D$):

$$CF = (\mathrm{NOI} - k_d D)(1 - t). \tag{12.1}$$

Here, for simplicity, we suppose that interest on the loan will be paid in equal shares $k_d D$ during all periods. Note that principal repayment is made at the end of the last period.

We will consider the case of discounting, when operating and financial flows are not separated and both are discounted, using the general rate (at which, obviously, the weighted average cost of capital (WACC) can be selected). In the case for long-term (perpetuity) projects, the Modigliani–Miller formula (Modigliani and Miller 1958, 1963, 1966) for WACC has been used (Brusov et al. 2018) and for projects of finite (arbitrary) duration Brusov–Filatova–Orekhova formula will be used (Brusov and Filatova 2011; Brusov et al. 2011a, b, c, 2012a, b, 2013a, b, 2014a, b; Filatova et al. 2008; Brusova 2011).

Note that debt capital is the least risky, because interest on credit is paid after taxes in the first place. Therefore, the cost of credit will always be less than the equity cost, whether of ordinary or of preference shares $k_e > k_d$; $k_p > k_d$. Here k_e are k_p are the equity cost of ordinary and that of preference shares, respectively.

12.2.1 *The Effectiveness of the Investment Project from the Perspective of the Equity Holders Only (Without Flows Separation)*

In this case operating and financial flows are not separated and are discounted, using the general rate (at which, obviously, WACC can be selected).

The credit reimbursable at the end of the project (at the end of the period (n)) can be discounted either at the same rate WACC or at the debt cost rate k_d. Now we choose a uniform rate and the first option.

$$\begin{aligned} \mathrm{NPV} &= -S + \sum_{i=1}^{n} \frac{\mathrm{NOI}(1-t) - k_d D(1-t)}{(1+\mathrm{WACC})^i} - \frac{D}{(1+\mathrm{WACC})^n} \\ &= -S + \frac{\mathrm{NOI}(1-t) - k_d D(1-t)}{\mathrm{WACC}}\left(1 - \frac{1}{(1+\mathrm{WACC})^n}\right) - \frac{D}{(1+\mathrm{WACC})^n}. \end{aligned} \tag{12.2}$$

At a Constant Value of Equity Capital (S = const)

Accounting that in the case S = const NOI is proportional to the invested capital, I, $\mathrm{NOI} = \beta I = \beta S(1 + L)$ and substituting $D = LS$, we get

$$\mathrm{NPV} = -S + \frac{\mathrm{NOI}(1-t) - k_{\mathrm{d}}D(1-t)}{\mathrm{WACC}}\left(1 - \frac{1}{(1+\mathrm{WACC})^n}\right) - \frac{D}{(1+\mathrm{WACC})^n}, \tag{12.3}$$

$$\mathrm{NPV} = -S\left[1 + \frac{Lk_{\mathrm{d}}(1-t)}{\mathrm{WACC}}\left(1 - \frac{1}{(1+\mathrm{WACC})^n}\right) + \frac{L}{(1+\mathrm{WACC})^n}\right] + \frac{\beta S(1+L)(1-t)}{\mathrm{WACC}}\left(1 - \frac{1}{(1+\mathrm{WACC})^n}\right). \tag{12.4}$$

$$\mathrm{NPV} = -S\left[1 + \frac{k_d L(1-t)}{\mathrm{WACC}}\left(1 - \frac{1}{(1+\mathrm{WACC})^n}\right) + \frac{L}{(1+\mathrm{WACC})^n}\right] + \frac{\beta S(1+L)(1-t)}{\mathrm{WACC}}\left(1 - \frac{1}{(1+\mathrm{WACC})^n}\right). \tag{12.5}$$

12.3 Incorporation of Financial Coefficients, Used in Project Rating, into Modern Investment Models, Describing the Investment Projects of Arbitrary Duration

Below for the first time we incorporate the financial coefficients, used in project rating, into modern investment models, describing the investment projects of arbitrary duration, created by authors. We will consider two kinds of financial coefficients: coverage ratios and leverage coefficients. In each group of financial coefficients, we incorporate three particular quantities.

For coverage ratios we incorporate: (1) coverage ratios of debt, $i_1 = \mathrm{NPV}/D$; (2) coverage ratios of interest on the credit $i_2 = \mathrm{NPV}/k_{\mathrm{d}}D$; and (3) coverage ratios of debt and interest on the credit $i_3 = (\mathrm{NPV})/(1 + k_{\mathrm{d}})D$.

For leverage ratios we incorporate: (1) leverage ratios of debt, $l_1 = D/\mathrm{NPV}$; (2) leverage ratios of interest on the credit $l_2 = k_{\mathrm{d}}D/\mathrm{NPV}$; and (3) leverage ratios of debt and interest on the credit $l_3 = (1 + k_{\mathrm{d}})D/\mathrm{NPV}$.

12.3.1 Coverage Ratios

12.3.1.1 Coverage Ratios of Debt

Let us first incorporate the coverage ratios, used in project rating, into modern investment models, describing the investment projects of arbitrary duration, created by authors. Dividing both parts of eq. (12.5) by D, one gets

$$\frac{\mathrm{NPV}}{D} = -\frac{1}{L} + \frac{(i_1 - k_\mathrm{d})(1-t)}{\mathrm{WACC}}\left(1 - \frac{1}{(1+\mathrm{WACC})^n}\right) - \frac{1}{(1+\mathrm{WACC})^n} \tag{12.6}$$

$$\text{Here} \quad i_1 = \frac{\mathrm{NPV}}{D} \tag{12.7}$$

12.3.1.2 Coverage Ratios of Interest on the Credit

Dividing both parts of eq. (12.5) by $k_\mathrm{d}D$, one gets

$$\frac{\mathrm{NPV}}{k_\mathrm{d}D} = -\frac{1}{k_\mathrm{d}L} + \frac{(i_2 - k_\mathrm{d})(1-t)}{\mathrm{WACC}}\left(1 - \frac{1}{(1+\mathrm{WACC})^n}\right) - \frac{1}{k_\mathrm{d}(1+\mathrm{WACC})^n} \tag{12.8}$$

$$\text{Here} \quad i_2 = \frac{\mathrm{NPV}}{k_\mathrm{d}D} \tag{12.9}$$

12.3.1.3 Coverage Ratios of Debt and Interest on the Credit

Dividing both parts of eq. (12.5) by $(1 + k_\mathrm{d})D$, one gets

$$\frac{\mathrm{NPV}}{(1+k_\mathrm{d})D} = \frac{1}{(1+k_\mathrm{d})} \times \left[-\frac{1}{L} + \frac{((1+k_\mathrm{d})i_3 - k_\mathrm{d})(1-t)}{\mathrm{WACC}}\left(1 - \frac{1}{(1+\mathrm{WACC})^n}\right) - \frac{1}{(1+\mathrm{WACC})^n}\right] \tag{12.10}$$

$$\text{Here} \quad i_3 = \frac{\mathrm{NPV}}{(1+k_\mathrm{d})D} \tag{12.11}$$

12.3.2 *Leverage Ratios*

12.3.2.1 Leverage Ratios for Debt

Now let us incorporate the leverage ratios, used in project rating, into modern investment models, created by authors.

Dividing both parts of eq. (12.5) by NOI, one gets

$$\frac{\text{NPV}}{\text{NOI}} = -\frac{l_1}{L} + \frac{(1 - k_d l_1)(1 - t)}{\text{WACC}}\left(1 - \frac{1}{(1 + \text{WACC})^n}\right) - \frac{l_1}{(1 + \text{WACC})^n} \tag{12.12}$$

$$\text{Here} \quad l_1 = \frac{D}{\text{NPV}} \tag{12.13}$$

12.3.2.2 Leverage Ratios for Interest on Credit

$$\frac{\text{NPV}}{\text{NOI}} = -\frac{l_2}{k_d L} + \frac{(1 - l_2)(1 - t)}{\text{WACC}}\left(1 - \frac{1}{(1 + \text{WACC})^n}\right) - \frac{l_2}{k_d(1 + \text{WACC})^n} \tag{12.14}$$

$$\text{Here} \quad l_2 = \frac{k_d D}{\text{NPV}} \tag{12.15}$$

12.3.2.3 Leverage Ratios for Debt and Interest on Credit

$$\frac{\text{NPV}}{\text{NOI}} = \frac{1}{1 + k_d} \times \left[-\frac{l_3}{L} + \frac{(1 + k_d - k_d l_3)(1 - t)}{\text{WACC}}\left(1 - \frac{1}{(1 + \text{WACC})^n}\right) - \frac{l_3}{(1 + \text{WACC})^n}\right] \tag{12.16}$$

$$\text{Here} \quad l_3 = \frac{(1 + k_d)D}{\text{NPV}}. \tag{12.17}$$

Let us investigate below the effectiveness of investment projects of arbitrary duration studying the dependence of NPV on coverage ratios and on leverage ratios. We make calculations for coefficients i_1 and l_1. Calculations for the rest of coefficients (i_2, i_3 and l_2, l_3) could be made in a similar way.

We start from the calculations of the dependence of NPV on coverage ratios. We consider different values of equity costs k_0, different values of debt costs k_d, and different values of leverage level $L = D/S$. Here t is tax on profit rate, which in our calculations is equal to 20%.

12.4 Results and Analysis

12.4.1 Dependence of NPV/D on Coverage Ratios

Below we calculate the dependence of NPV (in units of D)(NPV/D) on coverage ratio on debt i_1 at different equity costs k_0 (k_0 is the equity cost at zero leverage level $L = 0$). We will make calculations for two leverage levels L ($L = 1$ and $L = 3$), for two project durations ($n = 2$ and $n = 5$), and for different credit rates k_d. In our calculations, we use Excel technique in two aspects: (1) we calculate WACC at different values of equity costs k_0, different values of debt costs k_d, and different values of leverage level $L = D/S$, using the famous BFO formula, and (2) we calculate the dependences of NPV on coverage ratios as well as leverage ratios at different values of equity costs k_0, different values of debt costs k_d, and different values of leverage level L. We use typical values of equity costs k_0, of debt costs k_d, and of leverage level L.

For calculation of the dependence of NPV/D on coverage ratio on debt i_1 within BFO approximation (arbitrary duration projects), we use the formula (12.6)

$$\frac{\text{NPV}}{D} = -\frac{1}{L} + \frac{(i_1 - k_d)(1-t)}{\text{WACC}}\left(1 - \frac{1}{(1+\text{WACC})^n}\right) - \frac{1}{(1+\text{WACC})^n}$$

12.4.1.1 The Dependence of NPV on Coverage Ratio on Debt i_1

Below we investigate the dependence of NPV/D on coverage ratio on debt i_1 at different values of equity costs k_0, at different values of debt costs k_d at fixed value of equity cost, as well as at different values of leverage levels L.

Let us start our calculations from the case of equity cost $k_0 = 14\%$.

1. We calculate WACC, using the famous BFO formula (Brusov et al. 2015, 2018)

$$\frac{\left[1-(1+\text{WACC})^{-n}\right]}{\text{WACC}} = \frac{\left[1-(1+k_0)^{-n}\right]}{k_0 + \left[1 - w_d \times t \times \left(1-(1+k_d)^{-n}\right)\right]} \tag{12.18}$$

Here k_0 is equity costs, k_d is debt costs, $L = D/S$ is the leverage level, t is tax on profit rate, w_d is debt ratio, WACC is weighted average capital cost, and n is the project duration.

2. We calculate dependence of NPV/D (NPV in units D) on coverage ratio on debt i_1, using obtained value of WACC, which depends on k_0, k_d, t, n, L.
3. We calculate NPV/NOI (NPV in units NOI) on leverage ratio on debt l_1, using obtained value of WACC, which depends on k_0, k_d, t, n, L.

The results are shown in tables and figures.

Table 12.1 The dependence of NPV/D on coverage ratio on debt i_1 at $L = 1$, $k_0 = 14\%$; $k_d = 12\%$; $t = 20\%$, $n = 2$

w_d	L	k_0	k_d	t	i_1	n	NPV/D ($L = 1$)	WACC
0.5	1	0.14	0.12	0.2	0	2	−1.86035	0.185838
0.5	1	0.14	0.12	0.2	1	2	−0.61682	0.185838
0.5	1	0.14	0.12	0.2	2	2	0.626711	0.185838
0.5	1	0.14	0.12	0.2	3	2	1.870243	0.185838
0.5	1	0.14	0.12	0.2	4	2	3.113776	0.185838
0.5	1	0.14	0.12	0.2	5	2	4.357308	0.185838
0.5	1	0.14	0.12	0.2	6	2	5.600841	0.185838
0.5	1	0.14	0.12	0.2	7	2	6.844373	0.185838
0.5	1	0.14	0.12	0.2	8	2	8.087906	0.185838
0.5	1	0.14	0.12	0.2	9	2	9.331438	0.185838
0.5	1	0.14	0.12	0.2	10	2	10.57497	0.185838

Table 12.2 The dependence of NPV/D on coverage ratio on debt i_1 at $L = 1$, $k_0 = 14\%$; $k_d = 12\%$; $t = 20\%$, $n = 5$

L	k_0	k_d	t	i_1	n	NPV/D ($L = 1$)	WACC
1	0.14	0.12	0.2	0	5	−2.0942	0.072849
1	0.14	0.12	0.2	1	5	1.161083	0.072849
1	0.14	0.12	0.2	2	5	4.41637	0.072849
1	0.14	0.12	0.2	3	5	7.671658	0.072849
1	0.14	0.12	0.2	4	5	10.92694	0.072849
1	0.14	0.12	0.2	5	5	14.18223	0.072849
1	0.14	0.12	0.2	6	5	17.43752	0.072849
1	0.14	0.12	0.2	7	5	20.69281	0.072849
1	0.14	0.12	0.2	8	5	23.94809	0.072849
1	0.14	0.12	0.2	9	5	27.20338	0.072849
1	0.14	0.12	0.2	10	5	30.45867	0.072849

We see from the Tables 12.1, 12.2, 12.3, and 12.4 and from Fig. 12.1 that NPV (in units of D) (NPV/D) increases with i_1.

The features of this increase are the following:

1. The angle NPV(i_1) is determined by the project duration n: it increases with n.
2. With the increase of leverage level L, the curve NPV(i_1) shifts practically parallel up. Thus, NPV increases with debt financing.

This means that the influence of the project duration n on the dependence of NPV/D on coverage ratio on debt i_1 is more significant than the influence of leverage level L.

Table 12.3 The dependence of NPV/*D* on coverage ratio on debt i_1 at $L = 3$, $k_0 = 14\%$; $k_d = 12\%$; $t = 20\%$, $n = 2$

L	k_0	k_d	t	i_1	n	NPV/*D* ($L = 1$)	WACC
3	0.14	0.12	0.2	0	2	−1.19238	0.186786
3	0.14	0.12	0.2	1	2	0.049707	0.186786
3	0.14	0.12	0.2	2	2	1.291792	0.186786
3	0.14	0.12	0.2	3	2	2.533877	0.186786
3	0.14	0.12	0.2	4	2	3.775963	0.186786
3	0.14	0.12	0.2	5	2	5.018048	0.186786
3	0.14	0.12	0.2	6	2	6.260133	0.186786
3	0.14	0.12	0.2	7	2	7.502218	0.186786
3	0.14	0.12	0.2	8	2	8.744303	0.186786
3	0.14	0.12	0.2	9	2	9.986389	0.186786
3	0.14	0.12	0.2	10	2	11.22847	0.186786

Table 12.4 The dependence of NPV/*D* on coverage ratio on debt i_1 at $L = 3$, $k_0 = 14\%$; $k_d = 12\%$; $t = 20\%$, $n = 5$

w_d	L	k_0	k_d	t	i_1	n	NPV/*D* ($L = 1$)	WACC
0.25	3	0.14	0.12	0.2	0	5	−1.42302	0.073898
0.25	3	0.14	0.12	0.2	1	5	1.823185	0.073898
0.25	3	0.14	0.12	0.2	2	5	5.069387	0.073898
0.25	3	0.14	0.12	0.2	3	5	8.315588	0.073898
0.25	3	0.14	0.12	0.2	4	5	11.56179	0.073898
0.25	3	0.14	0.12	0.2	5	5	14.80799	0.073898
0.25	3	0.14	0.12	0.2	6	5	18.05419	0.073898
0.25	3	0.14	0.12	0.2	7	5	21.30039	0.073898
0.25	3	0.14	0.12	0.2	8	5	24.5466	0.073898
0.25	3	0.14	0.12	0.2	9	5	27.7928	0.073898
0.25	3	0.14	0.12	0.2	10	5	31.039	0.073898

12.4.1.2 The Dependence of NPV on Leverage Ratio on Debt l_1

We see from Tables 12.5, 12.6, 12.7, and 12.8 and from Fig. 12.2 that NPV (in units of NOI) (NPV/NOI) decreases with l_1.

The features of this decrease are the following:

1. The angle NPV(l_1) is determined by the leverage level *L*: it increases with *L*. Thus, NPV increases with debt financing.
2. With the increase of project duration *n*, the curve NPV(l_1) shifts practically parallel up.

This means that the influence of leverage level *L* on the dependence of NPV/NOI on leverage ratio on debt l_1 is more significant than the influence of the project duration n.

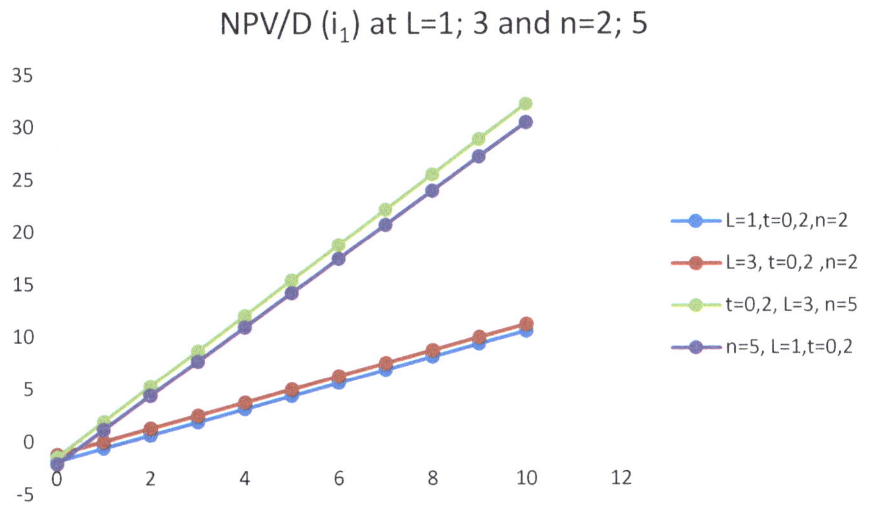

Fig. 12.1 The dependence of NPV/D on coverage ratio on debt i_1 at $L = 1; 3$, $k_0 = 14\%$; $k_d = 12\%$; $t = 20\%$, $n = 2; 5$

Table 12.5 The dependence of NPV/NOI on leverage ratio on debt l_1 at $L = 1$, $k_0 = 14\%$; $k_d = 12\%$; $t = 20\%$, $n = 2$

L	l_1	k_d	k_0	t	n	w_d	WACC	NPV/NOI ($L = 1$)
1	0	0.12	0.14	0.2	2	0.5	0.1231	1.346553406
1	1	0.12	0.14	0.2	2	0.5	0.1231	−0.6078321
1	2	0.12	0.14	0.2	2	0.5	0.1231	−2.5622176
1	3	0.12	0.14	0.2	2	0.5	0.1231	−4.5166031
1	4	0.12	0.14	0.2	2	0.5	0.1231	−6.47098861
1	5	0.12	0.14	0.2	2	0.5	0.1231	−8.42537411
1	6	0.12	0.14	0.2	2	0.5	0.1231	−10.3797596
1	7	0.12	0.14	0.2	2	0.5	0.1231	−12.3341451
1	8	0.12	0.14	0.2	2	0.5	0.1231	−14.2885306
1	9	0.12	0.14	0.2	2	0.5	0.1231	−16.2429161
1	10	0.12	0.14	0.2	2	0.5	0.1231	−18.1973016

One can see that the dependence of NPV/NOI on leverage ratio on debt l_1 is opposite to the dependence of NPV/D on coverage ratio on debt i_1:

1. The angle NPV(l_1) is determined by the leverage level L, while the angle NPV(i_1) is determined by the project duration n.
2. With the increase of project duration n, the curve NPV(l_1) shifts practically parallel up, while such kind of behavior is typical for the influence of the leverage level L in the case of the curve NPV(i_1).

The only one common thing for both curves NPV(l_1) and NPV(i_1) is that NPV increases with debt financing (or with the leverage level L).

Table 12.6 The dependence of NPV/NOI on leverage ratio on debt l_1 at $L = 3$, $k_0 = 14\%$; $k_d = 12\%$; $t = 20\%$, $n = 2$

L	l_1	k_d	k_0	t	n	w_d	WACC	NPV/NOI ($L = 1$)
3	0	0.12	0.14	0.2	2	0.25	0.13203	1.330967788
3	1	0.12	0.14	0.2	2	0.25	0.13203	0.057577565
3	2	0.12	0.14	0.2	2	0.25	0.13203	−1.21581266
3	3	0.12	0.14	0.2	2	0.25	0.13203	−2.48920288
3	4	0.12	0.14	0.2	2	0.25	0.13203	−3.7625931
3	5	0.12	0.14	0.2	2	0.25	0.13203	−5.03598332
3	6	0.12	0.14	0.2	2	0.25	0.13203	−6.30937355
3	7	0.12	0.14	0.2	2	0.25	0.13203	−7.58276377
3	8	0.12	0.14	0.2	2	0.25	0.13203	−8.85615399
3	9	0.12	0.14	0.2	2	0.25	0.13203	−10.1295442
3	10	0.12	0.14	0.2	2	0.25	0.13203	−11.4029344

Table 12.7 The dependence of NPV/NOI on leverage ratio on debt l_1 at $L = 1$, $k_0 = 14\%$; $k_d = 12\%$; $t = 20\%$, $n = 5$

L	l_1	k_d	k_0	t	n	w_d	WACC	NPV/NOI ($L = 1$)
1	0	0.12	0.14	0.2	5	0.5	0.121819	2.870871
1	1	0.12	0.14	0.2	5	0.5	0.121819	0.963526
1	2	0.12	0.14	0.2	5	0.5	0.121819	−0.94382
1	3	0.12	0.14	0.2	5	0.5	0.121819	−2.85116
1	4	0.12	0.14	0.2	5	0.5	0.121819	−4.75851
1	5	0.12	0.14	0.2	5	0.5	0.121819	−6.66585
1	6	0.12	0.14	0.2	5	0.5	0.121819	−8.5732
1	7	0.12	0.14	0.2	5	0.5	0.121819	−10.4805
1	8	0.12	0.14	0.2	5	0.5	0.121819	−12.3879
1	9	0.12	0.14	0.2	5	0.5	0.121819	−14.2952
1	10	0.12	0.14	0.2	5	0.5	0.121819	−16.2026

Table 12.8 The dependence of NPV/NOI on leverage ratio on debt l_1 at $L = 3$, $k_0 = 14\%$; $k_d = 12\%$; $t = 20\%$, $n = 5$

L	l_1	k_d	k_0	t	n	w_d	WACC	NPV/NOI ($L = 1$)
3	0	0.12	0.14	0.2	5	0.25	0.130962	2.807196
3	1	0.12	0.14	0.2	5	0.25	0.130962	1.596542
3	2	0.12	0.14	0.2	5	0.25	0.130962	0.385889
3	3	0.12	0.14	0.2	5	0.25	0.130962	−0.82476
3	4	0.12	0.14	0.2	5	0.25	0.130962	−2.03542
3	5	0.12	0.14	0.2	5	0.25	0.130962	−3.24607
3	6	0.12	0.14	0.2	5	0.25	0.130962	−4.45672
3	7	0.12	0.14	0.2	5	0.25	0.130962	−5.66738
3	8	0.12	0.14	0.2	5	0.25	0.130962	−6.87803
3	9	0.12	0.14	0.2	5	0.25	0.130962	−8.08868
3	10	0.12	0.14	0.2	5	0.25	0.130962	−9.29934

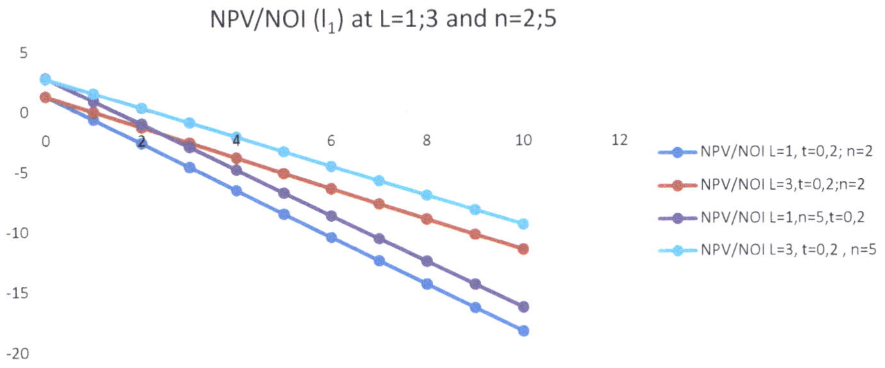

Fig. 12.2 The dependence of NPV/NOI on leverage ratio on debt l_1 at $L = 1$; 3, $k_0 = 14\%$; $k_d = 12\%$; $t = 20\%$, n = 2; 5

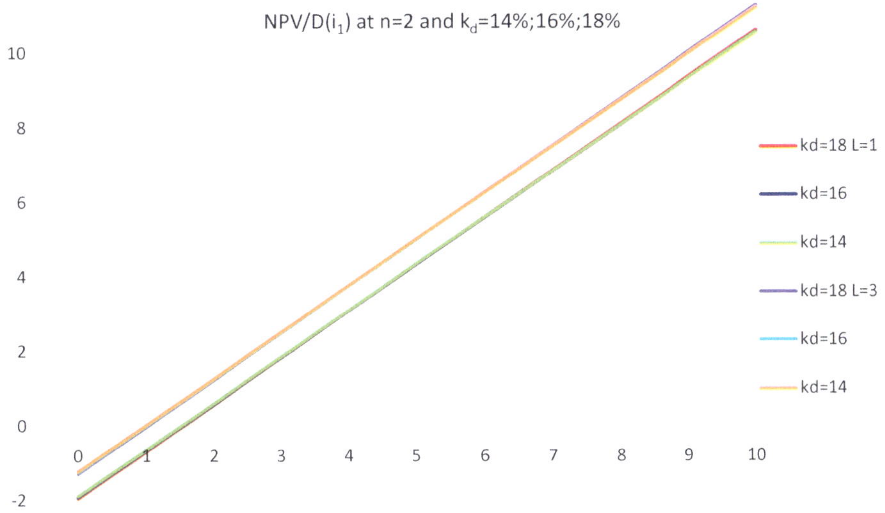

Fig. 12.3 The dependence of NPV/*D* on coverage ratio on debt i_1 at $L = 1$; 3, $k_0 = 20\%$; $k_d = 14\%$, 16%, 18%; $t = 20\%$, $n = 2$ (i_1 changes from 0 to 10)

12.4.1.3 The Dependence of NPV on Coverage Ratio on Debt i_1 at Different Values of k_d

Let us investigate the dependence of NPV/*D* on coverage ratio on debt i_1 at $L = 3$, $k_0 = 20\%$; $k_d = 18\%$; $t = 20\%$, $n = 2$ (Fig. 12.3 and Tables 12.9, 12.10, and 12.11).

The straight lines for different k_d practically merge, which means that the influence of the variation of k_d on such a scale of changes i_1 is insignificant. In order to evaluate the ordering of straight lines corresponding to different k_d, we increase the scale in the following figures, considering the values of i_1 not from 0 to

Table 12.9 The dependence of NPV/*D* on coverage ratio on debt i_1 at $L = 3$, $k_0 = 20\%$; $k_d = 18\%$; $t = 20\%$, $n = 2$

NPV/D	L	i_1	k_d	WACC	t	n
−1.281958725	3	0	0.18	0.176679108	0.2	2
−0.024284066	3	1	0.18	0.176679108	0.2	2
1.233390593	3	2	0.18	0.176679108	0.2	2
2.491065253	3	3	0.18	0.176679108	0.2	2
3.748739912	3	4	0.18	0.176679108	0.2	2
5.006414571	3	5	0.18	0.176679108	0.2	2
6.264089231	3	6	0.18	0.176679108	0.2	2
7.52176389	3	7	0.18	0.176679108	0.2	2
8.779438549	3	8	0.18	0.176679108	0.2	2
10.03711321	3	9	0.18	0.176679108	0.2	2
11.29478787	3	10	0.18	0.176679108	0.2	2

Table 12.10 The dependence of NPV/*D* on coverage ratio on debt i_1 at $L = 3$, $k_0 = 20\%$; $k_d = 16\%$; $t = 20\%$, $n = 2$

NPV	L	i_1	k_d	WACC	t	n
−1.249017883	3	0	0.16	0.18198583	0.2	2
0.000427777	3	1	0.16	0.18198583	0.2	2
1.249873438	3	2	0.16	0.18198583	0.2	2
2.499319098	3	3	0.16	0.18198583	0.2	2
3.748764758	3	4	0.16	0.18198583	0.2	2
4.998210418	3	5	0.16	0.18198583	0.2	2
6.247656078	3	6	0.16	0.18198583	0.2	2
7.497101739	3	7	0.16	0.18198583	0.2	2
8.746547399	3	8	0.16	0.18198583	0.2	2
9.995993059	3	9	0.16	0.18198583	0.2	2
11.24543872	3	10	0.16	0.18198583	0.2	2

Table 12.11 The dependence of NPV/*D* on coverage ratio on debt i_1 at $L = 3$, $k_0 = 20\%$; $k_d = 14\%$; $t = 20\%$, $n = 2$

NPV	L	i_1	k_d	WACC	t	n
−1.221437995	3	0	0.14	0.183805688	0.2	2
0.025207969	3	1	0.14	0.183805688	0.2	2
1.271853932	3	2	0.14	0.183805688	0.2	2
2.518499896	3	3	0.14	0.183805688	0.2	2
3.76514586	3	4	0.14	0.183805688	0.2	2
5.011791823	3	5	0.14	0.183805688	0.2	2
6.258437787	3	6	0.14	0.183805688	0.2	2
7.505083751	3	7	0.14	0.183805688	0.2	2
8.751729714	3	8	0.14	0.183805688	0.2	2
9.998375678	3	9	0.14	0.183805688	0.2	2
11.24502164	3	10	0.14	0.183805688	0.2	2

10, but from 0 to 1. In Fig. 12.4, we consider the case of different project duration n, while in Fig. 12.5 the case of different leverage level L.

One can see from Fig. 12.5 that the ordering of the NPV/D straight lines for different credit rates k_d and different leverage level L turns out to be the following:

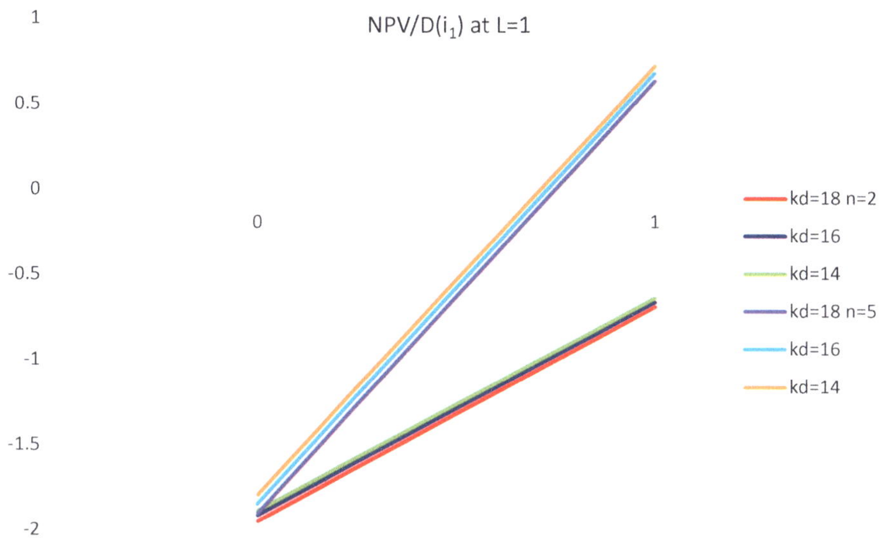

Fig. 12.4 The detailed dependence of NPV/D on coverage ratio on debt i_1 at $L = 1$, $k_0 = 20\%$; $k_d = 14\%$; 16%; 18%; $t = 20\%$, $n = 2$; 5

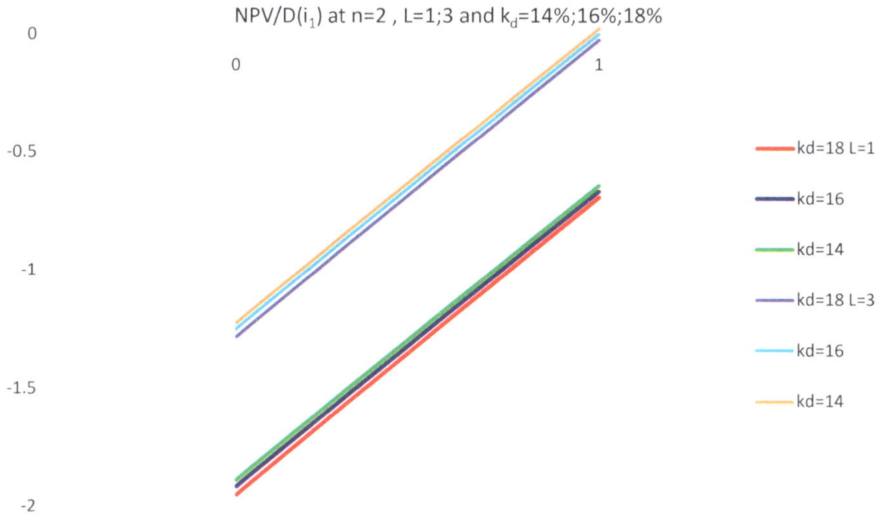

Fig. 12.5 The detailed dependence of NPV/D on coverage ratio on debt i_1 at $L = 1$; 3, $k_0 = 20\%$; $k_d = 14\%$, 16%, 18%; $t = 20\%$, $n = 2$ (i_1 changes from 0 to 1)

two triplets, corresponding to different leverage level L, are well distinguished and the upper triplet (with bigger NPV value) corresponds to bigger leverage level $L = 3$.

This means that NPV increases with debt financing. Within each triplet NPV decreases with credit rates k_d: the biggest NPV corresponds to $k_d = 14\%$ and the smallest one corresponds to $k_d = 18\%$.

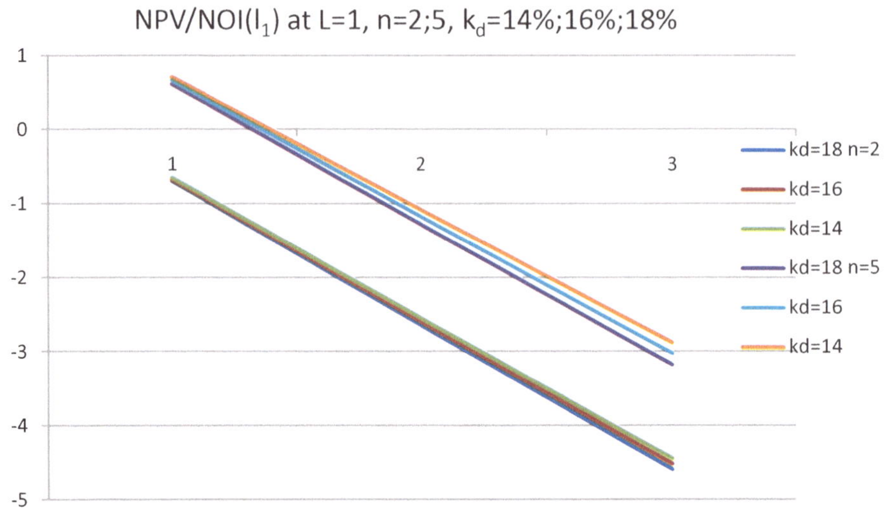

Fig. 12.6 The detailed dependence of NPV/NOI on leverage ratio on debt l_1 at $L = 1$; $k_0 = 20\%$; $k_d = 14\%$, 16%, 18%; $t = 20\%$, $n = 2$; 5 (i_1 changes from 0 to 3)

12.4.1.4 The Dependence of NPV/NOI on Leverage Ratio on Debt l_1 at Different Values of k_d

Let us investigate the dependence of NPV/NOI on leverage ratio on debt l_1 at $L = 1$, $k_0 = 20\%$; $k_d = 18\%$; $t = 20\%$, $n = 2$.

We show below the detailed dependence of NPV/NOI on leverage ratio on debt l_1 at $L = 1$; $k_0 = 20\%$; $k_d = 14\%$, 16%, 18%; $t = 20\%$, $n = 2$; 5 (i_1 changes from 0 to 3).

One can see from Fig. 12.6 that with the increase of project duration n the NPV/NOI(l_1) straight lines shift practically parallel up. The ordering of the NPV/NOI(l_1) straight lines for different credit rates k_d and different project duration n turns out to be the following: two triplets, corresponding to different project duration n, are well distinguished and the upper triplet (with bigger NPV value) corresponds to bigger project duration $n = 5$. Within each triplet NPV decreases with credit rates kd: the biggest NPV corresponds to $k_d = 14\%$ and the smallest one corresponds to $k_d = 18\%$. It is seen that the influence of the value of credit rates k_d increases with n, while in the case of NPV/D the shift of NPV turns out to be the same for different leverage level L.

12.5 Conclusion

In this chapter, we develop for the first time a new approach to ratings of the investment projects of arbitrary duration, applicable to energy projects. The ratings of such energy projects as "Turkish stream" and "Nord stream-2," energy projects relating to clean, renewable, and sustainable energy, as well as relating to pricing carbon emissions, could be done using new rating methodologies. The chapter generalizes the new approach to the ratings of the long-term investment projects, which has been developed in our previous chapter (Brusov et al. 2018).The important features of current consideration as well as in previous studies are (1) the adequate use of discounting financial flows virtually not used in existing rating methodologies and (2) the incorporation of rating parameters (financial "ratios"), used in project rating, into considered modern investment models.

We use the modern investment models, created by us, with incorporated financial "ratios" to study the dependence of NPV on rating parameters (financial "ratios") at different values of equity cost k_0, at different values of credit rates k_d, as well as at different values of on leverage level L and project duration n. We study the dependence of NPV on two types of financial "ratios": on the coverage ratios i_j and on the leverage ratios l_j. In our calculations, we use Excel technique in two aspects: (1) we calculate WACC at different values of equity costs k_0, different values of debt costs k_d, and different values of leverage level $L = D/S$, using the famous BFO formula, and (2) we calculate the dependences of NPV on coverage ratios as well as leverage ratios at different values of equity costs k_0, different values of debt costs k_d, and different values of leverage level L.

Analyzing obtained results we have found:

I. NPV (in units of D) (NPV/D) increases with i_1 with the following features:

   1. The angle NPV(i_1) is determined by the project duration n: it increases with n.
   2. With the increase of leverage level L, the curve NPV(i_1) shifts practically parallel up. Thus, NPV increases with debt financing.

This means that the influence of the project duration n on the dependence of NPV/D on coverage ratio on debt i_1 is more significant than the influence of leverage level L.

II. NPV (in units of NOI) (NPV/NOI) decreases with l_1 with the following features:

   1. The angle NPV(l_1) is determined by the leverage level L: it increases with L. Thus, NPV increases with debt financing.
   2. With the increase of project duration n, the curve NPV(l_1) shifts practically parallel up.

This means that the influence of leverage level L on the dependence of NPV/NOI on leverage ratio on debt l_1 is more significant than the influence of the project duration n.

One can see that the dependence of NPV/NOI on leverage ratio on debt l_1 is opposite to the dependence of NPV/D on coverage ratio on debt i_1:

1. The angle NPV(l_1) is determined by the leverage level L, while the angle NPV(i_1) is determined by the project duration n.

2. With the increase of project duration n, the curve NPV(l_1) shifts practically parallel up, while such kind of behavior is typical for the influence of the leverage level L in the case of the curve NPV(i_1).

The only one common thing for both curves NPV(l_1) and NPV(i_1) is that NPV increases with debt financing (or with the leverage level L). This means that debt financing of the projects of arbitrary duration favors effectiveness of the investment project as well as its creditworthiness.

The obtained results allow us to make adequate estimation of the effectiveness of the investment projects, NPV, knowing rating parameters (financial "ratios"). For all calculations we use the correct values of discount rate, WACC, which is calculated by the use of the modern theory of capital cost and capital structure (BFO theory) (Brusov et al. 2018).

Investigations, conducting in this chapter, create a new approach to rating methodology with respect to the ratings of the investment project of arbitrary duration. It allows us to use the financial "ratios" for adequate estimation of the effectiveness of the investment projects of arbitrary duration, including energy projects, such as "Turkish stream" and "Nord stream-2,", energy projects relating to clean, renewable, and sustainable energy.

References

Brusov P (2018a) Editorial: introduction on special issue on the banking system and financial markets of Russia and other countries: problems and prospects. J Rev Glob Econ 7:i–vi, SCOPUS

Brusov P (2018b) Editorial. J Rev Glob Econ 7:i–v, SCOPUS

Brusov PN, Filatova TV (2011) From Modigliani–Miller to general theory of capital cost and capital structure of the company. Finance Credit 435:2–8

Brusov P, Filatova T, Orehova N, Brusova A (2011a) Weighted average cost of capital in the theory of Modigliani–Miller, modified for a finite life-time company. Appl Financ Econ 21 (11):815–824

Brusov P, Filatova T, Orehova N et al (2011b) From Modigliani–Miller to general theory of capital cost and capital structure of the company. Res J Econ Bus ICT 2:16–21

Brusov P, Filatova T, Orehova N et al (2011c) Influence of debt financing on the effectiveness of the investment project within the Modigliani–Miller theory. Res J Econ Bus ICT (UK) 2:11–15

Brusov P, Filatova T, Eskindarov M, Orehova N (2012a) Influence of debt financing on the effectiveness of the finite duration investment project. Appl Financ Econ 22(13):1043–1052

Brusov P, Filatova T, Eskindarov M, Orehova N (2012b) Hidden global causes of the global financial crisis. J Rev Global Econ 1:106–111

Brusov P, Filatova P, Orekhova N (2013a) Absence of an optimal capital structure in the famous tradeoff theory! J Rev Global Econ 2:94–116

Brusov P, Filatova T, Orehova N (2013b) A qualitatively new effect in corporative finance: abnormal dependence of cost of equity of company on leverage. J Rev Global Econ 2:183–193

Brusov P, Filatova P, Orekhova N (2014a) Mechanism of formation of the company optimal capital structure, different from suggested by trade off theory. Cogent Econ Finance 2:1–13. http://dx.doi.org/ 10.1080/23322039.2014.946150

Brusov P, Filatova T, Orehova N (2014b) Inflation in Brusov–Filatova–Orekhova theory and in its perpetuity limit—Modigliani–Miller theory. J Rev Global Econ 3:175–185

Brusov P, Filatova T, Orekhova N, Eskindarov M (2015) Modern corporate finance, investments and taxation, Springer International Publishing, Switzerland, p 373. Monograph, SCOPUS. https://www.springer.com/gp/book/9783319147314

Brusov PN, Filatova TV, Orekhova NP (2018a) Modern corporate finance and investments, monograph. Knorus Publishing House, Moscow, p 517

Brusov P, Filatova T, Orekhova N, Eskindarov M (2018b) Modern corporate finance, investments, taxation and ratings, Springer Nature Publishing, Switzerland, p 571. Monograph

Brusov PN, Filatova TV, Orekhova NP, Kulik VL (2018c) Rating: new approach. J Rev Glob Econ 7:37–62. SCOPUS. https://doi.org/10.6000/1929-7092.2018.07.05

Brusov PN, Filatova TV, Orekhova NP, Kulik VL (2018d) A "golden age" of the companies: conditions of its existence. J Rev Glob Econ 7:88–103. SCOPUS. https://doi.org/10.6000/1929-7092.2018.07.07

Brusov PN, Filatova TV, Orekhova NP, Kulik VL (2018e) Rating methodology: new look and new horizons. J Rev Glob Econ 7:63–87. SCOPUS. https://doi.org/10.6000/1929-7092.2018.07.06

Brusov PN, Filatova TV, Orekhova NP, Kulik VL, Weil I (2018f) New meaningful effects in modern capital structure theory. J Rev Glob Econ 7:104–122. SCOPUS. https://doi.org/10.6000/1929-7092.2018.07.08

Brusov P, Filatova T, Orekhova N, Kulik V, Weil I, Brailov A (2018g) The impact of the central bank key rate and commercial banks credit rates on creating and maintaining of a favorable investment climate in the country. J Rev Glob Econ 7:360–376. SCOPUS. https://doi.org/10.6000/1929-7092.2018.07.31

Brusov PN, Filatova TV, Orekhova NP, Kulik VL, Weil I (2019) Ratings of the investment projects of arbitrary durations: new methodology. J Rev Glob Econ 8:437–448. SCOPUS. https://doi.org/10.6000/1929-7092.2019.08.37

Brusov PN, Filatova TV, Orekhova NP, Kulik VL, Chang S-I, Lin YCG (2020) Modification of the Modigliani–Miller theory for the case of advance payments of tax on profit. J Rev Global Econ 9:257–268

Brusova A (2011) A comparison of the three methods of estimation of weighted average cost of capital and equity cost of company. Financ Anal Prob Sol 34(76):36–42

Filatova T, Orehova N, Brusova A (2008) Weighted average cost of capital in the theory of Modigliani–Miller, modified for a finite lifetime company. Bull FU 48:68–77

Filatova TV, Brusov PN, Orekhova NP, Kulik VL (2018) Ratings of the long-term projects: new approach. J Rev Glob Econ 7:645–661, SCOPUS. https://doi.org/10.6000/1929-7092.2018.07.59

Modigliani F, Miller M (1958) The cost of capital, corporate finance, and the theory of investment. Am Econ Rev 48:261–297

Modigliani F, Miller M (1963) Corporate income taxes and the cost of capital: a correction. Am Econ Rev 53:147–175

Modigliani F, Miller M (1966) Some estimates of the cost of capital to the electric utility industry 1954–1957. Am Econ Rev 56:333–391

Chapter 13
Ratings of Investment Projects of Arbitrary Duration with a Uniform Debt Repayment: A New Approach

13.1 Introduction

Along with the rating of non-financial issuers, considered in Chaps. 6, 7, and 8, the rating of investment projects plays an important role in the modern economy and finance. It allows ranking and selection of the most effective investment projects, which is especially important for attracting both foreign and domestic investments. This chapter discusses the rating of investment projects of arbitrary duration with a uniform repayment of debt, the investment model for which is described in Chap. 10. The methodology for rating investment projects has been modified. A fundamentally new approach to the project rating methodology has been developed, the key factors of which are: (1) adequate application of discounting when discounting the financial flows, which is practically not used in existing project rating methodologies; (2) incorporation of financial ratios into modern investment models created by the authors; (3) use of rating parameters upon discounting; and (4) the determination of the correct discount rate, taking into account financial ratios. We use modern investment model created by the authors (see Chap. 10), the modern theory of capital cost and capital structure by Brusov–Filatova–Orekhova (BFO theory), its modification for rating needs, and rating coefficients. Various theories of capital cost and capital structure are described in Chaps. 3, 4, and 5.

The developed approach should be applied by rating agencies, both international and national ones, when rating investment projects.

The modification of the methodology of the existing project rating systems will improve the accuracy of ratings of investment projects and make them more objective. The use of powerful tools of well-developed theories opens up new opportunities for the rating industry, which gives the opportunity to switch from using primarily qualitative methods for assessing the effectiveness of investment projects to using mainly quantitative methods for evaluating them.

P. Brusov et al., *Ratings*, Contributions to Finance and Accounting,
https://doi.org/10.1007/978-3-030-56243-4_13

13.2 Incorporation of Financial Ratios Used in Project Rating Into Modern Investment Models with Uniform Repayment of Debt

Below we incorporate the financial coefficients, used in project rating, into modern investment models with a uniform repayment of debt, created by authors. We will consider two kinds of financial coefficients: coverage ratios and leverage coefficients. In each group of financial coefficients, we incorporate three particular quantities.

For coverage ratios we incorporate: (1) coverage ratios of debt, $i_1 = \frac{\mathrm{NPV}}{D}$; (2) coverage ratios of interest on the credit $i_2 = \frac{\mathrm{NPV}}{k_\mathrm{d}D}$; and (3) coverage ratios of debt and interest on the credit $i_3 = \frac{\mathrm{NPV}}{(1+k_\mathrm{d})D}$.

For leverage ratios we incorporate: (1) leverage ratios of debt, $l_1 = \frac{D}{\mathrm{NPV}}$; (2) leverage ratios of interest on the credit $l_2 = \frac{k_\mathrm{d}D}{\mathrm{NPV}}$; and (3) leverage ratios of debt and interest on the credit $l_3 = \frac{(1+k_\mathrm{d})D}{\mathrm{NPV}}$.

Note that the last type of ratios (i_3 and l_3) was introduced by us for the first time to more fully characterize the ability to repay debts and pay interest on them at the expense of operating income when implementing an investment project.

13.2.1 Coverage Ratios

13.2.1.1 Coverage Ratios of Debt

Let us first incorporate the coverage ratios, using in project rating, into modern investment models, created by authors. Dividing both parts of Eq. (10.9) by D, one gets for the net present value of the project, NPV (in units of D), the following expression:

$$\frac{\mathrm{NPV}}{D} = -\frac{1}{L} + \frac{i_1(1-t) - \frac{1}{n} - k_\mathrm{d}\frac{n+1}{n}(1-t)}{\mathrm{WACC}}\left(1 - \frac{1}{(1+\mathrm{WACC})^n}\right)$$
$$+\frac{k_\mathrm{d}}{n}(1-t)\left\{\frac{(1+\mathrm{WACC})[1-(1+\mathrm{WACC})^{-n}]}{\mathrm{WACC}^2} - \frac{n}{\mathrm{WACC}(1+\mathrm{WACC})^n}\right\} \tag{13.1}$$

Here $i_1 = \mathrm{NOI}/D$, $L = D/S$—leverage level.

13.2.1.2 Coverage Ratios of Interest on the Credit

Dividing both parts of Eq. (10.9) by $k_{\mathrm{d}}D$, one gets for the net present value of the project, NPV (in units of $k_{\mathrm{d}}D$), the following expression:

$$\frac{\mathrm{NPV}}{k_{\mathrm{d}}D}=\frac{1}{k_{\mathrm{d}}L}+\frac{i_2(1-t)-\dfrac{1}{k_{\mathrm{d}}n}-\dfrac{n+1}{n}(1-t)}{\mathrm{WACC}}\left(1-\frac{1}{(1+\mathrm{WACC})^n}\right)$$
$$+\frac{1}{n}(1-t)\left\{\frac{(1+\mathrm{WACC})[1-(1+\mathrm{WACC})^{-n}]}{\mathrm{WACC}^2}-\frac{n}{\mathrm{WACC}(1+\mathrm{WACC})^n}\right\} \tag{13.2}$$

Here $i_2 = \mathrm{NOI}/k_dD$.

13.2.1.3 Coverage Ratios of Debt and Interest on the Credit (New Parameter)

Dividing both parts of Eq. (10.9) by $(1 + k_{\mathrm{d}})D$, one gets for the net present value of the project, NPV (in units of $(1 + k_{\mathrm{d}})D$), the following expression:

$$\frac{\mathrm{NPV}}{D(1+k_{\mathrm{d}})}=\frac{1}{L(1+k_{\mathrm{d}})}+\frac{i_3(1-t)-\dfrac{1}{n(1+k_{\mathrm{d}})}-\dfrac{k_{\mathrm{d}}}{(1+k_{\mathrm{d}})}\dfrac{n+1}{n}(1-t)}{\mathrm{WACC}}\left(1-\frac{1}{(1+\mathrm{WACC})^n}\right)$$
$$\$\$+\frac{k_{\mathrm{d}}}{(1+k_{\mathrm{d}})}(1-t)\left\{\frac{(1+\mathrm{WACC})[1-(1+\mathrm{WACC})^{-n}]}{\mathrm{WACC}^2}-\frac{n}{\mathrm{WACC}(1+\mathrm{WACC})^n}\right. \tag{13.3}$$

Here $i_3 = \frac{\mathrm{NOI}}{D(1+k_{\mathrm{d}})}$.

Analyzing formulas (13.1), (13.2), and (13.3) we come to a very important conclusion that NPV (in units of D) $(\frac{\mathrm{NPV}}{D})$ depends only on equity cost k_0, on credit rates k_{d}, on leverage level L, as well as on one of the coverage ratios i_j and does not depend on equity value S, debt value D, and NOI. This means that results on the dependence of NPV (in units of D) $(\frac{\mathrm{NPV}}{D})$ on coverage ratios i_j at different equity costs k_0, at different credit rates k_{d}, and at different leverage levels L carry the universal character: these dependencies remain valid for investment projects with any equity value S, debt value D, and NOI.

13.2.2 Leverage Ratios

13.2.2.1 Leverage Ratios for Debt

Now let us incorporate the leverage ratios, used in project rating, into modern investment models, created by authors.

Dividing both parts of Eq. (10.9) by NOI, one gets for the net present value of the project, NPV (in units of NOI), the following expression:

$$\frac{\mathrm{NPV}}{\mathrm{NOI}} = \frac{l_1}{L} + \frac{(1-t) - \frac{l_1}{n} - k_\mathrm{d} l_1 \frac{n+1}{n}(1-t)}{\mathrm{WACC}}\left(1 - \frac{1}{(1+\mathrm{WACC})^n}\right)$$
$$+ \frac{k_\mathrm{d} l_1}{n}(1-t)\left\{\frac{(1+\mathrm{WACC})\cdot[1-(1+\mathrm{WACC})^{-n}]}{\mathrm{WACC}^2} - \frac{n}{\mathrm{WACC}(1+\mathrm{WACC})^n}\right\} \tag{13.4}$$

Here $l_1 = \frac{D}{\mathrm{NOI}}$.

13.2.2.2 Leverage Ratios for Interest on Credit

Dividing both parts of Eq. (10.9) by NOI, one gets for the net present value of the project, NPV (in units of NOI), the following expression:

$$\frac{\mathrm{NPV}}{\mathrm{NOI}} = -\frac{l_2}{k_\mathrm{d} L} + \frac{(1-t) - \frac{l_2}{k_\mathrm{d} n} - l_2 \frac{n+1}{n}(1-t)}{\mathrm{WACC}}\left(1 - \frac{1}{(1+\mathrm{WACC})^n}\right)$$
$$+ \frac{l_2}{n}(1-t)\left\{\frac{(1+\mathrm{WACC})[1-(1+\mathrm{WACC})^{-n}]}{\mathrm{WACC}^2} - \frac{n}{\mathrm{WACC}(1+\mathrm{WACC})^n}\right. \tag{13.5}$$

Here $l_2 = \frac{k_\mathrm{d} D}{\mathrm{NOI}}$.

13.2.2.3 Leverage Ratios for Debt and Interest on Credit

Dividing both parts of Eq. (10.9) by NOI, one gets for the net present value of the project, NPV (in units of NOI), the following expression:

$$\frac{\mathrm{NPV}}{\mathrm{NOI}}=-\frac{1}{L(1+k_\mathrm{d})}+\frac{(1-t)-\frac{l_3}{(1+k_\mathrm{d})\cdot n}-\frac{k_\mathrm{d}l_3}{(1+k_\mathrm{d})}\frac{n+1}{n}(1-t)}{\mathrm{WACC}}\left(1-\frac{1}{(1+\mathrm{WACC})^n}\right)$$
$$+\frac{k_\mathrm{d}l_3}{(1+k_\mathrm{d})\cdot n}(1-t)\left\{\frac{(1+\mathrm{WACC})[1-(1+\mathrm{WACC})^{-n}]}{\mathrm{WACC}^2}-\frac{n}{\mathrm{WACC}(1+\mathrm{WACC})^n}\right. \tag{13.6}$$

where $l_3=\frac{(1+k_d)D}{\mathrm{NOI}}$.

Analyzing formulas (13.4), (13.5), and (13.6) we come to a very important conclusion that NPV (in units of NOI) $(\frac{\mathrm{NPV}}{\mathrm{NOI}})$ depends only on equity cost k_0, on credit rates k_d, on leverage level L, as well as on one of the leverage ratios l_j and does not depend on equity value S, debt value D, and NOI. This means that results on the dependence of NPV (in units of NOI) $(\frac{\mathrm{NPV}}{\mathrm{NOI}})$ on leverage ratios l_j at different equity costs k_0, at different credit rates k_d, and at different leverage levels L carry the universal character: these dependencies remain valid for investment projects with any equity value S, debt value D, and NOI.

We investigate below the effectiveness of long-term investment projects studying the dependence of NPV on coverage ratios and on leverage ratios. We make calculations for coefficients i_1 and l_1. Calculations for the rest of coefficients (i_2, i_3 and l_2, l_3) could be made in a similar way.

We start from the calculations of the dependence of NPV on coverage ratios. We consider different values of equity costs k_0, of debt costs k_d, and of leverage level $L = D/S$. Here t is tax on profit rate, which in our calculations is equal to 20%.

13.2.3 Perpetuity Limit

In the perpetuity limit ($T = 0$) from Eq. (10.9), or as limit expressions (13.1–13.6), we can obtain the following expressions for NPV (in units of D) and NPV (in units of NOI):

$$\frac{\mathrm{NPV}}{D}=-\frac{1}{L}+\frac{i_1(1-t)-k_\mathrm{d}(1-t)}{\mathrm{WACC}} \tag{13.7}$$

$$\frac{\mathrm{NPV}}{\mathrm{NOI}}=\frac{l_1}{L}+\frac{(1-t)-k_\mathrm{d}l_1(1-t)}{\mathrm{WACC}} \tag{13.8}$$

Substituting instead of WACC its value in the theory of MM

$$\mathrm{WACC}=k_0\left(1-\frac{Lt}{1+L}\right), \tag{13.9}$$

one gets for NPV (in units D)

$$\frac{\mathrm{NPV}}{D} = -\frac{1}{L} - \frac{(k_{\mathrm{d}} - i_1)(1-t)}{k_0\left(1 - \frac{Lt}{1+L}\right)} \tag{13.10}$$

and for NPV (in units *NOI*)

$$\frac{\mathrm{NPV}}{\mathrm{NOI}} = \frac{-l_1}{L} + \frac{(1 - k_{\mathrm{d}} l_1)(1-t)}{k_0\left(1 - \frac{Lt}{1+L}\right)}. \tag{13.11}$$

Here k_0 is the equity cost at zero leverage. In the following paragraphs, we will study the dependence of the net present value, NPV, on financial ratios for companies of a given age n and for particular values of investment project parameters, demonstrating the possibility of performing calculations for companies of arbitrary age n and for any values of investment project parameters.

13.2.4 *The Study of the Dependence of the Net Present Value of the Project, NPV, on Rating Parameters*

13.2.4.1 Investigation of the Dependence of the Net Present Value of the Project, NPV (in Units of Debt *D*) on Coverage Ratios

First, we analyze the dependence of the net present value of the NPV/*D* project on coverage coefficients i_j for companies of arbitrary age n in the framework of the modern theory of value and capital structure by Brusov–Filatova–Orekhova using modern investment models created by the authors and described above.

We restrict ourselves to considering the dependence of NPV on the debt coverage coefficients i_1 described by Eq. (13.1). Calculations for other coverage coefficients described by Eqs. (13.2–13.3) are carried out similarly.

The calculations are carried out in two stages.

1. First, for a given set of project parameters according to the famous Brusov–Filatova–Orekhova formula

$$\frac{1 - (1 + \mathrm{WACC})^{-n}}{\mathrm{WACC}} = \frac{1 - (1 + k_0)^{-n}}{k_0 * (1 - w_{\mathrm{d}} * t * (1 - (1 + k_{\mathrm{d}})^{-n}))} \tag{13.12}$$

   weighted average cost of capital, WACC, is calculated by Microsoft Excel using the "matching parameter" function.
2. The found WACC value is used in Eq. (13.1) to study the dependence of NPV/*D* on debt coverage coefficient i_1.

Similar studies can be carried out for other coverage coefficients (i_2 and i_3).

When analyzing this formula, we will use the following parameter values: $L = 1$, 3; $t = 20\%$; n is 3; 5; $k_0 = 18\%$; $k_d = 12$, 14, 16%; $i_1 = 0, 1, 2, 3, 4, 5, 6, 7, 8, 9, 10$.

The following conclusions can be drawn from the data in Tables 13.1 and 13.2:

1. The net present value of the project NPV/D increases linearly with an increase of debt coverage ratio i_1.
2. The dependence NPV/D (i_1) for various values of the cost of debt capital k_d has interesting features: for values of the coverage ratio for debt i_1 from 0 to 3, an increase in the cost of debt capital k_d leads to a decrease in NPV/D, and for the values of the cost of borrowed capital k_d more than 3 (and up to 10) large values of the cost of borrowed capital k_d correspond to large values of NPV/D.

From Tables 13.1 and 13.2, it is also seen that the values of the net present value of the project, NPV/D, for various values of debt capital k_d (12, 14, 16%) differ slightly from each other (by approximately 0.02), due to that the graphs of the dependence NPV/D (i_1) practically coincide, as shown in Fig. 13.1.

To demonstrate the differences in the dependence of the net present value of the project NPV (in units of debt D) on the debt coverage ratio i_1 for various L and k_d, we give Fig. 13.1 on an enlarged scale (Fig. 13.2).

From Fig. 13.2 and from Tables 13.1 and 13.2, we can come to the following conclusions:

1. The slope of the straight line NPV/D (i_1) is determined by the duration of the project n and increases with the duration of the project. So, the slope of the straight line NPV/D (i_1) for a 5-year project is greater than for a 3-year project.
2. When the leverage level L changes, the line NPV/D (i_1) shifts almost in parallel: with the growth of L, the line shifts higher (in Fig. 13.2 it can be seen that for projects of the same term, lines with $L = 3$ lie above lines with $L = 1$.

13.2.4.2 Study of the Dependence of the Net Present Value of the Project NPV (in Units of Net Operating Income NOI) on Leverage Ratios

Now we analyze the dependence of the net present value of the project NPV/D on leverage coefficients l_j for companies of arbitrary age n in the framework of the modern theory of value and capital structure of Brusov–Filatova–Orekhova using modern investment models created by the authors and described above.

We restrict ourselves to considering the dependence of NPV on the leverage coefficient for debt l_1, described by Eq. (13.4). Calculations for other leverage coefficients (l_2 and l_3) described by Eqs. (13.5–13.6) are carried out similarly.

The calculations, as in the case of coverage coefficients, are carried out in two stages.

Table 13.1 The dependence of NPV/D on debt coverage ratio i_1 at $L = 1.3$ t = 20%, $n = 3$, $k_0 = 18\%$, $k_d = k_d = 12, 14, 16\%$

NPV/D	WACC	k_d (%)	$i_1 = 0$	1	2	3	4	5	6	7	8	9	10
$L = 1$	0.1574	16	−1.954	−0.1493	1.6549	3.4592	5.2634	7.0677	8.8719	10.6762	12.4804	14.2847	16.0890
$n = 3$	0.1596	14	−1.925	−0.1273	1.6705	3.4684	5.2663	7.0641	8.8620	10.6598	12.4577	14.2555	16.0534
	0.1619	12	−1.897	−0.1057	1.6854	3.4764	5.2675	7.0585	8.8495	10.6406	12.4316	14.2227	16.0137
$L = 3$	0.1461	16	−1.30	0.53	2.37	4.21	6.05	7.89	9.73	11.57	13.40	15.24	17.08
$n = 3$	0.1493	14	−1.274	0.5548	2.3833	4.2119	6.0405	7.8690	9.6976	11.5261	13.3548	15.1833	17.0119
	0.1528	12	−1.243	0.5749	2.3929	4.2109	6.0289	7.8469	9.6649	11.4830	13.3010	15.1190	16.9370

Table 13.2 The dependence of NPV/D on debt coverage ratio i_1 at $L = 1.3$ $t = 20\%$, $n = 5$, $k_0 = 18\%$, $k_d = k_d = 12, 14, 16\%$

NPV/D	WACC	k_d (%)	$i_1 = 0$	1	2	3	4	5	6	7	8	9	10
$L = 1$	0.1566	16	−1.938	0.7022	3.3423	5.9823	8.6224	11.2624	13.9025	16.5425	19.1825	21.8226	24.4626
$n = 5$	0.1586	14	−1.899	0.7288	3.3569	5.9849	8.6130	11.2410	13.8691	16.4971	19.1252	21.7532	24.3813
	0.1608	12	−1.861	0.7543	3.3692	5.9840	8.5989	11.2137	13.8286	16.4434	19.0583	21.6731	24.2880
$L = 3$	0.1448	16	−1.296	1.4190	4.1341	6.8492	9.5643	12.2794	14.9945	17.7096	20.4247	23.1398	25.8549
$n = 5$	0.1477	14	−1.255	1.4416	4.1378	6.8339	9.5300	12.2261	14.9222	17.6183	20.3144	23.0105	25.7067
	0.1510	12	−1.213	1.4626	4.1380	6.8133	9.4886	12.1639	14.8393	17.5146	20.1899	22.8653	25.5406

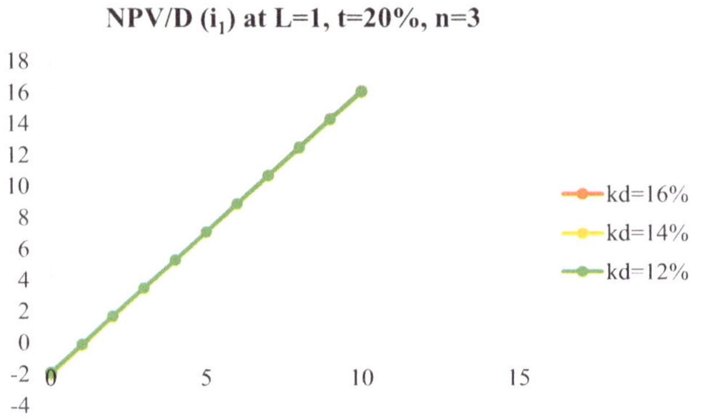

Fig. 13.1 The dependence of the net present value of the project NPV (in units of debt D) on the debt coverage ratio i_1

1. First, for a given set of project parameters according to the famous Brusov–Filatova–Orekhova formula:

$$\frac{1-(1+\text{WACC})^{-n}}{\text{WACC}} = \frac{1-(1+k_0)^{-n}}{k_0 * (1 - w_\text{d} * t * (1-(1+k_\text{d})^{-n}))} \tag{13.13}$$

weighted average cost of capital, WACC, is calculated by Microsoft Excel using the "matching parameter" function.
2. The found WACC value is used in Eq. (13.4) to study the dependence of NPV/NOI on the debt leverage coefficient l_1.

Similar studies can be carried out for other leverage coefficients (l_2 and l_3).

Let us analyze the dependence of the net present value of the project NPV (in units of net operating income NOI) on the leverage coefficient on debt l_1 for companies of a given age n and for specific values of investment project parameters, demonstrating the possibility of performing calculations for companies of arbitrary age n and for any values of investment project parameters.

When analyzing Eq. (13.4), we will use the following parameter values: $L = 1, 3$; $t = 0.20$; $n = 3.5$; $k_0 = 18$; $k_\text{d} = 16, 14, 12$; $l = 0, 1, 2, 3, 4, 5, 6, 7, 8, 9, 10$.

From the data of Tables 13.3 and 13.4 and Figs. 13.3 and 13.4, the following conclusions can be drawn:

1. The net present value of the project NPV/NOI decreases linearly with increasing leverage on debt ratio l_1.
2. The slope of the straight line NPV/NOI (l_1) is determined by the leverage level L, while the absolute value of the slope decreases with increasing L: thus, lines with $L = 3$ are closer to the axis l_1 than lines with $L = 1$.
3. An increase in the project duration n shifts the line NPV/NOI (l_1) almost parallel higher (Fig. 13.3 and 13.4 show that for projects with the same level of leverage L, lines with $n = 5$ lie above lines with $n = 3$).

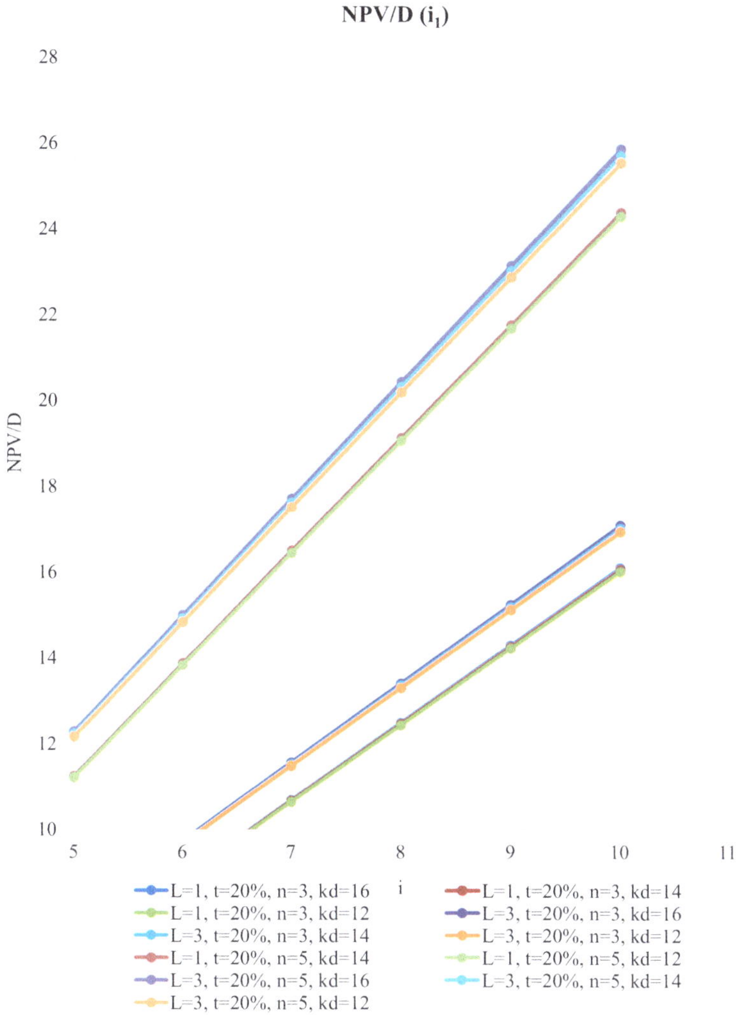

Fig. 13.2 Dependence of the net present value of the project NPV (in units of debt *D*) on the debt coverage ratio i_1 (increased scale)

4. For equal project duration n and equal leverage levels *L*, the line NPV/NOI (l_1) shifts almost parallel downward with an increase in the debt cost k_d (12, 14, 16%).

13.3 Conclusions

The chapter discusses the rating of investment projects of arbitrary duration with a uniform repayment of debt and a modification of the methodology of rating systems for investment projects. The development of a fundamentally new approach to the

Table 13.3 The dependence of the net present value of the project NPV (in units of net operating income NOI) on the leverage coefficient on debt l_1 at $L = 1.3$ $t = 20\%$, $n = 3$, $k_0 = 18\%$, $k_d = k_d = 12, 14, 16\%$

NPV/NOI	WACC	k_d (%)	$l_1 = 0$	1	2	3	4	5	6	7	8	9	10
$L = 1$	0.1574	16	18043	−0.149	−2.103	−4.057	−6.010	−7.964	−9.917	−11.871	−13.824	−15.778	−17.732
$n = 3$	0.1596	14	1.7979	−0.127	−2.053	−3.978	−5.903	−7.828	−9.753	−11.678	−13.603	−15.529	−17.454
	0.1619	12	1.7910	−0.106	−2.002	−3.899	−5.796	−7.692	−9.589	−11.486	−13.383	−15.279	−17.176
$L = 3$	0.1461	16	1.84	0.53	-0.77	-2.07	-3.38	-4.68	-5.99	-7.29	-8.60	-9.90	-11.21
$n = 3$	0.1493	14	1.83	0.55	-0.72	-1.99	-3.27	-4.54	-5.81	-7.09	-8.36	-9.64	-10.91
	0.1528	12	1.82	0.57	-0.67	-1.91	-3.15	-4.40	-5.64	-6.88	-8.13	-9.37	-10.61

Table 13.4 The dependence of the net present value of the project NPV (in units of net operating income NOI) on the leverage coefficient on debt l_1 at $L = 1.3$ $t = 20\%$, $n = 5$, $k_0 = 18\%$, $k_d = k_d = 12, 14, 16\%$

NPV/NOI	WACC	k_d (%)	$l_1 = 0$	1	2	3	4	5	6	7	8	9	10
$L = 1$	0.1566	16	2.64	0.70	−1.24	−3.17	−5.11	−7.05	−8.99	−10.92	−12.86	−14.80	−16.74
$n = 5$	0.1586	14	2.63	0.73	−1.17	−3.07	−4.97	−6.87	−8.77	−10.67	−12.57	−14.47	−16.36
	0.1608	12	2.61	0.75	−1.11	−2.97	−4.83	−6.69	−8.55	−10.41	−12.27	−14.13	−15.99
$L = 3$	0.1448	16	2.72	1.42	0.12	−1.17	−2.47	−3.77	−5.06	−6.36	−7.65	−8.95	−10.25
$n = 5$	0.1477	14	2.70	1.44	0.19	−1.07	−2.32	−3.58	−4.83	−6.09	−7.34	−8.59	−9.85
	0.1510	12	2.68	1.46	0.25	−0.96	−2.18	−3.39	−4.60	−5.81	−7.03	−8.24	−9.45

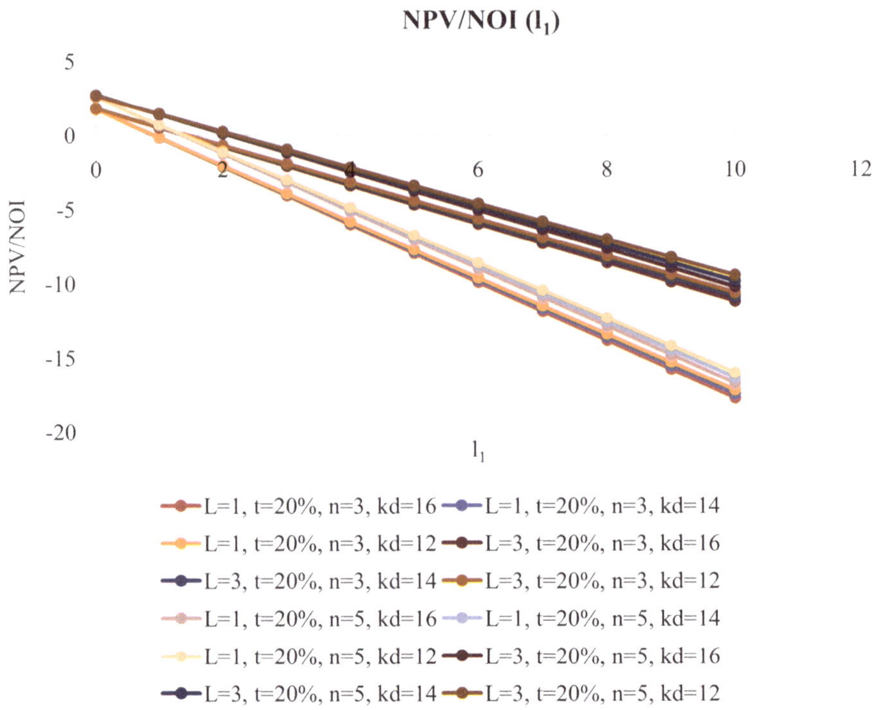

Fig. 13.3 Summary dependence of NPV/NOI on leverage ratio on debt *l*1 at different leverage level *L*, project duration *n*, and debt cost k_d

project rating methodology has been carried out, the key factors of which are: (1) adequate use of discounts when discounting the financial flows, which is practically not used in existing project rating methodologies; (2) incorporation of financial ratios into modern investment models created by the authors; (3) use of the rating parameters upon discounting; and (4) the correct determination of the discount rate, taking into account financial ratios.

We used modern investment models created by the authors, the modern theory of capital cost and capital structure by Brusov–Filatova–Orekhova (BFO theory) (Brusov et al. (2015), 2018a, 2019, 2020), Brusov (2018b), Filatova et al. (2018), Brusov et al. (2018c, d, e, f). Brusov (2018g), Brusov et al. (2018h), Filatova et al. (2008, 2018)), its modification for rating needs.

For the first time, incorporation of coverage ratios and leverage coefficients used in the rating was carried out into modern investment models created by the authors and designed to study the effectiveness of investment projects of arbitrary duration with uniform repayment of debt.

The dependence of the net present value of the project, NPV/NOI, on the coverage coefficients i_j (leverage coefficients l_j) for companies of arbitrary age n is analyzed.

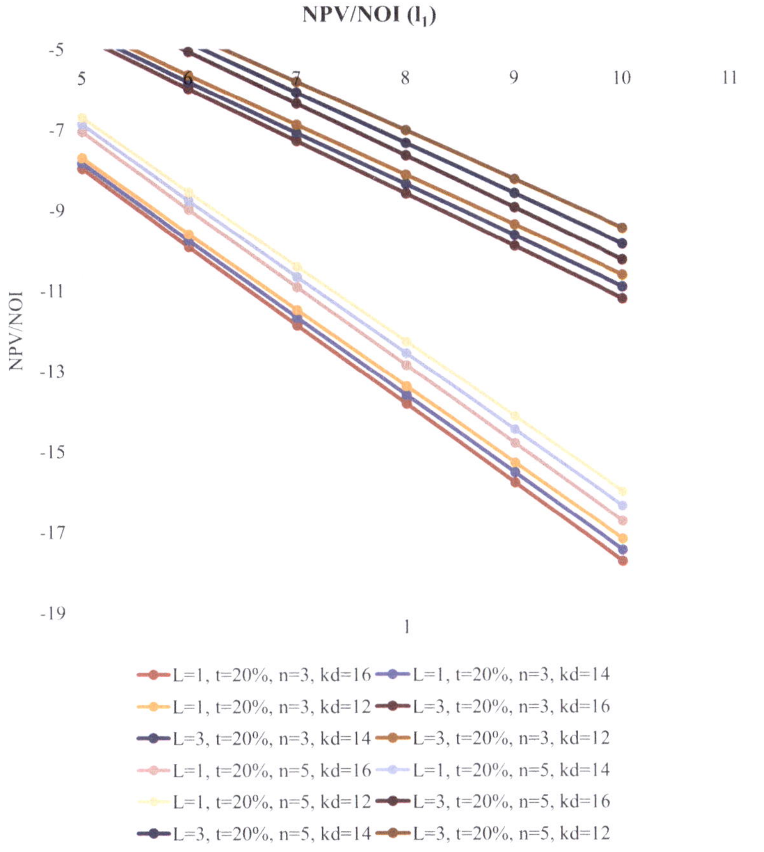

Fig. 13.4 Summary dependence of NPV/NOI on leverage ratio on debt l_1 at different leverage level L, project duration n, and debt cost k_d (in increased scale)

When studying the dependence of NPV/D on coverage ratios i_j, it was shown that the net present value of the project, NPV/D, increases linearly with increasing debt coverage ratio i_j. At the same time, the dependence NPV/D (i_1) for various values of the debt cost k_d has interesting features: for values of the coverage ratio for debt i_1 from 0 to 3, an increase in the cost of debt capital k_d leads to a decrease in NPV/D, and for values of the cost of debt capital k_d more than 3 (and up to 10) bigger values of the cost of debt capital k_d correspond to bigger values of NPV/D. At the same time, the values of the net present value of the project NPV/D at various values of the cost of debt capital k_d (12, 14, 16%) differ slightly from each other (by about 0.02), and therefore the NPV/D graphs (i_1) almost coincide.

The slope of the straight line NPV/D (i_1) is determined by the duration of the project n and increases with the duration of the project. So, the slope of the straight line NPV/D (i_1) for a 5-year project is greater than for a 3-year project. When the leverage level L changes, the line NPV/D (i_1) shifts almost in parallel: with the growth of L, the line shifts higher (for projects of the same term, lines with $L = 3$ lie above lines with $L = 1$).

When studying the dependence of NPV/NOI on leverage coefficients l_j, it is shown that the net present value of the project NPV/NOI decreases linearly with an increase of the leverage coefficient for debt l_1. In this case, the slope of the straight line NPV/NOI (l_1) is determined by the leverage level L, and the absolute value of the slope decreases with increasing L: thus, lines with $L = 3$ lie closer to the axis l_1 than lines with $L = 1$. An increase of the project duration n shifts the line NPV/NOI (l_1) almost parallel higher (for projects with the same level of leverage L, lines with $n = 5$ lie above lines with $n = 3$). With equal project times and equal leverage levels L, the direct NPV/D (i_1) shifts almost parallel downward with the growth of the debt cost k_d (12, 14, 16%).

It can be seen that the behavior of the NPV/NOI (l_j) dependence is qualitatively different from the behavior of the NPV/D (i_j) dependence. These dependencies should be taken into account and used when rating investment projects.

The modification of the methodology of the existing project rating systems will improve the accuracy of issued ratings of investment projects and make them more objective. The use of powerful tools of well-developed theories opens up new opportunities for the rating industry, which gives the opportunity to switch from using mainly qualitative methods for assessing the effectiveness of investment projects to using mainly quantitative methods for evaluating them.

References

Brusov P, Filatova T, Orekhova N, Eskindarov M (2015) Modern corporate finance, investments and taxation, Springer International Publishing, Switzerland, p 373. Monograph, SCOPUS. https://www.springer.com/gp/book/9783319147314

Brusov P, Filatova T, Orekhova N, Eskindarov M (2018a) Modern corporate finance, investments, taxation and ratings, Springer Nature Publishing, Switzerland, p 571. Monograph

Brusov PN, Filatova TV, Orekhova NP, Kulik VL, Chang S-I, Lin YCG (2020) Modification of the Modigliani–Miller theory for the case of advance payments of tax on profit. J Rev Glob Econ 9:257–268

Brusov PN, Filatova TV, Orekhova NP, Kulik VL, Weil I (2019) Ratings of the investment projects of arbitrary durations: new methodology. J Rev Glob Econ 8:437–448. SCOPUS. https://doi.org/10.6000/1929-7092.2019.08.37

Brusov P (2018a) Editorial: introduction on special issue on the banking system and financial markets of Russia and other countries: problems and prospects. J Rev Glob Econ 7:i–vi, SCOPUS

Filatova TV, Brusov PN, Orekhova NP, Kulik VL (2018a) Ratings of the long–term projects: new approach. J Rev Glob Econ 7:645–661, SCOPUS. https://doi.org/10.6000/1929-7092.2018.07.59

Brusov PN, Filatova TV, Orekhova NP, Kulik VL (2018b) Rating: new approach. J Rev Glob Econ 7:37–62. SCOPUS. https://doi.org/10.6000/1929-7092.2018.07.05

Brusov PN, Filatova TV, Orekhova NP, Kulik VL (2018c) A "golden age" of the companies: conditions of its existence. J Rev Glob Econ 7:88–103. SCOPUS. https://doi.org/10.6000/1929-7092.2018.07.07

Brusov PN, Filatova TV, Orekhova NP, Kulik VL (2018d) Rating methodology: new look and new horizons. J Rev Glob Econ 7:63–87. SCOPUS. https://doi.org/10.6000/1929-7092.2018.07.06

P.N. Brusov, T.V. Filatova, N.P. Orekhova, V.L. Kulik and I. Weil (2018e) New Meaningful effects in modern capital structure theory J Rev Glob Econ, 7, 104–122. SCOPUS. https://doi.org/10.6000/1929-7092.2018.07.08

Brusov P (2018b) Editorial. J Rev Glob Econ 7:i–v, SCOPUS

Brusov P, Filatova T, Orekhova N, Kulik V, Weil I, Brailov A (2018f) The impact of the central bank key rate and commercial banks credit rates on creating and maintaining of a favorable investment climate in the country. J Rev Glob Econ 7:360–376. SCOPUS. https://doi.org/10.6000/1929-7092.2018.07.31

Brusov PN, Filatova TV, Orekhova NP (2018g) Modern corporate finance and investments, monograph. Knorus Publishing House, Moscow, p 517

Filatova T, Orekhova N, Brusova A (2008) Weighted average cost of capital in the theory of Modigliani–Miller, modified for a finite life–time company. Bull FU 48:68–77

Filatova TV, Brusov PN, Orekhova NP, Kulik VL (2018b) Ratings of the long–term projects: new approach. J Rev Glob Econ 7:645–661, SCOPUS. https://doi.org/10.6000/1929-7092.2018.07.59

Part IV
New Meaningful Effects in Modern Capital Structure Theory (BFO Theory) Which Should Be Accounting in Rating Methodologies

Chapter 14
The Golden Age of the Company (Three Colors of Company's Time)

In Chaps. 14, 15, 16, 17, and 18, we describe new meaningful effects in modern capital structure theory (BFO theory), which should be accounted in rating methodologies. In this and the next chapter, we conduct a complete study of the effects we have discovered: the "golden" and "silver" age of the company and their conditions of existence. The effects of the "golden" and "silver" age of the company are that at a certain age of the company WACC value is lower than in the perpetuity limit of the BFO theory—Modigliani–Miller theory, and the company's capitalization, V, is greater than capitalization, V, in the theory of Modigliani–Miller. These effects should be considered when generating ratings. Since the cost of raising capital is used (should be used) in rating methodologies as the discount rate for discounting cash flows, the study of the dependence of WACC on the age of the company is very important for assessment procedures in rating and business valuation. Taking into account the effects of the company's "golden" and "silver" age can significantly change the credit rating of issuers. We study the dependence of the cost of raising capital on the age of the company n at various leverage levels and at different values of the equity and debt costs in order to determine the minimum cost of raising capital of the company. All calculations were performed within the framework of the modern theory of capital cost and capital structure by Brusov–Filatova–Orekhova (BFO theory). We study the dependence of the weighted average cost of capital of a company, WACC, on the company age n at various leverage levels L and at various values of the cost of capital (equity and debt).

It has been shown for the first time that the average weighted cost of capital of a company, WACC, in the theory of Modigliani–Miller (MM) is not minimal, and the estimate of Modigliani–Miller's capitalization of a company is not maximum, as all financiers have assumed: at some stage in the development of a company, the WACC turns out to be lower than Modigliani–Miller estimates, and company capitalization, V, turns out to be higher than V estimates in the Modigliani–Miller theory.

P. Brusov et al., *Ratings*, Contributions to Finance and Accounting,
https://doi.org/10.1007/978-3-030-56243-4_14

This and the following chapters conclude that the notions of the results of the Modigliani–Miller theory existing in these aspects turn out to be incorrect. The possibilities of using discovered effects in practice are discussed, in particular, when rating non-financial issuers.

14.1 Introduction

In this chapter, we describe a very important discovery, made by us recently (Brusov et al. 2015). We investigate the dependence of attracting capital cost on the company age n at various leverage levels and at various values of capital (equity and debt) costs with the aim of defining the minimum cost of attracting capital. All calculations have been done within the modern theory of capital cost and capital structure by Brusov–Filatova–Orekhova (Brusov and Filatova 2011; Brusov et al. 2011a, b, c, 2012a, b, 2013a, b, 2014a, b; Filatova et al. 2008; Brusova 2011, Brusov (2018a, b), Brusov et al. (2018a, b, c, d, e, f, g, 2019, 2020, Filatova et al. (2018a, b)).

It is shown for the first time that valuation of weighted average cost of capital (WACC) in the Modigliani–Miller theory (Modigliani and Miller 1958, 1963, 1966) **is not minimal and valuation of the company capitalization is not maximal, as all financiers assumed up to now**: ***at some age of the company, its WACC value turns out to be lower than in the Modigliani–Miller theory, and company capitalization V turns out to be greater than V in the Modigliani–Miller theory***.

It is shown that, from the point of view of cost of attracting capital, there are two types of dependences of WACC on the age of company n: monotonic decrease of WACC with n and decrease of WACC with passage through minimum, followed by a limited growth (Brusov et al. 2015). The companies with the latter type of dependence of WACC on the age of company n can take advantage of the benefits given at a certain stage of development by discovered effect. Moreover, since the "golden age" of company depends on the company's capital costs, k_e and k_d, by controlling them (e.g., by modifying the value of dividend payments that reflect the equity cost), the company may extend its "golden age" when the cost to attract capital becomes minimal (less than perpetuity limit) and the capitalization of companies becomes maximal (above than perpetuity assessment) up to a specified time interval.

It has been concluded that existing presentations concerning the results of the theory of Modigliani–Miller (Modigliani and Miller 1958, 1963, 1966) in these aspects are incorrect. We discuss the use of opened effects in economics.

It is well known that the company goes through several stages in its development process: adolescence, maturity, and old age. Within the modern theory of capital cost and capital structure by Brusov–Filatova–Orekhova (BFO theory) (Brusov and Filatova 2011; Brusov et al. 2011a, b, c, 2012a, b, 2013a, b, 2014a, b; Filatova et al. 2008; Brusova 2011), it is shown that the problem of the company development has an interpretation, which is absolutely different from the generally accepted one.

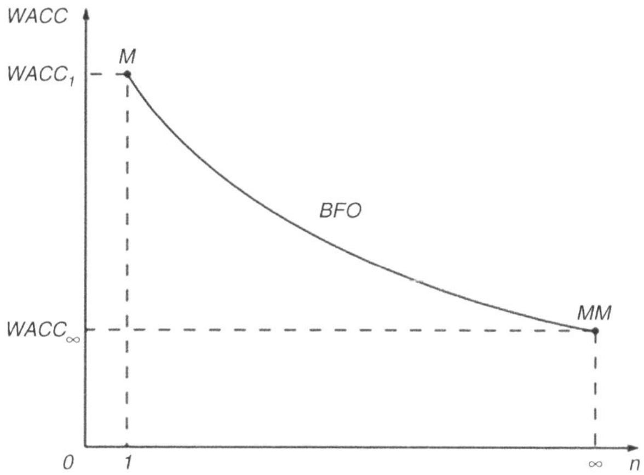

Fig. 14.1 Monotonic dependence of WACC on the lifetime (age) of the company *n*

One of the most important problems in corporate finance is the problem of capital cost and capital structure. Before 2008, there were just two kinds of valuations of cost of capital: the first one was the first quantitative theory by Nobel Prize winners Modigliani and Miller (1958, 1963, 1966), applicable to perpetuity (with infinite lifetime) companies, and the second one was the valuation applicable to 1-year companies by Steve Myers (1984).

So, before 2008, when the modern theory of capital cost and capital structure by Brusov–Filatova–Orekhova (BFO theory) has been created (Brusov and Filatova 2011; Brusov et al. 2011a, b, c, 2012a, b, 2013a, b, 2014a, b; Filatova et al. 2008; Brusova 2011), only two points in time interval have been known: 1 year and infinity. At that time, Steve Myers (1984) has assumed that the Modigliani–Miller (MM) theory (Modigliani and Miller 1958, 1963, 1966) gave the lowest assessment for WACC and, consequently, the highest assessment for company capitalization. This means that the WACC monotonically decreases with the time of life of company, *n*, approaching its perpetuity limit (Fig. 14.1), and, consequently, company capitalization monotonically increases, approaching its perpetuity limit (Fig. 14.3).

Created in 2008 the modern theory of capital cost and capital structure by Brusov–Filatova–Orekhova (BFO theory) (Brusov and Filatova 2011; Brusov et al. 2011a, b, c, 2012a, b, 2013a, b, 2014a, b; Filatova et al. 2008; Brusova 2011) turned out to be able to make valuation of capital cost and company capitalization for companies with arbitrary lifetime (of arbitrary age): this completes the whole time interval from $n = 1$ up to $n = \infty$. A lot of qualitative effects in corporate finance, investments, taxations, etc., have been made within the BFO theory.

In this chapter with BFO theory it is shown that Steve Myers' suggestion (Myers 1984) turns out to be wrong.

Choosing optimal capital structure of the company, i.e., proportion of debt and equity, which minimizes the weighted average cost of capital and maximizes the company capitalization, is one of the most important tasks of financial manager and the management of a company. The search for an optimal capital structure attracts

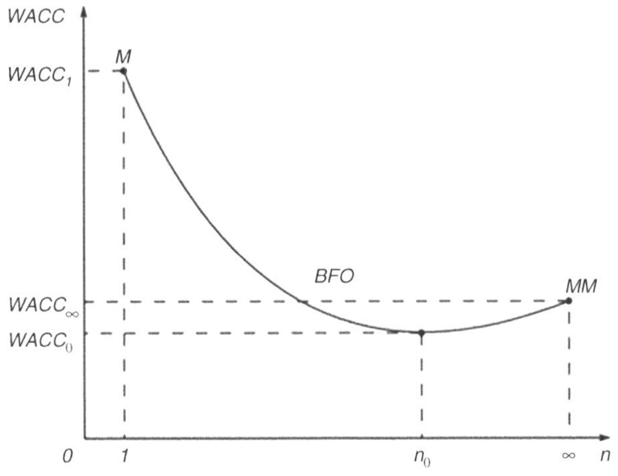

Fig. 14.2 Dependence of WACC on the lifetime (age) of the company n, showing decrease of WACC with passage through minimum and then showing a limited growth to perpetuity (MM) limit

the attention of economists and financiers during many tens of years. And it is clear why: one can, only by changing the proportion between the values of equity capital and debt of the company, significantly enhance the company capitalization, in other words fulfill the primary task, to reach the critical goal of business management. Spend a little less of your own, loan slightly more, or vice versa, and company capitalization reaches a maximum.

Before, the search for an optimal capital structure was made by studying the dependence of WACC on leverage level in order to determine the optimal leverage level L_0, at which the WACC is minimal and capitalization V is maximal. Here we apply an absolutely different method, studying the dependence of WACC on the time of life (age) of company n. Note that before the appearance of BFO theory, study of such kind of dependences was impossible due to the absence of "time" parameter in perpetuity Modigliani–Miller theory (Modigliani and Miller 1958, 1963, 1966).

As it is shown in this chapter, from the point of view of cost of capital, there are two types of dependences of WACC on the time of life (age) of company n: monotonic decrease of WACC with n and decrease of WACC with passage through minimum, followed by a limited growth (Figs. 14.1 and 14.2) (Brusov et al. 2015).

The first type of behavior is linked to the comment by Myers (1984) that the Modigliani–Miller (MM) theory (Modigliani and Miller 1958, 1963, 1966) gives the lowest assessment for WACC that, as shown by us within the BFO theory, is, generally speaking, incorrect. The second type of behavior of dependence of WACC on the time of life (age) of company n is decrease of WACC with passage through minimum, followed by a limited growth.

Thus, in the general case, the comment by Myers (1984) turns out to be wrong, and in the life of company there is a "golden age" or "the golden century" when the cost of attracting capital becomes minimal and company capitalization becomes maximal (Figs. 14.2 and 14.3) (Brusov et al. 2015). In the life of the company, the same number of stages as usual can be allocated: youth, maturity, and old age. In

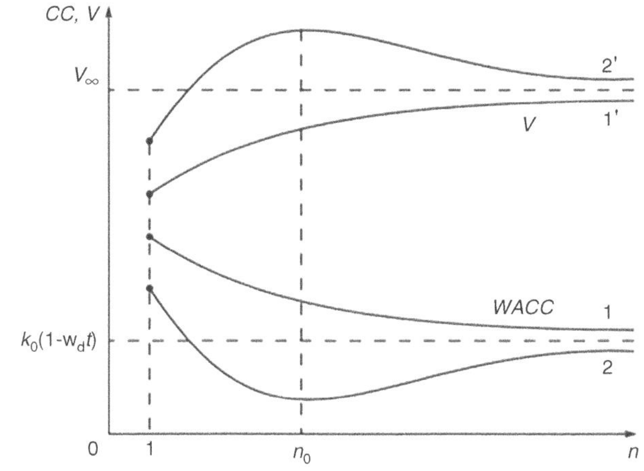

Fig. 14.3 Two kinds of dependences of WACC and company capitalization, V, on the lifetime (age) of the company n: 1–1′—monotonic decrease of WACC and monotonic increase of company capitalization, V, with the lifetime of the company n; 2–2′—decrease of WACC with passage through minimum and then showing a limited growth, and increase of V with passage through maximum (at n_0) and then a limited decrease to perpetuity (MM) limit

youth the WACC decreases with n, in maturity the value of attracting capital cost becomes minimal, and in old age this cost grows, approaching its perpetuity limit.

So, figuratively speaking, a current investigation transforms "black and white business world" (with monotonic decrease of WACC with the time of life of company n) into "color business world" (with decrease of WACC with n with passage through minimum, followed by a limited growth): really there are three colors of company's time.

The conclusion made in this chapter for the first time that **the assessment of the WACC in the theory of Modigliani and Miller (MM)** (Modigliani and Miller 1958, 1963, 1966) **is not the minimal and capitalization is not maximal seems to be very significant and important**.

14.1.1 Dependence of WACC on the Age of the Company n at Different Leverage Levels

In this section, we study the dependence of WACC on the age of the company n at different leverage levels.

For $L = 1$ one has
For $L = 2$ we have
For $L = 3$ one has
For $L = 5$ one has
For $L = 7$ one has

Table 14.1 Dependence of WACC on the age of the company n at $L = 1$

L	WACC	k_0	k_d	W_d	t	n	k_e
1	0.1843	0.2	0.15	0.5	0.2	1	0.2487
1	0.1798	0.2	0.15	0.5	0.2	2	0.2397
1	0.1780	0.2	0.15	0.5	0.2	3	0.2360
1	0.1772	0.2	0.15	0.5	0.2	4	0.2345
1	0.1769	0.2	0.15	0.5	0.2	5	0.2339
1	0.1769	0.2	0.15	0.5	0.2	6	0.2338
1	0.1770	0.2	0.15	0.5	0.2	7	0.2340
1	0.1771	0.2	0.15	0.5	0.2	8	0.2343
1	0.1773	0.2	0.15	0.5	0.2	9	0.2346
1	0.1775	0.2	0.15	0.5	0.2	10	0.2351

Table 14.2 Dependence of WACC on the age of the company n at $L = 2$

L	WACC	k_0	k_d	W_d	t	n	k_e
2	0.1791	0.2	0.15	0.66667	0.2	1	0.2974
2	0.1731	0.2	0.15	0.66667	0.2	2	0.2793
2	0.1706	0.2	0.15	0.66667	0.2	3	0.2719
2	0.1696	0.2	0.15	0.66667	0.2	4	0.2687
2	0.1692	0.2	0.15	0.66667	0.2	5	0.2675
2	0.1691	0.2	0.15	0.66667	0.2	6	0.2672
2	0.1692	0.2	0.15	0.66667	0.2	7	0.2675
2	0.1694	0.2	0.15	0.66667	0.2	8	0.2681
2	0.1696	0.2	0.15	0.66667	0.2	9	0.2689
2	0.1699	0.2	0.15	0.66667	0.2	10	0.2697

Table 14.3 Dependence of WACC on the age of the company n at $L = 3$

L	WACC	k_0	k_d	W_d	t	n	k_e
3	0.1765	0.2	0.15	0.75	0.2	1	0.3461
3	0.1697	0.2	0.15	0.75	0.2	2	0.3189
3	0.1669	0.2	0.15	0.75	0.2	3	0.3078
3	0.1657	0.2	0.15	0.75	0.2	4	0.3029
3	0.1653	0.2	0.15	0.75	0.2	5	0.3010
3	0.1651	0.2	0.15	0.75	0.2	6	0.3006
3	0.1653	0.2	0.15	0.75	0.2	7	0.3010
3	0.1655	0.2	0.15	0.75	0.2	8	0.3019
3	0.1658	0.2	0.15	0.75	0.2	9	0.3030
3	0.1661	0.2	0.15	0.75	0.2	10	0.3042

The analysis in Tables 14.1, 14.2, 14.3, 14.4, and 14.5 and Fig. 14.4 allows us to make the following conclusions:

1. In all examined cases (at all leverage levels), at current values of capital costs (equity, k_0, and debt, k_d, ones), the second type of behavior of dependence of WACC on the lifetime (age) of the company, n, takes place, namely, decrease of WACC with n with passage through minimum with subsequent limited growth.

Table 14.4 Dependence of WACC on the age of the company n at $L = 5$

L	WACC	k_0	k_d	W_d	t	n	k_e
5	0.1739	0.2	0.15	0.83333	0.2	1	0.4435
5	0.1663	0.2	0.15	0.83333	0.2	2	0.3980
5	0.1632	0.2	0.15	0.83333	0.2	3	0.3795
5	0.1619	0.2	0.15	0.83333	0.2	4	0.3713
5	0.1613	0.2	0.15	0.83333	0.2	5	0.3680
5	0.1612	0.2	0.15	0.83333	0.2	6	0.3672
5	0.1613	0.2	0.15	0.83333	0.2	7	0.3679
5	0.1615	0.2	0.15	0.83333	0.2	8	0.3693
5	0.1619	0.2	0.15	0.83333	0.2	9	0.3711
5	0.1622	0.2	0.15	0.83333	0.2	10	0.3732

Table 14.5 Dependence of WACC on the age of the company n at $L = 7$

L	WACC	k_0	k_d	W_d	t	n	k_e
7	0.1726	0.2	0.15	0.875	0.2	1	0.5409
7	0.1646	0.2	0.15	0.875	0.2	2	0.4771
7	0.1614	0.2	0.15	0.875	0.2	3	0.4511
7	0.1599	0.2	0.15	0.875	0.2	4	0.4396
7	0.1594	0.2	0.15	0.875	0.2	5	0.4349
7	0.1592	0.2	0.15	0.875	0.2	6	0.4338
7	0.1593	0.2	0.15	0.875	0.2	7	0.4347
7	0.1596	0.2	0.15	0.875	0.2	8	0.4366
7	0.1599	0.2	0.15	0.875	0.2	9	0.4392
7	0.1603	0.2	0.15	0.875	0.2	10	0.4421

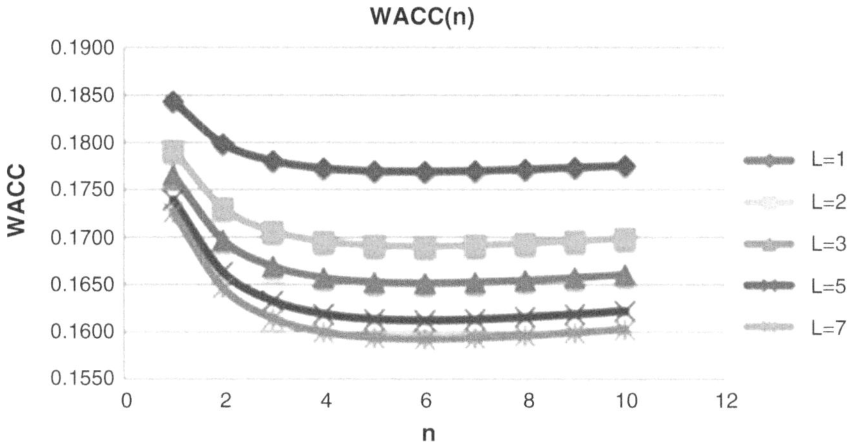

Fig. 14.4 Dependence of WACC on the age of the company n at different leverage levels

2. The minimum cost of attracting capital (WACC) is achieved at all leverage levels at the same company's age at $n = 6$ (only when $L = 1$, minimum is spread for 2 years ($n = 5$ and $n = 6$)).
3. The value of minimum WACC, at a fixed n, significantly depends on the level of leverage, L, and, of course, decreases with increasing L.

Table 14.6 Dependence of WACC on the age of the company n at $L = 1$, $k_0 = 8\%$, $k_d = 4\%$

L	WACC	k_0	k_d	W_d	t	n	k_e
1	0.0758	0.08	0.04	0.5	0.2	1	0.1197
1	0.0745	0.08	0.04	0.5	0.2	2	0.1170
1	0.0738	0.08	0.04	0.5	0.2	3	0.1157
1	0.0735	0.08	0.04	0.5	0.2	4	0.1149
1	0.0732	0.08	0.04	0.5	0.2	5	0.1144
1	0.0731	0.08	0.04	0.5	0.2	6	0.1141
1	0.0729	0.08	0.04	0.5	0.2	7	0.1139
1	0.0729	0.08	0.04	0.5	0.2	8	0.1137
1	0.0728	0.08	0.04	0.5	0.2	9	0.1136
1	0.0728	0.08	0.04	0.5	0.2	10	0.1135

Table 14.7 Dependence of WACC on the age of the company n at $L = 1$, $k_0 = 20\%$, $k_d = 15\%$

L	WACC	k_0	k_d	W_d	t	n	k_e
1	0.1843	0.2	0.15	0.5	0.2	1	0.2487
1	0.1798	0.2	0.15	0.5	0.2	2	0.2397
1	0.1780	0.2	0.15	0.5	0.2	3	0.2360
1	0.1772	0.2	0.15	0.5	0.2	4	0.2345
1	0.1769	0.2	0.15	0.5	0.2	5	0.2339
1	0.1769	0.2	0.15	0.5	0.2	6	0.2338
1	0.1770	0.2	0.15	0.5	0.2	7	0.2340
1	0.1771	0.2	0.15	0.5	0.2	8	0.2343
1	0.1773	0.2	0.15	0.5	0.2	9	0.2346
1	0.1775	0.2	0.15	0.5	0.2	10	0.2351

Table 14.8 Dependence of WACC on the age of the company n at $L = 3$, $k_0 = 20\%$, $k_d = 15\%$

L	WACC	k_0	k_d	W_d	t	n	k_e
3	0.1765	0.2	0.15	0.75	0.2	1	0.3461
3	0.1697	0.2	0.15	0.75	0.2	2	0.3189
3	0.1669	0.2	0.15	0.75	0.2	3	0.3078
3	0.1657	0.2	0.15	0.75	0.2	4	0.3029
3	0.1653	0.2	0.15	0.75	0.2	5	0.3010
3	0.1651	0.2	0.15	0.75	0.2	6	0.3006
3	0.1653	0.2	0.15	0.75	0.2	7	0.3010
3	0.1655	0.2	0.15	0.75	0.2	8	0.3019
3	0.1658	0.2	0.15	0.75	0.2	9	0.3030
3	0.1661	0.2	0.15	0.75	0.2	10	0.3042

Table 14.9 Dependence of WACC on the age of the company n at $L = 3$, $k_0 = 8\%$, $k_d = 4\%$

L	WACC	k_0	k_d	W_d	t	n	k_e
3	0.0738	0.08	0.04	0.75	0.2	1	0.1991
3	0.0717	0.08	0.04	0.75	0.2	2	0.1909
3	0.0707	0.08	0.04	0.75	0.2	3	0.1870
3	0.0702	0.08	0.04	0.75	0.2	4	0.1847
3	0.0698	0.08	0.04	0.75	0.2	5	0.1832
3	0.0696	0.08	0.04	0.75	0.2	6	0.1822
3	0.0694	0.08	0.04	0.75	0.2	7	0.1815
3	0.0693	0.08	0.04	0.75	0.2	8	0.1810
3	0.0692	0.08	0.04	0.75	0.2	9	0.1806
3	0.0691	0.08	0.04	0.75	0.2	10	0.1803

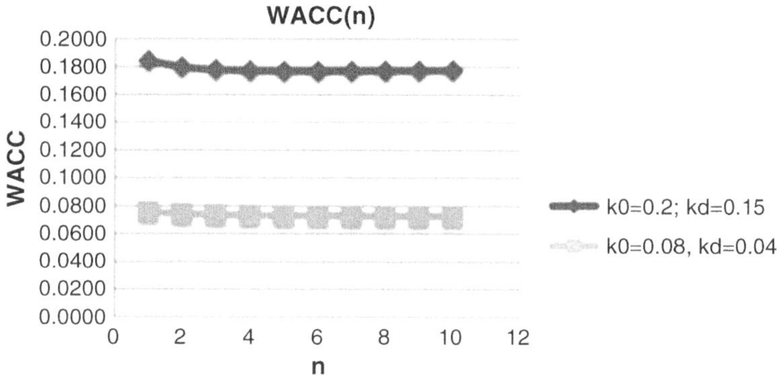

Fig. 14.5 Dependence of WACC on the age of the company n at different values of capital costs (equity, k_0, and debt, k_d, ones) and fixed leverage level $L = 1$

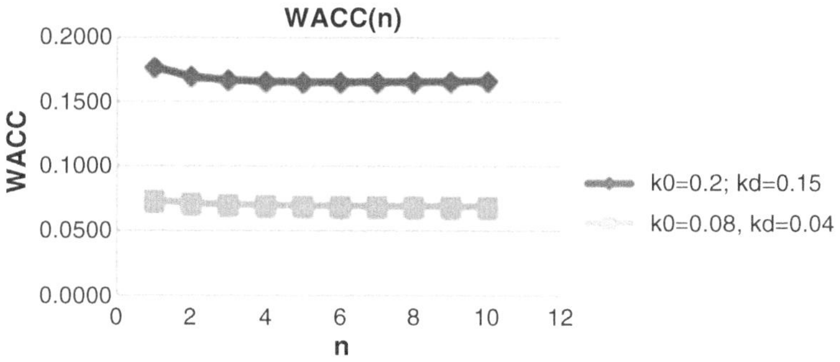

Fig. 14.6 Dependence of WACC on the age of the company n at different values of capital costs (equity, k_0, and debt, k_d) and fixed leverage level $L = 3$

14.1.2 Dependence of WACC on the Age of the Company n at Different Values of Capital Costs (Equity, k_0, and Debt, k_d) and Fixed Leverage Levels

The analysis in Tables 14.6, 14.7, 14.8, and 14.9 and Figs. 14.5 and 14.6 allows us to make the following conclusions:

1. The type of behavior of dependence of WACC on the age of the company, n, at fixed leverage level significantly depends on values of capital costs (equity, k_0, and debt, k_d). At the values of capital costs that are specific to developing countries (including Russia) ($k_0 = 20\%$, $k_d = 15\%$), there is a second type of dependence of WACC on the age of the company, n, namely, decrease of WACC with n with passage through minimum with subsequent limited growth. And at the capital cost values, characteristic in the West ($k_0 = 8\%$, $k_d = 4\%$), there is a first type of dependence of WACC on the age of company n, namely, the monotonic decrease of WACC with n.

Current suggestion has been made before the detailed investigation of condition of existing of gold age effect has been done. As we will see in the next chapter, the existence of the "golden age" of company does not depend on the value of capital costs of the company, but depends on the difference value between equity, k_0, and debt, k_d, costs.

2. The same features are observed in both considering cases: at the leverage values $L = 1$ and $L = 3$.

   Put $L = 3$.

14.1.3 Dependence of WACC on the Age of the Company n at Different Values of Debt Capital Cost, k_d, and Fixed Equity Cost, k_0, and Fixed Leverage Levels

In this section, we study the dependence of WACC on the age of the company n at different values of debt capital cost, k_d, and fixed equity cost, k_0, and fixed leverage levels.

Put first $L = 1$.

The analysis in Tables 14.10, 14.11, 14.12, 14.13, 14.14, 14.15, 14.16, and 14.17 and Figs. 14.7 and 14.8 allows us to make the following conclusions:

1. At fixed equity cost, k_0, and at fixed leverage level, the type of behavior of dependence of WACC on the age of the company, n, significantly depends on value of debt capital cost, k_d: with growth of k_d it is changing from monotonic decrease of WACC with n to decrease of WACC with n with passage through minimum with subsequent limited growth.

Table 14.10 Dependence of WACC on the age of the company n at $L = 1$, $k_0 = 20\%$, $k_d = 15\%$

L	WACC	k_0	k_d	W_d	t	n	k_e
1	0.1843	0.2	0.15	0.5	0.2	1	0.2487
1	0.1798	0.2	0.15	0.5	0.2	2	0.2397
1	0.1780	0.2	0.15	0.5	0.2	3	0.2360
1	0.1772	0.2	0.15	0.5	0.2	4	0.2345
1	0.1769	0.2	0.15	0.5	0.2	5	0.2339
1	0.1769	0.2	0.15	0.5	0.2	6	0.2338
1	0.1770	0.2	0.15	0.5	0.2	7	0.2340
1	0.1771	0.2	0.15	0.5	0.2	8	0.2343
1	0.1773	0.2	0.15	0.5	0.2	9	0.2346
1	0.1775	0.2	0.15	0.5	0.2	10	0.2351

Table 14.11 Dependence of WACC on the age of the company n at $L = 1$, $k_0 = 20\%$, $k_d = 12\%$

L	WACC	k_0	k_d	W_d	t	n	k_e
1	0.1871	0.2	0.12	0.5	0.2	1	0.2783
1	0.1832	0.2	0.12	0.5	0.2	2	0.2705
1	0.1815	0.2	0.12	0.5	0.2	3	0.2670
1	0.1807	0.2	0.12	0.5	0.2	4	0.2653
1	0.1802	0.2	0.12	0.5	0.2	5	0.2644
1	0.1799	0.2	0.12	0.5	0.2	6	0.2639
1	0.1798	0.2	0.12	0.5	0.2	7	0.2636
1	0.1798	0.2	0.12	0.5	0.2	8	0.2636
1	0.1798	0.2	0.12	0.5	0.2	9	0.2635
1	0.1798	0.2	0.12	0.5	0.2	10	0.2636

Table 14.12 Dependence of WACC on the age of the company n at $L = 1$, $k_0 = 20\%$, $k_d = 17\%$

L	WACC	k_0	k_d	W_d	t	n	k_e
1	0.1826	0.2	0.17	0.5	0.2	1	0.2291
1	0.1777	0.2	0.17	0.5	0.2	2	0.2194
1	0.1759	0.2	0.17	0.5	0.2	3	0.2158
1	0.1752	0.2	0.17	0.5	0.2	4	0.2144
1	0.1750	0.2	0.17	0.5	0.2	5	0.2141
1	0.1751	0.2	0.17	0.5	0.2	6	0.2143
1	0.1754	0.2	0.17	0.5	0.2	7	0.2148
1	0.1757	0.2	0.17	0.5	0.2	8	0.2154
1	0.1760	0.2	0.17	0.5	0.2	9	0.2160
1	0.1763	0.2	0.17	0.5	0.2	10	0.2167

2. At $k_d = 10\%$ and $k_d = 12\%$ ($k_0 = 20\%$), the monotonic decrease of WACC with n is observed, while at higher debt costs, $k_d = 15\%$ and $k_d = 17\%$ ($k_0 = 20\%$), decrease of WACC with n with passage through minimum with subsequent limited growth takes place. The optimum age of the company is growing with k_d decreasing: it is equal to 5 years at $k_d = 17\%$ and 6 years at $k_d = 15\%$.
3. The conclusions are saved at both considered values of leverage level: $L = 1$ and $L = 3$.

   Put than $L = 3$.

Table 14.13 Dependence of WACC on the age of the company n at $L = 1$, $k_0 = 20\%$, $k_d = 10\%$

L	WACC	k_0	k_d	W_d	t	n	k_e
1	0.1891	0.2	0.1	0.5	0.2	1	0.2982
1	0.1857	0.2	0.1	0.5	0.2	2	0.2913
1	0.1841	0.2	0.1	0.5	0.2	3	0.2881
1	0.1832	0.2	0.1	0.5	0.2	4	0.2864
1	0.1827	0.2	0.1	0.5	0.2	5	0.2853
1	0.1823	0.2	0.1	0.5	0.2	6	0.2846
1	0.1821	0.2	0.1	0.5	0.2	7	0.2842
1	0.1819	0.2	0.1	0.5	0.2	8	0.2838
1	0.1818	0.2	0.1	0.5	0.2	9	0.2836
1	0.1817	0.2	0.1	0.5	0.2	10	0.2834

Table 14.14 Dependence of WACC on the age of the company n at $L = 3$, $k_0 = 20\%$, $k_d = 15\%$

L	WACC	k_0	k_d	W_d	t	n	k_e
3	0.1765	0.2	0.15	0.75	0.2	1	0.3461
3	0.1697	0.2	0.15	0.75	0.2	2	0.3189
3	0.1669	0.2	0.15	0.75	0.2	3	0.3078
3	0.1657	0.2	0.15	0.75	0.2	4	0.3029
3	0.1653	0.2	0.15	0.75	0.2	5	0.3010
3	0.1651	0.2	0.15	0.75	0.2	6	0.3006
3	0.1653	0.2	0.15	0.75	0.2	7	0.3010
3	0.1655	0.2	0.15	0.75	0.2	8	0.3019
3	0.1658	0.2	0.15	0.75	0.2	9	0.3030
3	0.1661	0.2	0.15	0.75	0.2	10	0.3042

Table 14.15 Dependence of WACC on the age of the company n at $L = 3$, $k_0 = 20\%$, $k_d = 12\%$

L	WACC	k_0	k_d	W_d	t	n	k_e
3	0.1807	0.2	0.12	0.75	0.2	1	0.4349
3	0.1748	0.2	0.12	0.75	0.2	2	0.4113
3	0.1722	0.2	0.12	0.75	0.2	3	0.4009
3	0.1709	0.2	0.12	0.75	0.2	4	0.3955
3	0.1702	0.2	0.12	0.75	0.2	5	0.3927
3	0.1698	0.2	0.12	0.75	0.2	6	0.3911
3	0.1696	0.2	0.12	0.75	0.2	7	0.3903
3	0.1695	0.2	0.12	0.75	0.2	8	0.3900
3	0.1695	0.2	0.12	0.75	0.2	9	0.3899
3	0.1695	0.2	0.12	0.75	0.2	10	0.3900

Table 14.16 Dependence of WACC on the age of the company n at $L = 3$, $k_0 = 20\%$, $k_d = 17\%$

L	WACC	k_0	k_d	W_d	t	n	k_e
3	0.1738	0.2	0.17	0.75	0.2	1	0.2874
3	0.1665	0.2	0.17	0.75	0.2	2	0.2581
3	0.1637	0.2	0.17	0.75	0.2	3	0.2469
3	0.1626	0.2	0.17	0.75	0.2	4	0.2426
3	0.1624	0.2	0.17	0.75	0.2	5	0.2415
3	0.1625	0.2	0.17	0.75	0.2	6	0.2420
3	0.1628	0.2	0.17	0.75	0.2	7	0.2433
3	0.1633	0.2	0.17	0.75	0.2	8	0.2451
3	0.1638	0.2	0.17	0.75	0.2	9	0.2470
3	0.1643	0.2	0.17	0.75	0.2	10	0.2490

Table 14.17 Dependence of WACC on the age of the company n at $L = 3$, $k_0 = 20\%$, $k_d = 10\%$

L	WACC	k_0	k_d	W_d	t	n	k_e
3	0.1836	0.2	0.1	0.75	0.2	1	0.4945
3	0.1785	0.2	0.1	0.75	0.2	2	0.4739
3	0.1761	0.2	0.1	0.75	0.2	3	0.4642
3	0.1747	0.2	0.1	0.75	0.2	4	0.4588
3	0.1739	0.2	0.1	0.75	0.2	5	0.4556
3	0.1734	0.2	0.1	0.75	0.2	6	0.4535
3	0.1730	0.2	0.1	0.75	0.2	7	0.4520
3	0.1727	0.2	0.1	0.75	0.2	8	0.4510
3	0.1726	0.2	0.1	0.75	0.2	9	0.4502
3	0.1724	0.2	0.1	0.75	0.2	10	0.4496

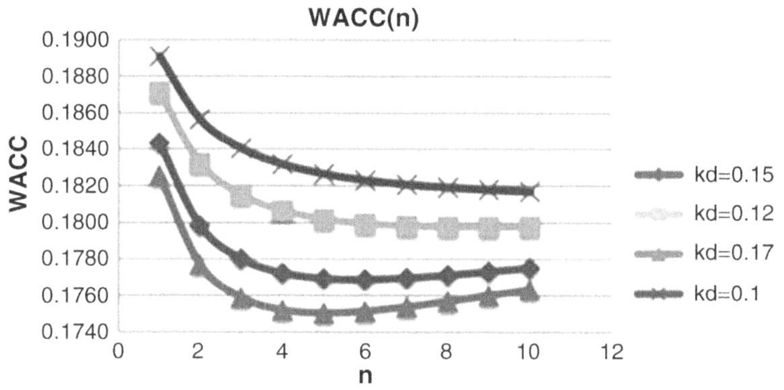

Fig. 14.7 Dependence of WACC on the age of the company n at different values of debt capital cost, k_d, and fixed equity cost, k_0, and fixed leverage level $L = 1$

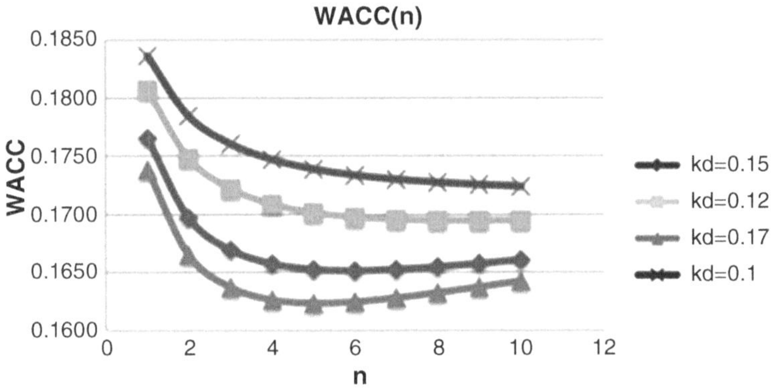

Fig. 14.8 Dependence of WACC on the age of the company n at different values of debt capital cost, k_d, and fixed equity cost, k_0, and fixed leverage level $L = 3$

Table 14.18 Dependence of WACC on the age of the company n at $L = 1$, $k_0 = 18\%$, $k_d = 15\%$

L	WACC	k_0	k_d	W_d	t	n	k_e
1	0.1646	0.18	0.15	0.5	0.2	1	0.2092
1	0.1602	0.18	0.15	0.5	0.2	2	0.2005
1	0.1585	0.18	0.15	0.5	0.2	3	0.1970
1	0.1578	0.18	0.15	0.5	0.2	4	0.1956
1	0.1576	0.18	0.15	0.5	0.2	5	0.1952
1	0.1576	0.18	0.15	0.5	0.2	6	0.1952
1	0.1578	0.18	0.15	0.5	0.2	7	0.1955
1	0.1580	0.18	0.15	0.5	0.2	8	0.1960
1	0.1583	0.18	0.15	0.5	0.2	9	0.1965
1	0.1585	0.18	0.15	0.5	0.2	10	0.1970

14.1.4 *Dependence of WACC on the Age of the Company* n *at Different Values of Equity Cost,* k_0*, and Fixed Debt Capital Cost,* k_d*, and Fixed Leverage Levels*

In this section, we study the dependence of WACC on the age of the company n at different values of equity cost, k_0, and fixed debt capital cost, k_d, and fixed leverage levels.

The analysis in Tables 14.18, 14.19, 14.20, 14.21, 14.22, and 14.23 and Figs. 14.9, and 14.10 allows us to make the following conclusions:

1. At fixed debt capital cost, k_d, and at fixed leverage level in all considered cases (at all equity costs k_0 and all leverage levels L), the second type of dependence of WACC on the age of the company, n, namely, decrease of WACC with n with passage through minimum with subsequent limited growth, takes place.
2. The "golden age" of the company slightly fluctuates under change of the equity value k_0; these fluctuations are described in Table 14.24 (age is in years).

   Put $L = 3$.

Table 14.19 Dependence of WACC on the age of the company n at $L = 1$, $k_0 = 20\%$, $k_d = 15\%$

L	WACC	k_0	k_d	W_d	t	n	k_e
1	0.1843	0.2	0.15	0.5	0.2	1	0.2487
1	0.1798	0.2	0.15	0.5	0.2	2	0.2397
1	0.1780	0.2	0.15	0.5	0.2	3	0.2360
1	0.1772	0.2	0.15	0.5	0.2	4	0.2345
1	0.1769	0.2	0.15	0.5	0.2	5	0.2339
1	0.1769	0.2	0.15	0.5	0.2	6	0.2338
1	0.1770	0.2	0.15	0.5	0.2	7	0.2340
1	0.1771	0.2	0.15	0.5	0.2	8	0.2343
1	0.1773	0.2	0.15	0.5	0.2	9	0.2346
1	0.1775	0.2	0.15	0.5	0.2	10	0.2351

Table 14.20 Dependence of WACC on the age of the company n at $L = 1$, $k_0 = 22\%$, $k_d = 15\%$

L	WACC	k_0	k_d	W_d	t	n	k_e
1	0.2041	0.22	0.15	0.5	0.2	1	0.2882
1	0.1994	0.22	0.15	0.5	0.2	2	0.2789
1	0.1975	0.22	0.15	0.5	0.2	3	0.2751
1	0.1967	0.22	0.15	0.5	0.2	4	0.2733
1	0.1963	0.22	0.15	0.5	0.2	5	0.2726
1	0.1962	0.22	0.15	0.5	0.2	6	0.2723
1	0.1962	0.22	0.15	0.5	0.2	7	0.2723
1	0.1962	0.22	0.15	0.5	0.2	8	0.2725
1	0.1964	0.22	0.15	0.5	0.2	9	0.2727
1	0.1965	0.22	0.15	0.5	0.2	10	0.2730

Table 14.21 Dependence of WACC on the age of the company n at $L = 3$, $k_0 = 18\%$, $k_d = 15\%$

L	WACC	k_0	k_d	W_d	t	n	k_e
3	0.1569	0.18	0.15	0.75	0.2	1	0.2677
3	0.1503	0.18	0.15	0.75	0.2	2	0.2412
3	0.1477	0.18	0.15	0.75	0.2	3	0.2307
3	0.1466	0.18	0.15	0.75	0.2	4	0.2264
3	0.1462	0.18	0.15	0.75	0.2	5	0.2249
3	0.1462	0.18	0.15	0.75	0.2	6	0.2250
3	0.1464	0.18	0.15	0.75	0.2	7	0.2258
3	0.1468	0.18	0.15	0.75	0.2	8	0.2271
3	0.1471	0.18	0.15	0.75	0.2	9	0.2286
3	0.1475	0.18	0.15	0.75	0.2	10	0.2302

Table 14.22 Dependence of WACC on the age of the company n at $L = 3$, $k_0 = 20\%$, $k_d = 15\%$

L	WACC	k_0	k_d	W_d	t	n	k_e
3	0.1765	0.2	0.15	0.75	0.2	1	0.3461
3	0.1697	0.2	0.15	0.75	0.2	2	0.3189
3	0.1669	0.2	0.15	0.75	0.2	3	0.3078
3	0.1657	0.2	0.15	0.75	0.2	4	0.3029
3	0.1653	0.2	0.15	0.75	0.2	5	0.3010
3	0.1651	0.2	0.15	0.75	0.2	6	0.3006
3	0.1653	0.2	0.15	0.75	0.2	7	0.3010
3	0.1655	0.2	0.15	0.75	0.2	8	0.3019
3	0.1658	0.2	0.15	0.75	0.2	9	0.3030
3	0.1661	0.2	0.15	0.75	0.2	10	0.3042

Table 14.23 Dependence of WACC on the age of the company n at $L = 3$, $k_0 = 22\%$, $k_d = 15\%$

L	WACC	k_0	k_d	W_d	t	n	k_e
3	0.1961	0.22	0.15	0.75	0.2	1	0.4245
3	0.1891	0.22	0.15	0.75	0.2	2	0.3965
3	0.1862	0.22	0.15	0.75	0.2	3	0.3848
3	0.1849	0.22	0.15	0.75	0.2	4	0.3795
3	0.1843	0.22	0.15	0.75	0.2	5	0.3770
3	0.1840	0.22	0.15	0.75	0.2	6	0.3762
3	0.1840	0.22	0.15	0.75	0.2	7	0.3761
3	0.1841	0.22	0.15	0.75	0.2	8	0.3766
3	0.1843	0.22	0.15	0.75	0.2	9	0.3773
3	0.1845	0.22	0.15	0.75	0.2	10	0.3781

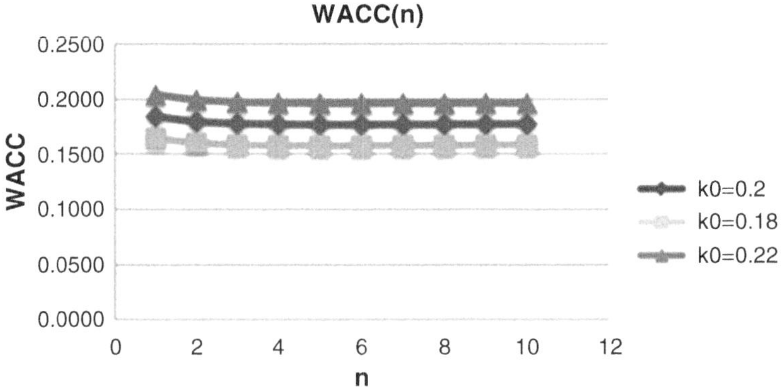

Fig. 14.9 Dependence of WACC on the age of the company n at different values of equity cost, k_0, and fixed debt capital cost, k_d, and fixed leverage level $L = 1$

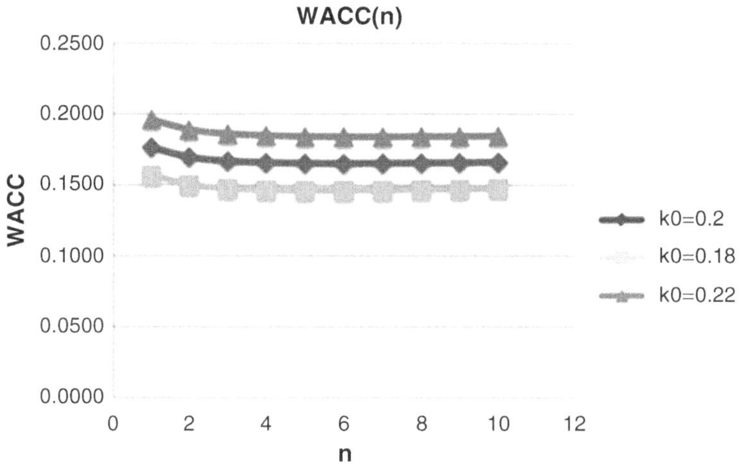

Fig. 14.10 Dependence of WACC on the age of the company n at different values of equity cost, k_0, and fixed debt capital cost, k_d, and fixed leverage level $L = 3$

Table 14.24 Dependence of "golden age" of the company n on L and k_0

	k_0		
L	18%	20%	22%
1	5–6	5–6	6–8
3	5–6	6	6–7

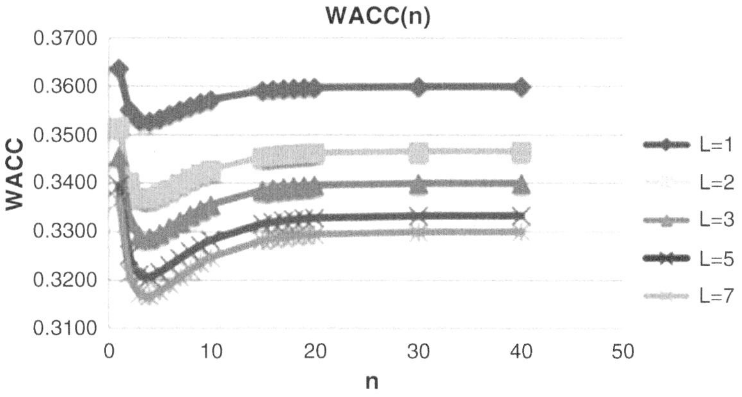

Fig. 14.11 Dependence of WACC on the age of the company n at high values of capital cost (equity, $k_0 = 40\%$, and debt, $k_d = 35\%$) at different leverage levels L (up to high values of lifetime of the company)

Table 14.25 The difference between the optimal (minimal) value of WACC and its perpetuity limit

L	1	2	3	5	7
ΔWACC, %	−0.72	−0.99	−1.12	−1.25	−1.33

14.1.5 Dependence of WACC on the Age of the Company n *at High Values of Capital Cost (Equity,* k_0*, and Debt,* k_d*) and High Lifetime of the Company*

Let us study the dependence of WACC on the age of the company n at high values of capital cost (equity, k_0, and debt, k_d) and higher age of the company.

14.1.5.1 At Fixed Leverage Level

From Fig. 14.11, it follows that:

1. In all considered cases (at all leverage levels L) at high values of capital cost (equity, $k_0 = 40\%$, and debt, $k_d = 35\%$), the second type of dependence of WACC on the age of the company, n, namely, decrease of WACC with n with passage through minimum with subsequent limited growth up to perpetuity limit, takes place.
2. A minimum value of attracting capital cost (WACC) is achieved at all leverage levels in the same age, when $n = 4$. This means that, at high value of capital costs, the company age, at which minimal value of attracting capital cost is achieved, is shifted forward lower (younger) values. We just remind that at $k_0 = 20\%$ and $k_d = 15\%$ (see above), the "golden age" was 6 years.
3. The shift of curves to lower values of WACC with the increase of leverage level L is associated with decrease of WACC with leverage.
4. An interesting thing is the analysis of the value of detected effect, i.e., how much is the difference between the minimum of the attracting capital, found in the BFO theory, and its perpetuity limit value, which has been considered as minimal value up to now. In Table 14.25, the dependence of the difference between the minimum of the attracting capital and its perpetuity limit value on leverage level L is shown.

Perpetuity limit value of WACC is calculated by using Modigliani–Miller formula (Modigliani and Miller 1958, 1963, 1966) with accounting of corporate taxes:

$$\text{WACC} = k_0(1 - w_d \cdot t) \tag{14.1}$$

From Fig. 14.11, it is seen that at high values of the age of the company ($n \geq 30$), the WACC practically does not differ from its perpetuity limit.

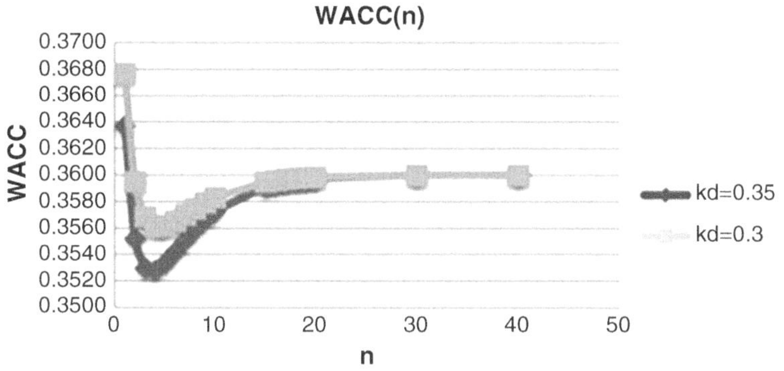

Fig. 14.12 Dependence of WACC on the age of the company n at fixed high value of equity cost, $k_0 = 40\%$, and two values of debt cost, $k_d = 30$ and 35%, at leverage level $L = 1$

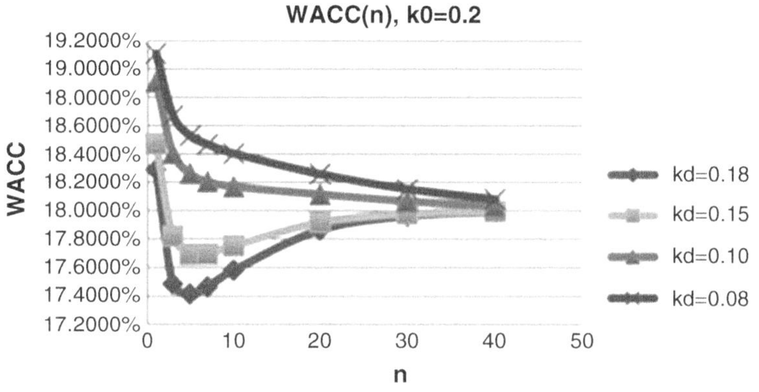

Fig. 14.13 Dependence of WACC on the age of the company n at fixed value of equity cost, $k_0 = 20\%$, and at four values of debt cost, $k_d = 8$, 10, 15, and 18%, at leverage level $L = 1$

From Table 14.25, it is seen that the gain value is from 0.7% up to 1.5% and grows with the increase of the leverage level of company, L.

14.1.5.2 Under Change of the Debt Capital Cost, k_d

Under change of the debt capital cost, k_d, a depth of pit in dependence of WACC on the age of the company, n, is changed as well: from Fig. 14.12, it is seen that pit (accounted from perpetuity value) is changed from 0.49% (at $k_d = 0.3$) up to 0.72% (at $k_d = 0.35$).

Note that as it is seen from Fig. 14.12, a perpetuity limit of WACC does not depend on debt cost, k_d, which is in accordance with the Modigliani–Miller formula (14.1) for WACC, which does not contain a debt capital cost, k_d, which means independence of perpetuity limit of WACC values from k_d, while the intermediate

Table 14.26 Dependence of WACC on the age of the company n at $L = 1$, $k_0 = 20\%$, $k_d = 18\%$

a (%)	k_0	k_d	L	n	t
14.2889	0.2	0.18	1	1	0.2
17.4859	0.2	0.18	1	3	0.2
17.4155	0.2	0.18	1	5	0.2
17.4654	0.2	0.18	1	7	0.2
17.5833	0.2	0.18	1	10	0.2
17.8641	0.2	0.18	1	20	0.2
17.9629	0.2	0.18	1	30	0.2
17.9909	0.2	0.18	1	40	0.2

Table 14.27 Dependence of WACC on the age of the company n at $L = 1$, $k_0 = 20\%$, $k_d = 15\%$

WACC (%)	k_0	k_d	L	n	t
14.4736	0.2	0.15	1	1	0.2
17.8200	0.2	0.15	1	3	0.2
17.6936	0.2	0.15	1	5	0.2
17.6967	0.2	0.15	1	7	0.2
17.7528	0.2	0.15	1	10	0.2
17.9192	0.2	0.15	1	20	0.2
17.9797	0.2	0.15	1	30	0.2
17.9957	0.2	0.15	1	40	0.2

Table 14.28 Dependence of WACC on the age of the company n at $L = 1$, $k_0 = 20\%$, $k_d = 12\%$

WACC (%)	k_0	k_d	L	n	t
14.6583	0.2	0.12	1	1	0.2
14.1511	0.2	0.12	1	3	0.2
14.0181	0.2	0.12	1	5	0.2
17.9817	0.2	0.12	1	7	0.2
17.9789	0.2	0.12	1	10	0.2
14.0145	0.2	0.12	1	20	0.2
14.0175	0.2	0.12	1	30	0.2
14.0099	0.2	0.12	1	40	0.2

Table 14.29 Dependence of WACC on the age of the company n at $L = 1$, $k_0 = 20\%$, $k_d = 10\%$

a (5)	k_0	k_d	L	n	t
14.9082	0.2	0.1	1	1	0.2
14.4030	0.2	0.1	1	3	0.2
14.2615	0.2	0.1	1	5	0.2
14.2045	0.2	0.1	1	7	0.2
14.1678	0.2	0.1	1	10	0.2
14.1146	0.2	0.1	1	20	0.2
14.0669	0.2	0.1	1	30	0.2
14.0330	0.2	0.1	1	40	0.2

WACC values (for finite lifetime (age) of company, n) depend on the debt capital cost, k_d [see BFO theory (Brusov and Filatova 2011; Brusov et al. 2011a, b, c, 2012a, b, 2013a, b, 2014a, b; Filatova et al. 2008)].

Table 14.30 Dependence of WACC on the age of the company n at $L = 1$, $k_0 = 20\%$, $k_d = 8\%$

WACC (%)	k_0	k_d	L	n	t
19.1087	0.2	0.08	1	1	0.2
14.6716	0.2	0.08	1	3	0.2
14.5297	0.2	0.08	1	5	0.2
14.4692	0.2	0.08	1	7	0.2
14.4040	0.2	0.08	1	10	0.2
14.2594	0.2	0.08	1	20	0.2
14.1532	0.2	0.08	1	30	0.2
14.0813	0.2	0.08	1	40	0.2

Table 14.31 Dependence of WACC on the age of the company n at $L = 1$, $k_0 = 25\%$, $k_d = 15\%$

WACC (%)	k_0	k_d	L	n	t
23.2477	0.25	0.15	1	1	0.2
22.6690	0.25	0.15	1	3	0.2
22.5117	0.25	0.15	1	5	0.2
22.4913	0.25	0.15	1	7	0.2
22.4933	0.25	0.15	1	10	0.2
22.5219	0.25	0.15	1	20	0.2
22.5136	0.25	0.15	1	30	0.2
22.5045	0.25	0.15	1	40	0.2

Table 14.32 Dependence of WACC on the age of the company n at $L = 1$, $k_0 = 22\%$, $k_d = 15\%$

WACC (%)	k_0	k_d	L	n	t
20.3006	0.22	0.15	1	1	0.2
19.7431	0.22	0.15	1	3	0.2
19.6171	0.22	0.15	1	5	0.2
19.6163	0.22	0.15	1	7	0.2
19.6514	0.22	0.15	1	10	0.2
19.7639	0.22	0.15	1	20	0.2
19.7960	0.22	0.15	1	30	0.2
19.8007	0.22	0.15	1	40	0.2

Table 14.33 Dependence of WACC on the age of the company n at $L = 1$, $k_0 = 20\%$, $k_d = 15\%$

WACC (%)	k_0	k_d	L	n	t
14.4717	0.2	0.15	1	1	0.2
17.8015	0.2	0.15	1	3	0.2
17.6938	0.2	0.15	1	5	0.2
17.6972	0.2	0.15	1	7	0.2
17.7592	0.2	0.15	1	10	0.2
17.9192	0.2	0.15	1	20	0.2
17.9797	0.2	0.15	1	30	0.2
17.9957	0.2	0.15	1	40	0.2

From Fig. 14.13 it is seen that with the increase of debt cost, k_d, the character of dependence of WACC on the age of the company n is changed from monotonic decrease of WACC with n to decrease of WACC with n with passage through

Table 14.34 Dependence of WACC on the age of the company n at $L = 1$, $k_0 = 18\%$, $k_d = 15\%$

WACC (%)	k_0	k_d	L	n	t
16.4350	0.18	0.15	1	1	0.2
15.8519	0.18	0.15	1	3	0.2
15.7610	0.18	0.15	1	5	0.2
15.7793	0.18	0.15	1	7	0.2
15.8561	0.18	0.15	1	10	0.2
16.0683	0.18	0.15	1	20	0.2
16.1586	0.18	0.15	1	30	0.2
16.1884	0.18	0.15	1	40	0.2

Table 14.35 Dependence of WACC on the age of the company n at $L = 1$, $k_0 = 16\%$, $k_d = 15\%$

WACC (%)	k_0	k_d	L	n	t
14.4304	0.16	0.15	1	1	0.2
13.9019	0.16	0.15	1	3	0.2
13.8278	0.16	0.15	1	5	0.2
13.8610	0.16	0.15	1	7	0.2
13.9481	0.16	0.15	1	10	0.2
14.2119	0.16	0.15	1	20	0.2
14.3324	0.16	0.15	1	30	0.2
14.3781	0.16	0.15	1	40	0.2

Table 14.36 Dependence of depth of gap ΔWACC on k_0 value

k_0	0.16	0.18	0.20	0.22	0.25
ΔWACC, %	0.55	0.43	0.30	0.18	0.03

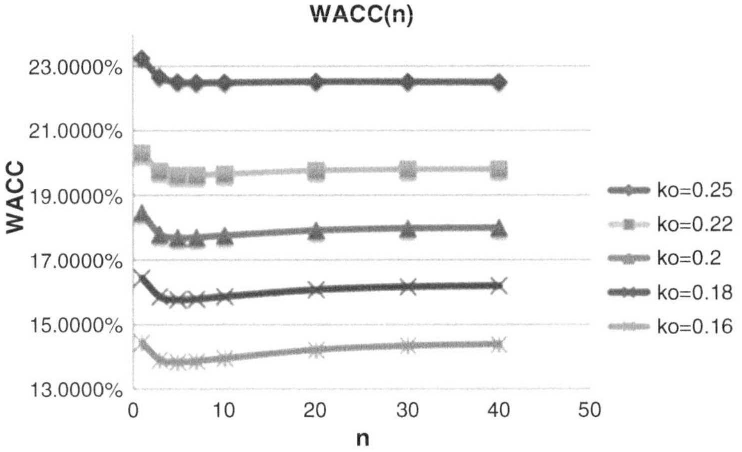

Fig. 14.14 Dependence of WACC on the age of the company n at fixed value of debt cost, $k_d = 15\%$, and five values of equity cost, $k_0 = 16$, 18, 20, 22, and 25%, at leverage level $L = 1$

Table 14.37 Dependence of WACC on the age of the company n at $L = 2$, $k_0 = 20\%$, $k_d = 15\%$, $t = 20\%$

L	WACC (%)	k_0	k_d	t	n
2	17.84	0.2	0.15	0.2	1
2	17.07	0.2	0.15	0.2	3
2	16.92	0.2	0.15	0.2	5
2	16.92	0.2	0.15	0.2	7
2	16.99	0.2	0.15	0.2	10
2	17.12	0.2	0.15	0.2	15
2	17.30	0.2	0.15	0.2	30
2	17.33	0.2	0.15	0.2	45

Table 14.38 Dependence of WACC on the age of the company n at $L = 2$, $k_0 = 20\%$, $k_d = 15\%$, $t = 40\%$

L	WACC (%)	k_0	k_d	t	n
2	15.72	0.2	0.15	0.4	1
2	14.09	0.2	0.15	0.4	3
2	13.76	0.2	0.15	0.4	5
2	13.73	0.2	0.15	0.4	7
2	13.86	0.2	0.15	0.4	10
2	14.13	0.2	0.15	0.4	15
2	14.56	0.2	0.15	0.4	30
2	14.65	0.2	0.15	0.4	45

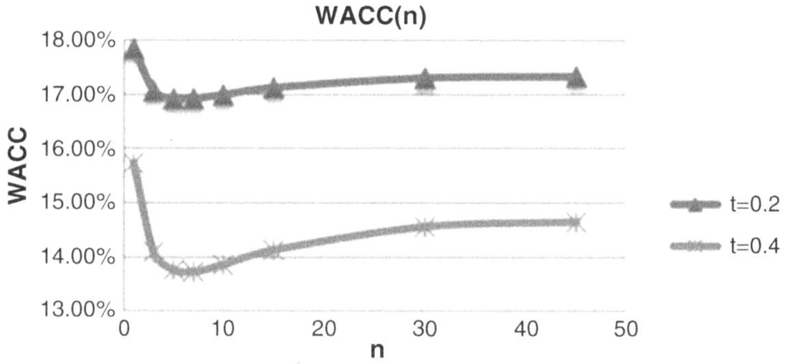

Fig. 14.15 Dependence of WACC on the age of the company n at fixed capital costs, $k_0 = 20\%$, $k_d = 15\%$, and two values of tax on profit rate $t = 0.2$ and $t = 0.4$ and at leverage level $L = 2$

minimum, followed by a limited growth (Tables 14.26, 14.27, 14.28, 14.29, and 14.30).

14.1.5.3 Under Change of the Equity Capital Cost, k_0 (Tables 14.31, 14.32, 14.33, 14.34, 14.35, and 14.36)

Depth of gap, ΔWACC, is decreased with equity cost, k_0 (Fig. 14.14).

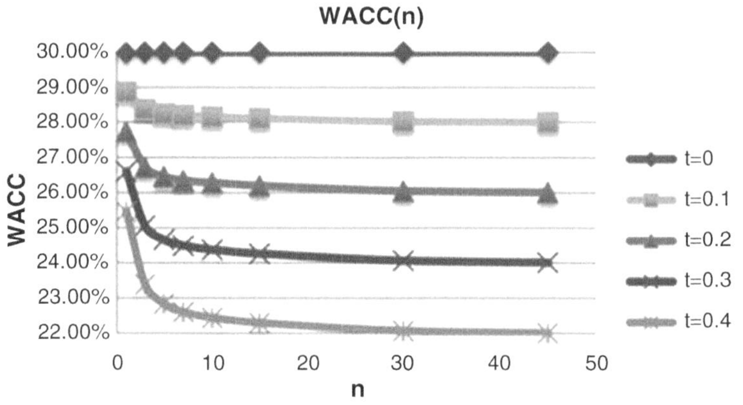

Fig. 14.16 Dependence of WACC on the age of the company n at fixed capital costs, $k_0 = 30\%$, $k_d = 15\%$, and different values of tax on profit rate $t = 0, 0.1, 0.2, 0.3$, and 0.4 and at leverage level $L = 2$

Table 14.39 Dependence of WACC on the age of the company n at $L = 1$, $k_0 = 25\%$, $k_d = 15\%$

L	t	k_0	k_d	n	W_d	WACC (%)
1	0.2	0.25	0.15	1	0.5	23.2270
1	0.2	0.25	0.15	3	0.5	22.6725
1	0.2	0.25	0.15	5	0.5	22.5184
1	0.2	0.25	0.15	7	0.5	22.4914
1	0.2	0.25	0.15	10	0.5	22.4934
1	0.2	0.25	0.15	20	0.5	22.5220
1	0.2	0.25	0.15	30	0.5	22.5137
1	0.2	0.25	0.15	40	0.5	22.5045
1	0.2	0.25	0.15	∞	0.5	21.50

14.1.5.4 Under Change of the Tax on Profit Rate, t (Tables 14.37 and 14.38)

The depth of gap in dependence of WACC on n, which is equal to 0.41% at $t = 0.2$, is increased 2.2 times and becomes equal to 0.92% at $t = 0.4$, i.e., it is increased 2.2 times, when tax on profit rate is increased two times (Fig. 14.15).

We see from Fig. 14.16 that at fixed capital costs, $k_0 = 30\%$, $k_d = 15\%$, and at different values of tax on profit rate, t, there is no minimum in WACC at finite age of the company: minimal value of WACC is reached at $n = \infty$. Note that this is a feature of particular values of capital costs (probably, too big difference between k_0 and k_d).

Table 14.40 Dependence of WACC on the age of the company n at $L = 2$, $k_0 = 25\%$, $k_d = 15\%$

L	t	k_0	k_d	n	W_d	WACC (%)
2	0.2	0.25	0.15	1	0.6667	22.8255
2	0.2	0.25	0.15	3	0.6667	21.8935
2	0.2	0.25	0.15	5	0.6667	21.6843
2	0.2	0.25	0.15	7	0.6667	21.6431
2	0.2	0.25	0.15	10	0.6667	21.6448
2	0.2	0.25	0.15	20	0.6667	21.6895
2	0.2	0.25	0.15	30	0.6667	21.6842
2	0.2	0.25	0.15	40	0.6667	21.6742
2	0.2	0.25	0.15	∞	0.6667	21.6665

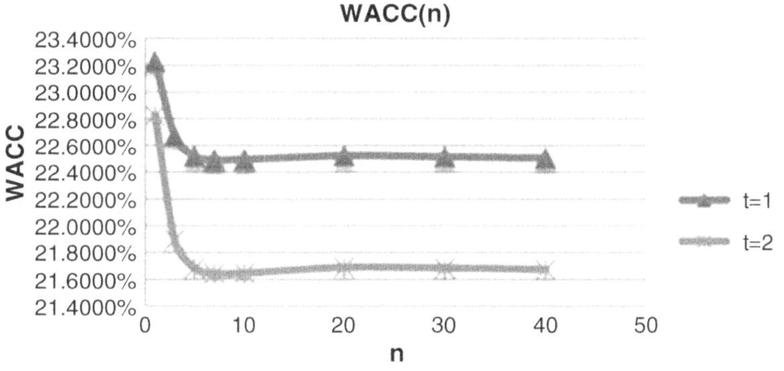

Fig. 14.17 Dependence of WACC on the age of the company n at fixed capital costs, $k_0 = 25\%$, $k_d = 15\%$, and different values of leverage level $L = 1$ and $L = 2$

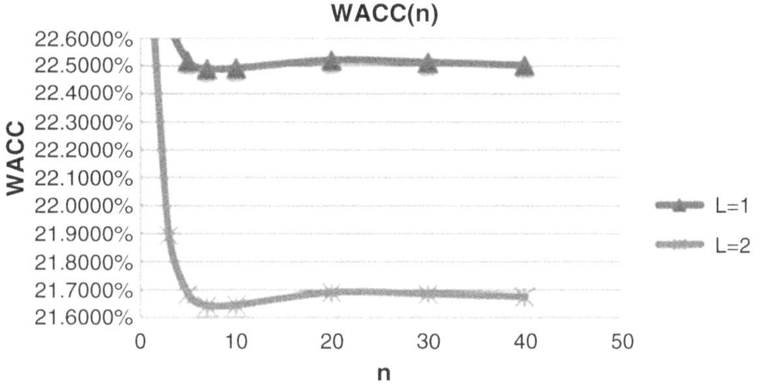

Fig. 14.18 Dependence of WACC on the age of the company n at fixed capital costs, $k_0 = 25\%$, $k_d = 15\%$, and different values of leverage level $L = 1$ and $L = 2$ (lager scale)

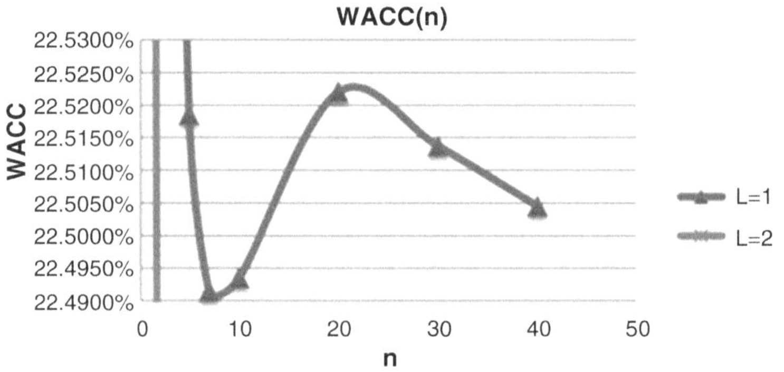

Fig. 14.19 Dependence of WACC on the age of the company n at fixed capital costs, $k_0 = 25\%$, $k_d = 15\%$, and different values of leverage level $L = 1$ and $L = 2$ (the largest scale)

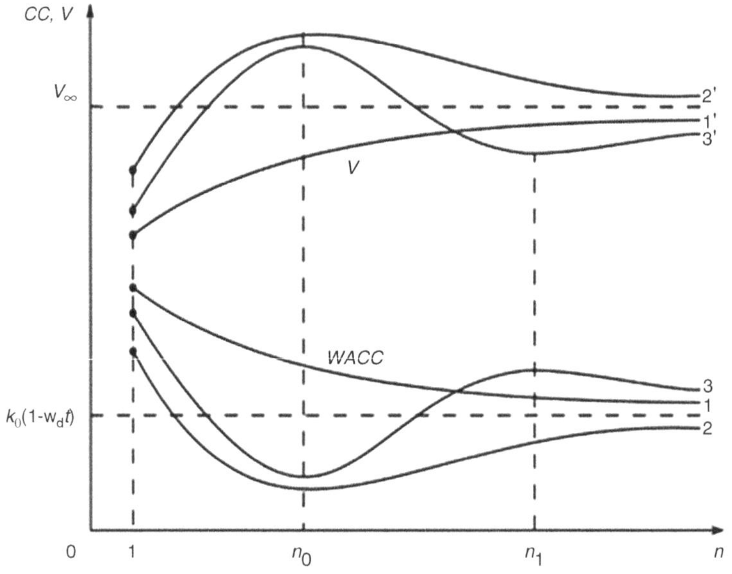

Fig. 14.20 "Kulik" effect: behavior 3 for WACC(n) and 3′ for $V(n)$

14.1.6 Further Investigation of Effect

During further investigation of effect, we have discovered one more interesting feature of dependence of WACC on n, WACC(n): we have called this effect "Kulik$_e$ffect" (Kulik is a graduate student of the Management Department of Financial University in Moscow, who has discovered this effect) (Brusov et al. 2015) (Tables 14.39 and 14.40).

Note that perpetuity limits for WACC(n), calculated by the Modigliani–Miller formula (Modigliani and Miller 1958, 1963, 1966) (14.1), are equal to:

For $L = 1$ WACC(∞) = 22.5%

For $L = 2$ WACC(∞) = 21.6665% (Figs. 14.17, 14.18, and 14.19)

It turns out that at particular values of capital costs, for example, at $k_0 = 25\%$, $k_d = 15\%$, a third modification of dependences of WACC on the age of the company n takes place: decrease of WACC with passage through minimum, followed by a growth with passage through maximum, and finally with trend to perpetuity limit from bigger values (note that at the second type of WACC(n) behavior, the curve WACC(n) tends to perpetuity limit from lower values). We have called this effect "Kulik$_e$ffect." It gives a third type of dependence of WACC on the age of the company n, which is represented at Fig. 14.20.

14.2 Conclusions

In this chapter, it is shown for the first time (Brusov et al. 2015) within the BFO theory (Brusov and Filatova 2011; Brusov et al. 2011a, b, c, 2012a, b, 2013a, b, 2014a, b; Filatova et al. 2008) that valuation of WACC in the Modigliani–Miller theory (Modigliani and Miller 1958, 1963, 1966) is not minimal and valuation of the company capitalization is not maximal, as all financiers assumed up to now: at some age of the company its WACC value turns out to be lower than in the Modigliani–Miller theory, and company capitalization V turns out to be greater than V in the Modigliani–Miller theory (Modigliani and Miller 1958, 1963, 1966). Thus, existing presentations concerning the results of the Modigliani–Miller theory in this aspect (Myers 1984) turn out to be incorrect (Brusov et al. 2015).

It is shown that from the point of view of cost of attracting capital, there are two (really three) types of dependences of WACC on the time of life (age) of company n: monotonic decrease of WACC with n and decrease of WACC with passage through minimum, followed by a limited growth [there is a third modification of dependences WACC(n) ("Kulik" behavior), which leaves all conclusions valid (Brusov et al. 2015)].

A hypothesis was put forward (Brusov et al. 2015) that the character of the WACC(n) dependence is determined by the equity cost k_0.The first type takes place for the companies with low-cost capital, characteristic for the Western companies. The second type takes place for higher-cost capital of the company, characteristic for companies from developing countries (including Russia). This means that the latter companies, in contrast to the Western ones, can take advantage of the benefits given at a certain stage of development by discovered effect (Brusov et al. 2015).

Whether or not this hypothesis turned out to be right we will see in Chap. 15, where we investigate the conditions of existing of "the golden age" of the company effect and discover a new important effect, which we called "the silver age" of the company.

It is important to note that since the "golden age" of company depends on the company's capital costs, by controlling them (e.g., by modifying the value of dividend payments that reflects the equity cost), the company may extend the "golden age" of the company when the cost to attract capital becomes minimal (less than perpetuity limit) and the capitalization of companies becomes maximal (above than perpetuity assessment) up to a specified time interval.

References

Brusov P (2018a) Editorial: introduction on special issue on the banking system and financial markets of Russia and other countries: problems and prospects. J Rev Glob Econ 7:i–vi. SCOPUS

Brusov P (2018b) Editorial. J Rev Glob Econ 7:i–v, SCOPUS

Brusov PN, Filatova TV (2011) From Modigliani–Miller to general theory of capital cost and capital structure of the company. Finance Credit 435:2–8

Brusov P, Filatova T, Orehova N, Brusova A (2011a) Weighted average cost of capital in the theory of Modigliani–Miller, modified for a finite life–time company. Appl Financ Econ 21 (11):815–824

Brusov P, Filatova T, Orehova N et al (2011b) From Modigliani–Miller to general theory of capital cost and capital structure of the company. Res J Econ Bus ICT 2:16–21

Brusov P, Filatova T, Orehova N et al (2011c) Influence of debt financing on the effectiveness of the investment project within the Modigliani–Miller theory. Res J Econ Bus ICT (UK) 2:11–15

Brusov P, Filatova T, Eskindarov M, Orehova N (2012a) Influence of debt financing on the effectiveness of the finite duration investment project. Appl Financ Econ 22(13):1043–1052

Brusov P, Filatova T, Eskindarov M, Orehova N (2012b) Hidden global causes of the global financial crisis. J Rev Global Econ 1:106–111

Brusov P, Filatova P, Orekhova N (2013a) Absence of an optimal capital structure in the famous tradeoff theory! J Rev Global Econ 2:94–116

Brusov P, Filatova T, Orehova N (2013b) A qualitatively new effect in corporative finance: abnormal dependence of cost of equity of company on leverage. J Rev Global Econ 2:183–193

Brusov P, Filatova P, Orekhova N (2014a) Mechanism of formation of the company optimal capital structure, different from suggested by trade off theory. Cogent Econ Finance 2:1–13. http://dx.doi.org/ 10.1080/23322039.2014.946150

Brusov P, Filatova T, Orehova N (2014b) Inflation in Brusov–Filatova–Orekhova theory and in its perpetuity limit—Modigliani–Miller theory. J Rev Global Econ 3:175–185

Brusov P, Filatova T, Orekhova N, Eskindarov M (2015) Modern corporate finance, investments and taxation. Springer International Publishing, Switzerland. p 373. Monograph. SCOPUS. https://www.springer.com/gp/book/9783319147314

Brusov P, Filatova T, Orekhova N, Eskindarov M (2018a), Modern corporate finance, investments, taxation and ratings. Springer Nature Publishing. Switzerland, p 571. Monograph

Brusov PN, Filatova TV, Orekhova NP, Kulik VL (2018b) Rating: new approach. J Rev Glob Econ 7:37–62. SCOPUS. https://doi.org/10.6000/1929-7092.2018.07.05

Brusov PN, Filatova TV, Orekhova NP, Kulik VL (2018c) A "golden age" of the companies: conditions of its existence. J Rev Glob Econ 7:88–103. SCOPUS. https://doi.org/10.6000/1929-7092.2018.07.07

Brusov PN, Filatova TV, Orekhova NP, Kulik VL (2018d) Rating methodology: new look and new horizons. J Rev Glob Econ 7:63–87. SCOPUS. https://doi.org/10.6000/1929-7092.2018.07.06

Brusov PN, Filatova TV, Orekhova NP, Kulik VL, Weil I (2018e) New meaningful effects in modern capital structure theory. J Rev Glob Econ 7:104–122. SCOPUS. https://doi.org/10.6000/1929-7092.2018.07.08

Brusov P, Filatova T, Orekhova N, Kulik V, Weil I, Brailov A (2018f) The impact of the central bank key rate and commercial banks credit rates on creating and maintaining of a favorable investment climate in the country. J Rev Glob Econ 7:360–376. SCOPUS. https://doi.org/10.6000/1929-7092.2018.07.31

Brusov PN, Filatova TV, Orekhova NP (2018g) Modern corporate finance and investments, monograph. Knorus Publishing House, Moscow, p 517

Brusov PN, Filatova TV, Orekhova NP, Kulik VL, Weil I (2019) Ratings of the investment projects of arbitrary durations: new methodology. J Rev Glob Econ 8:437–448. SCOPUS. https://doi.org/10.6000/1929-7092.2019.08.37

Brusov PN, Filatova TV, Orekhova NP, Kulik VL, Chang S-I, Lin YCG (2020) Modification of the Modigliani–Miller theory for the case of advance payments of tax on profit. J Rev Glob Econ 9:257–268

Brusova A (2011) A comparison of the three methods of estimation of weighted average cost of capital and equity cost of company. Financ Anal Prob Sol 34(76):36–42

Filatova T, Orehova N, Brusova A (2008) Weighted average cost of capital in the theory of Modigliani–Miller, modified for a finite lifetime company. Bull FU 48:68–77

Filatova TV, Brusov PN, Orekhova NP, Kulik VL (2018a) Ratings of the long-term projects: new approach. J Rev Glob Econ 7:645–661. SCOPUS. https://doi.org/10.6000/1929-7092.2018.07.59

Filatova TV, Brusov PN, Orekhova NP, Kulik VL (2018b) Ratings of the long-term projects: new approach. J Rev Glob Econ 7:645–661. SCOPUS. https://doi.org/10.6000/1929-7092.2018.07.59

Modigliani F, Miller M (1958) The cost of capital, corporate finance, and the theory of investment. Am Econ Rev 48:261–297

Modigliani F, Miller M (1963) Corporate income taxes and the cost of capital: a correction. Am Econ Rev 53:147–175

Modigliani F, Miller M (1966) Some estimates of the cost of capital to the electric utility industry 1954–1957. Am Econ Rev 56:333–391

Chapter 15
A "Silver Age" of the Companies. Conditions of Existence of "Golden Age" and "Silver Age" Effects

In this chapter, we continue to study the effect of the "golden age" of the company, which we described in Chap. 14. As it was shown for the first time (Brusov et al. 2015), the valuation of the weighted average cost of capital, WACC, in the Modigliani–Miller theory (Modigliani and Miller 1958, 1963, 1966) is not minimal and valuation of the company capitalization is not maximal, as all financiers assumed up to this discovery: at some age of the company its WACC value turns out to be lower than in the Modigliani–Miller theory, and company capitalization V turns out to be greater than V in the Modigliani–Miller theory. It was shown that, from the point of view of cost of attracting capital there are two types of dependences of weighted average cost of capital, WACC, on the company age n: monotonic decrease with n and decrease with passage through minimum, followed by a limited growth. In practice, there are companies with both types of dependences of WACC on the company age n.

In this chapter, we investigate which companies have the "golden age," i.e., obey the latter type of dependence of WACC on n (Brusov 2018b). With this aim we study the dependence of WACC on the age of company n at various leverage levels within the wide spectrum of capital cost values as well as the dependence of WACC on leverage level L at fixed company age n. All calculations have been done within modern theory of capital cost and capital structure BFO by Brusov–Filatova–Orekhova (Brusov et al. 2011a, b, c, 2012a, b, 2013a, b, 2014a, b; Filatova et al. 2008; Brusov (2018a); Brusov et al. (2018b, c, d, e, f, g); Brusov et al. (2019); Brusov et al. (2020); Filatova (2018)).

We have shown that existence of the "golden age" of the company does not depend on the value of capital costs of the company, but depends on the difference between equity k_0 and debt k_d costs. The "golden age" of the company exists at small enough difference between k_0 and k_d costs, while at high value of this difference the "golden age" of the company is absent: curve WACC(n) monotonically decreases with n. For the companies with the "golden age" curve WACC(L) for perpetuity companies lies between curves WACC(L) for company ages $n = 1$ and $n = 3$, while

P. Brusov et al., *Ratings*, Contributions to Finance and Accounting,
https://doi.org/10.1007/978-3-030-56243-4_15

for the companies without the ""golden age" curve WACC(L) for perpetuity companies is the lowest one.

In our paper (Brusov et al. 2015), we have also found a third type of WACC (n) dependence: decrease with passage through minimum, which lies below the perpetuity limit value, then going through maximum followed by a limited decrease. We called this effect "Kulik effect." In this chapter, we have found a type of "Kulik effect": decrease with passage through minimum of WACC, which lies above the perpetuity limit value, then going through maximum followed by a limited decrease. We call this company age, where WACC has a minimum, which lies above the perpetuity limit value, "a silver age" of the company.

Because the cost of attracting capital is used in rating methodologies as discounting rate under discounting of cash flows, study of WACC behavior is very important for rating procedures. Taking account of effects of the "golden (silver) age" could change the valuation of creditworthiness of issuers.

Note that, since the "golden age" of the company depends on the company's capital costs, by controlling them (e.g., by modifying the value of dividend payments, which reflect the equity cost), company may extend the "golden age" of the company, when the cost to attract capital becomes minimal (less than perpetuity limit), and capitalization of companies becomes maximal (above than perpetuity assessment) up to a specified time interval. We discuss the use of discovered effects in finance, in economics, and, in particular, in rating methodologies.

15.1 Introduction

In this chapter, we answer the following question: which companies have "a golden age,"" i.e., obey the following type of dependence of WACC on n: WACC (n) decreases with passage through minimum, followed by a limited growth. With this aim we study the dependence of WACC on the age of company n at various leverage levels within the wide spectrum of capital cost values as well as the dependence of WACC on leverage level L at fixed company age n. All calculations have been done within modern theory of capital cost and capital structure BFO by Brusov–Filatova–Orekhova (Brusov et al. 2011a, b, c, 2012a, b, 2013a, b, 2014a, b, Filatova et al. 2008). We make calculations for equity cost k_0 (at $L = 0$) between 6% and 30% and debt cost k_d between 4% and 28% for a lot of pairs (k_0, k_d), accounting that the inequality $k_0 \geq k_d$ is always valid via the fact that equity cost is more risky than debt one. We present in paper only some examples of our calculations (1–2 in each group) and readers should understand that other results in each group give more or less qualitatively similar results.

We have shown that existence of the "golden age" of the company depends not on the value of capital costs of the company, but on the difference between equity k_0 and debt k_d costs. The "golden age" of the company exists at small enough difference between k_0 and k_d costs, while at high value of this difference the "golden age" of the company is absent: curve WACC(n) monotonically decrease with n. For the

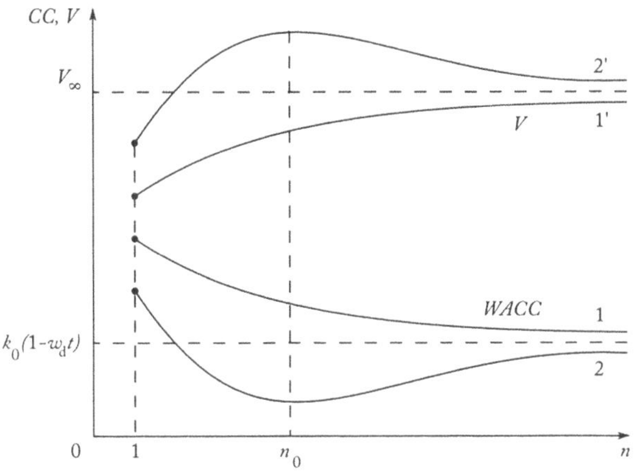

Fig. 15.1 Two kinds of dependences of weighted average cost of capital, WACC, and company capitalization, V, on lifetime of the company n: 1–1'—monotonic dependence of weighted average cost of capital, WACC, and company capitalization, V, on lifetime of the company n; 2–2'—showing decrease of WACC with n and with the passage through a minimum and then a limited growth and increase of V with the passage through a maximum (at n_0) and then a limited decrease

companies with the "golden age" curve WACC(L) for perpetuity limit ($n = \infty$) lies between curves WACC(L) for one year ($n = 1$) and three years ($n = 3$) companies, while for the companies without the "golden age" curve WACC(L) for perpetuity limit is the lowest one.

The problem of the existence of the "golden age" of the company is very important in ratings because the discount rate (WACC value), used in discounting of cash flows in ratings, depends on the existence or the nonexistence of the "golden age" of the company (Fig. 15.1).

15.2 Companies without the "Golden Age" (Large Difference between k_0 and k_d Costs)

As an example of companies without the "golden age" (with large difference between k_0 and k_d costs) we present the calculations for equity cost k_0 (at $L = 0$) equal to 20% and debt cost k_d equal to 9%.

15.2.1 Dependence of Weighted Average Cost of Capital, WACC, on the Company Age n at Different Leverage Levels

We study below the dependence of weighted average cost of capital, WACC, on the company age n at different leverage levels ($L = 1, 2, 3$), using the BFO formula

$$\frac{[1-(1+WACC)^{-n}]}{WACC} = \frac{[1-(1+k_0)^{-n}]}{k_0[1-\omega_d t(1-(1+k_d)^{-n})]} \tag{15.1}$$

Leverage level L is presented in BFO formula through the share of debt capital $w_d = L/(1+L)$.

The results of our calculations are shown below in Tables and Figures.

For $L = 1$ one has

For $L = 2$, we have

For $L = 3$, one has

It is seen from Tables 15.1, 15.2 and 15.3 and Fig. 15.2 that 1–1'-behavior (from Fig. 15.1) takes place: monotonic dependence of weighted average cost of capital, WACC, and company capitalization, V, on the company age n for all considered leverage levels (L=1, 2, 3); this means that the "golden age" of the company is absent. The ordering of curves is the following: the lower curve corresponds to the greater leverage level.

From Tables 15.4, 15.5 and 15.6 and Fig. 15.3, it is seen that the ordering of curves WACC(L) is the following: the lower curve corresponds to the greater company age n. We will see below that under existence the "golden age" of the company this ordering will be a different one. We keep here the case of $n = 45$ as the

Table 15.1 Dependence of WACC on the age of the company n at $L = 1$, $k_0 = 20\%$, $k_d = 9\%$

n	t	L	WACC (L=1)	ko	kd	wd	$A(n)$	БФО
1	0.2	1	0.19001348	0.2	0.09	0.50	0.840271	0.000055264
2	0.2	1	0.18679105	0.2	0.09	0.50	1.552355	0.000242408
3	0.2	1	0.18521681	0.2	0.09	0.50	2.155589	0.000643588
4	0.2	1	0.18453895	0.2	0.09	0.50	2.666482	0.000008562
5	0.2	1	0.18398934	0.2	0.09	0.50	3.099102	0.000019534
6	0.2	1	0.18361179	0.2	0.09	0.50	3.465420	0.000038686
7	0.2	1	0.18333561	0.2	0.09	0.50	3.775614	0.000068644
8	0.2	1	0.18312210	0.2	0.09	0.50	4.038322	0.000111902
9	0.2	1	0.18294855	0.2	0.09	0.50	4.260871	0.000170582
10	0.2	1	0.18280097	0.2	0.09	0.50	4.449469	0.000246231
20	0.2	1	0.18181178	0.2	0.09	0.50	5.305460	0.000013165
30	0.2	1	0.18103559	0.2	0.09	0.50	5.486207	0.000041589
40	0.2	1	0.18052092	0.2	0.09	0.50	5.532205	0.000065502

Table 15.2 Dependence of WACC on the age of the company n at $L = 2$, $k_0 = 20\%$, $k_d = 9\%$

n	*t*	*L*	WACC (*L*=2)	*ko*	*kd*	*wd*	*A*(*n*)	*БФО*
1	0.2	2	0.18670845	0.2	0.09	0.67	0.8426098	0.000057189
2	0.2	2	0.18242414	0.2	0.09	0.67	1.5607236	0.000239282
3	0.2	2	0.18033977	0.2	0.09	0.67	2.1724715	0.000618675
4	0.2	2	0.17935211	0.2	0.09	0.67	2.6934467	0.000007915
5	0.2	2	0.17860838	0.2	0.09	0.67	3.1370358	0.000018207
6	0.2	2	0.17809570	0.2	0.09	0.67	3.5147106	0.000036130
7	0.2	2	0.17771992	0.2	0.09	0.67	3.8362859	0.000064261
8	0.2	2	0.17742943	0.2	0.09	0.67	4.1101468	0.000105021
9	0.2	2	0.17719390	0.2	0.09	0.67	4.3434469	0.000160484
10	0.2	2	0.17699457	0.2	0.09	0.67	4.5422818	0.000232186
20	0.2	2	0.17567694	0.2	0.09	0.67	5.4686271	0.000012229
30	0.2	2	0.17467722	0.2	0.09	0.67	5.6790746	0.000039727
40	0.2	2	0.17401430	0.2	0.09	0.67	5.7372042	0.000064124

Table 15.3 Dependence of WACC on the age of the company n at $L = 3$, $k_0 = 20\%$, $k_d = 9\%$

n	*t*	*L*	WACC (*L*=3)	*ko*	*kd*	*wd*	*A*(*n*)	*БФО*
1	0.2	3	0.18506498	0.2	0.09	0.75	0.8437839	0.000051714
2	0.2	3	0.18024369	0.2	0.09	0.75	1.5649420	0.000228517
3	0.2	3	0.17789664	0.2	0.09	0.75	2.1810121	0.000607678
4	0.2	3	0.17675215	0.2	0.09	0.75	2.7071344	0.000007660
5	0.2	3	0.17590910	0.2	0.09	0.75	3.1563532	0.000017650
6	0.2	3	0.17532683	0.2	0.09	0.75	3.5398852	0.000035095
7	0.2	3	0.17489950	0.2	0.09	0.75	3.8673589	0.000062558
8	0.2	3	0.17456914	0.2	0.09	0.75	4.1470258	0.000101532
9	0.2	3	0.17430145	0.2	0.09	0.75	4.3859468	0.000155351
10	0.2	3	0.17407533	0.2	0.09	0.75	4.5901557	0.000225050
20	0.2	3	0.17259416	0.2	0.09	0.75	5.5540330	0.000011720
30	0.2	3	0.17148952	0.2	0.09	0.75	5.7806846	0.000038586
40	0.2	3	0.17075742	0.2	0.09	0.75	5.8455083	0.000063263

case which is close to perpetuity limit. An alternative method is the use of Modigliani–Miller formula

$$\mathrm{WACC} = k_0(1 - \omega_d t), \tag{15.2}$$

which follows from BFO formula (15.1) for perpetuity limit.

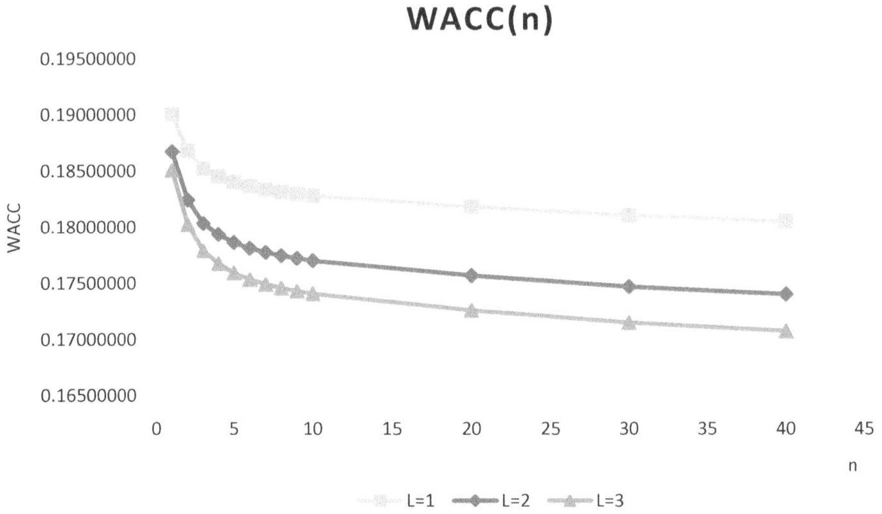

Fig. 15.2 The dependence of weighted average cost of capital, WACC, on the company age n at different leverage levels ($L = 1, 2, 3$)

Table 15.4 Dependence of WACC on the leverage level at the company age $n = 1$, $k_0 = 20\%$, $k_d = 9\%$

n	t	L	WACC (n=1)	ko	kd	wd	$A(n)$	*БФО*
1	0.2	0	0.19990871	0.2	0.09	0.00	0.833333	0.000063399
1	0.2	1	0.18989673	0.2	0.09	0.50	0.840271	0.000137715
1	0.2	2	0.18675471	0.2	0.09	0.67	0.842610	0.000024342
1	0.2	3	0.18504185	0.2	0.09	0.75	0.843784	0.000068187
1	0.2	4	0.18395964	0.2	0.09	0.80	0.844490	0.000133490
1	0.2	5	0.18323424	0.2	0.09	0.83	0.844961	0.000179952
1	0.2	6	0.18270822	0.2	0.09	0.86	0.845298	0.000218846
1	0.2	7	0.18230907	0.2	0.09	0.88	0.845551	0.000251369
1	0.2	8	0.18203277	0.2	0.09	0.89	0.845748	0.000252248
1	0.2	9	0.18178544	0.2	0.09	0.90	0.845906	0.000271780
1	0.2	10	0.18158213	0.2	0.09	0.91	0.846034	0.000288455

15.3 Companies with the "Golden Age" (Small Difference between k_0 and k_d Costs)

As an example of companies with the "golden age" (with small difference between k_0 and k_d costs) we present the calculations for equity cost k_0 (at $L = 0$) equal to 27% and debt cost k_d equal to 25% (Fig. 15.4).

It is seen from Tables 15.7, 15.8 and 15.9 and Fig. 15.5 that 2–2'-behavior (from Fig. 15.1) takes place: decrease of WACC with n and with the passage through a minimum and then a limited growth and increase of V with the passage through a

Table 15.5 Dependence of WACC on the leverage level at the company age $n = 3$, $k_0 = 20\%$, $k_d = 9\%$

n	*t*	*L*	WACC (*n*=3)	*ko*	*kd*	*wd*	*A(n)*	*БФО*
3	0.2	0	0.19978349	0.2	0.09	0.00	2.106481	0.000714376
3	0.2	1	0.18521867	0.2	0.09	0.50	2.155589	0.000637220
3	0.2	2	0.18034194	0.2	0.09	0.67	2.172471	0.000611094
3	0.2	3	0.17789941	0.2	0.09	0.75	2.181012	0.000597961
3	0.2	4	0.17643254	0.2	0.09	0.80	2.186169	0.000590059
3	0.2	5	0.17545407	0.2	0.09	0.83	2.189620	0.000584783
3	0.2	6	0.17475488	0.2	0.09	0.86	2.192092	0.000581010
3	0.2	7	0.17423034	0.2	0.09	0.88	2.193950	0.000578178
3	0.2	8	0.17382227	0.2	0.09	0.89	2.195397	0.000575974
3	0.2	9	0.17349576	0.2	0.09	0.90	2.196556	0.000574210
3	0.2	10	0.17322858	0.2	0.09	0.91	2.197505	0.000572766

Table 15.6 Dependence of WACC on the leverage level at the company age $n = 45$, $k_0 = 20\%$, $k_d = 9\%$

n	*t*	*L*	WACC (*n*=45)	*ko*	*kd*	*wd*	*A*(*n*)	*БФО*
45	0.2	0	0.19999699	0.2	0.09	0.00	4.998633	0.000075004
45	0.2	1	0.18035710	0.2	0.09	0.50	5.541296	0.000073385
45	0.2	2	0.17380207	0.2	0.09	0.67	5.749351	0.000072648
45	0.2	3	0.17052242	0.2	0.09	0.75	5.859349	0.000072233
45	0.2	4	0.16855385	0.2	0.09	0.80	5.927391	0.000071966
45	0.2	5	0.16724112	0.2	0.09	0.83	5.973638	0.000071780
45	0.2	6	0.16630328	0.2	0.09	0.86	6.007115	0.000071642
45	0.2	7	0.16559980	0.2	0.09	0.88	6.032471	0.000071536
45	0.2	8	0.16505258	0.2	0.09	0.89	6.052340	0.000071451
45	0.2	9	0.16461477	0.2	0.09	0.90	6.068330	0.000071382
45	0.2	10	0.16425654	0.2	0.09	0.91	6.081476	0.000071325

maximum (at $n_0 \approx 4$) and then a limited decrease. This means the presence of the "golden age" of the company. The ordering of curves is the following: the lower curve corresponds to the greater leverage level.

From Tables 15.10, 15.11 and 15.12 and Fig. 15.6, the ordering of curves WACC (L) is the following: the top curve corresponds to the company age $n = 1$, the middle one corresponds to perpetuity company $n_0 = \infty$ (we use $n = 49$ to approximate perpetuity limit), and the bottom one corresponds to the company age $n = 3$. Thus, the curve WACC(L) for perpetuity company lies between curves corresponding to the company age $n = 1$ and n-3.

Note that this ordering is quite different from the case when the "golden age" of the company is absent: in that case the lower curve corresponds to the greater company age n: the top curve corresponds to the company age $n = 1$, the middle one corresponds to the company age $n = 3$, and the bottom one corresponds to the perpetuity company.

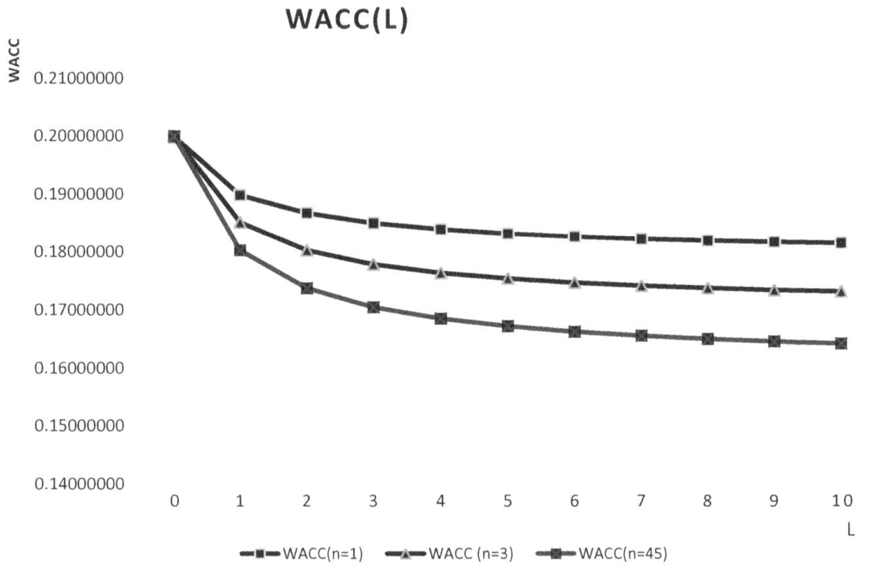

Fig. 15.3 The dependence of weighted average cost of capital, WACC, on the leverage level at different company age n (n=1, 3, 45)

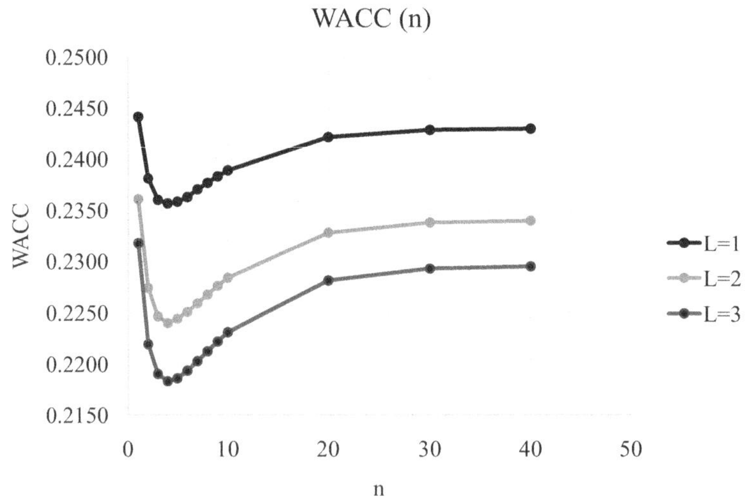

Fig. 15.4 The dependence of weighted average cost of capital, WACC, on the company age n at different leverage levels (L = 1, 2, 3)

Table 15.7 Dependence of WACC on the age of the company n at $L = 1$, $k_0 = 27\%$, $k_d = 25\%$

n	t	L	WACC	K_0	K_d	W_d	$A(n)$	BFO
1	0.2	1	0.2441	0.27	0.25	0.50	0.8035	0.000292
2	0.2	1	0.2381	0.27	0.25	0.50	1.4600	0.000038
3	0.2	1	0.2360	0.27	0.25	0.50	1.9928	0.000286
4	0.2	1	0.2357	0.27	0.25	0.50	2.4231	0.000046
5	0.2	1	0.2359	0.27	0.25	0.50	2.7688	0.000319
6	0.2	1	0.2363	0.27	0.25	0.50	3.0457	0.000877
7	0.2	1	0.2371	0.27	0.25	0.50	3.2668	0.000033
8	0.2	1	0.2377	0.27	0.25	0.50	3.4430	0.000070
9	0.2	1	0.2383	0.27	0.25	0.50	3.5830	0.000127
10	0.2	1	0.2389	0.27	0.25	0.50	3.6941	0.000204
20	0.2	1	0.2422	0.27	0.25	0.50	4.0755	0.000005
30	0.2	1	0.2429	0.27	0.25	0.50	4.1115	0.000009
40	0.2	1	0.2430	0.27	0.25	0.50	4.1149	0.000010

Table 15.8 Dependence of WACC on the age of the company n at $L = 2$, $k_0 = 27\%$, $k_d = 25\%$

n	t	L	WACC	K_0	K_d	W_d	$A(n)$	BFO
1	0.2	2	0.2361	0.27	0.25	0.67	0.8090	0.000024
2	0.2	2	0.2274	0.27	0.25	0.67	1.4784	0.000164
3	0.2	2	0.2246	0.27	0.25	0.67	2.0275	0.000411
4	0.2	2	0.2239	0.27	0.25	0.67	2.4748	0.000753
5	0.2	2	0.2244	0.27	0.25	0.67	2.8370	−0.000018
6	0.2	2	0.2251	0.27	0.25	0.67	3.1288	−0.000026
7	0.2	2	0.2259	0.27	0.25	0.67	3.3630	−0.000037
8	0.2	2	0.2267	0.27	0.25	0.67	3.5504	−0.000046
9	0.2	2	0.2276	0.27	0.25	0.67	3.6999	−0.000054
10	0.2	2	0.2284	0.27	0.25	0.67	3.8189	−0.000063
20	0.2	2	0.2328	0.27	0.25	0.67	4.2301	−0.000110
30	0.2	2	0.2338	0.27	0.25	0.67	4.2694	−0.000124
40	0.2	2	0.2340	0.27	0.25	0.67	4.2731	−0.000128

15.4 Companies with Abnormal "Golden Age" (Intermediate Difference between k_0 and k_d Costs)

One example, which is different from two considered above cases will be studied below, where we present the calculations for equity cost k_0 (at $L = 0$) equal to 27% and debt cost k_d equal to 16%.

While in this case the "golden age" of the company is present, but it is less pronounced: the minimal WACC value (at some leverage value: in this case at $L = 1$) lies above the perpetuity WACC value. We call this situation the "silver age" of the company (Tables 15.13, 15.14 and 15.15).

Table 15.9 Dependence of WACC on the age of the company n at $L = 3$, $k_0 = 27\%$, $k_d = 25\%$

n	t	L	WACC	K_0	K_d	W_d	$A(n)$	BFO
1	0.2	3	0.2318	0.27	0.25	0.75	0.8118	0.000064
2	0.2	3	0.2219	0.27	0.25	0.75	1.4877	0.000412
3	0.2	3	0.2190	0.27	0.25	0.75	2.0453	−0.000020
4	0.2	3	0.2183	0.27	0.25	0.75	2.5015	−0.000044
5	0.2	3	0.2186	0.27	0.25	0.75	2.8723	−0.000076
6	0.2	3	0.2193	0.27	0.25	0.75	3.1721	−0.000112
7	0.2	3	0.2203	0.27	0.25	0.75	3.4133	−0.000154
8	0.2	3	0.2212	0.27	0.25	0.75	3.6067	−0.000195
9	0.2	3	0.2222	0.27	0.25	0.75	3.7612	−0.000234
10	0.2	3	0.2231	0.27	0.25	0.75	3.8845	−0.000271
20	0.2	3	0.2281	0.27	0.25	0.75	4.3120	−0.000497
30	0.2	3	0.2293	0.27	0.25	0.75	4.3530	−0.000570
40	0.2	3	0.2295	0.27	0.25	0.75	4.3569	−0.000590

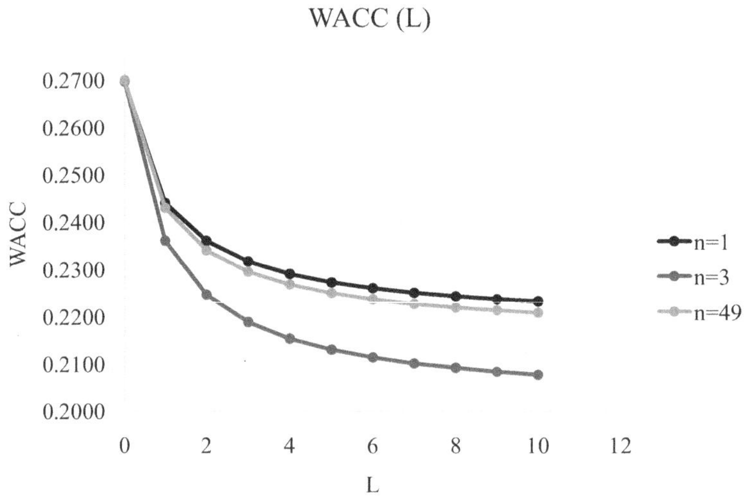

Fig. 15.5 The dependence of weighted average cost of capital, WACC, on leverage level L at different company age n ($n = 1, 3, 49$)

To be sure that the minimal WACC value at leverage level $L = 1$ lies above the perpetuity WACC value, we make more detailed calculations for this case (see Table 15.16). We see that the minimal WACC value at $n = 8.2$ is equal to 0.243095889, while perpetuity limit is equal to 0.243 and lies below.

Let us study the dependence of weighted average cost of capital, WACC, on the leverage level at different company age n ($n = 1, 3, \infty$)

It is seen from Tables 15.14 and 15.15 and Fig. 15.6 that the following behavior takes place for $L = 2$ and 3: a third modification of dependences of weighted average cost of capital, WACC, on the company age n takes place: decrease of WACC with

Table 15.10 Dependence of WACC on the leverage level at the company age $n = 1$, $k_0 = 27\%$, $k_{\text{d}} = 25\%$

n	t	L	WACC	K_0	K_d	W_d	$A(n)$	BFO
1	0.2	0	0.2697	0.27	0.25	0.00	0.7874	0.000188
1	0.2	1	0.2441	0.27	0.25	0.50	0.8035	0.000292
1	0.2	2	0.2360	0.27	0.25	0.67	0.8090	0.000064
1	0.2	3	0.2317	0.27	0.25	0.75	0.8118	0.000153
1	0.2	4	0.2290	0.27	0.25	0.80	0.8134	0.000216
1	0.2	5	0.2273	0.27	0.25	0.83	0.8146	0.000263
1	0.2	6	0.2260	0.27	0.25	0.86	0.8154	0.000298
1	0.2	7	0.2251	0.27	0.25	0.88	0.8160	0.000326
1	0.2	8	0.2243	0.27	0.25	0.89	0.8164	0.000349
1	0.2	9	0.2237	0.27	0.25	0.90	0.8168	0.000367
1	0.2	10	0.2232	0.27	0.25	0.91	0.8171	0.000382

Table 15.11 Dependence of WACC on the leverage level at the company age $n = 3$, $k_0 = 27\%$, $k_{\text{d}} = 25\%$

n	t	L	WACC	K_0	K_d	W_d	$A(n)$	BFO
3	0.2	0	0.2697	0.27	0.25	0.00	1.8956	0.000832
3	0.2	1	0.2361	0.27	0.25	0.50	1.9928	0.000174
3	0.2	2	0.2246	0.27	0.25	0.67	2.0275	0.000411
3	0.2	3	0.2188	0.27	0.25	0.75	2.0453	0.000542
3	0.2	4	0.2154	0.27	0.25	0.80	2.0561	0.000631
3	0.2	5	0.2131	0.27	0.25	0.83	2.0634	0.000694
3	0.2	6	0.2114	0.27	0.25	0.86	2.0687	0.000741
3	0.2	7	0.2102	0.27	0.25	0.88	2.0726	0.000778
3	0.2	8	0.2092	0.27	0.25	0.89	2.0757	0.000807
3	0.2	9	0.2084	0.27	0.25	0.90	2.0781	0.000830
3	0.2	10	0.2078	0.27	0.25	0.91	2.0802	0.000850

Table 15.12 Dependence of WACC on the leverage level at the company age $n = 49$, $k_0 = 27\%$, $k_{\text{d}} = 25\%$

n	t	L	WACC	K_0	K_d	W_d	$A(n)$	BFO
49	0.2	0	0.2700	0.27	0.25	0.00	3.7037	−0.000037
49	0.2	1	0.2430	0.27	0.25	0.50	4.1152	0.000041
49	0.2	2	0.2340	0.27	0.25	0.67	4.2735	0.000159
49	0.2	3	0.2295	0.27	0.25	0.75	4.3572	0.000273
49	0.2	4	0.2268	0.27	0.25	0.80	4.4091	0.000368
49	0.2	5	0.2250	0.27	0.25	0.83	4.4444	0.000444
49	0.2	6	0.2237	0.27	0.25	0.86	4.4699	0.000505
49	0.2	7	0.2227	0.27	0.25	0.88	4.4893	0.000556
49	0.2	8	0.2220	0.27	0.25	0.89	4.5045	0.000598
49	0.2	9	0.2214	0.27	0.25	0.90	4.5167	0.000633
49	0.2	10	0.2209	0.27	0.25	0.91	4.5267	0.000664

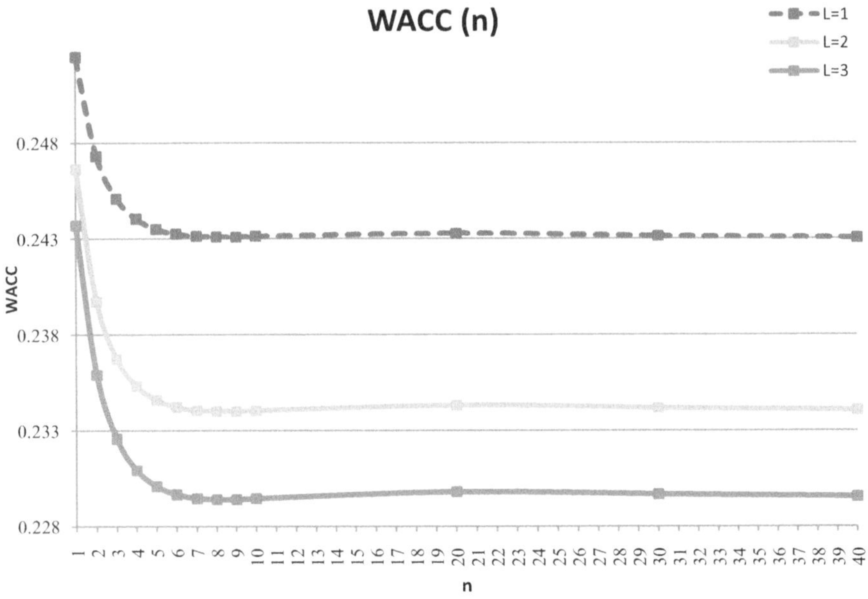

Fig. 15.6 The dependence of weighted average cost of capital, WACC, on the company age n at different leverage levels ($L = 1, 2, 3$)

Table 15.13 Dependence of WACC on the age of the company n at $L = 1$, $k_0 = 27\%$, $k_d = 16\%$

n	t	L	K_0	K_d	W_d	WACC
1	0.2	1	0.27	0.16	0.5	0.252483428
2	0.2	1	0.27	0.16	0.5	0.247301552
3	0.2	1	0.27	0.16	0.5	0.245105573
4	0.2	1	0.27	0.16	0.5	0.244045922
5	0.2	1	0.27	0.16	0.5	0.243511488
6	0.2	1	0.27	0.16	0.5	0.243250247
7	0.2	1	0.27	0.16	0.5	0.24313388
8	0.2	1	0.27	0.16	0.5	0.243097298
9	0.2	1	0.27	0.16	0.5	0.243103247
10	0.2	1	0.27	0.16	0.5	0.243130071
20	0.2	1	0.27	0.16	0.5	0.243291667
30	0.2	1	0.27	0.16	0.5	0.243146312
40	0.2	1	0.27	0.16	0.5	0.243048121
∞	0.2	1	0.27	0.16	0.5	0.243

passage through minimum at $n = 8$, followed by a growth with passage through maximum at $n = 20$ and finally with trend to perpetuity limit from bigger values (note that at the second type of WACC(n) behavior, the curve WACC(n) tends to perpetuity limit from lower values). We have called this effect "Kulik effect."

The ordering of curves is the following: the lower curve corresponds to the greater leverage level (Fig. 15.7).

Table 15.14 Dependence of WACC on the age of the company n at $L = 2$, $k_0 = 27\%$, $k_d = 16\%$

n	t	L	K_0	K_d	W_d	WACC
1	0.2	2	0.27	0.16	0.6(6)	0.246644883
2	0.2	2	0.27	0.16	0.6(6)	0.239710388
3	0.2	2	0.27	0.16	0.6(6)	0.236752006
4	0.2	2	0.27	0.16	0.6(6)	0.235311829
5	0.2	2	0.27	0.16	0.6(6)	0.234578628
6	0.2	2	0.27	0.16	0.6(6)	0.23421254
7	0.2	2	0.27	0.16	0.6(6)	0.234046353
8	0.2	2	0.27	0.16	0.6(6)	0.233991091
9	0.2	2	0.27	0.16	0.6(6)	0.233996344
10	0.2	2	0.27	0.16	0.6(6)	0.234032536
20	0.2	2	0.27	0.16	0.6(6)	0.234316362
30	0.2	2	0.27	0.16	0.6(6)	0.234174539
40	0.2	2	0.27	0.16	0.6(6)	0.234059889
∞	0.2	2	0.27	0.16	0.6(6)	0.234

Table 15.15 Dependence of WACC on the age of the company n at $L = 3$, $k_0 = 27\%$, $k_d = 16\%$

n	t	L	K_0	K_d	W_d	WACC
1	0.2	3	0.27	0.16	0.75	0.243725045
2	0.2	3	0.27	0.16	0.75	0.235910011
3	0.2	3	0.27	0.16	0.75	0.232564477
4	0.2	3	0.27	0.16	0.75	0.230926014
5	0.2	3	0.27	0.16	0.75	0.230090888
6	0.2	3	0.27	0.16	0.75	0.229669501
7	0.2	3	0.27	0.16	0.75	0.229475982
8	0.2	3	0.27	0.16	0.75	0.229409857
9	0.2	3	0.27	0.16	0.75	0.229414009
10	0.2	3	0.27	0.16	0.75	0.229454135
20	0.2	3	0.27	0.16	0.75	0.229812629
30	0.2	3	0.27	0.16	0.75	0.229682914
40	0.2	3	0.27	0.16	0.75	0.229564113
∞	0.2	3	0.27	0.16	0.75	0.2295

From Tables 15.16, 15.17, 15.18 and 15.19 and Fig. 15.6 it is seen that for $L = 1$ the following behavior takes place: decrease of WACC with passage through minimum at $n = 8.2$ (which is higher than perpetuity limit), followed by a growth with passage through maximum at $n = 20$ and finally with trend to perpetuity limit from bigger values. This means that the "golden age" in its purest form presents at leverage levels for $L = 2$ and 3, while at $L = 1$ one has different effects: we call it the "silver age."

The ordering of curves is the following: the lower curve corresponds to the greater company age.

It turns out that at particular values of capital costs, for example, at $k_0 = 27\%$; $k_d = 16\%$, a third modification of dependences of weighted average cost of capital, WACC, on the company age n takes place: decrease of WACC with passage through

Table 15.16 Dependence of WACC (more detailed) on the age of the company n at $L = 1$, $k_0 = 27\%$, $k_d = 16\%$

L	K_0	K_d	t	n	W_d	WACC	BFO
1	0.27	0.16	0.2	7	0.50	0.243133854	0.000
1	0.27	0.16	0.2	7.2	0.50	0.243121633	0.000
1	0.27	0.16	0.2	7.4	0.50	0.243112185	0.000
1	0.27	0.16	0.2	7.6	0.50	0.243105150	0.000
1	0.27	0.16	0.2	7.8	0.50	0.243100256	0.000
1	0.27	0.16	0.2	8	0.50	0.243097246	0.000
1	0.27	0.16	0.2	8.2	0.50	0.243095889	0.000
1	0.27	0.16	0.2	8.4	0.50	0.243095979	0.000
1	0.27	0.16	0.2	8.6	0.50	0.243097328	0.000
1	0.27	0.16	0.2	8.8	0.50	0.243099771	0.000
1	0.27	0.16	0.2	9	0.50	0.243103156	0.000
1	0.27	0.16	0.2	∞	0.50	0.243	0.000

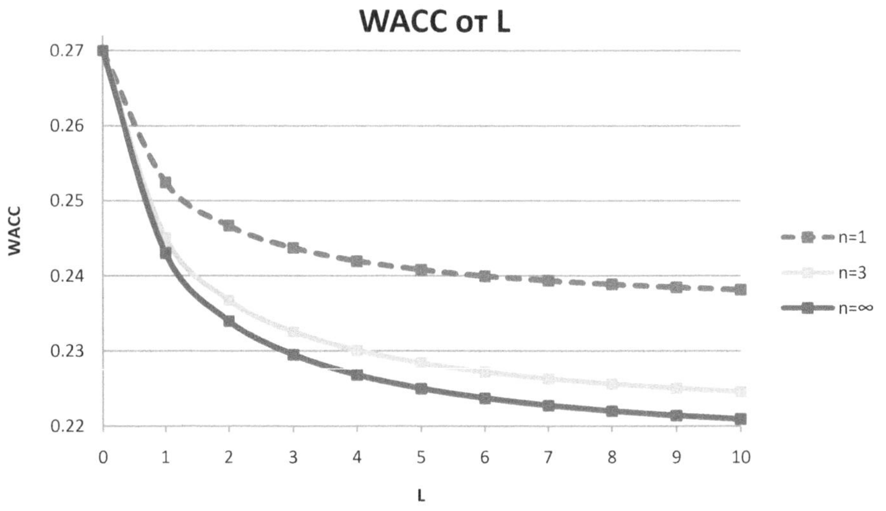

Fig. 15.7 The dependence of weighted average cost of capital, WACC, on the leverage level at different company age n (n=1, 3, ∞)

minimum, followed by a growth with passage through maximum and finally with trend to perpetuity limit from bigger values (note that at the second type of WACC (n) behavior, the curve WACC(n) tends to perpetuity limit from lower values). We have called this effect "Kulik effect."

Table 15.17 Dependence of WACC on the leverage level L at age of the company $n = 1$, $k_0 = 27\%$, $k_d = 16\%$

n	t	L	K_0	K_d	W_d	WACC
1	0.2	0	0.27	0.16	0	0.270000213
1	0.2	1	0.27	0.16	0.5	0.252483428
1	0.2	2	0.27	0.16	0.6(6)	0.246644883
1	0.2	3	0.27	0.16	0.75	0.243725045
1	0.2	4	0.27	0.16	0.8	0.241973361
1	0.2	5	0.27	0.16	0.8(3)	0.24080557
1	0.2	6	0.27	0.16	0.857	0.239971433
1	0.2	7	0.27	0.16	0.875	0.239345829
1	0.2	8	0.27	0.16	0.8(8)	0.238859248
1	0.2	9	0.27	0.16	0.9	0.238469982
1	0.2	10	0.27	0.16	0(90)	0.238151492

Table 15.18 Dependence of WACC on the leverage level L at age of the company $n = 3$, $k_0 = 27\%$, $k_d = 16\%$

n	t	L	K_0	K_d	W_d	WACC
3	0.2	0	0.27	0.16	0	0.270000842
3	0.2	1	0.27	0.16	0.5	0.245105573
3	0.2	2	0.27	0.16	0.6(6)	0.236752006
3	0.2	3	0.27	0.16	0.75	0.232564477
3	0.2	4	0.27	0.16	0.8	0.230048473
3	0.2	5	0.27	0.16	0.8(3)	0.228369673
3	0.2	6	0.27	0.16	0.857	0.22716981
3	0.2	7	0.27	0.16	0.875	0.226269517
3	0.2	8	0.27	0.16	0.(8)	0.225569054
3	0.2	9	0.27	0.16	0.9	0.225008535
3	0.2	10	0.27	0.16	0(90)	0.224549831

Table 15.19 Dependence of WACC on the leverage level L for the perpetuity company ($n = \infty$) at $k_0 = 27\%$, $k_d = 16\%$

n	t	L	K_0	K_d	W_d	WACC
∞	0.2	0	0.27	0.16	0	0.27
∞	0.2	1	0.27	0.16	0.5	0.243
∞	0.2	2	0.27	0.16	0(6)	0.234
∞	0.2	3	0.27	0.16	0.75	0.2295
∞	0.2	4	0.27	0.16	0.8	0.2268
∞	0.2	5	0.27	0.16	0.8(3)	0.225
∞	0.2	6	0.27	0.16	0.857	0.223714286
∞	0.2	7	0.27	0.16	0.875	0.22275
∞	0.2	8	0.27	0.16	0.(8)	0.222
∞	0.2	9	0.27	0.16	0.9	0.2214
∞	0.2	10	0.27	0.16	0(90)	0.220909091

15.5 Comparing with Results from the Previous Chapter

15.5.1 *Under Change of the Debt Capital Cost,* k_d

From Fig. 15.8 it is seen that with the increase of debt cost, k_d, the character of dependence of weighted average cost of capital, WACC, on the company age n is changed from monotonic decrease of WACC with n to decrease of WACC with n with passage through minimum, followed by a limited growth. It is seen from Table 15.20 that the gap depth ΔWACC (the difference between the optimal (minimal) value of weighted average cost of capital, WACC, and its perpetuity limit) decreases with $\Delta k = k_0 - k_d$ from 3.38% at $\Delta k = 0.02$ up to 1.89% at $\Delta k = 0.5$. At $\Delta k = 0.10$ and $\Delta k = 0.12$ the minimum in dependence of WACC(n) is absent (too big value of $\Delta k = k_0 - k_d$). This coincides with our conclusions in this chapter.

The same conclusion could be made from Fig. 15.9 and Table 15.21 for higher values of capital costs: it is seen that with the increase of debt cost, k_d at fixed k_0, i.e., with decrease $\Delta k = k_0 - k_d$ the gap depth ΔWACC is increased from 1.08% at

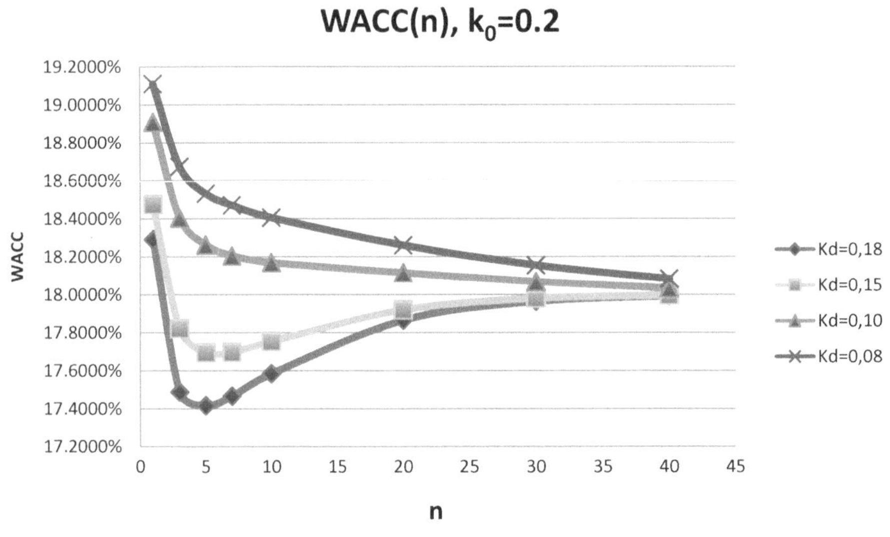

Fig. 15.8 Dependence of weighted average cost of capital, WACC, on lifetime of the company n at fixed value of equity cost, $k_0 = 20\%$, and at four values of debt cost, $k_d = 8\%$; 10%;15%, and 18% at leverage level $L = 1$

Table 15.20 Dependence of Δk and ΔWACC on kd at fixed value of equity cost, k0 = 20%, and at four values of debt cost, kd = 8%; 10%;15%, and 18% at leverage level L = 1

k_d	0.18	0.15	0.10	0.08
$\Delta k = k_0 - k_d$	0.02	0.05	0.10	0.12
ΔWACC, %	3.38	1.89	NA	NA

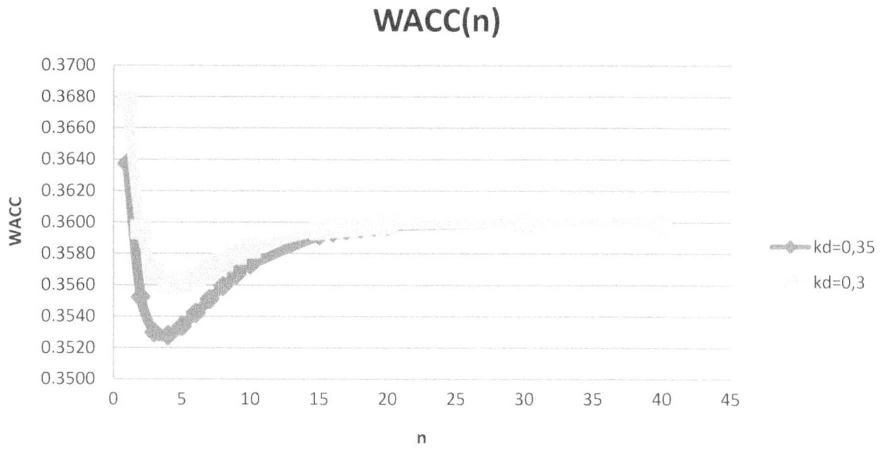

Fig. 15.9 Dependence of weighted average cost of capital, WACC, on lifetime of the company n at fixed high value of equity cost, $k_0 = 40\%$, and two values of debt cost, $k_d = 30\%$ and 35% at leverage level $L = 1$

Table 15.21 Dependence of Δk and ΔWACC on k at fixed high value of equity cost, k0 = 40%, and two values of debt cost, kd = 30% and 35% at leverage level L = 1

$k_0 = 0, 4; k_d$	0.35	0.3
$\Delta k = k_0 - k_d$	0.05	0.10
ΔWACC, %	1.85	1.08

$\Delta k = 0.10$ up to 1.85% at $\Delta k = 0.05$. This as well coincides with our conclusions in this paper.

15.5.2 *Under Change of the Equity Capital Cost*, k_0

From Fig. 15.10 and Table 15.22, it is seen that the gap depth ΔWACC (the difference between the optimal (minimal) value of weighted average cost of capital, WACC, and its perpetuity limit) decreases with $\Delta k = k_0 - k_d$ from 0.55% at $\Delta k = 0.01$ up to 0.03% at $\Delta k = 0.10$. This as well coincides with our conclusions in this paper.

In conclusion, we present in Fig. 15.11 both cases of "Kulik" effect: "the golden age" of the company and the "silver age" of the company.

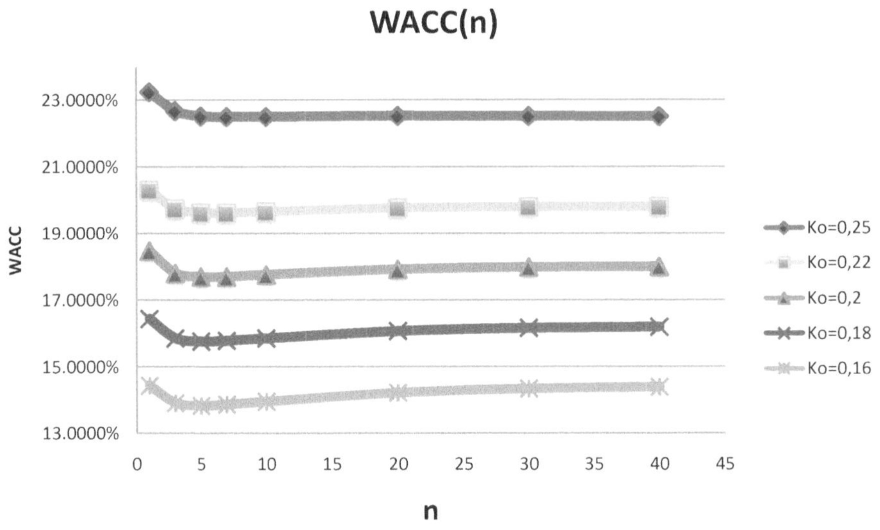

Fig. 15.10 Dependence of weighted average cost of capital, WACC, on lifetime of the company n at fixed value of debt cost, $k_d = 15\%$, and five values of equity cost, $k_0 = 16\%, 18\%, 20\%, 22\%$, and 25% at leverage level $L = 1$

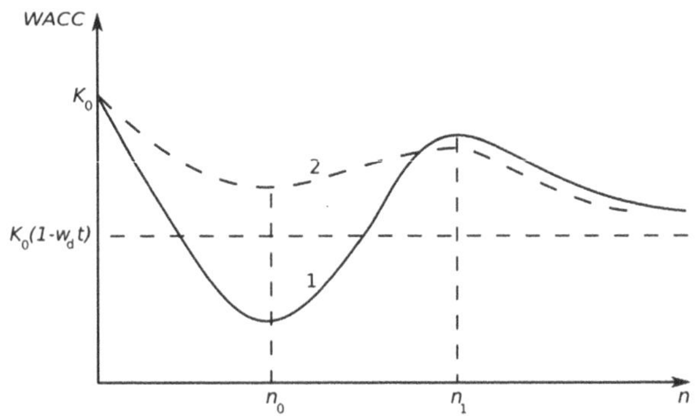

Fig. 15.11 Dependence of weighted average cost of capital, WACC, on company age of the company n, which illustrates the presence of "the golden age" of the company (curve 1) and of "the silver age" of the company (curve 2) under existence of "Kulik" effect. Here n_0 is "the golden (silver) age" of the company and n_1 is the age of local maximum in dependence of WACC(n)

Table 15.22 Dependence of Δk and ΔWACC on k0 at fixed value of debt cost, kd = 15%, and five values of equity cost, k0 = 16%, 18%, 20%, 22%, and 25% at leverage level L = 1

k_0	0.16	0.18	0.20	0.22	0.25
$\Delta k = k_0 - k_d$	0.01	0.03	0.05	0.07	0.10
ΔWACC, %	0.55	0.43	0.30	0.18	0.03

15.6 Conclusions

In our previous paper a few years ago (Brusov et al. 2015) we have discovered the effect of the "golden age" of the company: it was shown for the first time that valuation of the weighted average cost of capital, WACC, in the Modigliani–Miller theory (Modigliani and Miller 1958, 1963, 1966) is not minimal and valuation of the company capitalization is not maximal, as all financiers assumed up to this discovery: at some age of the company, its WACC value turns out to be lower than in the Modigliani–Miller theory and company capitalization V turns out to be greater than V in the Modigliani–Miller theory (see the previous chapter). It was shown that, from the point of view of cost of attracting capital there are two types of dependences of weighted average cost of capital, WACC, on the company age n: monotonic decrease with n and decrease with passage through minimum, followed by a limited growth. In practice, there are companies with both types of dependences of WACC on the company age n.

In this chapter, we have continued the study of the effect of the "golden age" of the company and have investigated which companies have the "golden age," i.e., obey the latter type of dependence of WACC on n. With this aim we study the dependence of WACC on the age of company n at various leverage levels within the wide spectrum of capital cost values as well as the dependence of WACC on leverage level L at fixed company age n. All calculations have been done within modern theory of capital cost and capital structure BFO by Brusov–Filatova–Orekhova (Brusov et al. 2011a, b, c, 2012a, b, 2013a, b, 2014a, b; Filatova et al. 2008).

We have shown that existence of the "golden age" of the company does not depend on the value of capital costs of the company (as it was assumed in the previous chapter), but depends on the difference value between equity, k_0, and debt, k_d, costs. The "golden age" of the company exists at small enough difference between k_0 and k_d costs, while at high value of this difference the "golden age" of the company is absent: curve WACC(n) monotonically decreases with company age n. For the companies with the "golden age" curve WACC(L) for perpetuity limit lies between curves WACC(L) at $n = 1$ and $n = 3$, while for the companies without the "golden age" curve WACC(L) for perpetuity limit ($n = \infty$) is the lowest one. In other words, the ordering of curves WACC(L) is different for the companies with the "golden age" and without it.

In the previous chapter, we have also found a third type of WACC(n) dependence: decrease with passage through minimum, which lies below the perpetuity limit value, then going through maximum followed by a limited decrease. We called this effect "Kulik effect" (this is the last name of the student who has discovered this effect). In this paper, we have found a type of "Kulik effect": decrease with passage through minimum of WACC, which lies above the perpetuity limit value, then going through maximum followed by a limited decrease. We call this company age n, at which WACC has a minimum, which lies above the perpetuity limit value, "the silver age" of the company. It takes place at intermediate difference value between equity k_0 and debt k_d costs.

Because the cost of attracting capital is used in rating methodologies as discounting rate under discounting of cash flows, study of WACC behavior is very important for rating procedures. Taking account effects of the "golden (silver) age" could change the valuation of creditworthiness of issuers.

Note that, since the "golden age" of the company depends on the company's capital costs, by controlling them (e.g., by modifying the value of dividend payments, which reflect the equity cost), company may extend the "golden (silver) age" of the company, when the cost to attract capital becomes minimal (less (above) than perpetuity limit), and capitalization of companies becomes maximal (above (below) than perpetuity assessment) up to a specified time interval.

References

Brusov P (2018a) Editorial: introduction on special issue on the Banking System and financial markets of Russia and other countries: problems and prospects. J Rev Global Econ 7:i–vi. SCOPUS

Brusov P (2018b) Editorial. J Rev Global Econ 7:i–v. SCOPUS

Brusov PN, Filatova TV (2011) From Modigliani–Miller to general theory of capital cost and capital structure of the company. Finance Credit 435:2–8

Brusov P, Filatova T, Orehova N, Brusova A (2011a) Weighted average cost of capital in the theory of Modigliani–Miller, modified for a finite life-time company. Appl Financ Econ 21(11):815–824

Brusov P, Filatova T, Orehova N et al (2011b) From Modigliani–Miller to general theory of capital cost and capital structure of the company. Res J Econ Bus ICT 2:16–21

Brusov P, Filatova T, Orehova N et al (2011c) Influence of debt financing on the effectiveness of the investment project within the Modigliani–Miller theory. Res J Econ Bus ICT (UK) 2:11–15

Brusov P, Filatova T, Eskindarov M, Orehova N (2012a) Influence of debt financing on the effectiveness of the finite duration investment project. Appl Financ Econ 22(13):1043–1052

Brusov P, Filatova T, Eskindarov M, Orehova N (2012b) Hidden global causes of the global financial crisis. J Rev Global Econ 1:106–111

Brusov P, Filatova P, Orekhova N (2013a) Absence of an optimal capital structure in the famous tradeoff theory! J Rev Global Econ 2:94–116

Brusov P, Filatova T, Orehova N (2013b) A qualitatively new effect in corporative finance: abnormal dependence of cost of equity of company on leverage. J Rev Global Econ 2:183–193

Brusov P, Filatova P, Orekhova N (2014a) Mechanism of formation of the company optimal capital structure, different from suggested by trade off theory. Cogent Econ Finance 2:1–13. https://doi.org/10.1080/23322039.2014.946150

Brusov P, Filatova T, Orehova N (2014b) Inflation in Brusov–Filatova–Orekhova theory and in its perpetuity limit—Modigliani–Miller theory. J Rev Global Econ 3:175–185

Brusov PN, Filatova TV, Orekhova NP (2018d) Modern corporate finance and investments, monograph. Knorus Publishing House, Moscow, 517 p

Brusov P, Filatova T, Orekhova N, Eskindarov M (2015) Modern corporate finance, investments and taxation. Springer International Publishing, Switzerland, 373 p. monograph. SCOPUS. https://www.springer.com/gp/book/9783319147314

Brusov P, Filatova T, Orekhova N, Eskindarov M (2018c) Modern corporate finance, investments, taxation and ratings. Springer Nature Publishing, Switzerland, 571 p. monograph

Brusov PN, Filatova TV, Orekhova NP, Kulik VL (2018e) Rating: new approach. J Rev Global Econ 7:37–62. SCOPUS. https://doi.org/10.6000/1929-7092.2018.07.05

Brusov PN, Filatova TV, Orekhova NP, Kulik VL (2018f) A "golden age" of the companies: conditions of its existence. J Rev Global Econ 7:88–103. SCOPUS. https://doi.org/10.6000/1929-7092.2018.07.07

Brusov PN, Filatova TV, Orekhova NP, Kulik VL (2018g) Rating methodology: new look and new horizons. J Rev Global Econ 7:63–87. SCOPUS. https://doi.org/10.6000/1929-7092.2018.07.06

Brusov PN, Filatova TV, Orekhova NP, Kulik VL, Weil I (2018b) New meaningful effects in modern capital structure theory. J Rev Global Econ 7:104–122. SCOPUS. https://doi.org/10.6000/1929-7092.2018.07.08

Brusov PN, Filatova TV, Orekhova NP, Kulik VL, Weil I (2019) Ratings of the investment projects of arbitrary durations: new methodology. J Rev Global Econ 8:437–448. SCOPUS. https://doi.org/10.6000/1929-7092.2019.08.37

Brusov PN, Filatova TV, Orekhova NP, Kulik VL, Chang S-I, Lin YCG (2020) Modification of the Modigliani–Miller theory for the case of advance payments of tax on profit. J Rev Global Econ 9:257–268

Brusov P, Filatova T, Orekhova N, Kulik V, Weil I, Brailov A (2018a) The impact of the central bank key rate and commercial banks credit rates on creating and maintaining of a favorable investment climate in the country. J Rev Global Econ 7:360–376. SCOPUS. https://doi.org/10.6000/1929-7092.2018.07.31

Filatova T, Orehova N, Brusova A (2008) Weighted average cost of capital in the theory of Modigliani–Miller, modified for a finite life-time company. Bull FU 48:68–77

Filatova TV, Brusov PN, Orekhova NP, Kulik VL (2018) Ratings of the long–term projects: new approach. J Rev Global Econ 7:645–661. SCOPUS. https://doi.org/10.6000/1929-7092.2018.07.59

Modigliani F, Miller M (1958) The cost of capital, corporate finance, and the theory of investment. Am Econ Rev 48:261–297

Modigliani F, Miller M (1963) Corporate income taxes and the cost of capital: a correction. Am Econ Rev 53:147–175

Modigliani F, Miller M (1966) Some estimates of the cost of capital to the electric utility industry 1954–1957. Am Econ Rev 56:333–391

Chapter 16
Inflation in Brusov–Filatova–Orekhova Theory and in Its Perpetuity Limit–Modigliani–Miller Theory

This chapter examines the effect of inflation on the company's cost of capital and its capitalization in the framework of the Modigliani–Miller theory, which is currently outdated, but still used in the West, and in the framework of the modern theory of value and capital structure of Brusov–Filatova–Orekhova (BFO) (Brusov and Filatova 2011; Brusov et al. 2011a, b, c, 2012a, b, 2013a, b, 2014a, b; Filatova et al. 2008; Brusova 2011). It is shown that inflation not only increases the value of the company's equity capital and the weighted average cost of capital, but also changes their dependence on leverage. In particular, it increases the growth rate of the equity value of a leverage company. The company's capitalization is reduced when accounting for inflation.

We will first consider the role of inflation in the framework of the Modigliani–Miller (MM) theory, excluding corporate income taxes, then taking into account taxes, and, finally, in the framework of the modern Brusov–Filatova–Orekhova (BFO) theory (Brusov and Filatova 2011; Brusov et al. 2011a, b, c, 2012a, b, 2013a, b, 2014a, b; Filatova et al. 2008; Brusova 2011; Brusov (2018a, b, 2015), Brusov et al. (2018a, b, c, d, e, f, g, 2019, 2020); Filatova et al. (2018a, b)).

In this chapter, the influence of inflation on capital cost and capitalization of the company within the modern theory of capital cost and capital structure (Brusov–Filatova–Orekhova theory—BFO theory) (Brusov and Filatova 2011; Brusov et al. 2011a, b, c, 2012a, b, 2013a, b, 2014a, b; Filatova et al. 2008; Brusova 2011) and within its perpetuity limit (Modigliani–Miller theory) (Modigliani and Miller 1958, 1963, 1966) is investigated. By direct incorporation of inflation into both theories, it is shown for the first time that inflation not only increases the equity cost and the weighted average cost of capital, but as well it changes their dependence on leverage. In particular, it increases the growth rate of equity cost with leverage. Capitalization of the company is decreased under inflation (Fig. 16.1).

Inflation is one of the most important indicators taken into account when issuing issuer ratings. It affects the weighted average cost of capital WACC and the cost of equity k_0, which are used (should be used) as the discount rate for discounting financial flows in the ratings. Inflation also affects the dependence of discount rates

P. Brusov et al., *Ratings*, Contributions to Finance and Accounting,
https://doi.org/10.1007/978-3-030-56243-4_16

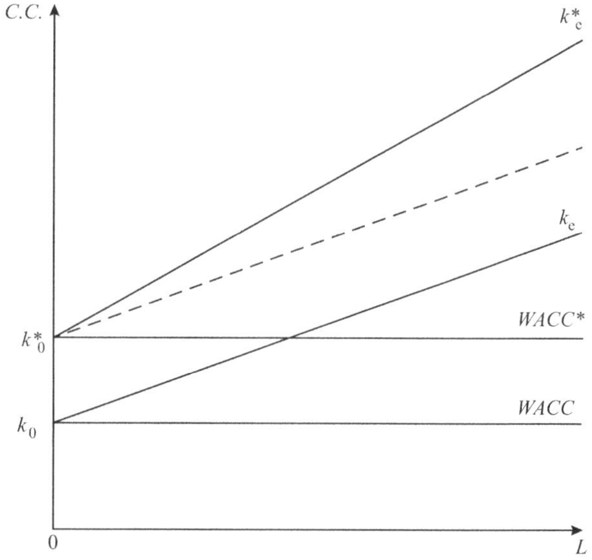

Fig. 16.1 Dependence of the equity cost and the weighted average cost of capital on leverage in the Modigliani–Miller theory without taxing under inflation. It is seen that growth rate of equity cost increases with leverage. Axis *y* means capital costs—CC

(WACC and k_0) on the leverage level L. Adequate accounting of inflation will contribute to the issuance of correct issuer ratings.

This chapter examines the effect of inflation on the company's cost of capital and its capitalization in the framework of the Modigliani–Miller theory, which is currently outdated, but still used in the West, and in the framework of the modern theory of value and capital structure of Brusov–Filatova–Orekhova (BFO) (Brusov and Filatova 2011; Brusov et al. 2011a, b, c, 2012a, b, 2013a, b, 2014a, b; Filatova et al. 2008; Brusova 2011). It is shown that inflation not only increases the value of the company's equity capital and the weighted average cost of capital, but also changes their dependence on leverage. In particular, it increases the growth rate of the equity value of a leverage company. The company's capitalization is reduced when accounting for inflation.

We will first consider the role of inflation in the framework of the Modigliani–Miller (MM) theory, excluding corporate income taxes, then taking into account taxes, and, finally, in the framework of the modern Brusov–Filatova–Orekhova (BFO) theory (Brusov and Filatova 2011; Brusov et al. 2011a, b, c, 2012a, b, 2013a, b, 2014a, b; Filatova et al. 2008; Brusova 2011; Brusov 2018a, b, 2015; Brusov et al. 2018a, b, c, d, e, f, g, 2019, 2020); Filatova et al. 2018a, b).

In this chapter, the influence of inflation on capital cost and capitalization of the company within the modern theory of capital cost and capital structure (Brusov–Filatova–Orekhova theory—BFO theory) (Brusov and Filatova 2011; Brusov et al. 2011a, b, c, 2012a, b, 2013a, b, 2014a, b; Filatova et al. 2008; Brusova 2011) and within its perpetuity limit (Modigliani–Miller theory) (Modigliani and Miller 1958, 1963, 1966) is investigated. By direct incorporation of inflation into both theories, it is shown for the first time that inflation not only increases the equity cost and the weighted average cost of capital, but as well it changes their dependence on leverage.

In particular, it increases the growth rate of equity cost with leverage. Capitalization of the company is decreased under inflation (Fig. 16.1).

16.1 Introduction

Created more than half a century ago by Nobel Prize winners Modigliani and Miller, the theory of capital cost and capital structure (Modigliani and Miller 1958, 1963, 1966) did not take into account a lot of factors of a real economy, such as taxing, bankruptcy, unperfected capital markets, inflation, and many others. But while taxes have been taken into consideration by authors themselves and some other limitations have been taken off by their followers, direct incorporation of inflation to Modigliani–Miller theory is absent till now.

In this chapter, the influence of inflation on valuation of capital cost of company and its capitalization is investigated within the Modigliani–Miller theory (MM) (Modigliani and Miller 1958, 1963, 1966, which is now outdated but still widely used in the West, as well as within the modern theory of capital cost and capital structure—Brusov–Filatova–Orekhova theory (BFO theory) (Brusov and Filatova 2011; Brusov et al. 2011a, b, c, 2012a, b, 2013a, b, 2014a, b; Filatova et al. 2008), which should replace the Modigliani–Miller theory (Modigliani and Miller 1958, 1963, 1966). It is shown that inflation not only increases the equity cost and the weighted average cost of capital, but as well changes their dependence on leverage. In particular, it increases the growth rate of equity cost with leverage. Capitalization of the company is decreased under inflation.

We start from the study of inflation within the Modigliani–Miller theory without taxes (Modigliani and Miller 1958), then with taxes (Modigliani et al. 1963), and finally within the modern theory of capital cost and capital structure—Brusov–Filatova–Orekhova theory (BFO theory) (Brusov and Filatova 2011; Brusov et al. 2011a, b, c, 2012a, b, 2013a, b, 2014a, b; Filatova et al. 2008).

16.1.1 Accounting of Inflation in Modigliani–Miller Theory without Taxes

Note that any modification of Modigliani–Miller theory, as well as of any other one, requires going beyond the frame of modifying theory. Thus, in the current case, we should go beyond the frame of perpetuity of the company (to remind the reader that the Modigliani–Miller theory describes only perpetuity companies—companies with infinite lifetime), consider the companies with finite lifetime, make necessary calculations, and then use the perpetuity limit.

As known, in profit approach, capitalization of the company is equal to discounted sum of profits of the company. Suppose that profit is constant for all periods and equal to CF, one gets for capitalization of the financially independent company V_0, existing n-years at market,

$$V_0 = \frac{\mathrm{CF}}{1+k_0} + \frac{\mathrm{CF}}{(1+k_0)^2} + \cdots + \frac{\mathrm{CF}}{(1+k_0)^n}, \tag{16.1}$$

where k_0 is the capital cost of the financially independent company.

Under inflation with rate α, the capitalization of the financially independent company V_0^* becomes equal to

$$V_0^* = \frac{\mathrm{CF}}{(1+k_0)(1+\alpha)} + \frac{\mathrm{CF}}{[(1+k_0)(1+\alpha)]^2} + \cdots + \frac{\mathrm{CF}}{[(1+k_0)(1+\alpha)]^n}. \tag{16.2}$$

Using the formula for sum of the terms of indefinitely diminishing geometrical progression with the first term

$$a_1 = \frac{\mathrm{CF}}{(1+k_0)(1+\alpha)} \tag{16.3}$$

and denominator

$$q = \frac{1}{(1+k_0)(1+\alpha)}, \tag{16.4}$$

one gets for capitalization of the financially independent company, V_0^*, the following expression:

$$V_0^* = \frac{a_1}{1-q} = \frac{\mathrm{CF}}{(1+k_0)(1+\alpha)\left[1-((1+k_0)(1+\alpha))^{-1}\right]}$$
$$= \frac{\mathrm{CF}}{(1+k_0)(1+\alpha)-1} = \frac{\mathrm{CF}}{k_0(1+\alpha)+\alpha}.$$

$$V_0^* = \frac{\mathrm{CF}}{k_0(1+\alpha)+\alpha}. \tag{16.5}$$

It is seen that under inflation, the capitalization of the company decreases.

At discount rate $k_0 = 10\%$ and inflation rate $\alpha = 3\%$, the decrease is equal to 5.7%, and at discount rate $k_0 = 15\%$ and inflation rate $\alpha = 7\%$, the decrease is equal to 35%. One can see that the influence of inflation on the company capitalization could be significant enough and is always negative.

For leverage company (using debt capital) capitalization, one has without inflation

$$V_L = \frac{\mathrm{CF}}{1+\mathrm{WACC}} + \frac{\mathrm{CF}}{(1+\mathrm{WACC})^2} + \cdots + \frac{\mathrm{CF}}{(1+\mathrm{WACC})^n} \tag{16.6}$$

and in perpetuity limit,

$$V_L = \frac{\mathrm{CF}}{\mathrm{WACC}}. \tag{16.7}$$

Under inflation, the capitalization of the company is equal to

$$V_L^* = \frac{\mathrm{CF}}{(1+\mathrm{WACC})(1+\alpha)} + \frac{\mathrm{CF}}{[(1+\mathrm{WACC})(1+\alpha)]^2} + \cdots + \frac{\mathrm{CF}}{[(1+\mathrm{WACC})(1+\alpha)]^n}. \tag{16.8}$$

Summing the infinite set, we get for leverage company capitalization under inflation in Modigliani–Miller limit

$$V_{\mathrm{L}}^* = \frac{a_1}{1-q} = \frac{\mathrm{CF}}{(1+\mathrm{WACC})(1+\alpha)\left[1-((1+\mathrm{WACC})(1+\alpha))^{-1}\right]}$$
$$= \frac{\mathrm{CF}}{(1+\mathrm{WACC})(1+\alpha)-1} = \frac{\mathrm{CF}}{\mathrm{WACC}(1+\alpha)+\alpha},$$
$$V_L^* = \frac{\mathrm{CF}}{\mathrm{WACC}(1+\alpha)+\alpha}. \tag{16.9}$$

It is seen that similar to the case of the financially independent company, inflation decreases the company capitalization, and the decrease could be significant. From formulas (Eqs. 16.7 and 16.9), it follows that effective values of capital costs (equity cost and WACC) are equal to:

$$k_0^* = k_0(1+\alpha)+\alpha, \tag{16.10}$$

$$\mathrm{WACC}^* = \mathrm{WACC}\cdot(1+\alpha)+\alpha. \tag{16.11}$$

Note that both capital costs increase under inflation.

We can compare obtained results with Fisher formula for inflation.

$$i^* = \frac{i-\alpha}{1+\alpha}. \tag{16.12}$$

Solving this equation with respect to nominal rate i, one gets equation, similar to (Eqs. 16.10 and 16.11),

$$i = i^* \cdot (1 + \alpha) + \alpha. \tag{16.13}$$

Thus, effective capital costs in our case have meaning of nominal ones, accounting for inflation.

From the Modigliani–Miller theorem, which states the weighted average cost of capital WACC does not depend on leverage level (without taxing), formulating under inflation, it is easy to get expression for the equity cost:

$$\text{WACC}^* = k_0^* = k_e^* w_e + k_d^* w_d. \tag{16.14}$$

Finding from here k_e^*, one gets:

$$\begin{aligned} k_e^* = \frac{k_0^*}{w_e} - k_d^* \frac{w_d}{w_e} = \frac{k_0^*(S+D)}{S} - k_d^* \frac{D}{S} = k_0^* + \left(k_0^* - k_d^*\right)\frac{D}{S} \\ = k_0^* + \left(k_0^* - k_d^*\right)L \end{aligned} \tag{16.15}$$

Putting instead of k_0^*, k_d^* in their expressions, one gets finally

$$\begin{aligned} k_e^* = k_0^* + \left(k_0^* - k_d^*\right)L = k_0(1+\alpha) + \alpha \\ + L(k_0 - k_d)(1+\alpha) = (1+\alpha)[k_0 + \alpha + L(k_0 - k_d)] \\ k_e^* = k_0(1+\alpha) + \alpha + L(k_0 - k_d)(1+\alpha). \end{aligned} \tag{16.16}$$

It is seen that inflation not only increases the equity cost, but as well changes its dependence on leverage. In particular, it increases the growth rate of equity cost with leverage by multiplier $(1 + \alpha)$. The growth rate of equity cost with leverage, which is equal to $(k_0 - k_d)$ without inflation, becomes equal to $(k_0 - k_d)(1 + \alpha)$ with accounting of inflation.

Thus, we come to the conclusion that it is necessary to modify the second statement of the Modigliani–Miller theory (Modigliani and Miller 1958) concerning the equity cost of leverage company.

16.1.1.1 Second Original MM Statement

Equity cost of leverage company k_e could be found as equity cost of financially independent company k_0 of the same group of risk, plus premium for risk, the value of which is equal to production of difference $(k_0 - k_d)$ on leverage level L.

16.1.1.2 Second Modified MM-BFO Statement

Under existence of inflation with rate α, equity cost of leverage company k_e could be found as equity cost of financially independent company k_0 of the same

group of risk, multiplied by (1 + α), plus inflation rate α and plus premium for risk, the value of which is equal to production of difference $(k_0 - k_d)$ on leverage level L and on multiplier $(1 + \alpha)$.

16.1.2 *Accounting of Inflation in Modigliani–Miller Theory with Corporate Taxes*

Let us calculate first the tax shield for perpetuity company under inflation

$$(\mathrm{PV})_{\mathrm{TS}} = k_d^* DT \sum_{t=1}^{\infty} \left(1 + k_d^*\right)^{-t} = DT \ . \tag{16.17}$$

It is interesting to note that in spite of the dependence of each term of set on effective credit rate k_d^*, tax shield turns out to be independent of it and equal to "inflationless" value DT, and Modigliani–Miller theorem under inflation takes the following form (Modigliani and Miller 1963):

$$V_L^* = V_0^* + DT. \tag{16.18}$$

Substituting $D = w_d V_L^*$,
one gets

$$V_L^* = \mathrm{CF}/k_0^* + w_d V_L^* T \tag{16.19}$$

or

$$V_L^*(1 - w_d T) = \mathrm{CF}/k_0^*. \tag{16.20}$$

Because leverage company capitalization is equal to
$V_L^* = \mathrm{CF}/\mathrm{WACC}^*$, for the weighted average cost of capital, one has

$$\mathrm{WACC}^* = k_0^*(1 - w_d T). \tag{16.21}$$

From (Eq. 16.21), we get the dependence of WACC* on leverage level $L = D/S$:

$$\mathrm{WACC}^* = k_0^*(1 - LT/(1 + L)),$$
$$\mathrm{WACC}^* = [k_0(1 + \alpha) + \alpha] \cdot (1 - w_d T). \tag{16.22}$$

By definition of the weighted average cost of capital with accounting of the tax shield, one has

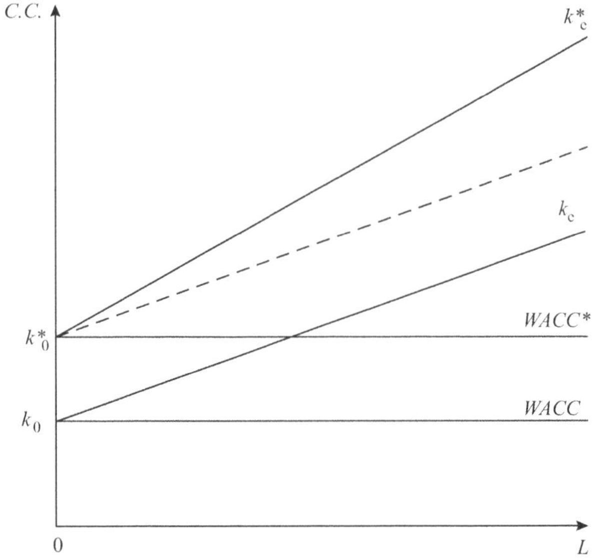

Fig. 16.2 Dependence of the equity cost and the weighted average cost of capital on leverage in the Modigliani–Miller theory with taxes under inflation. It is seen that the growth rate of equity cost increases with leverage. Axis *y* means capital costs—CC

$$\mathrm{WACC}^* = k_0^* w_e + k_d^* w_d (1 - T). \tag{16.23}$$

Equating right-hand parts of expressions (Eqs. 16.21 and 16.23), we get

$$k_0^*(1 - w_d T) = k_0^* w_e + k_d^* w_d (1 - T), \tag{16.24}$$

from where one obtains the following expression for equity cost:

$$k_e^* = k_0^* \frac{(1 - w_d T)}{w_e} - k_d^* \frac{w_d}{w_e}(1 - T) = k_e^* \frac{1}{w_e} - k_0^* \frac{w_d}{w_e} T - k_d^* \frac{D}{S}(1 - T)$$
$$= k_0^* \frac{D + S}{S} - k_0^* \frac{D}{S} T - k_d^* \frac{D}{S}(1 - T) = k_0^* + L(1 - T)\left(k_0^* - k_d^*\right),$$

$$\begin{aligned} k_e^* &= k_0^* + L(1 - T)\left(k_0^* - k_d^*\right) \\ &= [k_0(1 + \alpha) + \alpha] + L(1 - T)(k_0 - k_d)(1 + \alpha). \end{aligned} \tag{16.25}$$

It is seen that similar to the case without taxes, inflation not only increases the equity cost, but as well changes its dependence on leverage (Fig. 16.2). In particular, it increases the growth rate of equity cost with leverage by multiplier $(1 + \alpha)$. The growth rate of equity cost with leverage, which is equal to $(k_0 - k_d)(1 - T)$ without inflation, becomes equal to $(k_0 - k_d)(1 + \alpha)(1 - T)$ with accounting of inflation.

We can now reformulate the fourth statement of the Modigliani–Miller theory (Modigliani and Miller 1963) concerning the equity cost of leverage company for the case of accounting of inflation.

16.1.2.1 Fourth Original MM Statement

Equity cost of leverage company k_e paying tax on profit could be found as equity cost of financially independent company k_0 of the same group of risk, plus premium for risk, the value of which is equal to production of difference $(k_0 - k_d)$ on leverage level L and on tax shield $(1 - T)$ and on multiplier $(1 + \alpha)$.

16.1.2.2 Fourth Modified MM-BFO Statement

Equity cost of leverage company k_e paying tax on profit under existence of inflation with rate α could be found as equity cost of financially independent company k_0 of the same group of risk, multiplied by $(1 + \alpha)$, plus inflation rate α and plus premium for risk, the value of which is equal to production of difference $(k_0 - k_d)$ on leverage level L, on tax shield $(1 - T)$, and on multiplier $(1 + \alpha)$.

16.1.3 Accounting of Inflation in Brusov–Filatova–Orekhova Theory with Corporate Taxes

16.1.3.1 Generalized Brusov–Filatova–Orekhova Theorem

Brusov–Filatova–Orekhova generalized the Modigliani–Miller theory for the case of the companies with arbitrary lifetime (of arbitrary age) (Brusov and Filatova 2011; Brusov et al. 2011a, b, c, 2012a, b, 2013a, b, 2014a, b; Filatova et al. 2008) and have proved the following important theorem in the case of absence of corporate taxing:

Without corporate taxing, the equity cost k_0, as well as the weighted average cost of capital WACC, does not depend on company's lifetime and is equal to

$$k_e = k_0 + L(k_0 - k_d) \text{ and } \quad \text{WACC} = k_0. \tag{16.26}$$

consequently.

Thus, the theorem has proved that without corporate taxes (say, in offshore zones), the Modigliani–Miller results for capital costs, in spite of the fact that they have been obtained in perpetuity limit, remain in force for companies with arbitrary lifetime, described by Brusov–Filatova–Orekhova theory (BFO theory). To prove this theorem, Brusov, Filatova, and Orekhova, of course, had to go beyond Modigliani–Miller approximation.

Under inflation, we can generalize this theorem (Brusov and Filatova 2011; Brusov et al. 2011a, b, c, 2012a, b, 2013a, b, 2014a, b; Filatova et al. 2008):

Generalized Brusov–Filatova–Orekhova Theorem

Under inflation without corporate taxing, the equity cost k_0^*, as well as the weighted average cost of capital WACC*, ***does not depend on company's lifetime and is equal to***

$$k_e^* = k_0^* + L(k_0^* - k_d^*) = k_0(1+\alpha) + \alpha + L(k_0 - k_d)(1+\alpha)$$

and

$$\mathrm{WACC}^* = k_0^* = k_0(1+\alpha) + \alpha \tag{16.27}$$

consequently.

Following Brusov–Filatova–Orekhova (Brusov and Filatova 2011; Brusov et al. 2011a, b, c, 2012a, b, 2013a, b, 2014a, b; Filatova et al. 2008), let us consider the situation for companies of arbitrary age with accounting of corporate taxing. They have derived the famous formula for weighted average cost of capital of companies of arbitrary age

$$\frac{1-(1+\mathrm{WACC})^{-n}}{\mathrm{WACC}} = \frac{1-(1+k_0)^{-n}}{k_0[1-\omega_d T(1-(1+k_d)^{-n})]}. \tag{16.28}$$

The application of BFO formula (16.29) ***is very wide: authors have applied it in corporate finance, in investments, in taxing, in business valuation, in banking, and in some other areas (Brusov*** **et al.** 2011a, b, 2013a)***. Using this formula (***16.28***), one can study the dependence of the weighted average cost of capital, WACC, as well as the equity cost, k_e, on leverage level, L, on tax on profit rate, t, on lifetime of the company, n, and on relation between equity and debt cost. The qualitatively new effect in corporate finance has been discovered: decrease of the equity cost k_e with leverage level L, which is quite important for corporate finance in general and, in particular, for creating the adequate dividend policy.***

Below we generalize formula (16.28) under existence of inflation.

16.1.4 Generalized Brusov–Filatova–Orekhova Formula Under Existence of Inflation

Under existence of inflation, it is necessary to replace all capital costs: the equity, the debt, and the weighted average cost of capital k_0, k_d, WACC by effective ones k_0^*, k_d^*, WACC*,

where

$$k_0^* = k_0(1+\alpha)+\alpha,$$
$$k_d^* = k_d(1+\alpha)+\alpha,$$
$$\mathrm{WACC}^* = \mathrm{WACC}\cdot(1+\alpha)+\alpha.$$

Rewriting the equations for tax shield $(\mathrm{TS})_n$, capitalization of financially independent company V_0^*, as well as for financially dependent company V_L^* for the case of existence of inflation, one gets

$$(\mathrm{PV})_{\mathrm{TS}} = (TS)_n = k_d^* DT\sum_{t=1}^{n}\left(1+k_d^*\right)^{-t} = DT\left[1-\left(1+k_d^*\right)^{-n}\right] \tag{16.29}$$

$$V_0^* = \mathrm{CF}\sum_{t=1}^{n}\left(1+k_0^*\right)^{-t} = \mathrm{CF}\left[1-\left(1+k_0^*\right)^{-n}\right]/k_0^*, \tag{16.30}$$

$$V_L^* = \mathrm{CF}\sum_{t=1}^{n}(1+\mathrm{WACC}^*)^{-t} = \mathrm{CF}[1-(1+\mathrm{WACC}^*)^{-n}]/\mathrm{WACC}^*, \tag{16.31}$$

$$V_L^* = V_0^* + (\mathrm{TS})_n. \tag{16.32}$$

After substitution $D = w_d V_L^*$, we have

$$V_L^* = \mathrm{CF}/k_0^* + w_d V_L^* T. \tag{16.33}$$

From here, after some transformations we get generalized Brusov–Filatova–Orekhova formula under existence of inflation

$$\frac{1-(1+\mathrm{WACC}^*)^{-n}}{\mathrm{WACC}^*} = \frac{1-\left(1+k_0^*\right)^{-n}}{k_0^*\left[1-\omega_d T\left(1-\left(1+k_d^*\right)^{-n}\right)\right]}, \tag{16.34}$$

or after substitutions,

$$k_0^* = k_0(1+\alpha)+\alpha; \quad k_d^* = k_d(1+\alpha)+\alpha,$$

one gets finally

$$\frac{1-(1+\mathrm{WACC}^*)^{-n}}{\mathrm{WACC}^*} = \frac{1-[(1+k_0)(1+\alpha)]^{-n}}{(k_0(1+\alpha)+\alpha)\cdot\left[1-\omega_d T(1-((1+k_d)(1+\alpha))^{-n})\right]}. \tag{16.35}$$

Formula (16.35) is the generalized Brusov–Filatova–Orekhova formula under existence of inflation.

Let us show some figures, illustrating obtained results.

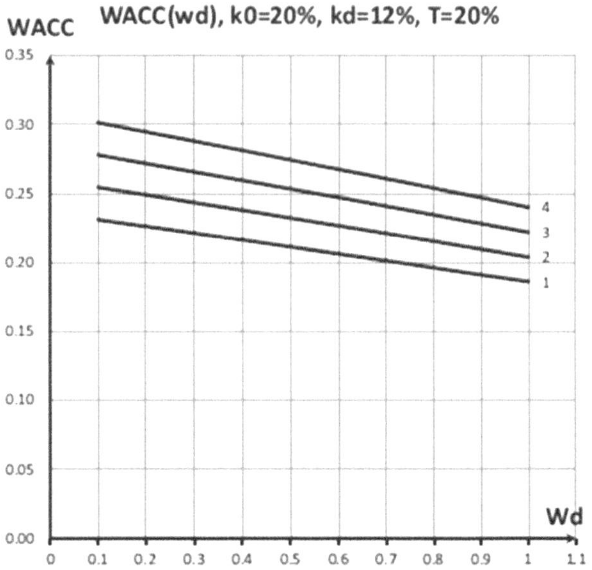

Fig. 16.3 Dependence of the weighted average cost of capital WACC on debt fraction w_d at different inflation rates α (1, $\alpha = 3\%$; 2, $\alpha = 5\%$; 3, $\alpha = 7\%$; and 4, $\alpha = 9\%$) for 5-year company

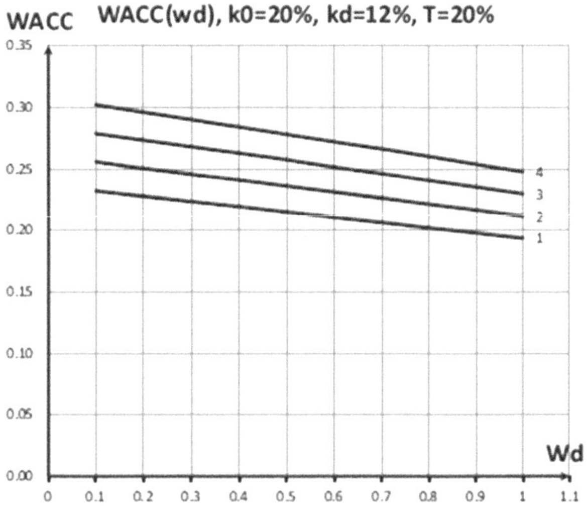

Fig. 16.4 Dependence of the weighted average cost of capital WACC on debt fraction w_d at different inflation rates α (1, $\alpha = 3\%$; 2, $\alpha = 5\%$; 3, $\alpha = 7\%$; and 4, $\alpha = 9\%$) for 2-year company

In Figs. 16.3 and 16.4, the dependence of the weighted average cost of capital WACC on debt fraction w_d at different inflation rates α (1, $\alpha = 3\%$; 2, $\alpha = 5\%$; 3, $\alpha = 7\%$; 4, $\alpha = 9\%$) for 5-year company as well as for 2-year company is seen. It is seen that with increase of inflation rate lines, showing the dependence, WACC (w_d) shift practically homogeneously to higher values.

It is seen that difference in results for 2-year company and 5-year company is very small. More obviously, it could be observed from Tables 16.1 and 16.2).

Table 16.1 Dependence of the weighted average cost of capital WACC on debt fraction w_d at different inflation rates $\alpha = 3; 5; 7;$ and 9% for 2-year company

α/w_d	0.1	0.2	0.3	0.4	0.5	0.6	0.7	0.8	0.9	1
0.03	0.2318	0.2276	0.2233	0.2191	0.2149	0.2106	0.2064	0.2021	0.1979	0.1937
0.05	0.2557	0.2503	0.2455	0.2406	0.2358	0.2309	0.2261	0.2212	0.2164	0.2115
0.07	0.2786	0.2733	0.2679	0.2626	0.2573	0.2514	0.2459	0.2404	0.2350	0.2295
0.09	0.3020	0.2960	0.2900	0.2839	0.2779	0.2720	0.2661	0.2602	0.2537	0.2476

Table 16.2 Dependence of the weighted average cost of capital WACC on debt fraction w_d at different inflation rates $\alpha = 3$; 5; 7; and 9% for 5-year company

α/w_d	0.1	0.2	0.3	0.4	0.5	0.6	0.7	0.8	0.9	1
0.03	0.2311	0.2262	0.2213	0.2163	0.2113	0.2064	0.2013	0.1963	0.1912	0.1863
0.05	0.2546	0.2491	0.2434	0.2379	0.2323	0.2267	0.2210	0.2154	0.2097	0.2040
0.07	0.2781	0.2718	0.2657	0.2595	0.2534	0.2472	0.2408	0.2346	0.2283	0.2219
0.09	0.3015	0.2947	0.2879	0.2812	0.2744	0.2676	0.2608	0.2539	0.2471	0.2400

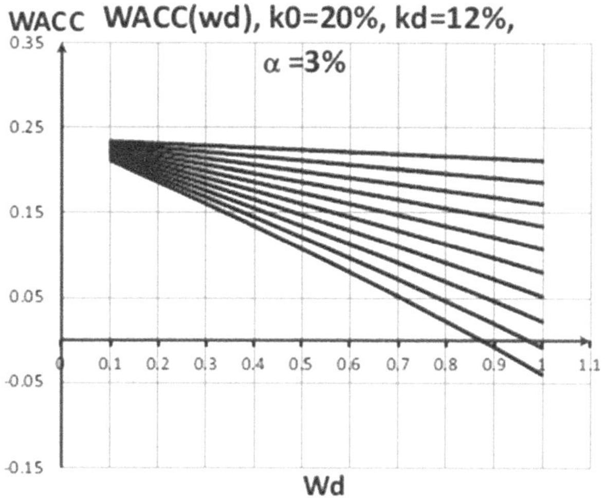

Fig. 16.5 Dependence of the weighted average cost of capital WACC on debt fraction w_d at different tax on profit rate at inflation rate $\alpha = 3\%$ for 5-year company. Tax on profit rate increases from $T = 0.1$ (*upper line*) up to $T = 1$ (*lower line*) with step 0.1

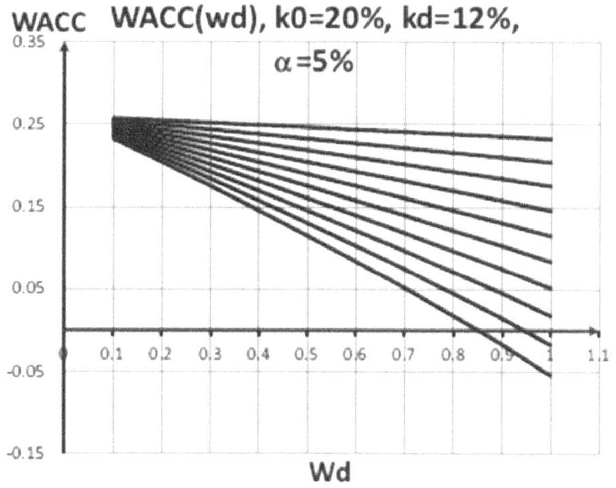

Fig. 16.6 Dependence of the weighted average cost of capital WACC on debt fraction w_d at different tax on profit rate at inflation rate $\alpha = 5\%$ for 5-year company. Tax on profit rate increases from $T = 0.1$ (*upper line*) up to $T = 1$ (*lower line*) with step 0.1

Below we show the dependences of the weighted average cost of capital WACC on debt fraction w_d at different tax on profit rate from $T = 10\%$ up to $T = 100\%$ at different inflation rates $\alpha = 3$, 5, 7, and 9% for 5-year company (Figs. 16.5, 16.6, 16.7, and 16.8) as well as for 2-year company (Figs. 16.9, 16.10, 16.11, and 16.12). Tax on profit rate increases from $T = 0.1$ (upper line) up to $T = 1$ (lower line) with step 0.1.

The analysis of Figs. 16.5, 16.6, 16.7, 16.8, 16.9, 16.10, 16.11, and 16.12 shows that the weighted average cost of capital WACC decreases with debt fraction w_d and faster with increase of tax on profit rate. The space between lines, corresponding to different tax on profit rates, increases with inflation rate. The variation range of WACC increases with inflation rate as well as with the company's age.

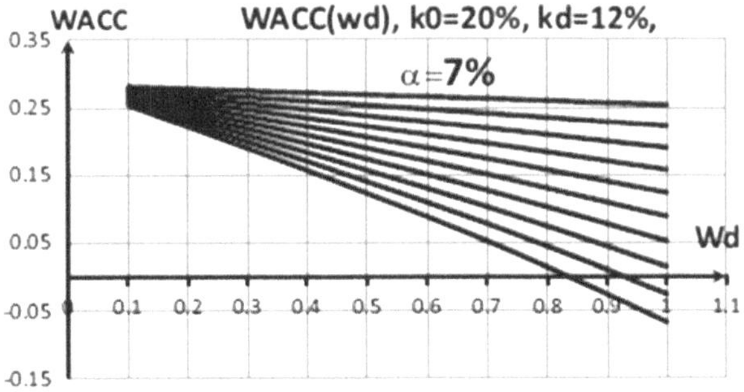

Fig. 16.7 Dependence of the weighted average cost of capital WACC on debt fraction w_d at different tax on profit rate at inflation rate $\alpha = 7\%$ for 5-year company. Tax on profit rate increases from $T = 0.1$ (*upper line*) up to $T = 1$ (*lower line*) with step 0.1

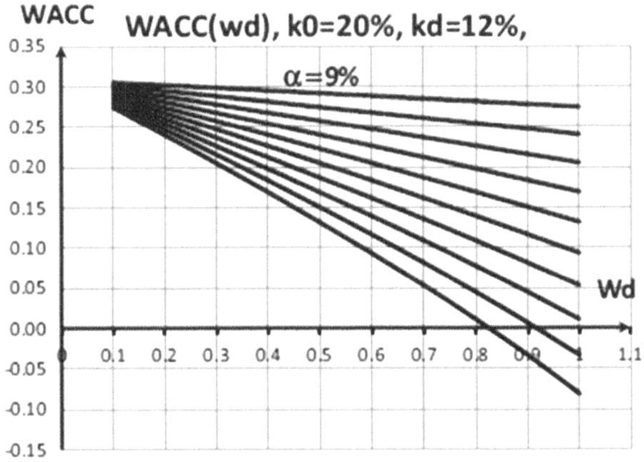

Fig. 16.8 Dependence of the weighted average cost of capital WACC on debt fraction w_d at different tax on profit rate at inflation rate $\alpha = 9\%$ for 5-year company. Tax on profit rate increases from $T = 0.1$ (*upper line*) up to $T = 1$ (*lower line*) with step 0.1

16.1.5 Irregular Inflation

Above we considered inflation rate as constant. Really, as a rule, the inflation rate is a variable. It is possible to generalize all the above considerations for the case of nonhomogeneous inflation, introducing effective inflation for a few periods.

The effective inflation rate for a few periods $t = t_1 + t_2 + \cdots + t_n$ is equal to

$$\alpha = (1 + \alpha_1)(1 + \alpha_2)\ldots(1 + \alpha_n) - 1, \tag{16.36}$$

where $\alpha_1, \alpha_2, \ldots, \alpha_n$ are inflation rates for periods $t_1, t_2, \ldots, t_n$.

The proof of the formula (16.36) will be done below in Sect. 16.1.6.

In the case of nonhomogeneous inflation, it could be accounted in both theories: Modigliani–Miller and Brusov–Filatova–Orekhova theory (BFO theory) either through effective inflation rate or directly upon discounting of financial flow.

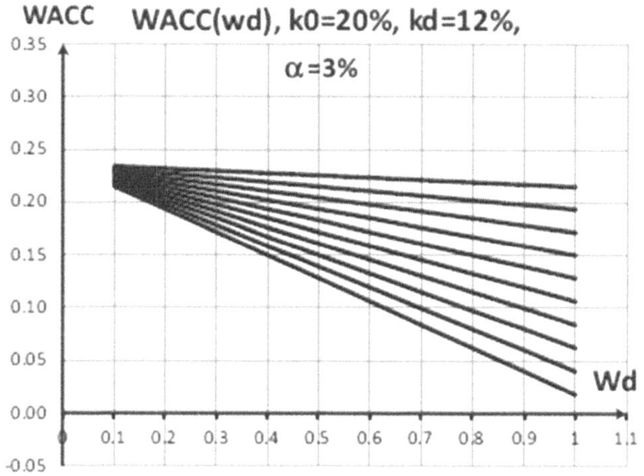

Fig. 16.9 Dependence of the weighted average cost of capital WACC on debt fraction w_d at different tax on profit rate at inflation rate $\alpha = 3\%$ for 2-year company. Tax on profit rate increases from $T = 0.1$ (*upper line*) up to $T = 1$ (*lower line*) with step 0.1

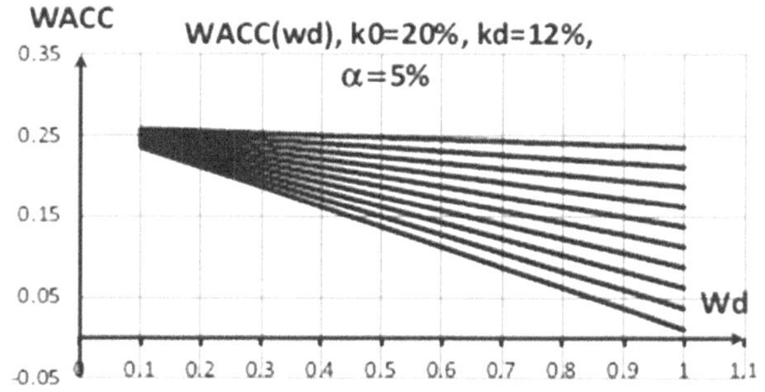

Fig. 16.10 Dependence of the weighted average cost of capital WACC on debt fraction w_d at different tax on profit rate at inflation rate $\alpha = 5\%$ for 2-year company. Tax on profit rate increases from $T = 0.1$ (*upper line*) up to $T = 1$ (*lower line*) with step 0.1

16.1.6 Inflation Rate for a Few Periods

Suppose that the inflation rate for the consistent time periods $t_1, t_2, \ldots, t_n$ is equal to $\alpha_1, \alpha_2, \ldots, \alpha_n$, respectively. Let us find the inflation rate α for total time period $t = t_1 + t_2 + \cdots + t_n$.

Common sense dictates that inflation rate is an additive value, so that α, at least approximately, is equal to the sum of the inflation rates $\alpha_1, \alpha_2, \ldots, \alpha_n$

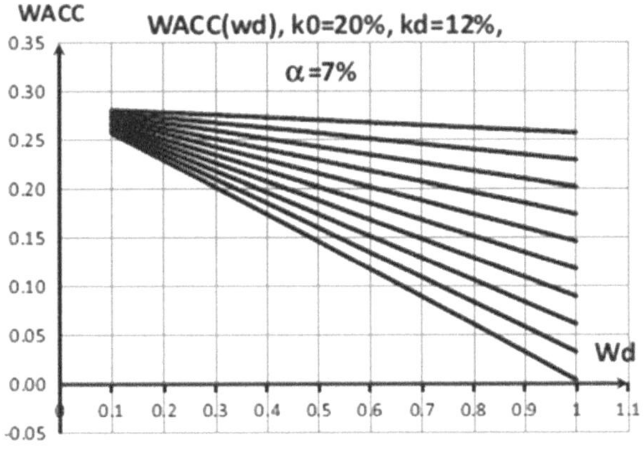

Fig. 16.11 Dependence of the weighted average cost of capital WACC on debt fraction w_d at different tax on profit rate at inflation rate $\alpha = 7\%$ for 2-year company. Tax on profit rate increases from $T = 0.1$ (*upper line*) up to $T = 1$ (*lower line*) with step 0.1

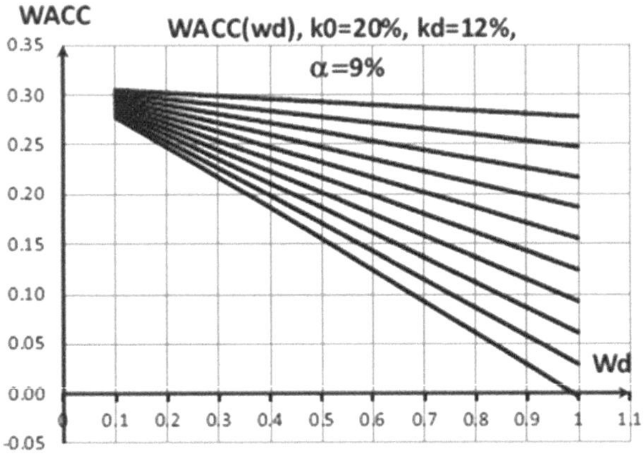

Fig. 16.12 Dependence of the weighted average cost of capital WACC on debt fraction w_d at different tax on profit rate at inflation rate $\alpha = 9\%$ for 2-year company. Tax on profit rate increases from $T = 0.1$ (*upper line*) up to $T = 1$ (*lower line*) with step 0.1

$$\alpha \approx \alpha_1 + \alpha_2 + \cdots + \alpha_n. \tag{16.37}$$

Below we will get an exact expression for inflation rate for the total period of time, t, and will see how it is different from an intuitive result (16.37).

At the end of the first commitment period, the gained sum will be equal to the amount $S_1 = S_0(1 + i)$, and with accounting of inflation, $S_{1\alpha} = S_0(1+i)^{t_1}/(1+\alpha_1)$. At the end of the second commitment period, the gained sum will be equal to the amount $S_2 = S_0(1+i)^{t_1+t_2}$, and with accounting of inflation, $S_{2\alpha} = S_0(1+i)^{t_1+t_2}/(1+\alpha_1)(1+\alpha_2)$. At the end of the n-th commitment period, the gained sum will be equal to the amount $S_n = S_0(1+i)^{t_1+t_2+\ldots+t_n}$, and with accounting of inflation,

$$S_{n\alpha} = S_0(1+i)^{t_1+t_2+\ldots+t_n}/(1+\alpha_1)(1+\alpha_2)\cdot\ldots\cdot(1+\alpha_n). \tag{16.38}$$

On the other hand, at inflation rate α for the total period at $t = t_1 + t_2 + \cdots + t_n$ at the end of this period t, gained sum will be equal to

$$S_{n\alpha} = S_0(1+i)^t/(1+\alpha). \tag{16.39}$$

Equating the right-hand part of (16.38) and (16.39), we get

$$(1+\alpha_1)(1+\alpha_2)\cdot\ldots\cdot(1+\alpha_n) = 1+\alpha. \tag{16.40}$$

From where,

$$\alpha = (1+\alpha_1)(1+\alpha_2)\cdot\ldots\cdot(1+\alpha_n) - 1. \tag{16.41}$$

It is easy to get a strict proof of this formula by the method of mathematical induction. Note that inflation rate for the n-periods does not depend on both the length of constituting periods and the period t.

For equal inflation rates $\alpha_1 = \alpha_2 = \cdots = \alpha_n$ (it is interesting to note that herewith the time intervals $t_1, t_2, \ldots, t_n$ can be arbitrary and do not equal each other), one has

$$\alpha = (1+\alpha_1)^n - 1. \tag{16.42}$$

16.2 Conclusions

Inflation is one of the most important indicators taken into account when issuing issuer ratings. It affects the weighted average cost of capital of WACC and the cost of equity k_0, which are used (should be used) as the discount rate for discounting of financial flows in the ratings. Inflation also affects the dependence of discount rates (WACC and k_0) on the leverage level L. Adequate accounting of inflation will contribute to the issuance of correct issuer ratings.

In this chapter, the influence of inflation on capital cost and capitalization of the company within the modern theory of capital cost and capital structure—Brusov–Filatova–Orekhova theory (BFO theory) (Brusov and Filatova 2011; Brusov et al. 2011a, b, c, 2012a, b, 2013a, b, 2014a, b; Filatova et al. 2008) and in its perpetuity limit—Modigliani–Miller theory (Modigliani and Miller 1958, 1963, 1966), which is now outdated, but still widely used in the West, is investigated. All basic results of Modigliani–Miller theory were modified. It is shown that inflation not only increases the equity cost and the weighted average cost of capital, but as well changes their dependence on leverage. In particular, it increases the growth rate of equity cost with leverage. Capitalization of the company is decreased with accounting of inflation.

Within the modern theory of capital cost and capital structure—Brusov–Filatova–Orekhova theory (BFO theory), the modified equation for the weighted average cost of capital, WACC, applicable to companies with arbitrary lifetime under inflation has been derived. Modified BFO equation allows us to investigate the dependence of the weighted average cost of capital, WACC, and equity cost, k_e, on leverage level, L, on tax on profit rate, t, on age of the company, n, on equity cost of financially independent company, k_0, and debt cost, k_d, as well as on inflation rate α.

Using modified BFO equation, the analysis of the dependence of the weighted average cost of capital WACC on debt fraction, w_d, at different tax on profit rate t, as well as inflation rate α, has been done.

It has been shown that WACC decreases with debt fraction, w_d, and faster at bigger tax on profit rates t. The space between lines, corresponding to different values of tax on profit rate at the same step (10%), increases with inflation rate α. The variation region (with change of tax on profit rate t) of the weighted average cost of capital, WACC, increases with inflation rate α, as well as with the age of the company n.

References

Brusov PN, Filatova TV (2011) From Modigliani–Miller to general theory of capital cost and capital structure of the company. Finance Credit 435:2–8

Brusov P, Filatova T, Orehova N, Brusova A (2011a) Weighted average cost of capital in the theory of Modigliani–Miller, modified for a finite life–time company. Appl Financ Econ 21(11):815–824

Brusov P, Filatova T, Orehova N et al (2011b) From Modigliani–Miller to general theory of capital cost and capital structure of the company. Res J Econ Bus ICT 2:16–21

Brusov P, Filatova T, Orehova N et al (2011c) Influence of debt financing on the effectiveness of the investment project within the Modigliani–Miller theory. Res J Econ Bus ICT (UK) 2:11–15

Brusov P, Filatova T, Eskindarov M, Orehova N (2012a) Influence of debt financing on the effectiveness of the finite duration investment project. Appl Financ Econ 22(13):1043–1052

Brusov P, Filatova T, Eskindarov M, Orehova N (2012b) Hidden global causes of the global financial crisis. J Rev Global Econ 1:106–111

Brusov P, Filatova P, Orekhova N (2013a) Absence of an optimal capital structure in the famous tradeoff theory! J Rev Global Econ 2:94–116

Brusov P, Filatova T, Orehova N (2013b) A qualitatively new effect in corporative finance: abnormal dependence of cost of equity of company on leverage. J Rev Global Econ 2:183–193

Brusov P, Filatova P, Orekhova N (2014a) Mechanism of formation of the company optimal capital structure, different from suggested by trade off theory. Cogent Econ Finance 2:1–13. https://doi.org/10.1080/23322039.2014.946150

Brusov P, Filatova T, Orehova N (2014b) Inflation in Brusov–Filatova–Orekhova theory and in its perpetuity limit—Modigliani–Miller theory. J Rev Global Econ 3:175–185

Brusov P (2018a) Editorial: introduction on special issue on the banking system and financial markets of Russia and other countries: problems and prospects. J Rev Glob Econ 7:i–vi, SCOPUS

Brusov P (2018b) Editorial. J Rev Glob Econ 7:i–v, SCOPUS

Brusov P, Filatova T, Orekhova N, Eskindarov M (2015) Modern corporate finance, investments and taxation, Springer International Publishing, Switzerland, p 373. Monograph, SCOPUS. https://www.springer.com/gp/book/9783319147314

Brusov P, Filatova T, Orekhova N, Eskindarov M (2018a) Modern corporate finance, investments, taxation and ratings, Springer Nature Publishing, Switzerland, p 571. Monograph

Brusov PN, Filatova TV, Orekhova NP, Kulik VL (2018b) Rating: new approach. J Rev Glob Econ 7:37–62. SCOPUS. https://doi.org/10.6000/1929-7092.2018.07.05

Brusov PN, Filatova TV, Orekhova NP, Kulik VL (2018c) A "golden age" of the companies: conditions of its existence. J Rev Glob Econ 7:88–103. SCOPUS. https://doi.org/10.6000/1929-7092.2018.07.07

Brusov PN, Filatova TV, Orekhova NP, Kulik VL (2018d) Rating methodology: new look and new horizons. J Rev Glob Econ 7:63–87. SCOPUS. https://doi.org/10.6000/1929-7092.2018.07.06

Brusov PN, Filatova TV, Orekhova NP, Kulik VL, Weil I (2018e) New meaningful effects in modern capital structure theory. J Rev Glob Econ 7:104–122. SCOPUS. https://doi.org/10.6000/1929-7092.2018.07.08

Brusov P, Filatova T, Orekhova N, Kulik V, Weil I, Brailov A (2018f) The impact of the central bank key rate and commercial banks credit rates on creating and maintaining of a favorable investment climate in the country. J Rev Glob Econ 7:360–376. SCOPUS. https://doi.org/10.6000/1929-7092.2018.07.31

Brusov PN, Filatova TV, Orekhova NP (2018g) Modern corporate finance and investments, monograph. Knorus Publishing House, Moscow, p 517

Brusov PN, Filatova TV, Orekhova NP, Kulik VL, Weil I (2019) Ratings of the investment projects of arbitrary durations: new methodology. J Rev Glob Econ 8:437–448. SCOPUS. https://doi.org/10.6000/1929-7092.2019.08.37

Brusov PN, Filatova TV, Orekhova NP, Kulik VL, Chang S-I, Lin YCG (2020) Modification of the Modigliani–Miller theory for the case of advance payments of tax on profit. J Rev Glob Econ 9:257–268

Filatova T, Orehova N, Brusova A (2008) Weighted average cost of capital in the theory of Modigliani–Miller, modified for a finite lifetime company. Bull FU 48:68–77

Filatova TV, Brusov PN, Orekhova NP, Kulik VL (2018a) Ratings of the long-term projects: new approach. J Rev Glob Econ 7:645–661, SCOPUS. https://doi.org/10.6000/1929-7092.2018.07.59

Modigliani F, Miller M (1958) The cost of capital, corporate finance, and the theory of investment. Am Econ Rev 48:261–297

Modigliani F, Miller M (1963) Corporate income taxes and the cost of capital: a correction. Am Econ Rev 53:147–175

Modigliani F, Miller M (1966) Some estimates of the cost of capital to the electric utility industry 1954–1957. Am Econ Rev 56:333–391

Myers S (2001) Capital structure. J Econ Perspect 15(2):81–102

Chapter 17
A Qualitatively New Effect in Corporate Finance: Abnormal Dependence of Equity Cost of Company on Leverage Level

For some ratios between equity and debt cost values, the discovered effect occurs at the tax on profit rate existing in Western countries and Russia, which provides practical value to the effect. Its accounting is important when improving tax legislation and can change the dividend policy of a company, the accounting of which is extremely important in rating when assessing the creditworthiness of issuers.

The validity of the dividend policy of the company, its assessment, is determined by comparing the amount of paid dividends with their economically sound value, which is the cost of equity of the company. Calculating the latter is rather a difficult task. The BFO theory allows us to make correct estimates of the cost of the company's equity and thereby compare the amount of dividends paid by the company with their economically sound value; this allows us to assess the validity of the dividend policy, which is undoubtedly associated with the issuer's creditworthiness.

In this chapter, a complete study of the effect found in the framework of the Brusov–Filatova–Orekhova theory (Brusov and Filatova 2011; Brusov et al. 2011a, b, c, 2012a, b, 2013a, b, 2014a, b; Filatova et al. 2008; Brusova 2011) is carried out. It is shown that the absence of effect for some ratios between the parameters is due to the fact that T^* in these cases exceeds 100% (the income tax rate is in the "non-financial" region).Taking into account the company's dividend policy is extremely important in rating when assessing the creditworthiness of issuers. Qualitatively new effect in corporative finance, which could radically change the approach to the formation of the company's dividend policy, is discovered: decrease of equity cost k_e with leverage level L. This effect, which is absent in perpetuity Modigliani–Miller limit (Modigliani and Miller 1958, 1963, 1966), takes place on account of finite age of the company at tax on profit rate, which exceeds some value T^* (Brusov and Filatova 2011; Brusov et al. 2011a, b, c, 2012a, b, 2013a, b, 2014a, b; Filatova et al. 2008).

For some ratios between equity and debt cost values, the discovered effect occurs at the tax on profit rate existing in Western countries and Russia, which provides

P. Brusov et al., *Ratings*, Contributions to Finance and Accounting,
https://doi.org/10.1007/978-3-030-56243-4_17

practical value to the effect. Its accounting is important when improving tax legislation and can change the dividend policy of a company, the accounting of which is extremely important in rating when assessing the creditworthiness of issuers.

The validity of the dividend policy of the company, its assessment, is determined by comparing the amount of paid dividends with their economically sound value, which is the cost of equity of the company. Calculating the latter is rather a difficult task. The BFO theory allows us to make correct estimates of the cost of the company's equity and thereby compare the amount of dividends paid by the company with their economically sound value; this allows us to assess the validity of the dividend policy, which is undoubtedly associated with the issuer's creditworthiness.

In this chapter, a complete study of the effect found in the framework of the Brusov–Filatova–Orekhova theory (Brusov and Filatova 2011; Brusov et al. 2011a, b, c, 2012a, b, 2013a, b, 2014a, b; Filatova et al. 2008; Brusova 2011) is carried out. It is shown that the absence of effect for some ratios between the parameters is due to the fact that T^* in these cases exceeds 100% (the income tax rate is in the "non-financial" region).

17.1 Introduction

The structure of this chapter is as follows: first, we consider the value of the equity cost k_e in the theory of Modigliani and Miller, its dependence on leverage L, and tax on profit rate T to show that in thih s perpetuity limit, the equity cost k_e is always growing with leverage (for any tax on profit rate T).

Then, we consider the equity cost k_e within the modern Brusov–Filatova–Orekhova theory and show that for companies of arbitrary age, a qualitatively new effect takes place: decrease of the equity cost with the leverage. The effect takes place at tax on profit rate T, exceeding some critical value T^*.

Next, we make a complete study of the discovered effect: we investigate the dependence of T^* on company's age n, on equity cost of financially independent company k_0, and on debt cost k_d as well as on ratio of these parameters.

We separately consider a 1-year company and analyze its special feature in connection with the discussed effect. An explanation of the absence of this effect for such companies will be given. In conclusion, the importance of the discovered effect in various areas, including improving tax legislation and dividend policies of companies, as well as the practical value of the effect is discussed.

17.1.1 Equity Cost in the Modigliani–Miller Theory

For weighted average cost of capital WACC in the Modigliani–Miller theory, the following expression has been obtained (Modigliani and Miller 1958, 1963, 1966):

$$\text{WACC} = k_0(1 - w_d T). \tag{17.1}$$

Dependence of WACC on financial leverage $L = D/S$ is described by the formula

$$\text{WACC} = k_0(1 - LT/(1 + L)) \ . \tag{17.2}$$

In accordance with the definition of the weighted average cost of capital taking into account the tax shield, one has

$$\text{WACC} = k_0 w_e + k_d w_d(1 - T). \tag{17.3}$$

Equating (Eqs. 17.1–17.3), we get

$$k_0(1 - w_d T) = k_0 w_e + k_d w_d(1 - T). \tag{17.4}$$

From where, for equity cost, one has

$$k_e = k_0 + L(1 - T)(k_0 - k_d). \tag{17.5}$$

Note that formula (Eq. 17.5) is different from the corresponding formula without tax only by multiplier $(1 - T)$ in terms of premium for risk. As the multiplier is less than unit, the appearance of corporate tax on profit leads to the fact that equity cost increases with leverage slower than in the case of tax absence.

Analysis of formulas (Eqs. 17.1 and 17.5) leads to the following conclusions.

17.1.1.1 With the Increase of Financial Leverage

1. Value of the company is increased.
2. Weighted average cost of capital is decreased from k_0 (at $L = 0$) up to $k_0(1 - T)$ (at $L = \infty$, when the company is funded solely by borrowing or its equity capital is negligible).
3. Equity cost is increased linearly from k_0 (at $L = 0$) up to ∞ (at $L = \infty$).

Let us analyze now the influence of taxes on equity cost in the Modigliani–Miller theory by studying the dependence of equity cost on tax on profit rate.

For this, we will analyze the formula (Fig. 17.1)

$$k_e = k_0 + L(1 - T)(k_0 - k_d). \tag{17.6}$$

It is seen that dependence is linear: equity cost is decreased linearly with tax on profit rate. The module of negative tilt angle tangent $tg\gamma = -L(k_0 - k_d)$ is increased with leverage, and besides, all dependences at different leverage levels L_i, coming from different points $k_e = k_0 + L_i(k_0 - k_d)$ at $T = 0$ and at $T = 1$, are converged at the point k_0 (Fig. 17.2).

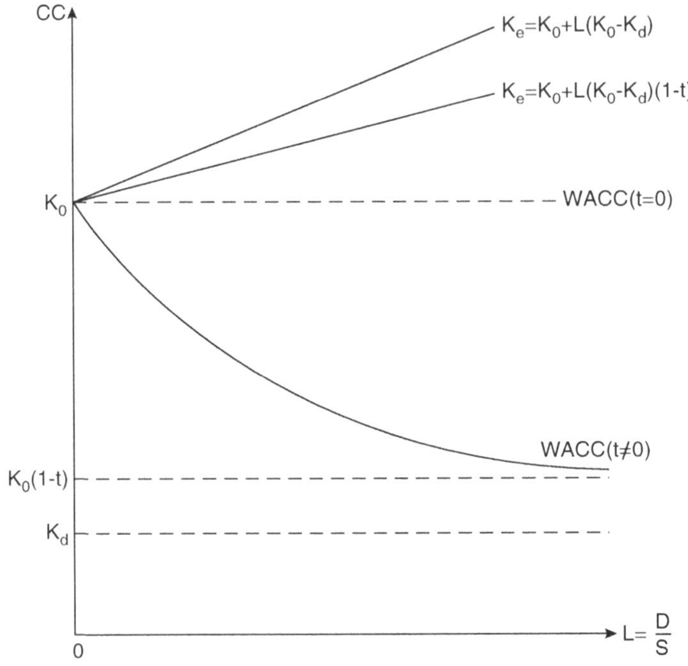

Fig. 17.1 Dependence of equity cost, debt cost, and WACC on leverage without taxes ($t = 0$) and with taxes ($t \neq 0$)

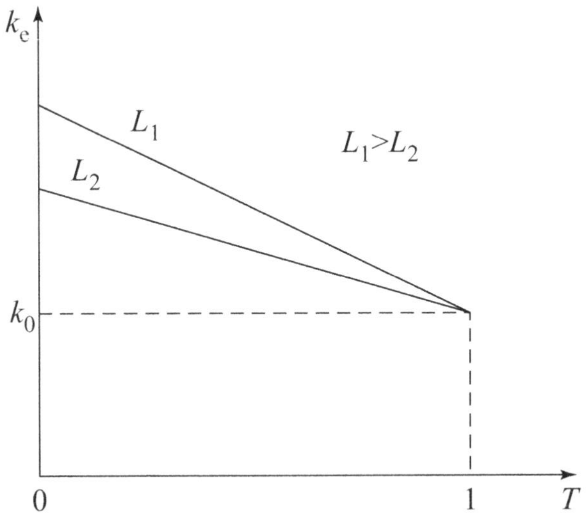

Fig. 17.2 Dependence of equity cost on tax on profit rate T at different leverage levels L_i

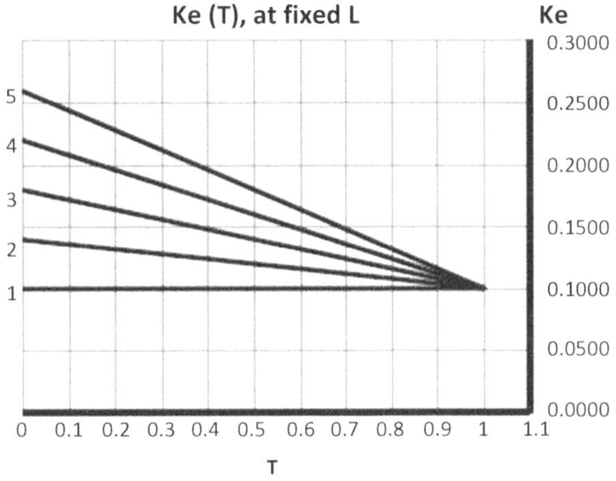

Fig. 17.3 Dependence of equity cost on tax on profit rate T at different leverage levels L_i for the case $k_0 = 10\%$; $k_d = 8\%$: (1) $L = 0$; (2) $L = 2$; (3) $L = 4$; (4) $L = 6$; and (5) $L = 8$

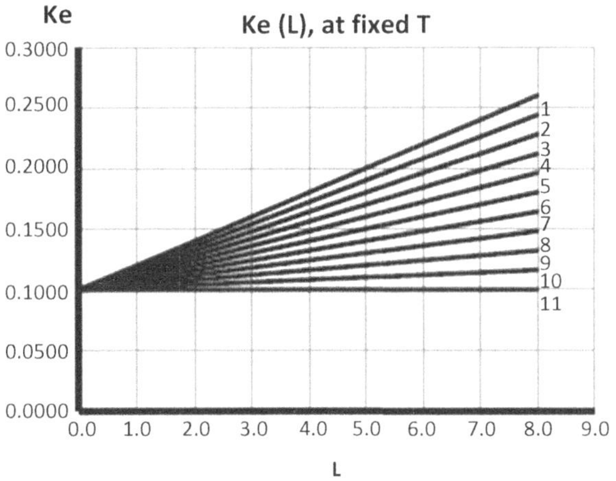

Fig. 17.4 Dependence of equity cost on leverage L at different tax on profit rates T for the case $k_0 = 10\%$; $k_d = 8\%$: (1) $T = 0$; (2) $T = 0.1$; (3) $T = 0.2$; (4) $T = 0.3$; (5) $T = 0.4$; (6) $T = 0.5$; (7) $T = 0.6$; (8) $T = 0.7$; (9, 10) $T = 0.9$; and (11) $T = 1$

This means that the difference in equity cost at different leverage levels L_i is decreased with tax on profit rate T, disappearing at $T = 1$.

Let us illustrate these general considerations by the example $k_0 = 10\ \%$; $k_d = 8\ \%$ (Figs. 17.3, 17.4, and 17.5).

From Fig. 17.2, it is seen that dependence is linear: equity cost is decreased linearly with tax on profit rate. The module of negative tilt angle tangent $tg\gamma = -L(k_0 - k_d)$ is increased with leverage, and besides, all dependences at different leverage levels L_i, coming from different points $k_e = k_0 + L_i(k_0 - k_d)$ at $T = 0$ and at $T = 1$, are converged at the point k_0 (Fig. 17.2).

From Fig. 17.4, it is seen that equity cost is increased linearly from k_0 (at $L = 0$) up to ∞ (at $L = \infty$), and besides, tilt angle tangent is decreased with tax on profit rate T, becoming zero at $T = 100\%$.

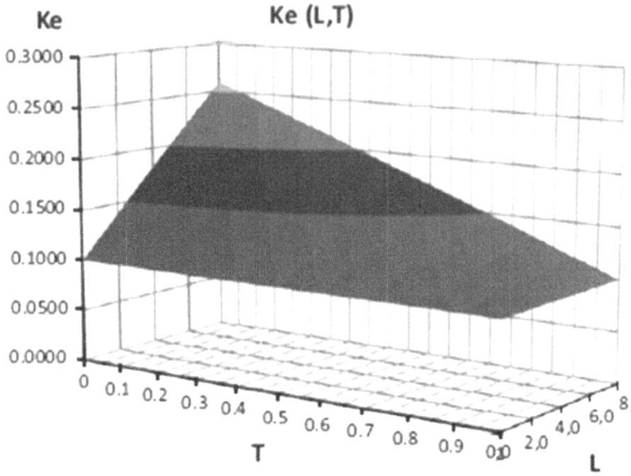

Fig. 17.5 Dependence of equity cost on leverage L and on tax on profit rate T for the case $k_0 = 10\ \%$; $k_d = 8\%$

In other words, with increase of tax on profit rate T, dependence of equity cost on leverage L becomes smaller, disappearing at $T = 100\%$, i.e., within perpetuity Modigliani–Miller theory, any anomaly effect, announced in the title of this chapter, is absent.

In conclusion, here is a three-dimensional graph of dependence of equity cost on leverage L and on tax on profit rate T for the case $k_0 = 10\ \%$; $k_d = 8\%$.

17.1.2 Equity Cost Capital Within Brusov–Filatova–Orekhova Theory

The general solution of the problem of weighted average cost of capital and the equity cost for the company of arbitrary age or with finite lifetime has been received for the first time by Brusov–Filatova–Orekhova (Brusov and Filatova 2011; Brusov et al. 2011a, b, c, 2012a, b, 2013a, b, 2014a, b; Filatova et al. 2008; Brusova 2011). They have gotten (now already famous) formula for WACC (BFO formula)

$$\frac{1-(1+\mathrm{WACC})^{-n}}{\mathrm{WACC}} = \frac{1-(1+k_0)^{-n}}{k_0[1-\omega_d T(1-(1+k_d)^{-n})]}. \qquad (17.7)$$

At $n = 1$, one gets Myers formula (Myers 2001) for 1-year company, which represents the particular case of Brusov–Filatova–Orekhova formula (Eq. 17.7)

$$\mathrm{WACC} = k_0 - \frac{1+k_0}{1+k_d} k_d w_d T. \qquad (17.8)$$

We will study the dependence of equity cost k_e on tax on profit rate T and on leverage level L by three methods:

1. We will study the dependence of equity cost k_e on tax on profit rate T at fixed leverage level L for different lifetime (age) n of the company.
2. We will study the dependence of equity cost k_e on leverage level L at fixed tax on profit rate T for different lifetime (age) n of the company.
3. We will explore the influence of simultaneous change of leverage level L and tax on profit rate T on equity cost k_e for different lifetime (age) n of the company. In this case, the results will be presented as 3D graphs.

In these studies, a qualitatively new effect has been discovered, and it is visible in each of the applicable types of studies (1–3).

17.1.2.1 Dependence of Equity Cost k_e on Tax on Profit Rate T at Different Fixed Leverage Levels L

Dependence of Equity Cost k_e on Tax on Profit Rate T at Fixed Leverage Level L Below we show three figures (Figs. 17.6, 17.7, and 17.8) of the dependence of equity cost k_e on tax on profit rate T at different fixed leverages L for different sets of parameters n, k_0, k_d.

On the basis of the analysis of the three figures (Figs. 17.6, 17.7, and 17.8) and other data, we come to the following conclusions:

1. All dependences are linear: equity cost decreases linearly with tax on profit rate.
2. The initial values of k_e grow significantly with the level of leverage (the share of debt capital w_d) and exceed k_0.
3. Lines corresponding to the different values of leverage level (the share of debt capital w_d) intersect at one point (at some value of tax on profit rate T^*), depending on parameters n, k_0, k_d (Figs. 17.7 and 17.8).

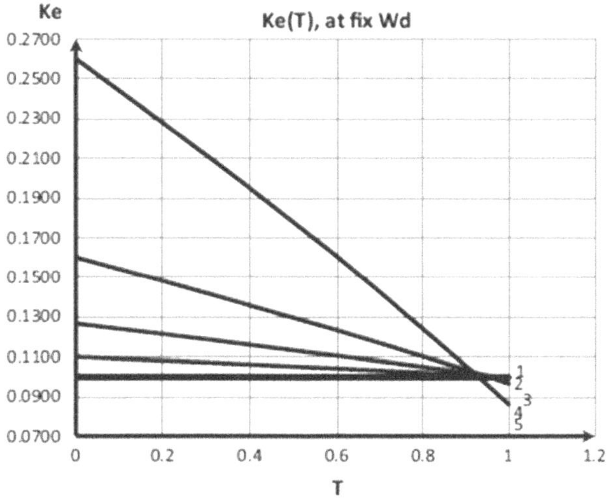

Fig. 17.6 Dependence of equity cost k_e on tax on profit rate T at different fixed leverage levels L ($n = 5$, $k_0 = 10\ \%$, $k_d = 6\%$): (1) $w_d = 0$; (2) $w_d = 0.2$; (3) $w_d = 0.4$; (4) $w_d = 0.6$; and (5) $w_d = 0.8$

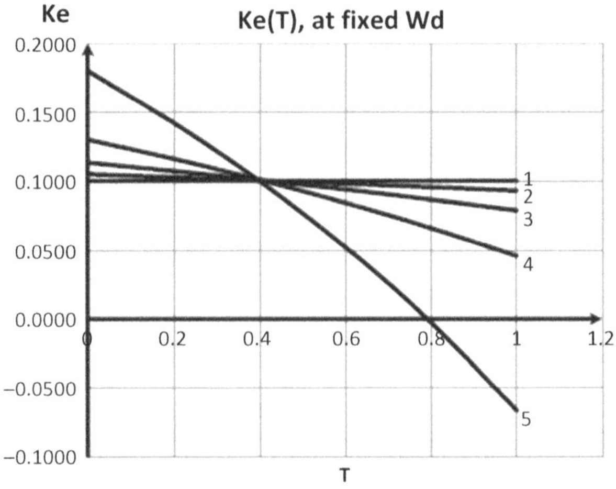

Fig. 17.7 Dependence of equity cost k_e on tax on profit rate T at different fixed leverage levels L ($n = 10$, $k_0 = 10\ \%$, $k_d = 8\%$): (1) $w_d = 0$; (2) $w_d = 0.2$; (3) $w_d = 0.4$; (4) $w_d = 0.6$; and (5) $w_d = 0.8$)

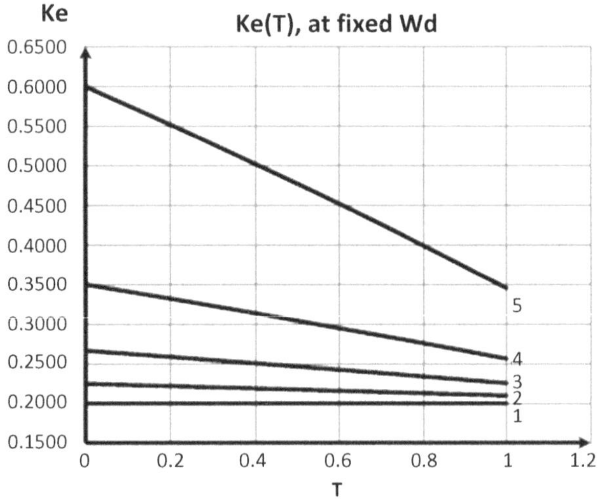

Fig. 17.8 Dependence of equity cost k_e on tax on profit rate T at different fixed leverage levels L ($n = 3$, $k_0 = 20\ \%$, $k_d = 10\%$): (1) $w_d = 0$; (2) $w_d = 0.2$; (3) $w_d = 0.4$; (4) $w_d = 0.6$; and (5) $w_d = 0.8$)

At fixed tax on profit rate $T > T^*$ increasing of leverage level corresponds to moving from line 1–2,3, 4, and 5, i.e., decreasing k_e; this means the discovery of ***qualitatively new effect in corporative finance: decreasing of equity cost*** k_e ***with leverage.*** In a more obvious form, it will manifest itself in studies depending on equity cost of the company on the leverage level, carried out by us below.

At some values of parameters n, k_0, k_d, the intersection of all lines at one point could not happen at any tax on profit rate $0 < T \leq 100\%$. From Fig. 17.9, it is seen that with a large gap between k_0 and k_d, the intersection of the lines lies in the nonexistent ("non-financial") region $T^* > 100\%$ (for data of Fig. 17.9 $T^* \approx 162\%$).

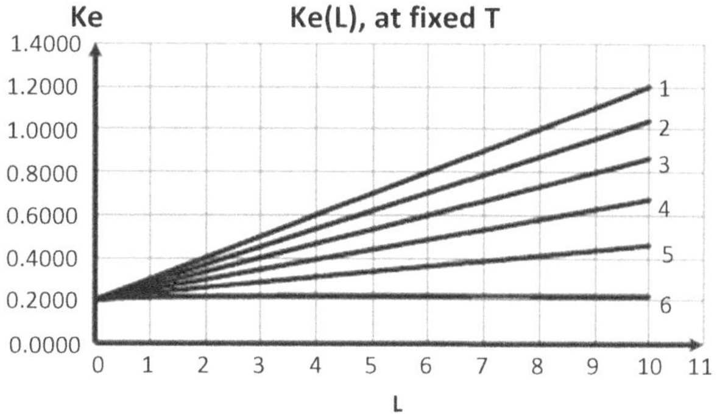

Fig. 17.9 Dependence of equity cost k_e on leverage level L at different tax on profit rate T ($n = 7$, $k_0 = 20\ \%$, $k_d = 10\%$): (1) $T = 0$; (2) $T = 0.2$; (3) $T = 0.4$; (4) $T = 0.6$; (5) $T = 0.8$; and (6) $T = 1$

17.1.2.2 Dependence of Equity Cost k_e on Leverage Level L (the Share of Debt Capital w_d) at Different Fixed Tax on Profit Rate T

Below we show the results of calculation of dependence of equity cost k_e on leverage level L (the share of debt capital w_d) in Excel at different fixed tax on profit rate T in the form of a table, and in the form of a graph for the case $n = 7$, $k_0 = 20\ \%$, $k_d = 10\%$, as well as in the form of a graph for the case $n = 5$, $k_0 = 10\ \%$, $k_d = 8\%$ (Table 17.1).

From Fig. 17.9, it is seen that dependence of equity cost k_e on leverage level L with a good accuracy is linear. The tilt angle decreases with tax on profit rate like the perpetuity case.

However, for the companies of arbitrary age along with the behavior $k_e(L)$, similar to the perpetuity behavior of the Modigliani–Miller case (Fig. 17.9), for some sets of parameters n, k_0, k_d, there is an otherwise behavior $k_e(L)$.

From Fig. 17.10, it is seen that starting from some values of tax on profit rate T^* (in this case, from $T^* = 40\%$, although at other sets of parameters n, k_0, k_d critical values of tax on profit rate T^* could be lower) there is no rise in the equity cost of the company with leverage, but decreases. Once again, the presence or the absence of such an effect depends on a set of parameters k_0, k_d, n.

This effect has been observed above in dependence of equity cost k_e on tax on profit rate T at fixed leverage level, but it is more clearly visible, depending on value of equity cost of the company on the leverage for various values of tax on profit rate T.

Note that this is a new effect, which may take place only for the companies of arbitrary finite age and which is not observed in perpetuity Modigliani–Miller limit.

It is easy to see from the Modigliani–Miller formula (17.5)

$$k_e = k_0 + L(1 - T)(k_0 - k_d),$$

that at $T = 1(100\%)$ equity cost k_e does not change with leverage: $k_e = k_0$, i.e., there is no decrease of k_e with leverage at any k_0 and k_d.

Table 17.1 Dependence of equity cost k_e on leverage level L at different fixed tax on profit rates T for the case $n = 7$, $k_0 = 20\ \%$, $k_d = 10\%$

T/L	0.0	1.0	2.0	3.0	4.0	5.0	6.0	7.0	17.0	9.0	10
0	0.2000	0.3000	0.4000	0.5000	0.6000	0.7000	0.8000	0.9000	1.0000	1.1000	1.2000
0.2	0.2000	0.2842	0.3682	0.4522	0.5362	0.6202	0.7042	0.7874	0.8713	0.9551	1.0389
0.4	0.2000	0.2677	0.3344	0.4008	0.4672	0.5335	0.5998	0.6661	0.7323	0.7986	0.8649
0.6	0.2000	0.2504	0.2984	0.3457	0.3928	0.4397	0.4865	0.5334	0.5802	0.6265	0.6731
0.8	0.2000	0.2323	0.2601	0.2861	0.3117	0.3369	0.3619	0.3867	0.4116	0.4364	0.4612
1	0.2000	0.2132	0.2185	0.2210	0.2223	0.2229	0.2231	0.2233	0.2231	0.2228	0.2224

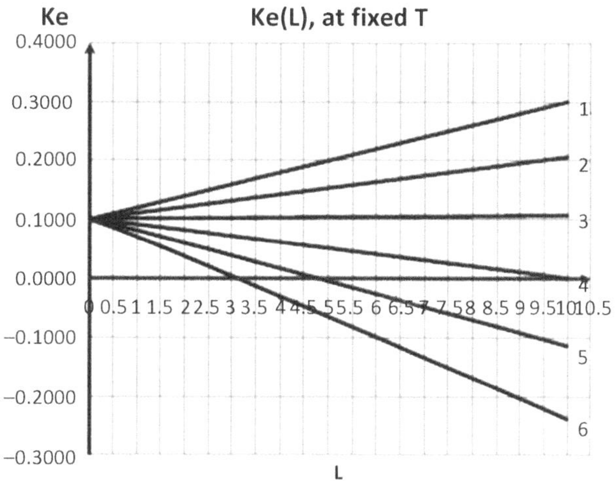

Fig. 17.10 Dependence of equity cost k_e on leverage level L at different tax on profit rate T ($n = 5$, $k_0 = 10\ \%$, $k_d = 8\%$): (1) $T = 0$; (2) $T = 0.2$; (3) $T = 0.4$; (4) $T = 0.6$; (5) $T = 0.8$; and (6) $T = 1$

Table 17.2 The dependence of the critical value of tax on profit rate T^* on the age of the company under variation of the difference between k_0 and k_d

$k_e(t)/n$	2	3	5	7	10	15	20	25
$k_d = 6\%$, $k_0 = 8\%$	0.9575	0.6600	0.5200	0.4800	0.4640	0.4710	0.4903	0.5121
$k_d = 6\%$, $k_0 = 10\%$			0.9110	0.8225	0.7650	0.7332	0.7249	0.7260
$k_d = 6\%$, $k_0 = 12\%$					0.9800	0.9040	0.8693	0.8504
$k_d = 6\%$, $k_0 = 14\%$							0.9671	0.9324
$k_d = 6\%$, $k_0 = 16\%$								
$k_d = 6\%$, $k_0 = 20\%$								
$k_d = 6\%$, $k_0 = 24\%$								

17.1.3 Dependence of the Critical Value of Tax on Profit Rate T^* on Parameters N, k_0, k_d of the Company

In this section, we study the dependence of the critical value of tax on profit rate T^* on parameters n, k_0, k_d of the company. First, we study the dependence of the critical value of tax on profit rate T^* on the company age under variation of the difference between k_0 and k_d.

The results of calculations are shown in Table 17.2; empty cells mean that the critical value of tax on profit rate $T^* > 100\%$, i.e., we are in "non-financial" region.

The conclusions from Fig. 17.11 are as follows:

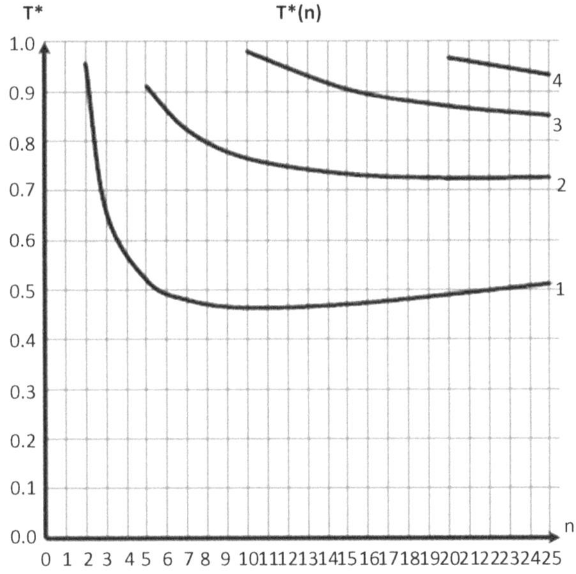

Fig. 17.11 The dependence of the critical value of tax on profit rate T^* on the age of the company under variation of the difference between k_0 and k_d ($\Delta k = k_0 - k_d = 2\ \%$; $4\ \%$; $6\ \%$; 8%): (1) $k_d = 6\%$, $k_0 = 8\%$; (2) $k_d = 6\%$, $k_0 = 10\%$; (3) $k_d = 6\%$, $k_0 = 12\%$; and (4) $k_d = 6\%$, $k_0 = 14\%$

1. It is seen that the critical value of tax on profit rate T^* increases with the difference $\Delta k = k_0 - k_d$; therefore, a small difference between the value of equity cost (at $L = 0$) k_0 of the company and the credit rate k_d favors the existence of a new effect.
2. The critical value of tax on profit rate T^* decreases monotonically with the age of the company (only for 10 years in the case of $\Delta k = k_0 - k_d = 2\%$ it has a minimum). Therefore, the probability of the anomaly effect is higher for "adult" companies.
3. Recapitulating 1 and 2, one can note that a small difference between the value of equity cost (at $L = 0$) k_0 of the company and the credit rate k_d as well as old enough age of the company favors the existence of a new effect.

We calculated as well T^* at different values of k_0 and k_d at constant difference between them $\Delta k = k_0 - k_d = 2\%$. The data are shown in Table 17.3 (Fig. 17.12).

The conclusions in the current case are as follows:

1. All curves are convex and the critical value of tax on profit rate T^* reaches minimum, the value of which decreases with k_0.

Min $T^* = 22.2\%$ at $k_0 = 24\%$, min $T^* = 24.35\%$ at $k_0 = 20\%$, min $T^* = 217.1\%$ at $k_0 = 16\%$, min $T^* = 30.43\%$ at $k_0 = 14\%$, min $T^* = 33.92\%$ at $k_0 = 12\%$, min $T^* = 317.92\%$ at $k_0 = 10\%$, min $T^* = 46.4\%$ at $k_0 = 8\%$. Therefore, the higher value of k_0 and the higher value of k_d at constant difference between them $\Delta k = k_0 - k_d =$ const favor the existence of a new effect.

Table 17.3 The dependence of the critical value of tax on profit rate T^* on the age of the company under different values of k_0 and k_d at constant difference between them $\Delta k = k_0 - k_d = 2\%$

$k_e(t)/n$	2	3	5	7	10	15	20	25
$k_d = 6\%$, $k_0 = 8\%$	0.9575	0.6600	0.5200	0.4800	0.4640	0.4710	0.4903	0.5121
$k_d = 8\%$, $k_0 = 10\%$	0.7313	0.5125	0.4140	0.3905	0.3892	0.4138	0.4453	0.4803
$k_d = 10\%$, $k_0 = 12\%$	0.6000	0.4280	0.3510	0.3392	0.3467	0.3840	0.4285	0.4733
$k_d = 12\%$, $k_0 = 14\%$	0.5125	0.3687	0.3110	0.3043	0.3218	0.3697	0.4239	0.4788
$k_d = 14\%$, $k_0 = 16\%$	0.4437	0.3266	0.2810	0.2821	0.3043	0.3636	0.4277	0.4904
$k_d = 18\%$, $k_0 = 20\%$	0.3625	0.2710	0.2435	0.2549	0.2895	0.3677	0.4468	0.5221
$k_d = 22\%$, $k_0 = 24\%$	0.3100	0.2370	0.2220	0.2400	0.2875	0.3818	0.4759	0.5588

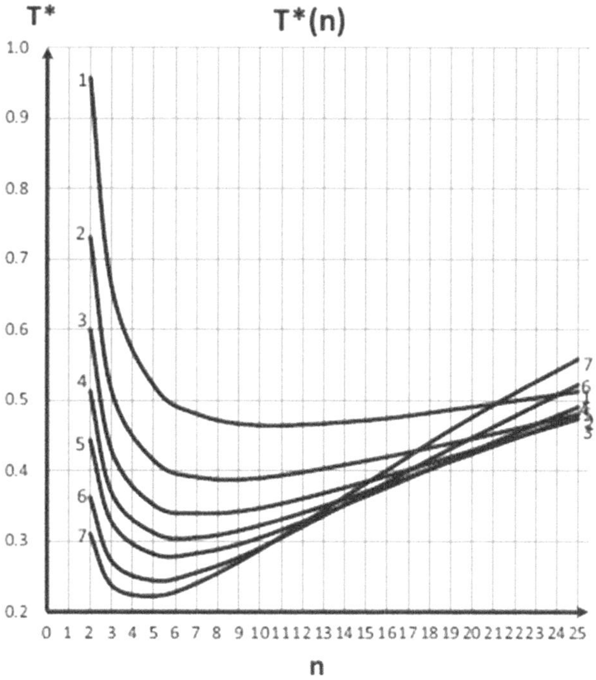

Fig. 17.12 The dependence of the critical value of tax on profit rate T^* on the age of the company under different values of k_0 and k_d at constant difference between them $\Delta k = k_0 - k_d = 2\%$: (1) $k_0 = 8\%$; (2) $k_0 = 10\%$; (3) $k_0 = 12\%$; (4) $k_0 = 14\%$; (5) $k_0 = 16\%$; (6) $k_0 = 20\%$; and (7) $k_0 = 24\%$

2. The critical value of tax on profit rate T^* reaches minimum at company age, decreasing with k_0: $n = 4.5$ years at $k_0 = 24\%$, $n = 5.5$ years at $k_0 = 16\%$, $n = 6.5$ years at $k_0 = 12\%$, and $n = 10.5$ years at $k_0 = 8\%$.
3. Thus, a parallel shift of rates k_0 and k_d favors a new effect, while the company's age, favorable for a new effect, decreases with k_0.

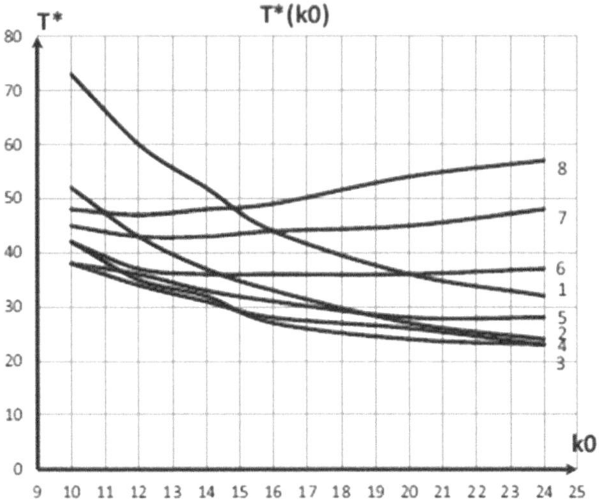

Fig. 17.13 The dependence of the critical value of tax on profit rate T^* on k_0 at constant difference between k_0 and k_d $\Delta k = k_0 - k_d = 2\%$: (1) $n = 2$; (2) $n = 3$; (3) $n = 5$; (4) $n = 7$; (5) $n = 10$; (6) $n = 15$; (7) $n = 20$; and (8) $n = 25$

Now let us investigate the dependence of critical value of tax on profit rate T^* on k_0 for the second considerable case (at constant difference between k_0 and k_d $\Delta k = k_0 - k_d = 2\%$).

For this, we consider Fig. 17.13.

For companies of the age up to 10–15 years, the decrease of critical value of tax on profit rate T^* with k_0 is observed. On further increase of company's age, one observes in dependence of T^* on k_0 a smooth transition to a low growing function T^* on k_0.

So, for companies of age up to 10–15 years, monotonic growth of k_0 favors a new effect, while for companies with bigger age rates of order $k_0 \approx 12$–15% favor a new effect.

17.1.4 Practical Value of Effect

What is the practical value of effect? Does it exist in real life or its discovery has a purely theoretical interest?

Because a new effect takes place at tax on profit rate, which exceeds some value T^*, it is necessary to compare this value with real tax on profit rates established in the different countries.

The biggest tax on profit rate for corporation is in the USA—39.2%. In Japan, it exceeds a little bit, 38%. In France, tax on profit rate varies from 33.3% for small and medium-sized companies, up to 36% for large companies. In England, tax on profit rate is in the range of 21–28%. In the Russian Federation, tax on profit rate amounts to 20%.

In the examples considered by us, the value of T^* strongly depends on the ratio between k_0, k_d, n and reaches a minimal value of 22.2%, and it is quite likely for even lower values of T^* with other ratios of values k_0, k_d, n.

In this way, we come to the conclusion that at some ratios of values of equity cost, debt cost, and company's age k_0, k_d, n, the effect discovered by us takes place at tax on profit rate established in most developed countries, which provides the practical value of the effect.

Taking it into account is important in improving tax legislation and may change dividend policies of the company.

Opening the effect expands our view of the rules of the game in the economy.

If prior to that it was widely known that with the rising of leverage the equity cost is always growing, which is associated with the decrease of financial sustainability of the companies, with an increase in the share of borrowing, then the shareholders require a higher rate of return on the share.

But now it becomes clear that this is not always the case, and the dependence of equity cost on leverage depends on the ratio between the parameters k_0, k_d, n and, ultimately, on the tax on profit rate.

This effect has never been known; therefore, it was not taken into account by tax legislation, but opportunities here are tremendous.

The effect is also important for the development of the dividend policy of the company.

It turns out that the rule taken by the shareholders since time immemorial—to require higher rate of return on the share with an increase of the portion of debt capital—now does not always work. This will allow the company management to hold a more realistic dividend policy, limiting appetites of shareholders by economically founded value of dividends.

17.1.5 Equity Cost of 1-Year Company

The dependence of the equity cost on tax on profit rate T for 1-year company has some features, considered below. Interest in the 1-year companies is associated also with the fact that a great number of companies, both in developed countries and in developing ones, are becoming bankrupt or no longer exist in the first year or two after the creation.

For 1-year company, the Brusov–Filatova–Orekhova (BFO) equation for weighted average cost of capital is simplified and can be expressed in apparent form (Brusov and Filatova 2011; Brusov et al. 2011a, b, c, 2012a, b, 2013a, b, 2014a, b; Filatova et al. 2008) (Eq. 17.8)

$$\mathrm{WACC} = k_0 - \frac{1 + k_0}{1 + k_d} k_d w_d T.$$

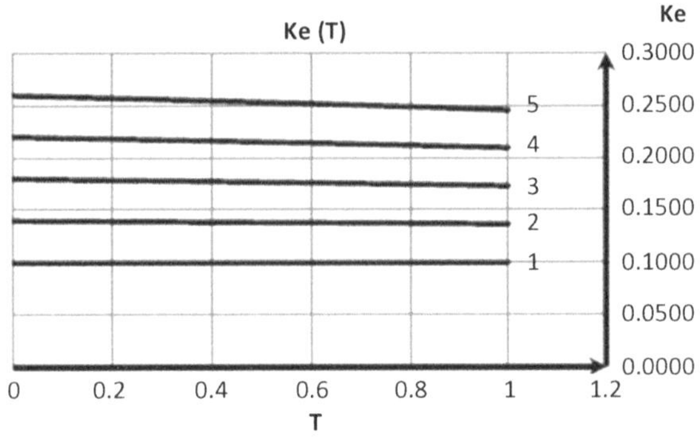

Fig. 17.14 Dependence of equity cost k_e of the company on tax on profit rate T at fixed leverage level for 1-year company ($n = 1$, $k_0 = 10\ \%$, $k_d = 8\%$)

This formula has been obtained for the first time by Myers (2001) and represents the particular case of the Brusov–Filatova–Orekhova (BFO) equation at $n = 1$.

By definition, for weighted average cost of capital taking into account "the tax shield," one has

$$\text{WACC} = k_e w_e + k_d w_d (1 - T). \tag{17.9}$$

Substituting here the expression for WACC of 1-year company, let us find the expression for equity cost k_e of the company

$$k_e = \frac{\text{WACC} - w_d k_d (1 - T)}{w_e} = k_0 + L(k_0 - k_d)\left(1 - T\frac{k_d}{1 + k_d}\right). \tag{17.10}$$

It is seen that equity cost k_e decreases linearly with tax on profit rate. The module of negative tilt angle tangent is equal to

$$tg\alpha = L(k_0 - k_d)\frac{k_d}{1 + k_d} \tag{17.11}$$

However, the calculation for the case $k_0 = 10\ \%$, $k_d = 8\%$ gives practically independence of equity cost k_e of the company's tax on profit rate T at fixed leverage level (Fig. 17.14).

This is due to the low value of coefficient $(k_0 - k_d)\frac{k_d}{1+k_d}$, which in our case is equal to 0.001417. Therefore, the decrease becomes visible only at significantly higher leverage (Fig. 17.14).

Note that such a weak dependence (virtually independence) of equity cost k_e of the company on tax on profit rate T at fixed leverage level takes place for 1-year company only.

Already for 2-year company with the same parameters, dependence of equity cost k_e of the company on tax on profit rate T at fixed leverage level becomes significant.

Below we give an example for 2-year company with other parameters $n = 2$, $k_0 = 24\ \%$, $k_d = 22\%$ (Fig. 17.15).

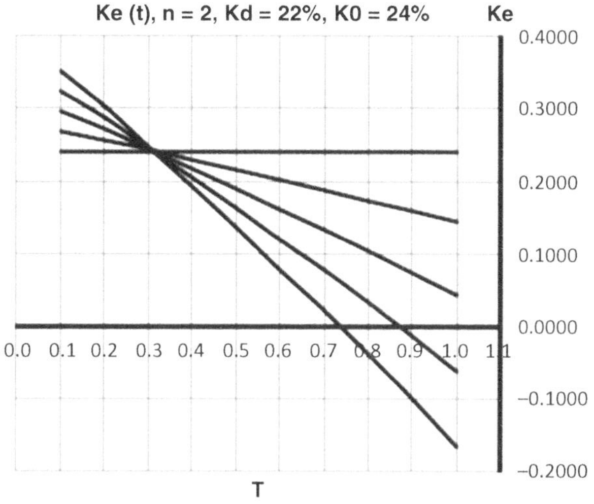

Fig. 17.15 Dependence of equity cost k_e of the company on tax on profit rate T at fixed leverage level for 2-year company ($n = 2$, $k_0 = 24\ \%$, $k_d = 22\%$)

17.2 Finding a Formula for T^*

In the case of 1-year company, it is easy to find a formula for T^*.

Putting in (Eq. 17.10) $k_e = k_0$, one gets

$$k_0 = k_0 + L(k_0 - k_d)\left(1 - T\frac{k_d}{1 + k_d}\right) \tag{17.12}$$

From where

$$T^* = \frac{1 + k_d}{k_d} \tag{17.13}$$

It is seen that T^* does not depend on L, i.e., all the direct lines, corresponding to different L, intersect at a single point. From the data for the older companies ($n > 1$ year), it follows that similar situation takes place for them as well; however, it becomes more difficult to prove this fact and, in the case $n > 3$, practically impossible.

Note that Eq. (17.13) allows us to evaluate the value of T^*, which depends now on credit rate only and is equal to:

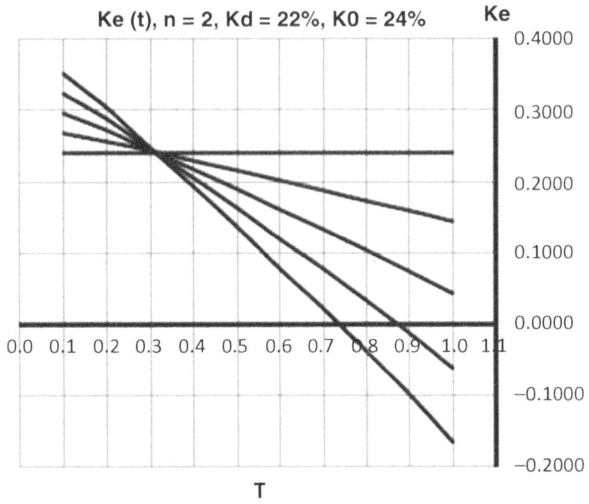

Fig. 17.16 Dependence of equity cost k_e of the company on tax on profit rate T and leverage level L ($n = 1$, $k_0 = 10\ \%$, $k_d = 8\%$)

for $k_d = 8\%$ $T^* = 13.5$
for $k_d = 10\%$ $T^* = 11$
for $k_d = 15\%$ $T^* = 7.7$
for $k_d = 25\%$ $T^* = 5$

It is clear that for all (reasonable and unreasonable) credit rate values, tax on profit rate T^* is situated in "non-financial" region (which exceeds 1 (100%)), which is the cause of the absence of effect.

Analysis of formula (Eq. 17.13) shows that at very large credit rate values T, T^* tends to be 1(100%), always remaining greater than 1. This means that the effect found by us is absent for 1-year company.

Let us show the 3D picture for dependence of equity cost k_e of the company on tax on profit rate T and leverage level L for 1-year company (Fig. 17.16).

It is seen that all dependences of equity cost k_e of the company on tax on profit rate T and leverage level L are linear, and abnormal effect for 1-year company (as well as for perpetuity one) is absent.

17.3 Conclusions

Taking into account the company's dividend policy is extremely important in rating when assessing the creditworthiness of issuers. Qualitatively new effect in corporative finance, which could radically change the approach to the formation of the company's dividend policy, is discovered: decrease of equity cost k_e with leverage level L. This effect, which is absent in perpetuity Modigliani–Miller limit

(Modigliani and Miller 1958, 1963, 1966), takes place on account of finite age of the company at tax on profit rate, which exceeds some value T^* (Brusov and Filatova 2011; Brusov et al. 2011a, b, c, 2012a, b, 2013a, b, 2014a, b; Filatova et al. 2008).

For some ratios between equity and debt cost values, the discovered effect occurs at the tax on profit rate existing in Western countries and Russia, which provides practical value to the effect. Its accounting is important when improving tax legislation and can change the dividend policy of a company, the accounting of which is extremely important in rating when assessing the creditworthiness of issuers.

The validity of the dividend policy of the company, its assessment, is determined by comparing the amount of paid dividends with their economically sound value, which is the cost of equity of the company. Calculating the latter is rather a difficult task. The BFO theory allows us to make correct estimates of the cost of the company's equity and thereby compare the amount of dividends paid by the company with their economically sound value; this allows us to assess the validity of the dividend policy, which is undoubtedly associated with the issuer's creditworthiness.

In this chapter, the complete and detailed investigation of the discussed effect, discovered within the Brusov–Filatova–Orekhova (BFO) theory, has been done (Brusov and Filatova 2011; Brusov et al. 2011a, b, c, 2012a, b, 2013a, b, 2014a, b; Filatova et al. 2008; Brusov 2018a, b; Brusov et al. 2015, 2018a, b, c, d, e, f, g, 2019, 2020; Filatova et al. 2018a, b). It has been shown that the absence of the effect at some particular set of parameters is connected to the fact that in these cases, T^* exceeds 100% (tax on profit rate is situated in a "non-financial" region).

In future, the papers and monographs will be devoted to discussion of discovered abnormal effect, but it is already clear now that we will have to abandon some of the established views in corporative finance, as well as change some approaches in rating methodologies.

References

Brusov PN, Filatova TV (2011) From Modigliani–Miller to general theory of capital cost and capital structure of the company. Finance Credit 435:2–8

Brusov P, Filatova T, Orehova N, Brusova A (2011a) Weighted average cost of capital in the theory of Modigliani–Miller, modified for a finite life–time company. Appl Financ Econ 21(11):815–824

Brusov P, Filatova T, Orehova N et al (2011b) From Modigliani–Miller to general theory of capital cost and capital structure of the company. Res J Econ Bus ICT 2:16–21

Brusov P, Filatova T, Orehova N et al (2011c) Influence of debt financing on the effectiveness of the investment project within the Modigliani–Miller theory. Res J Econ Bus ICT (UK) 2:11–15

Brusov P, Filatova T, Eskindarov M, Orehova N (2012a) Influence of debt financing on the effectiveness of the finite duration investment project. Appl Financ Econ 22(13):1043–1052

Brusov P, Filatova T, Eskindarov M, Orehova N (2012b) Hidden global causes of the global financial crisis. J Rev Global Econ 1:106–111

Brusov P, Filatova P, Orekhova N (2013a) Absence of an optimal capital structure in the famous tradeoff theory! J Rev Global Econ 2:94–116

Brusov P, Filatova T, Orehova N (2013b) A qualitatively new effect in corporative finance: abnormal dependence of cost of equity of company on leverage. J Rev Global Econ 2:183–19

Brusov P, Filatova P, Orekhova N (2014a) Mechanism of formation of the company optimal capital structure, different from suggested by trade off theory. Cogent Econ Finance 2:1–13. http://dx.doi.org/ 10.1080/23322039.2014.946150

Brusov P, Filatova T, Orehova N (2014b) Inflation in Brusov—1Filatova—Orekhova theory and in its perpetuity limit—Modiglian—Miller theory. J Rev Global Econ 3:175–185

Brusov P (2018a) Editorial: introduction on special issue on the banking system and financial markets of Russia and other countries: problems and prospects. J Rev Glob Econ 7:i–vi. SCOPUS

Brusov P (2018b) Editorial. J Rev Glob Econ 7:i–v. SCOPUS

Brusov P, Filatova T, Orekhova N, Eskindarov M (2015) Modern corporate finance, investments and taxation. Springer International Publishing, Switzerland, p373. Monograph. SCOPUS. https://www.springer.com/gp/book/9783319147314

Brusov P, Filatova T, Orekhova N, Eskindarov M (2018a) Modern corporate finance, investments, taxation and ratings. Springer Nature Publishing, Switzerland, p 571. Monograph

Brusov PN, Filatova TV, Orekhova NP, Kulik VL (2018b) Rating: New approach. J Rev Glob Econ 7:37–62. SCOPUS. https://doi.org/10.6000/1929-7092.2018.07.05

Brusov PN, Filatova TV, Orekhova NP, Kulik VL (2018c) A "golden age" of the companies: Conditions of its existence. J Rev Glob Econ 7:88–103. SCOPUS. https://doi.org/10.6000/1929-7092.2018.07.07

Brusov PN, Filatova TV, Orekhova NP, Kulik VL (2018d) Rating methodology: New look and new horizons. J Rev Glob Econ 7:63–87. SCOPUS. https://doi.org/10.6000/1929-7092.2018.07.06

Brusov PN, Filatova TV, Orekhova NP, Kulik VL, Weil I (2018e) New meaningful effects in modern capital structure theory. J Rev Glob Econ 7:104–122. SCOPUS. https://doi.org/10.6000/1929-7092.2018.07.08

Brusov P, Filatova T, Orekhova N, Kulik V, Weil I, Brailov A (2018f) The impact of the central bank key rate and commercial banks credit rates on creating and maintaining of a favorable investment climate in the country. J Rev Glob Econ 7:360–376. SCOPUS. https://doi.org/10.6000/1929-7092.2018.07.31

Brusov PN, Filatova TV, Orekhova NP (2018g) Modern corporate finance and investments, monograph. Knorus Publishing House, Moscow, p 517

Brusov PN, Filatova TV, Orekhova NP, Kulik VL, Weil I (2019) Ratings of the investment projects of arbitrary durations: New methodology. J Rev Glob Econ 8:437–448. SCOPUS. https://doi.org/10.6000/1929-7092.2019.08.37

Brusov PN, Filatova TV, Orekhova NP, Kulik VL, Chang S-I, Lin YCG (2020) Modification of the Modigliani–Miller theory for the case of advance payments of tax on profit. J Rev Glob Economics 9:257–268

Filatova T, Orekhova N, Brusova A (2008) Weighted average cost of capital in the theory of Modigliani–Miller, modified for a finite lifetime company. Bull FU 48:68–77

Filatova TV, Brusov PN, Orekhova NP, Kulik VL (2018a) Ratings of the long-term projects: New approach. J Rev Global Econ 7:645–661. SCOPUS. https://doi.org/10.6000/1929-7092.2018.07.59

Filatova TV, Brusov PN, Orekhova NP, Kulik VL (2018b) Ratings of the long-term projects: New approach. J Rev Global Econ 7:645–661. SCOPUS. https://doi.org/10.6000/1929-7092.2018.07.59

Modigliani F, Miller M (1958) The cost of capital, corporate finance, and the theory of investment. Am Econ Rev 48:261–297

Modigliani F, Miller M (1963) Corporate income taxes and the cost of capital: a correction. Am Econ Rev 53:147–175

Modigliani F, Miller M (1966) Some estimates of the cost of capital to the electric utility industry 1954–1957. Am Econ Rev 56:333–391

Chapter 18
The Impact of Taxing and Leverage in Evaluation of Capital Cost, Capitalization of the Company and Issued Ratings

Estimates (according to the BFO methodology) of the impact of the level of borrowed financing and the level of taxation on the effectiveness of investment projects for different values of capital costs can be used in project rating: in rating of the investment projects and investment programs of companies.

Taxation significantly affects the rating of issuers. Estimates (according to the BFO methodology) of the effect of taxation (the value of the corporate income tax rate) on the financial performance of the company and on the effectiveness of investment projects can be used in ratings of the companies and of the investment programs of companies, investment projects, and in the face of changes in the corporate income tax rate also for forecasting and in analysis of country risk.

Estimates (according to the BFO methodology) of the impact of the Central Bank's base rate, credit rates of the commercial bank on the effectiveness of investment projects, andcreation of a favorable investment climate in the country can be used for forecasting, as well as in analysis of country risk, which is taken into account in ratings.

In this chapter, the role of tax shield, taxes, and leverage in the modern theory of corporative finance and, in particular, in rating methodologies is investigated. Modigliani–Miller theory and modern theory of capital cost and capital structure by Brusov–Filatova–Orekhova are considered. It is shown that the equity cost, as well as the weighted average cost of capital, decreases with the tax on profit rate, while capitalization increases. The detailed investigation of the dependence of the weighted average cost of capital WACC and the equity cost k_e on the tax on profit rate at fixed leverage (debt capital fraction w_d) and on the leverage level at fixed tax on profit rate, as well as the dependence of WACC and k_e on company age, is made. We have introduced the concept of tax operation leverage. For companies with finite age, a number of important qualitative effects, which have no analogies for perpetuity companies, are found.

Currently, rating agencies take into account the leverage level L only from the standpoint of assessing financial stability and the risk of bankruptcy. In fact, the

P. Brusov et al., *Ratings*, Contributions to Finance and Accounting,
https://doi.org/10.1007/978-3-030-56243-4_18

leverage level L significantly affects the main financial indicators of the company: the cost of equity k_e and WACC—in other words, the cost of raising capital, which is used (should be used) for discounting of the financial flows in the ratings, as well as for the valuation of the company's capitalization. Failure to take this influence into account when analyzing financial statements leads to incorrect conclusions and incorrect ratings. Simultaneous accounting of the leverage level L and income taxes may be important in rating: in the BFO theory a whole series of qualitative effects of their mutual influence are discovered.

Estimates (according to the BFO methodology) of the impact of the level of borrowed financing and the level of taxation on the effectiveness of investment projects for different values of capital costs can be used in project rating: in rating of the investment projects and investment programs of companies.

Taxation significantly affects the rating of issuers. Estimates (according to the BFO methodology) of the effect of taxation (the value of the corporate income tax rate) on the financial performance of the company and on the effectiveness of investment projects can be used in ratings of the companies and of the investment programs of companies, investment projects, and in the face of changes in the corporate income tax rate also for forecasting and in analysis of country risk.

Estimates (according to the BFO methodology) of the impact of the Central Bank's base rate, credit rates of the commercial bank on the effectiveness of investment projects, creation of a favorable investment climate in the country can be used for forecasting, as well as in analysis of country risk, which is taken into account in ratings.

In this chapter, the role of tax shield, taxes, and leverage in the modern theory of corporative finance and, in particular, in rating methodologies is investigated. Modigliani–Miller theory and modern theory of capital cost and capital structure by Brusov–Filatova–Orekhova are considered. It is shown that the equity cost, as well as the weighted average cost of capital, decreases with the tax on profit rate, while capitalization increases. The detailed investigation of the dependence of the weighted average cost of capital WACC and the equity cost k_e on the tax on profit rate at fixed leverage (debt capital fraction w_d) and on the leverage level at fixed tax on profit rate, as well as the dependence of WACC and k_e on company age, is made. We have introduced the concept of tax operation leverage. For companies with finite age, a number of important qualitative effects, which have no analogies for perpetuity companies, are found.

In Chap. 3, it has been noted that Modigliani and Miller in their paper in 1958 (Modigliani and Miller 1958) have come to conclusions which are fundamentally different from the conclusions of traditional approach. They have shown that, in the framework of assumptions made by them, the ratio between equity and debt capital in the company neither affects the cost of capital nor the company value.

In the context of the study of the impact of tax on profit rate on the cost of capital and on the company capitalization, we make among the numerous assumptions of Modigliani and Miller two of the most important:

1. Corporate taxes and taxes on personal income of investors are absent.
2. All financial flows are perpetuity ones.

Modigliani and Miller subsequently rejected the first of these assumptions and have modified their theory to the case of presence of corporate taxes and taxes on personal income of investors that have significantly altered the conclusions of their theory (Modigliani and Miller 1963, 1966).

The failure of the second assumption has led to the creation of modern theory of capital cost and capital structure by Brusov–Filatova–Orekhova (BFO theory) (Brusov and Filatova 2011; Brusov et al. 2011a, b, c, 2012a, b, 2013a, b, 2014a, b; Filatova et al. 2008; Brusova 2011).

18.1 The Role of Taxes in Modigliani–Miller Theory

We analyze now the role of taxes in the Modigliani–Miller theory, studying the dependence of weighted average cost of capital WACC and the equity cost k_e of tax on profit rate T.

With this purpose, we analyze the following formulas:

1. For weighted average cost of capital WACC, one has

$$\mathrm{WACC} = k_0(1 - w_d T), \tag{18.1}$$
$$\mathrm{WACC} = k_0(1 - LT/(1 + L));$$

2. For the equity cost k_e, one has

$$k_e = k_0 + L(1 - T)(k_0 - k_d). \tag{18.2}$$

Both dependences are linear: both costs of capital decrease linearly with the increase of tax on profit rate T.

For dependence of weighted average cost of capital WACC on tax on profit rate T, negative tangent of tilt angle in $tg\beta = -k_0L/(1 + L)$ is growing in the module with the increase of the leverage level, L, achieving maximum, equal to k_0 at an infinite leverage level $L = \infty$ (share of equity capital is insignificantly small compared with the fraction of debt funds) (Fig. 18.1).

Let us give a few examples:

1. In accordance with expression $tg\beta = -k_0L/(1 + L)$, one gets that at $k_0 = 10\%$ and $L = 1$, i.e., $D = S$, an increase of tax on profit rate T on 10% leads to a decrease of weighted average cost of capital WACC on 0.5%.
2. This dependence of weighted average cost of capital WACC on tax on profit rate T will be even more significant at a higher leverage level L and higher value k_0.

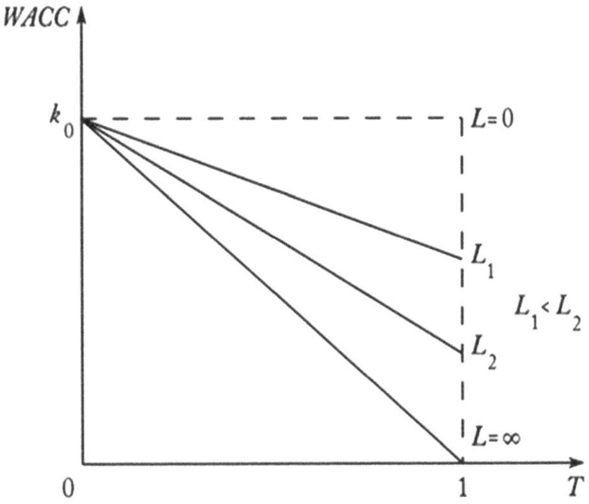

Fig. 18.1 The dependence of weighted average cost of capital WACC on tax on profit rate T at different fixed leverage levels L

For example, at $k_0 = 20\%$ and $L = 2$, the increase in T on 10% leads to a decrease in WACC on 1.33%.

For dependence of the equity cost k_e on tax on profit rate T (from the analysis of formula $k_e = k_0 + L(1 - T)(k_0 - k_d)$), it is seen that negative tangent of tilt angle $tg\gamma = -L(k_0 - k_d)$ also increases in the module with the increase of the leverage level; in this connection all dependences at the different leverage levels L_i, based on the different points $k_e = k_0 + L_i(k_0 - k_d)$ when $T = 0$, at $T = 1$ converge at the point k_0.

1. In accordance with the formula $tg\gamma = -L(k_0 - k_d)$, we get that when $k_0 - k_d = 6\%$ and $L = 1$, i.e., $D = S$, the increase of tax on profit rate T on 10% leads to a reduction in the equity capital cost k_e on 0.6%.
2. This dependence of the equity cost k_e on tax on profit rate T will be even more significant at a higher leverage level L and higher value $k_0 - k_d$. For example, at $k_0 - k_d = 10\%$ and $L = 2$, the increase in T on 10% leads to a decrease in k_e on 2%.

It should be noted that with the increase of tax on profit rate T, the difference in the equity cost k_e at various levels of leverage decreases, disappearing at $T = 1$.

This procedure recalls ***operational analysis***, which examined dependence of financial results of the activities of the company on the costs and volumes of production and the implementation of the products, goods, and services. The key elements of operational analysis of any enterprise are operating lever, the threshold of cost-effectiveness, and stock financial strength of enterprise. The operational arm is reflected in the fact that any change proceeding from the disposal always gives rise to a more severe change in earnings.

In the present case, as the effects of ***tax operational lever*** can be taken as the ratio of change of weighted average cost of capital WACC to the change of tax on profit

Fig. 18.2 Dependence of equity capital cost k_e on tax on profit rate T at different leverage level L

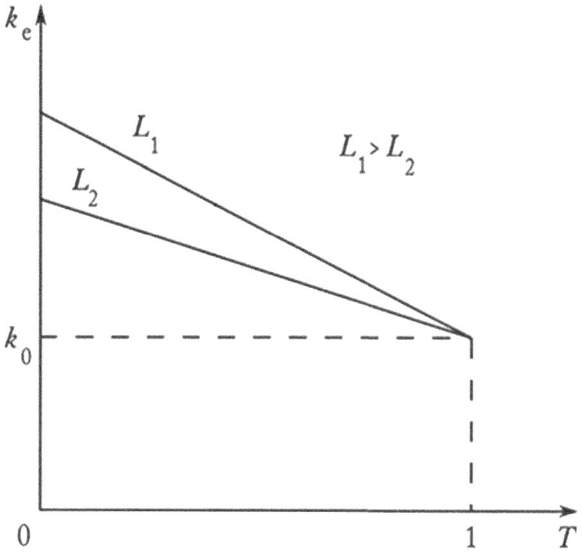

rate T, and the ratio of change of equity capital cost k_e to the change of tax on profit rate T, we can introduce for the first time two tax operating levers:

- For weighted average cost of capital WACC:

$$L_{\mathrm{WACC}} = \Delta\mathrm{WACC}/\Delta T;$$

- For equity capital cost k_e:

$$L_{k_e} = \Delta k_e/\Delta T.$$

For the earlier examples, the power of the lever is:

1. $L_{\mathrm{WACC}} = 0.05$;
2. $L_{\mathrm{WACC}} = 0.133$;
3. $L_{k_e} = 0.06$;
4. $L_{k_e} = 0.2$.

The higher value of the tax operational lever causes the greater change in capital cost of the company at fixed change of tax on profit rate T (Fig. 18.2).

18.2 The Role of Taxes in Brusov–Filatova–Orekhova Theory

The solution of the problem of evaluation of the weighted average cost of capital WACC for companies of arbitrary age or with arbitrary lifetime, as it was noted in Chap. 3, has been done for the first time by Brusov–Filatova–Orekhova (Brusov and Filatova 2011, Brusov et al. 2011a, b, c, 2012a, b, 2013a, b, 2014a, b; Filatova et al. 2008).

Following them, consider the situation for the arbitrary age of the company. In this case, the Modigliani–Miller theorem

$$V_L = V_0 + DT$$

is changed by

$$V = V_0 + (PV)_{TS} = V_0 + DT[1 - (1 + k_d)^{-n}], \qquad (18.3)$$

where

$$(PV)_{TS} = k_d DT \sum_{t=1}^{n} (1 + k_d)^{-t} = DT[1 - (1 + k_d)^{-n}], \qquad (18.4)$$

represents a tax shield for n-years.

It is seen that the capitalization of financially dependent (leverage) company linearly increases with the growth of the tax on profit rate (as well as in the limited case of Modigliani–Miller); however, the tilt angle of the linear function $V_L(T)$ is less than in the perpetuity case:

$$tg\delta = T[1 - (1 + k_d)^{-n}] \leq T. \qquad (18.5)$$

We will carry out the study of the dependence of weighted average cost of capital of the company WACC and its equity cost k_e on tax on profit rate in two ways:

1. We will study the dependence of weighted average cost of capital of the company WACC and its equity cost k_e on tax on profit rate at fixed leverage level and at different ages of the company.
2. We will study the dependence of weighted average cost of capital of the company WACC and its equity cost k_e on leverage level at fixed tax on profit rate and at different ages of the company.

In both cases, we will use Brusov–Filatova–Orekhova formula for weighted average cost of capital of the company WACC (Brusov and Filatova 2011; Brusov et al. 2011a, b, c, 2012a, b, 2013a, b, 2014a, b; Filatova et al. 2008):

$$\frac{1-(1+\mathrm{WACC})^{-n}}{\mathrm{WACC}}=\frac{1-(1+k_0)^{-n}}{k_0[1-\omega_\mathrm{d}T(1-(1+k_\mathrm{d})^{-n})]}. \tag{18.6}$$

18.2.1 Weighted Average Cost of Capital of the Company WACC

18.2.1.1 Dependence of Weighted Average Cost of Capital of the Company WACC on Tax on Profit Rate T at Fixed Leverage Level L

For $n = 2$, $k_0 = 18\ \%$, $k_\mathrm{d} = 10\%$, the dependences of weighted average cost of capital of the company WACC on tax on profit rate T at fixed leverage level L (fraction of debt capital w_d) are shown in Fig. 18.3.

It is quite obvious that dependences are very similar to that in Fig. 18.1, differing by the tilt angle α and the distance between curves (in fact, the dependences are very close to the linear ones). With the increase of debt capital fraction w_d (or leverage level L), the curves become more steep and the relevant tax operating lever decreases, which means the rise of the impact of the change of the tax on profit rate on the weighted average cost of capital.

18.2.1.2 Dependence of Weighted Average Cost of Capital of the Company WACC on Debt Capital Fraction w_d at Fixed Tax on Profit Rate T

Dependences of weighted average cost of capital of the company WACC on debt capital fraction w_d at fixed tax on profit rate T turn out to be linear ones as well. For

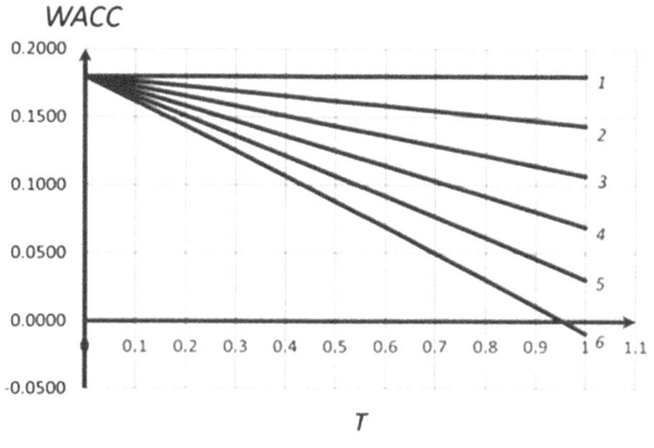

Fig. 18.3 Dependence of weighted average cost of capital of the company WACC on tax on profit rate T at fixed leverage level L (fraction of debt capital w_d): (1) $w_\mathrm{d} = 0$; (2) $w_\mathrm{d} = 0.2$; (3) $w_\mathrm{d} = 0.4$; (4) $w_\mathrm{d} = 0.6$; (5) $w_\mathrm{d} = 0.8$; (6) $w_\mathrm{d} = 1$

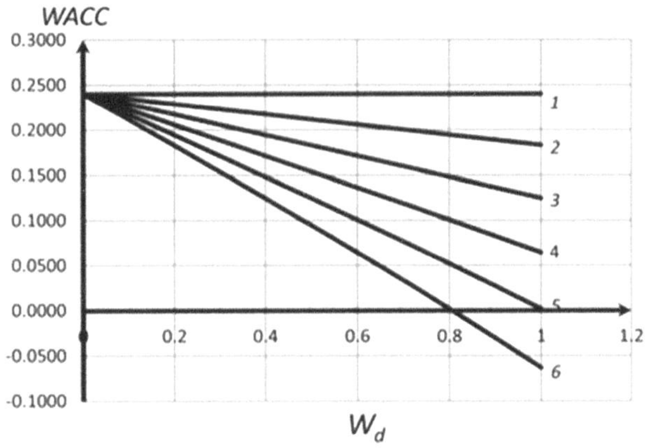

Fig. 18.4 Dependence of weighted average cost of capital of the company WACC on debt capital fraction w_d at different tax on profit rates T: (1) $T = 0$; (2) $T = 0.2$; (3) $T = 0.4$; (4) $T = 0.6$; (5) $T = 0.8$; and (6) $T = 1$

example, for $n = 3$, $k_0 = 24\ \%$, $k_d = 20\%$, we got the dependences, represented in Fig. 18.4.

The dependences shown in Fig. 18.4 are not surprising because the fraction of debt capital and tax on profit rate are included in the Brusov–Filatova–Orekhova formula (Eq. 18.5) in a symmetrical manner. With the increase of the tax on profit rate T, the curves become more steep, which means the rise of the impact of the change of the debt capital fraction w_d on the weighted average cost of capital WACC.

18.2.1.3 Dependence of Weighted Average Cost of Capital of the Company WACC on Leverage Level *L* at Fixed Tax on Profit Rate *T*

Dependence of weighted average cost of capital of the company WACC on leverage level L at fixed tax on profit rate T becomes essentially nonlinear.

For example, for $n = 3$; $k_0 = 18\ \%$, $k_d = 12\%$, we got the dependences, represented in Fig. 18.5.

With the increase of the tax on profit rate T, the curve of the dependence of weighted average cost of capital of the company WACC on leverage level L becomes more steep, i.e., at the same leverage level L; its change leads to bigger change of WACC at higher tax on profit rate T.

At tax on profit rate $T \leq 40\%$, weighted average cost of capital of the company WACC locates within $k_d \leq \text{WACC} \leq k_0$.

At tax on profit rate $T \geq 40\%$, weighted average cost of capital of the company WACC falls below k_d at certain leverage level L^*, which decreases with increase of T.

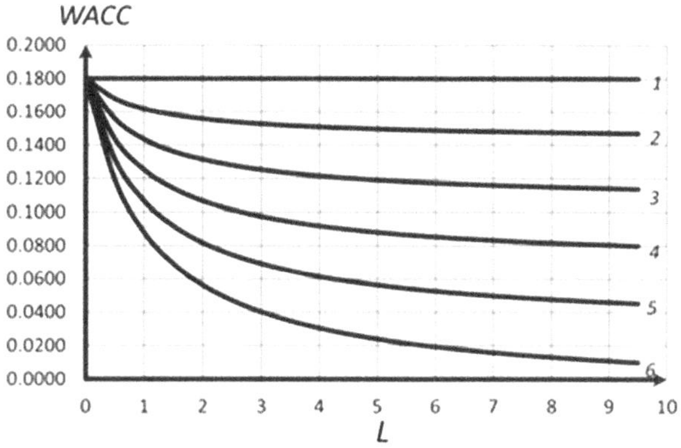

Fig. 18.5 Dependence of weighted average cost of capital of the company WACC on leverage level L at different fixed tax on profit rates T: (1) $T = 0$; (2) $T = 0.2$; (3) $T = 0.4$; (4) $T = 0.6$; (5) $T = 0.8$; and (6) $T = 1$

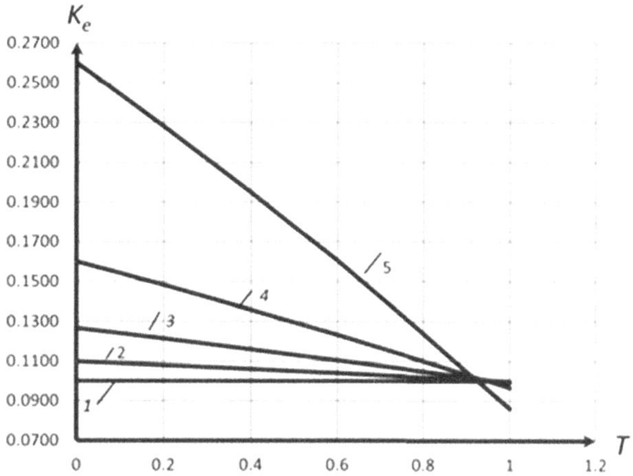

Fig. 18.6 Dependence of equity cost k_e of the company on tax on profit rate T at fixed debt capital fraction w_d ($n = 5$, $k_0 = 10\ \%$, $k_d = 6\%$): (1) $w_d = 0$; (2) $w_d = 0.2$; (3) $w_d = 0.4$; (4) $w_d = 0.6$; and (5) $w_d = 0.8$

18.2.2 *Equity Cost* k$_e$ *of the Company*

18.2.2.1 Dependence of Equity Cost k_e of the Company on Tax on Profit Rate T at Fixed Leverage Level L

Here are three figures, showing the dependence of equity cost k_e on tax on profit rate at different (fixed) leverage levels (debt capital fraction w_d) for different parameter sets n, k_0, k_d (Figs. 18.6, 18.7, and 18.8).

1. It should be noted that:
2. All dependencies are linear, and k_e decreases with increasing tax on profit rate T.
3. With the increase of the debt capital fraction w_d, initial values of k_e significantly grow and exceed k_0.
4. Lines, corresponding to the different values of the debt capital fraction w_d, intersect at the same point (at a certain value of tax on profit rate T^*), dependent on parameters n, k_0, k_d (Figs. 18.6 and 18.7).

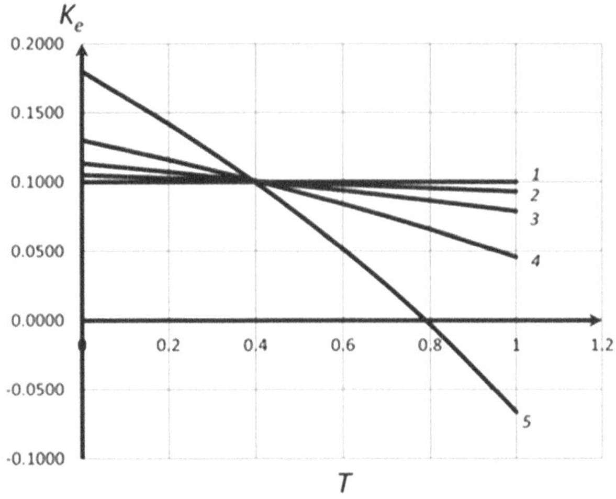

Fig. 18.7 Dependence of equity cost k_e of the company on tax on profit rate T at fixed debt capital fraction w_d ($n = 10$, $k_0 = 10\ \%$, $k_d = 8\%$): (1) $w_d = 0$; (2) $w_d = 0.2$; (3) $w_d = 0.4$; (4) $w_d = 0.6$; and (5) $w_d = 0.8$

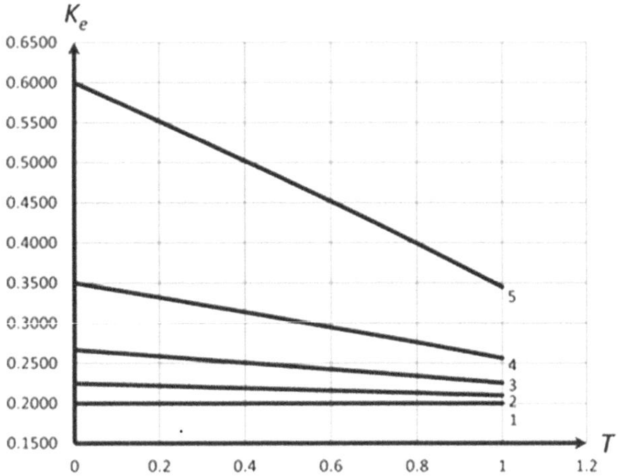

Fig. 18.8 Dependence of equity cost k_e of the company on tax on profit rate T at fixed debt capital fraction w_d ($n = 3$, $k_0 = 20\ \%$, $k_d = 10\%$): (1) $w_d = 0$; (2) $w_d = 0.2$; (3) $w_d = 0.4$; (4) $w_d = 0.6$; and (5) $w_d = 0.8$

5. At some values of parameters n, k_0, k_d, the crossing of all lines at a single point cannot take place at any tax on profit rate $0 < T \le 100\%$. With a large gap between k_0 and k_d, a point of crossing of all the lines lies in the nonexistent (the "non-financial") region $T^* > 100\%$ (Fig. 18.8). For data of Fig. 18.8, $T^* \approx 162\%$.

18.2.2.2 Dependence of Equity Cost k_e of the Company on Leverage Level L on Fixed Tax on Profit Rate T

The results of the calculations of dependence of equity cost k_e of the company on the leverage level L in Excel for the case, $n = 7$, $k_0 = 20\ \%$, $k_d = 10\%$ (at a fixed tax on profit rate T), are presented in Table 18.1 and in Fig. 18.9.

Table 18.1 Dependence of equity cost k_e of the company on leverage level L on fixed tax on profit rate T for the case $n = 7$, $k_0 = 20\ \%$, $k_d = 10\%$

	L										
T	0.0	1.0	2.0	3.0	4.0	5.0	6.0	18.0	8.0	9.0	10
0.0	0.2000	0.3000	0.4000	0.5000	0.6000	0.7000	0.8000	0.9000	1.0000	1.1000	1.2000
0.2	0.2000	0.2842	0.3682	0.4522	0.5362	0.6202	0.7042	0.7874	0.8713	0.9551	1.0389
0.4	0.2000	0.2677	0.3344	0.4008	0.4672	0.5335	0.5998	0.6661	0.7323	0.7986	0.8649
0.6	0.2000	0.2504	0.2984	0.3457	0.3928	0.4397	0.4865	0.5334	0.5802	0.6265	0.6731
0.8	0.2000	0.2323	0.2601	0.2861	0.3117	0.3369	0.3619	0.3867	0.4116	0.4364	0.4612
1.0	0.2000	0.2132	0.2185	0.2210	0.2223	0.2229	0.2231	0.2233	0.2231	0.2228	0.2224

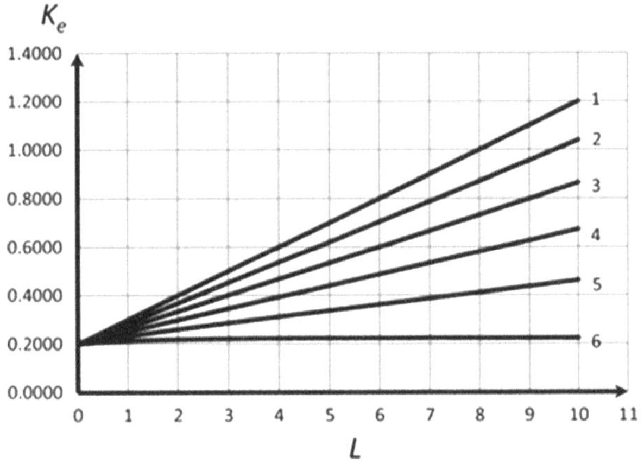

Fig. 18.9 Dependence of equity cost k_e of the company on leverage level L on fixed tax on profit rate T for the case $n = 7$, $k_0 = 20\ \%$, $k_d = 10\%$: (1) $T = 0$; (2) $T = 0.2$; (3) $T = 0.4$; (4) T = 0.6; (5) T = 0.8; and (6) $T = 1$

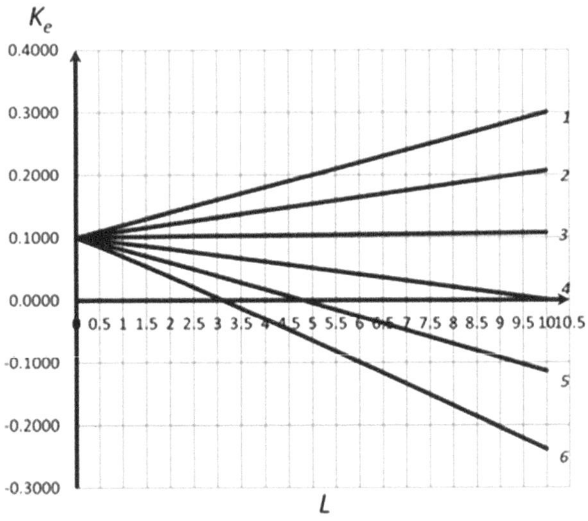

Fig. 18.10 Dependence of equity cost k_e of the company on leverage level L on fixed tax on profit rate T for the case: $n = 5$, $k_0 = 10\ \%$, $k_d = 8\%$: (1) $T = 0$; (2) $T = 0.2$; (3) $T = 0.4$; (4) $T = 0.6$; (5) $T = 0.8$; and (6) $T = 1$

Dependence of equity cost k_e of the company on leverage level L on fixed tax on profit rate T with a good accuracy is linear. When the tilt angle decreases with increasing tax on profit rate T, as in the perpetuity case (Fig. 18.9).

However, for companies of finite age, along with the behavior $k_e(L)$, similar to behavior in the case of Modigliani–Miller perpetuity companies (Fig. 18.9), for some sets of parameters n, k_0, k_d, there is a different dependence $k_e(L)$.

For example, starting with some of the values of tax on profit rate T^* (in this case, $T^* = 40\%$, although for the other parameter sets n, k_0, k_d, a critical tax on profit rate T^* could be even less), one has not the growth of the equity capital cost of the company with leverage level, but it is descending (Fig. 18.10). Let us repeat once more that existence or absence of this effect depends on a set of parameters k_0, k_d, n.

Note that this is a principally new effect, which may take place only for the company of finite age and which is not observed in perpetuity limit. For example, from the formula

$$k_e = k_0 + L(1 - T)(k_0 - k_d), \tag{18.7}$$

it follows that at $T = 1(100\%)$, equity cost k_e does not change with leverage: $k_e = k_0$, i.e., decrease of equity cost k_e with leverage, does not occur at any tax on profit rate T. Thus, discovered effect does NOT take place in perpetuity Modigliani–Miller limit.

18.2.3 Dependence of WACC and k_e on the Age of Company

The issue of dependency of WACC and k_e on the age of the company or on the lifetime or age of the company within the theory of Modigliani–Miller even though it is not possible: in their theory, the parameter "time" is absent, since all the companies are perpetuity ones.

Within the modern Brusov–Filatova–Orekhova theory, it becomes possible to study the dependence of WACC and k_e on the company's age. Below, we will undertake a detailed study of this problem: the dependences WACC(n) and $k_e(n)$ will be examined at different tax on profit rate T and leverage level L for different sets of parameters k_0, k_d, T, w_d.

18.2.3.1 Dependence of Weighted Average Cost of Capital of the Company WACC on Company Age at Different Fixed Tax on Profit Rate T

Considering dependence is shown in Fig. 18.11.

Weighted average cost of capital of the company WACC decreases with increase of the company age n tending to its perpetuity limit. The initial values of WACC

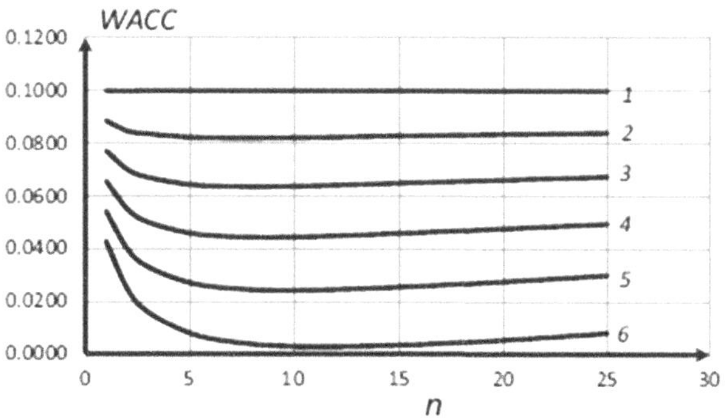

Fig. 18.11 Dependence of weighted average cost of capital of the company WACC on company age at different fixed tax on profit rate T ($w_d = 0.7$, $k_0 = 10\ \%$, $k_d = 8\%$): (1) $T = 0$; (2) $T = 0.2$; (3) $T = 0.4$; (4) $T = 0.6$; (5) $T = 0.8$; and (6) $T = 1$

(at $n = 1$) will decrease with the increase of tax on profit rate T (in accordance with the previously received dependences WACC(T)) and a range of WACC changes is growing with increasing T.

18.2.3.2 Dependence of Weighted Average Cost of Capital of the Company WACC on the Company Age at Different Fixed Fractions of Debt Capital w_d

Considering dependence is shown in Fig. 18.12.

The weighted average cost of capital of the company WACC decreases with the lifetime of company n, tending to its perpetuity limit. The initial values of WACC (at $n = 1$) decrease with the increase of fraction of debt capital [in accordance with the previously received dependences WACC(w_d)], and a range of WACC changes is growing with increase of w_d.

18.2.3.3 Dependence of Equity Cost of the Company k_e on the Company Age n at Different Fixed Fractions of Debt Capital w_d

Considering dependence is represented in Fig. 18.13.

The equity cost of the company k_e decreases with the company age n, tending to its perpetuity limit. The initial values of k_e (at $n = 1$) decrease significantly with the increase of fraction of debt capital w_d. A range of k_e changes is growing with increase of w_d.

It should be noted that the differences in equity cost of the company at a fixed n, starting from $w_d = 0.5$, become and remain significant (and constant for a fixed change in the fraction of debt capital Δw_d and at $n \geq 6$).

The situation will change with increase of tax on profit rate T. To demonstrate this fact we show the similar data, increasing tax on profit rate T twice (from 20% up to 40%) (Fig. 18.14).

It can be observed that with the increase in tax on profit rates in two times, the regions, where the differences in equity cost of capital k_e of the company are at

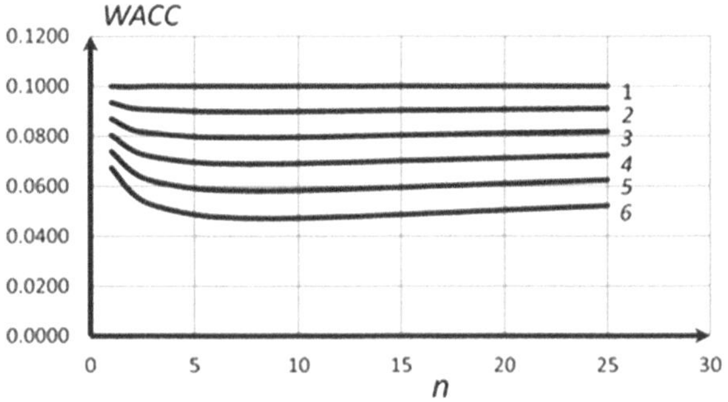

Fig. 18.12 Dependence of weighted average cost of capital of the company WACC on company age at different fixed fractions of debt capital w_d ($T = 40\ \%$, $k_0 = 10\ \%$, $k_d = 8\%$): (1) $w_d = 0$; (2) $w_d = 0.2$; (3) $w_d = 0.4$; (4) $w_d = 0.6$; and (5) $w_d = 0.8$

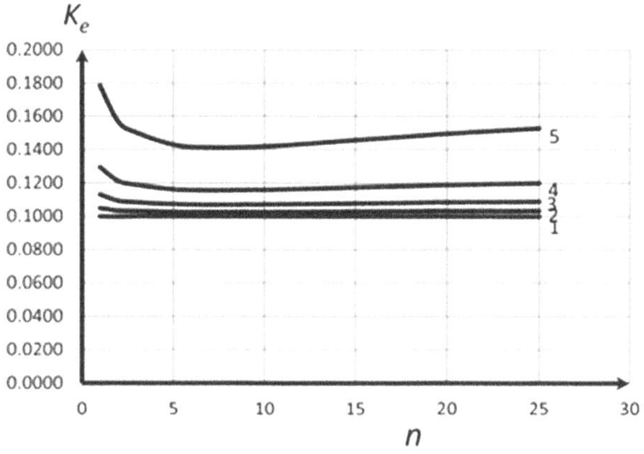

Fig. 18.13 Dependence of equity cost of the company k_e on company age n at different fixed fractions of debt capital w_d ($T = 20\ \%$, $k_0 = 10\ \%$, $k_d = 8\%$): (1) $w_d = 0$; (2) $w_d = 0.2$; (3) $w_d = 0.4$; (4) $w_d = 0.6$; and (5) $w_d = 0.8$

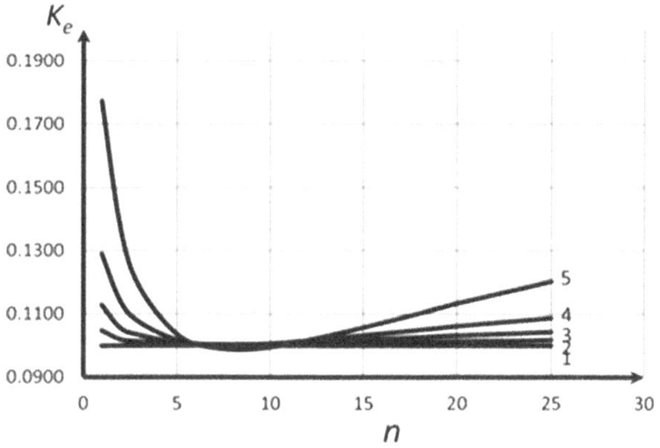

Fig. 18.14 Dependence of equity cost of the company k_e on company age n at different fixed fractions of debt capital w_d ($T = 40\ \%$, $k_0 = 10\ \%$, $k_d = 8\%$): (1) $w_d = 0$; (2) $w_d = 0.2$; (3) $w_d = 0.4$; (4) $w_d = 0.6$; and (5) $w_d = 0.8$

various fractions of debt capital w_d, have narrowed down to 6 years, while at $n \geq 6$, equity cost of capital k_e remains virtually equal to k_0 and only slightly fluctuates around this value.

18.2.3.4 Dependence of Equity Cost of the Company k_e on Company Age n at Different Fixed Tax on Profit Rate T

Considering dependence is represented in Fig. 18.15.

The equity cost of the company k_e decreases with the company age, n, tending to its perpetuity limit. With an increase in tax on profit rates T, the equity cost of the company k_e decreases (at fixed fraction of debt capital w_d), while range of k_e changes increases.

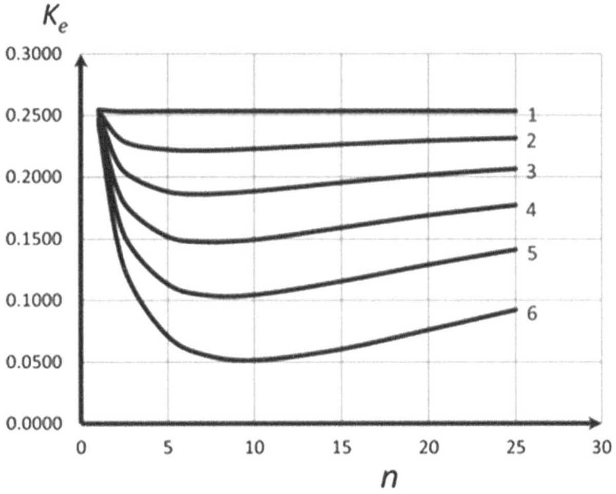

Fig. 18.15 Dependence of equity cost of the company k_e on company age n at different fixed tax on profit rates T ($w_d = 0.7$, $k_0 = 16\ \%$, $k_d = 12\%$): (1) $T = 0$; (2) $T = 0.2$; (3) $T = 0.4$; (4) $T = 0.6$; (5) $T = 0.8$; and (6) $T = 1$

18.3 Conclusions

Currently, rating agencies take into account the leverage level L only from the standpoint of assessing financial stability and the risk of bankruptcy. In fact, the leverage level L significantly affects the main financial indicators of the company: the cost of equity ke and WACC—in other words, the cost of raising capital, which is used (should be used) for discounting of the financial flows in the ratings, as well as for the valuation of the company's capitalization. Failure to take this influence into account when analyzing financial statements leads to incorrect conclusions and incorrect ratings. Simultaneous accounting of the leverage level L and income taxes may be important in rating: in the BFO theory a whole series of qualitative effects of their mutual influence are discovered.

Estimates (according to the BFO methodology) of the impact of the level of borrowed financing and the level of taxation on the effectiveness of investment projects for different values of capital costs can be used in project rating: in rating of the investment projects and investment programs of companies.

Taxation significantly affects the rating of issuers. Estimates (according to the BFO methodology) of the effect of taxation (the value of the corporate income tax rate) on the financial performance of the company and on the effectiveness of investment projects can be used in ratings of the companies and of the investment programs of companies, investment projects, and in the face of changes in the corporate income tax rate also for forecasting and in analysis of country risk.

Estimates (according to the BFO methodology) of the impact of the Central Bank's base rate, credit rates of the commercial bank on the effectiveness of investment projects, and creation of a favorable investment climate in the country can be used for forecasting, as well as in analysis of country risk, which is taken into account in ratings.

In this chapter, the role of tax shields, taxes, and leverage is investigated within the theory of Modigliani–Miller as well as within the modern theory of corporate finance by Brusov–Filatova–Orekhova (Brusov 2018a, b; Brusov et al. 2015, 2018a, b, c, d, e, f, g, 2019, 2020; Filatova et al. 2018a, b; Brusov and Filatova 2011; Brusov et al. 2011a, b, c, 2012a, b, 2013a, b, 2014a, b; Filatova et al. 2008). It is shown that equity cost of the company as well as weighted average cost of capital decreases with the growth of tax on profit rates. A detailed study of the dependence of weighted average cost of capital WACC and equity cost of the company k_e on tax on profit rates at fixed leverage level (fixed debt capital fraction w_d) as well as on leverage level (debt capital fraction w_d) at fixed tax on profit rate has been done. The dependences of weighted average cost of capital WACC and equity cost of the company k_e on company's age have been investigated as well.

The concept of "tax operating lever" has been introduced. For companies of arbitrary age, a number of important qualitative effects that do not have analogues for perpetuity companies have been detected.

One such effect—decrease of equity cost with leverage level at values of tax on profit rate T, which exceeds some critical value T^*—is described in detail in Chap. 17 (at certain ratios between the debt cost and equity capital cost, discovered effect takes place at tax on profit rate, existing in the Western countries and in Russia, which provides practical value of the effect). Taking it into account is important in improving tax legislation and may change dividend policy of the company significantly.

For more detailed investigation of the dependence of attracting capital cost on the age of company n at various leverage levels and at various values of capital costs with the aim of defining minimum cost of attracting capital, see Chap. 17, where new qualitative effects have been discussed.

References

Brusov PN, Filatova TV (2011) From Modigliani–Miller to general theory of capital cost and capital structure of the company. Finance Credit 435:2–8

Brusov P, Filatova T, Orehova N, Brusova A (2011a) Weighted average cost of capital in the theory of Modigliani–Miller, modified for a finite life-time company. Appl Financ Econ 21(11):815–824

Brusov P, Filatova T, Orehova N et al (2011b) From Modigliani–Miller to general theory of capital cost and capital structure of the company. Res J Econ Bus ICT 2:16–21

Brusov P, Filatova T, Orehova N et al (2011c) Influence of debt financing on the effectiveness of the investment project within the Modigliani–Miller theory. Res J Econ Bus ICT (UK) 2:11–15

Brusov P, Filatova T, Eskindarov M, Orehova N (2012a) Influence of debt financing on the effectiveness of the finite duration investment project. Appl Financ Econ 22(13):1043–1052

Brusov P, Filatova T, Eskindarov M, Orehova N (2012b) Hidden global causes of the global financial crisis. J Rev Global Econ 1:106–111

Brusov P, Filatova P, Orekhova N (2013a) Absence of an optimal capital structure in the famous tradeoff theory! J Rev Global Econ 2:94–116

Brusov P, Filatova T, Orehova N (2013b) A qualitatively new effect in corporative finance: abnormal dependence of cost of equity of company on leverage. J Rev Global Econ 2:183–193
Brusov P, Filatova P, Orekhova N (2014a) Mechanism of formation of the company optimal capital structure, different from suggested by trade off theory. Cogent Econ Finance 2:1–13. http://dx.doi.org/ 10.1080/23322039.2014.946150
Brusov P, Filatova T, Orehova N (2014b) Inflation in Brusov—Filatova—Orekhova theory and in its perpetuity limit—Modigliani—Miller theory. J Rev Global Econ 3:175–185
Brusov P (2018a) Editorial: introduction on special issue on the banking system and financial markets of Russia and other countries: problems and prospects. J Rev Glob Econ 7:i–vi. SCOPUS
Brusov P (2018b) Editorial. J Rev Glob Econ 7:i–v. SCOPUS
Brusov P, Filatova T, Orekhova N, Eskindarov M (2015) Modern corporate finance, investments and taxation. Springer International Publishing, Switzerland, p373. Monograph. SCOPUS. https://www.springer.com/gp/book/9783319147314
Brusov P, Filatova T, Orekhova N, Eskindarov M (2018a) Modern corporate finance, investments, taxation and ratings. Springer Nature Publishing, Switzerland, p 571. Monograph
Brusov PN, Filatova TV, Orekhova NP, Kulik VL (2018b) Rating: New approach. J Rev Glob Econ 7:37–62. SCOPUS. https://doi.org/10.6000/1929-7092.2018.07.05
Brusov PN, Filatova TV, Orekhova NP, Kulik VL (2018c) A "golden age" of the companies: Conditions of its existence. J Rev Glob Econ 7:88–103. SCOPUS. https://doi.org/10.6000/1929-7092.2018.07.07
Brusov PN, Filatova TV, Orekhova NP, Kulik VL (2018d) Rating methodology: New look and new horizons. J Rev Glob Econ 7:63–87. SCOPUS. https://doi.org/10.6000/1929-7092.2018.07.06
Brusov PN, Filatova TV, Orekhova NP, Kulik VL, Weil I (2018e) New meaningful effects in modern capital structure theory. J Rev Glob Econ 7:104–122. SCOPUS. https://doi.org/10.6000/1929-7092.2018.07.08
Brusov P, Filatova T, Orekhova N, Kulik V, Weil I, Brailov A (2018f) The impact of the central bank key rate and commercial banks credit rates on creating and maintaining of a favorable investment climate in the country. J Rev Glob Econ 7:360–376. SCOPUS. https://doi.org/10.6000/1929-7092.2018.07.31
Brusov PN, Filatova TV, Orekhova NP (2018g) Modern corporate finance and investments, monograph. Knorus Publishing House, Moscow, p 517
Brusov PN, Filatova TV, Orekhova NP, Kulik VL, Weil I (2019) Ratings of the investment projects of arbitrary durations: New methodology. J Rev Glob Econ 8:437–448. SCOPUS. https://doi.org/10.6000/1929-7092.2019.08.37
Brusov PN, Filatova TV, Orekhova NP, Kulik VL, Chang S-I, Lin YCG (2020) Modification of the Modigliani–Miller theory for the case of advance payments of tax on profit. J Rev Glob Econ 9:257–268
Brusova A (2011) A comparison of the three methods of estimation of weighted average cost of capital and equity cost of company. Financ Anal Prob Sol 34(76):36–42
Filatova T, Orekhova N, Brusova A (2008) Weighted average cost of capital in the theory of Modigliani–Miller, modified for a finite lifetime company. Bull FU 48:68–77
Filatova TV, Brusov PN, Orekhova NP, Kulik VL (2018a) Ratings of the long-term projects: New approach. J Rev Glob Econ 7:645–661. SCOPUS. https://doi.org/10.6000/1929-7092.2018.07.59
Filatova TV, Brusov PN, Orekhova NP, Kulik VL (2018b) Ratings of the long-term projects: New approach. J Rev Glob Econ 7:645–661. SCOPUS. https://doi.org/10.6000/1929-7092.2018.07.59
Modigliani F, Miller M (1958) The cost of capital, corporate finance, and the theory of investment. Am Econ Rev 48:261–297
Modigliani F, Miller M (1963) Corporate income taxes and the cost of capital: a correction. Am Econ Rev 53:147–175
Modigliani F, Miller M (1966) Some estimates of the cost of capital to the electric utility industry 1954–1957. Am Econ Rev 56:333–391

Chapter 19
Recommendations to International Rating Agencies (Big Three (Standard & Poor's, Fitch, and Moody's), European, and National Ones (ACRA, Chinese, etc.))

The studies performed in this monograph provide a new basis for the rating methodology. Rating agencies, both international and national, should apply the developed approach when assessing the creditworthiness of issuers.

The proposed improvement of the rating methodology of existing rating systems will improve the accuracy of generated ratings and make them more objective. Using in rating methods the modern theory of corporate finance allows us to move in the rating industry from using mainly qualitative rating methods to using mainly quantitative methods, which opens up new horizons in ratings of issuers and in methods for determining their creditworthiness.

The proposed fundamentally new approach to the rating methodology includes an adequate application of discounting, which is practically not used in existing rating methodologies when discounting the financial flows; the use of rating parameters upon discounting; and the correct determination of discount rates taking into account financial ratios.

Based on the results of this monograph, we give some recommendations to international rating agencies (Big Three (Standard & Poor's, Fitch, and Moody's), European, and national ones (ACRA, Chinese, etc.)

19.1 Discounting and Discount Rates

One of the major flaws of all existing rating methodologies is a failure or a very narrow use of discounting. But even in those rare cases where it is used, it is not quite correct, since the discount rate when discounting financial flows is chosen incorrectly.

The need to take into account the time factor in terms of discounting is obvious, because it is associated with the time value of money. The financial part of the rating is based on a comparison of generated income with the value of the debt and the

P. Brusov et al., *Ratings*, Contributions to Finance and Accounting,
https://doi.org/10.1007/978-3-030-56243-4_19

interest payable. Because income and disbursement of debt and interest are separated in time, the use of discounting when comparing revenues with the value of debt and interest is absolutely necessary for assigning credit ratings for issuers.

1. In existing rating methodologies, despite their breadth and detail, there are a lot of shortcomings. One of the major flaws of all existing rating methodologies is a failure or a very narrow use of discounting. But even in those rare cases where it is used, it is not quite correct, since the discount rate when discounting financial flows is chosen incorrectly.

The need to take into account the time factor in terms of discounting is obvious, because it is associated with the time value of money. The need to take into account the time factor in terms of discounting is obvious, because it is associated with the time value of money. The financial part of the rating is based on a comparison of generated income with the value of the debt and the interest payable. Because income and disbursement of debt and interest are separated in time, the use of discounting when comparing revenues with the value of debt and interest is absolutely necessary for assigning credit ratings for issuers.

This raises the question about the discount rate. This question has always been one of the major and extremely difficult in many areas of finance: corporate finance and investment; it is particularly important in business valuation, where a slight change in the discount rate leads to significant changes in estimates of capitalization of the company, which is used by unscrupulous appraisers for artificial bankruptcy of companies. As well it is essential in rating, and when assigning a rating to an issuer, and forecasting. The method of valuation of discount rate developed in this monograph using modified BFO theory for rating needs taking into account financial ratios allows us to make correct assessment of the creditworthiness of issuers.

Therefore, as soon as we talk about financial flows, it is necessary to take account of discounting; otherwise the time value of money is not taken into account, i.e., any analysis of financial flows should take account of discounting.

2. When we talk about using the rating reports for the three or five (GAAP) years, assuming that the behavior indicators beyond that period are "equal," discounting must be taken into account.

19.2 Dividend Policy of the Company

1. Dividend policy of the company must be taken into account (and account) when rating, because the financial policy is taken into account in rating. However, the existing methodologies for ranking estimate only the stability of the dividend policy and do not estimate its reasonableness: how reasonable is the value of dividend payouts and how do they relate to the economically reasonable dividend values.

2. The reasonableness of dividend policy, its score, is determined by comparing the values of paid dividends with their economically reasonable value, which is the cost of equity capital k_e of the company. The calculation of k_e is a rather difficult task.

BFO theory (Brusov 2018a, b; Brusov et al. 2015, 2018a, b, c, d, e, f, 2019, 2020; Filatova et al. 2008, 2018) allows you to make the correct assessment of the value of the equity capital cost of the company and thus to compare values of the dividend paid by the company with their economically reasonable value; it allows you to assess the reasonableness of dividend policy, which is clearly linked to the creditworthiness of the issuer.

3. For example, one of the varieties "cash flow," taking into account the amount of paid dividends (Discretionary cash flow (DCF) S&P), should be compared with the economically reasonable dividend values, and this will affect the rating.

19.3 Leverage Level

1. Currently the rating agencies take into account the leverage level only from the perspective of assessing the financial stability and risk of bankruptcy. In fact, the leverage level significantly affects the main financial indicators of the company's activity: the cost of equity capital k_e, WACC—in other words, the cost of attracting of capital, as well as the capitalization of the company. The failure of this effect in the analysis of financial reports leads to incorrect conclusions based on it.

Evaluation (by the BFO method) of the influence of the debt financing level on the effectiveness of investment projects for different values of capital costs can be used in the rating of investment projects and investment programs of companies.

19.4 Taxation

1. Taxation affects the rating of the issuers. Evaluation (by the BFO method) of the influence of taxation (tax on profit rate of company) on the financial performance of the company and on the effectiveness of investment projects can be used when rating companies and their investment programs, investment projects, as well as in the context of change of tax on profit rate of company for forecast predictions and in analysis of country risk.

2. Evaluation (by the BFO method) of the influence of the Central Bank key rate, credit rates of commercial banks on the effectiveness of investment projects, and creation of a favorable investment climate in the country can be used to forecast predictions, as well as in country risk analysis.

19.5 Account of the Industrial Specifics of the Issuer

Industrial specifics of the issuer in the existing rating methodologies, especially in newly established ones and taking into account the experience of predecessors, are ignored. So in "the methodology of ACRA for assigning of credit ratings for non-financial companies on a national scale for the Russian Federation," creditworthiness is determined by taking into account the characteristics of the industry in which the company operates. To assess the factor of the industry risk profile, ACRA subdivides the industry into five groups according to their cyclical, barriers to entry, and industry risk statistics, as well as trends and prospects.

The weight of the factor of industry risk profile is determined individually for each group and varies depending on the level of credit risk. This creates a certain rating threshold for companies from industries with high risk and slightly rewards low risk industry.

However, the existing accounting of industry specifics of issuer is clearly insufficient. Rating methodologies should better integrate industry peculiarities in the organization of finance of issuers. In particular, it is very important to define business needs in working capital, from the size of which financial soundness indicators, solvency and creditworthiness depend directly. The latter is the key indicator in rating.

19.6 Neglect of Taking into Account the Particularities of the Issuer

In existing rating methodologies the taking into account the particularities of the issuer, features of financial reports, taxation, legal and financial system is neglected in favor of achieving full comparability of financial reports, they smooth the distinctions (see Moody's rating methodologies).

19.7 Financial Ratios

1. A necessary and sufficient quantity and mix of financial ratios are not determined, it appears that such questions are even not raised though valuation of the financial risk, the financial condition of the issuer largely depend on the quantity and quality of financial ratios, their correlation or independence.

2. Some financial ratios define ambiguously the state of the issuer. For example, the ratio of cash flow/leverage is high at high cash flow value as well as at low leverage value. The question is how these two different states of the issuer, which is attributed to one value of financial risk, is really equally relate to credit risk.

3. As recognized in the ACRA methodology "in some cases it is possible that individual characteristics of factor/subfactor simultaneously fall into several categories of evaluation, particularly for qualitative factors. In this case, the score is based on expert opinion, taking into account the most important parameters."

4. In connection with paragraph 3 it should be noted that the formalization of expert opinions is one of the most important tasks in improving of the rating methodology, in making a peer review process more objective. There are a few ways to solve this problem: using results of modern theory of measurement, using of the formalism of fuzzy sets, fuzzy logic, and others.

Table 19.1 Score of funding and liquidity (after ACRA)

Assessment of funding		Liquidity assessment				
		1	**2**	**3**	**4**	**5**
	1	1	2	2	3	4
	2	1	2	3	3	4
	3	2	2	3	4	5
	4	3	3	3	4	5
	5	3	3	4	5	5

5. Tabulate the composition of various risks, for example, CICRA (in S&P methodology) gives 6 × 6 matrix, which has 36 elements, i.e. generally CICRA should have 36 different values, but their total number is equal to 6. The question is how this is justified. The fact that total number is equal exactly to 6 shows that not very justified, or there are other considerations, but they must be well grounded.

Similar examples abound. So in "the ACRA methodology for assigning credit ratings for microfinance organizations on a national scale for the Russian Federation" (table 10) "Score of funding and liquidity" provides 5 × 5 matrix that has 25 elements, i.e., generally should be 25 different states, but their total number is equal to 5. The question is whether it is justified. The fact that the total number is exactly equal to 5 shows that it is not very justified (Table 19.1).

6. Tabulation of mixes of different ratios in determining the financial risk has been done not quite correctly:

	FFO/debt (%)	Debt/EBITDA (x)	FFO/cash interest (x)	EBITDA/interest (x)	CFO/debt (%)	FOCF/deb (%)	DCF/debt (%)
Minimal	60+	Less than 1.5	More than 13	More than 15	More than 50	40+	25+
Modest	45–60	1.5–2	9–13	10–15	35–50	25–40	15–25
Intermediate	30–45	2–3	6–9	6–10	25–35	15–25	10–15
Significant	20–30	3–4	4–6	3–6	15–25	10–15	5–10
Aggressive	12–20	4–5	2–4	2–3	10–15	5–10	2–5
Highly leveraged	Less than 12	Greater than 5	Less than 2	Less than 2	Less than 10	Less than 5	Less than 2

ratios at least not completely correlated but used as fully correlated. So, one can see that the two lines

Minimal	60+	Less than 1.5	More than 13	More than 15	More than 50	40+	25+
Modest	45–60	1.5–2	9–13	10–15	35–50	25–40	15–25

do not allow mixing between parameters of lines, although such mixing can occur, for example,

	60+	1.5–2	More than 13	More than 15	More than 50	40+	25+

All these points are limiting the applicability of rating agencies methods. They were introduced by the rating agencies for the purpose of simplifying the procedure of ranking (with or without understanding) and unifying the methods used in different reporting systems of different countries, with the objective of making results comparable. Mentioned ambiguity of evaluations already occurred when S&P has assigned a rating to Gazprom.

References

Brusov P (2018a) Editorial: introduction on special issue on the Banking System and financial markets of Russia and other countries: problems and prospects. J Rev Global Econ 7:i–vi. SCOPUS

Brusov P (2018b) Editorial. J Rev Global Econ 7:i–v. SCOPUS

Brusov P, Filatova T, Orekhova N, Eskindarov M (2015) Modern corporate finance, investments and taxation. Springer International Publishing, Switzerland, 373 p. monograph. SCOPUS. https://www.springer.com/gp/book/9783319147314

Brusov PN, Filatova TV, Orekhova NP, Kulik VL (2018a) Rating: new approach. J Rev Global Econ 7:37–62. SCOPUS. https://doi.org/10.6000/1929-7092.2018.07.05

Brusov PN, Filatova TV, Orekhova NP, Kulik VL (2018b) A "golden age" of the companies: conditions of its existence. J Rev Global Econ 7:88–103. SCOPUS. https://doi.org/10.6000/1929-7092.2018.07.07

Brusov PN, Filatova TV, Orekhova NP, Kulik VL (2018c) Rating methodology: new look and new horizons. J Rev Global Econ 7:63–87. SCOPUS. https://doi.org/10.6000/1929-7092.2018.07.06

Brusov PN, Filatova TV, Orekhova NP (2018d) Modern corporate finance and investments, monograph. Knorus Publishing House, Moscow, 517 p

Brusov P, Filatova T, Orekhova N, Eskindarov M (2018e) Modern corporate finance, investments, taxation and ratings. Springer Nature Publishing, Switzerland, 571 p. monograph

Brusov PN, Filatova TV, Orekhova NP, Kulik VL, Weil I (2018f) New meaningful effects in modern capital structure theory. J Rev Global Econ 7:104–122. SCOPUS. https://doi.org/10.6000/1929-7092.2018.07.08

Brusov PN, Filatova TV, Orekhova NP, Kulik VL, Weil I (2019) Ratings of the investment projects of arbitrary durations: new methodology. J Rev Global Econ 8:437–448. SCOPUS. https://doi.org/10.6000/1929-7092.2019.08.37

Brusov PN, Filatova TV, Orekhova NP, Kulik VL, Chang S-I, Lin YCG (2020) Modification of the Modigliani–Miller theory for the case of advance payments of tax on profit. J Rev Global Econ 9:257–268

Brusov P, Filatova T, Orekhova N, Kulik V, Weil I, Brailov A (2018) The impact of the central bank key rate and commercial banks credit rates on creating and maintaining of a favorable investment climate in the country. J Rev Global Econ 7:360–376. SCOPUS. https://doi.org/10.6000/1929-7092.2018.07.31

Filatova T, Orehova N, Brusova A (2008) Weighted average cost of capital in the theory of Modigliani–Miller, modified for a finite life–time company. Bull FU 48:68–77

Filatova TV, Brusov PN, Orekhova NP, Kulik VL (2018) Ratings of the long–term projects: new approach. J Rev Global Econ 7:645–661. SCOPUS. https://doi.org/10.6000/1929-7092.2018.07.59

Chapter 20
Conclusions

In this monograph, new modern methodologies for rating of non-financial issuers and project ratings have been developed, based on the application in ratings of the modern theory of cost and capital structure (BFO theory (Brusov–Filatova–Orekhova theory)) (Brusov 2018a, b; Brusov et al. 2018; Brusov et al. 2015; Brusov et al. 2018; Brusov et al. (2018a, b, c); Brusov et al. 2018; Brusov et al. 2019; Brusov et al. 2020; Brusov et al. 2018; Filatova et al. 2008; Filatova et al. 2018), and its perpetuity limits (Modigliani–Miller theory (MM theory)(Modigliani and Miller 1958; Modigliani and Miller 1963; Modigliani and Miller 1966; Myers 2001) and new modified Modigliani–Miller theory (MMM theory), as well as modern investment models created by authors.

In order to modify and improve existing rating methodologies to increase the objectivity and accuracy of rating assessments, a critical analysis of the methodological and systemic shortcomings of the existing credit ratings of non-financial issuers and project rating has been carried out. The modern theory of capital cost and capital structure (BFO theory) for companies of arbitrary age and its two perpetuity limits (Modigliani–Miller theory and modified Modigliani–Miller theory) have been modified for rating needs. The incorporation of financial indicators used in the rating methodology, both into the BFO theory and into the Modigliani–Miller theory, has been carried out. Within the framework of the modified Brusov–Filatova–Orekhova theory (BFO theory) for rating needs, a complete and detailed study of the dependence of the weighted average cost of capital of WACC, used as the discount rate for discounting financial flows, on the financial ratios used in the rating, on the age of the company, on the leverage level, and on the level of taxation was conducted in a wide range of values of equity cost and debt cost for companies of arbitrary age. This allows us to carry out the correct assessment of the discount rate, taking into account the values of financial ratios.

To assess the creditworthiness of issuers, two models have been created that take into account the discounting of financial flows: a single-period model and a multi-period model.

P. Brusov et al., *Ratings*, Contributions to Finance and Accounting,
https://doi.org/10.1007/978-3-030-56243-4_20

The incorporation of rating ratios into the modern theory of capital cost and capital structure, Brusov–Filatova–Orekhova theory (BFO theory), and its perpetuity limit allows the use of powerful tools of these well-developed theories for credit rating of non-financial issuers, while discounting financial flows using the correct discount rates taking into account the values of financial ratios. The quantitative analysis in the rating has been expanded by expanding the range of financial indicators, introducing a number of new financial indicators. All this is a qualitatively new basis for creating a modern methodology for rating of non-financial issuers, and it increases the objectivity and accuracy of ratings.

The authors have modified created by them models of long-term (perpetuity) investment projects and projects of arbitrary duration with various debt repayment schemes (at the end of the project duration, uniform payments of debt) for rating needs.

The incorporation of financial indicators used in the rating methodology (coverage ratios and leverage ratios) into the model of long-term (perpetuity) investment projects and projects of arbitrary duration with various debt repayment schemes (at the end of the project duration, uniform payments of debt) was carried out.

For long-term (perpetuity) investment projects and projects of arbitrary duration with various debt repayment schemes (at the end of the project duration, uniform payments of debt), a complete and detailed study of the dependence of the main performance indicator, NPV, on financial ratios used in the rating (coverage ratios and leverage ratios), on the level of debt financing, and on the project duration in a wide range of values of equity cost and debt capital cost was carried out. This creates a new methodological basis for modern project rating.

The use of tools of well-developed corporate finance theories (BFO theory and its perpetuity limit) opens up new horizons in the rating industry, which gives the opportunity to switch from using mainly qualitative methods for determining the creditworthiness of issuers to using mainly quantitative methods in rating, which will undoubtedly improve the quality and accuracy of the rating score.

Recommendations have been developed to the rating agencies: the Big Three (Standard & Poor's, Fitch, and Moody's), ACRA, European, Chinese, and others on modifying the methodologies for rating of non-financial issuers and for project rating. All these rating agencies should use results obtained in this monograph for improving the rating methodologies and increasing the correctness of ratings issued by them.

References

Brusov P (2018a) Editorial: introduction on special issue on the Banking System and financial markets of Russia and other countries: problems and prospects. J Rev Global Econ 7:i–vi. SCOPUS

Brusov P (2018b) Editorial. J Rev Global Econ 7:i–v. SCOPUS

Brusov P, Filatova T, Orekhova N, Eskindarov M (2015) Modern corporate finance, investments and taxation. Springer International Publishing, Switzerland, 373 p. monograph. SCOPUS. https://www.springer.com/gp/book/9783319147314

Brusov PN, Filatova TV, Orekhova NP, Kulik VL (2018a) Rating: new approach. J Rev Global Econ 7:37–62. SCOPUS. https://doi.org/10.6000/1929-7092.2018.07.05

Brusov PN, Filatova TV, Orekhova NP, Kulik VL (2018b) A "golden age" of the companies: conditions of its existence. J Rev Global Econ 7:88–103. SCOPUS. https://doi.org/10.6000/1929-7092.2018.07.07

Brusov PN, Filatova TV, Orekhova NP, Kulik VL (2018c) Rating methodology: new look and new horizons. J Rev Global Econ 7:63–87. SCOPUS. https://doi.org/10.6000/1929-7092.2018.07.06

Brusov PN, Filatova TV, Orekhova NP (2018d) Modern corporate finance and investments, monograph. Knorus Publishing House, Moscow, 517 p

Brusov P, Filatova T, Orekhova N, Eskindarov M (2018e) Modern corporate finance, investments, taxation and ratings. Springer Nature Publishing, Switzerland, 571 p. monograph

Brusov PN, Filatova TV, Orekhova NP, Kulik VL, Weil I (2018f) New meaningful effects in modern capital structure theory. J Rev Global Econ 7:104–122. SCOPUS. https://doi.org/10.6000/1929-7092.2018.07.08

Brusov PN, Filatova TV, Orekhova NP, Kulik VL, Weil I (2019) Ratings of the investment projects of arbitrary durations: new methodology. J Rev Global Econ 8:437–448. SCOPUS. https://doi.org/10.6000/1929-7092.2019.08.37

Brusov PN, Filatova TV, Orekhova NP, Kulik VL, Chang S-I, Lin YCG (2020) Modification of the Modigliani–Miller theory for the case of advance payments of tax on profit. J Rev Global Econ 9:257–268

Brusov P, Filatova T, Orekhova N, Kulik V, Weil I, Brailov A (2018) The impact of the central bank key rate and commercial banks credit rates on creating and maintaining of a favorable investment climate in the country. J Rev Global Econ 7:360–376. SCOPUS. https://doi.org/10.6000/1929-7092.2018.07.31

Filatova T, Orehova N, Brusova A (2008) Weighted average cost of capital in the theory of Modigliani–Miller, modified for a finite life–time company. Bull FU 48:68–77

Filatova TV, Brusov PN, Orekhova NP, Kulik VL (2018) Ratings of the long–term projects: new approach. J Rev Global Econ 7:645–661. SCOPUS. https://doi.org/10.6000/1929-7092.2018.07.59

Modigliani F, Miller M (1958) The cost of capital, corporate finance, and the theory of investment. Am Econ Rev 48:261–297

Modigliani F, Miller M (1963) Corporate income taxes and the cost of capital: a correction. Am Econ Rev 53:147–175

Modigliani F, Miller M (1966) Some estimates of the cost of capital to the electric utility industry 1954–1957. Am Econ Rev 56:333–391

Myers S (2001) Capital structure. J Econ Perspect 15(2):81–102

The manufacturer's authorised representative in the EU is Springer Nature Customer Service Centre GmbH, Europaplatz 3, 69115 Heidelberg, Germany. If you have any concerns regarding our products, please contact ProductSafety@springernature.com

Printed and bound by CPI Group (UK) Ltd, Croydon, CR0 4YY
30/09/2026
02225452-0014